Nationalism in Modern Europe

Nationalism in Modern Europe

Politics, Identity, and Belonging since the French Revolution

Derek Hastings

Bloomsbury Academic
An imprint of Bloomsbury Publishing Plc

BLOOMSBURY
LONDON • OXFORD • NEW YORK • NEW DELHI • SYDNEY

Bloomsbury Academic

An imprint of Bloomsbury Publishing Plc

50 Bedford Square	1385 Broadway
London	New York
WC1B 3DP	NY 10018
UK	USA

www.bloomsbury.com

BLOOMSBURY and the Diana logo are trademarks of Bloomsbury Publishing Plc

First published 2018

British Library Cataloguing-in-Publication Data
A catalog record for this book is available from the British Library.

ISBN:	HB:	978-1-4742-1338-7
	PB:	978-1-4742-1339-4
	ePDF:	978-1-4742-1340-0
	eBook:	978-1-4742-1341-7

Library of Congress Cataloging-in-Publication Data
Names: Hastings, Derek (Derek Keith), author.
Title: Nationalism in modern Europe : politics, identity and belonging since
the French Revolution / Derek Hastings.
Description: London ; New York : Bloomsbury Academic, 2017. |
Includes bibliographical references and index.
Identifiers: LCCN 2017027163 (print) | LCCN 2017054650 (ebook) |
ISBN 9781474213400 (ePDF) | ISBN 9781474213417 (ePub) |
ISBN 9781474213387 (hardback) | ISBN 9781474213394 (paperback)
Subjects: LCSH: Nationalism–Europe–History. |
Group identity–Europe–History. | Europe–Politics and government–1789-1900. |
Europe–Politics and goverment–20th century. | Europe–Politics and
government–1989- | BISAC: HISTORY / Europe / General. | HISTORY / Modern / General. |
POLITICAL SCIENCE / Political Ideologies / Nationalism.
Classification: LCC D363 (ebook) | LCC D363 .H225 2017 (print) | DDC 320.54094–dc23
LC record available at https://lccn.loc.gov/2017027163

Cover design: Scott Graham, www.cyandesign.co.uk
Cover images: (top) The Festival of the Supreme Being at the Champ de Mars
on June 8, 1794. Photo By DEA/G. DAGLI ORTI/De Agostini/Getty Images.
(bottom) League of German Girls Dancing during the Reichs Party Congress.
Photo by Hugo Jaeger/Timepix/The LIFE Picture Collection/Getty Images.

Typeset by Integra Software Services Pvt. Ltd.
Printed and bound in Great Britain

To find out more about our authors and books visit www.bloomsbury.com.
Here you will find extracts, author interviews, details of forthcoming events and
the option to sign up for our newsletters.

CONTENTS

LIST OF ILLUSTRATIONS

Figures

Maps

1

Introduction

On March 11, 1882, Ernest Renan delivered a lecture at the Sorbonne in Paris that, while largely overlooked during his lifetime, has subsequently come to assume a central place in virtually every academic study of nationalism. Entitled *What Is a Nation?*, the lecture was formulated as a brief reflection on French attitudes toward France itself in the aftermath of the country's stunning defeat in the Franco-Prussian War, the previous decade. Many of the ideas and phrases introduced that day by Renan—that the nation represents a "daily plebiscite," that the nation is created through a voluntary act of identification on the part of its constituents, that historical "forgetting" is as important for a nation as commemoration—have become indispensable hallmarks in the scholarly literature on nationalism. At the time of the Sorbonne lecture, however, Renan was best known not as a theorist of nationalism but as the author of a best-selling and controversial history of the life of Jesus, which was published in 1863 and almost immediately translated into a number of other languages.[1] That book's stormy reception had led to Renan's dismissal from his position as Professor of Hebrew at the College de France, but the financial stability it provided enabled him to devote his time and energy to producing a vast array of works on topics both scholarly and popular, ranging from historical dramas to philological and linguistic works to multivolume surveys of Christianity, Judaism, and Buddhism. He was also a prolific essayist. By 1882, Renan was without question one of France's leading intellectual celebrities, but his reflections on the nation have typically been viewed as peripheral to his broader body of work.[2] And while Renan's fame drew a respectable crowd to the Sorbonne, the initial publication of *What Is a Nation?* in pamphlet form received surprisingly little attention. When choosing to reissue the piece as part of a broader collection of essays published in 1887, Renan reflected on both the personal significance he attached to the text and his strong desire that his words not be forgotten: "I have weighed each word of it with the utmost care; it is my profession of faith in all that concerns human affairs, and, when modern civilization has foundered as a result of the fatal misunderstanding of the words 'nation,' 'nationality' and 'race,' I hope these twenty pages will be remembered."[3] While the earliest biographies that appeared shortly after his death in 1892 almost universally ignored those twenty pages, Renan would be pleased, and perhaps even surprised, to see the extent to which his ideas continue to reverberate throughout scholarly discussions of nationalism well more than a century later.[4]

Renan was a polymath, and the study of nationalism since Renan's day has been a truly interdisciplinary affair, with generations of sociologists, anthropologists, and political scientists employing an impressive array of theoretical tools to analyze and compare the development of nationalism across vast expanses of space and time. For all of the sophistication of these analyses, however, it is my contention that nationalism cannot be understood fully in abstract isolation from the specific temporal and geographical contexts in which it is manifested, much in the same way that musical harmony cannot be grasped if one note is singled out for examination at the expense of surrounding notes. So the text at hand approaches nationalism from a specifically historical perspective, emphasizing context and prioritizing descriptive narrative. In that sense, it differs not only from theoretical approaches in the social sciences more generally, but also from many accounts written by historians.[5] By emphasizing narrative description over abstract theorizing, I am in agreement with the philosopher David Carr, who has argued that narrative is not merely an artificial device employed by scholars in an attempt to impose order on the unruly past. It also reflects, in a very real sense, the ways in which historical actors envisioned their own actions: framed against the backdrop of earlier exemplars, but with a clear eye toward their own potential commemoration by future chroniclers.[6] In the chapters that follow, then, I strive to offer readers, in words used by Simon Schama to describe his own narrative style, an "exercise in animated description."[7] It is hoped that this approach will be of benefit not only to history students and interested lay readers but also to students in more theoretically inclined disciplines who, against the introductory backdrop provided here, can proceed to engage in more analytical and schematic pursuits with a firmer empirical grounding. The text also strives, particularly in the notes, to point readers to some of the most significant features in a vast and ever-expanding historiographical landscape. The scope of the literature and the intended readership of this book have led to an emphasis on English-language works, although some reference will be made to major works in other European languages.

But before beginning the narrative journey through the history of nationalism in modern Europe, a few words of contextualization are in order regarding our object of study and the ways in which scholars have approached it over the decades.

Definitions and debates

Nationalism, put in simplest terms, is a form of group identity rooted in a powerful sense of belonging, a sense so compelling that, when fully articulated, it overrides all (or almost all) individual attachments and markers of identification. The object of that sense of belonging, the nation, can perhaps best be seen as a colossal ideational construct constituted by an act of creative projection on the part of its members, who come to see themselves and their individual fates as intricately intertwined with the lives of huge numbers of perceived compatriots they are incapable of ever knowing personally, yet with whom they feel an intimate bond. Thus, in Benedict Anderson's ubiquitous phrase, nations are indeed "imagined communities."[8] While humans have for millennia organized themselves into various collectivities—ranging from families and clans to tribes and kingdoms—nations are in fact quite recent in origin (this point is disputed by some scholars, as will be discussed below). Despite drawing much of their appeal from a largely artificial sense of primordial self-evidence, nations are essentially products of the modern era, the period beginning in the late eighteenth century. They are no less real for being imagined and no less modern for appearing ancient.

Yet as Ernest Gellner noted, nationalism is also a "political principle, which holds that the political and the national unit should be congruent."[9] In this sense, nationalism involves not only the identities and self-projections of individuals but also the tangible structures and institutions of nation-states as expressions of political legitimacy. In cases where the state's governing structures do not match the identity of the nation being governed (the "imagined community" of people), the political principle of nationalism is transgressed. So the study of nationalism necessarily entails an examination both of nationalist movements that advocate a correlation between the state and the nation and of the processes whereby the structures of the desired nation-states are built. Furthermore, within established nation-states, nationalist activists have at various points taken it upon themselves to define and disseminate normative visions of the collective identity of the nation—its purported strengths, its unique characteristics, and its historical mission. Thus, the study of nationalism is also, in part, the study of articulations of national identity (which are often, it should be noted, contested). These articulations have often been related to earlier visions of "patriotism," but devotion to the *patria* has, throughout most of history, applied mainly to narrower entities such as a city or region.[10] A historical understanding of nationalism also requires an intelligible framework within which to apprehend nationalist ideals as they emerge and circulate within their own specific (and often messy) contexts. With some qualification, I believe an evocative and at times even impressionistic narrative serves this purpose more effectively than airtight categorizations and typologies. Specifically, rather than engaging in an extended analysis of the precise conditions under which certain groups of people "qualify" to be counted as nations and others not, the present work essentially accepts, with appropriate historical skepticism, the self-designations of the historical actors themselves.[11]

The emphasis on ideology and identity leads us to one of the book's central, albeit far from novel, arguments: that much of the appeal of modern nationalism stems from its superlative ability to address the fundamental human desire for belonging and meaning—the drive to be part of something larger than oneself and to transcend one's own personal interests.[12] Humans can be seen as strikingly "religious" creatures in a certain sense, craving community and deriving sustenance from experiences that lift them out of their mundane daily routines. Thus, they have searched for various forms of transcendence, not necessarily in any organized or dogmatic or supernatural mode, of course, and not even along the lines of Freud's "oceanic feeling," but in the near-universal yearning for meaning beyond level of mere subsistence and survival.[13] For millions of Europeans, beginning in the era of the French Revolution but especially in the decades that followed, the nation emerged as the most compelling repository for those yearnings, leading a number of scholars to identify nationalism as a form of "political religion." In the vacuum created by the process of secularization and within the context of new ideals of popular sovereignty, the nation came to be elevated to a position of divinity, inspiring soaring devotion but also requiring tribute in the form of loyalty and sacrifice.[14] It must be remembered, though, that religious forms of attachment did not simply disappear in the face of modernization and secularization, and thus the interplay between religion and nationalism remained complex throughout the entire period under examination here.

It is important not only to place nationalist ideals within the context of religious attachments but also to examine their interaction with other markers of identity, such as gender. The success of nationalist discourse often stemmed from (and depended on) its ability to co-opt alternative modes of attachment and to mobilize them in the service of the nation. Rather than melting away, religious identity, gender, and even regionalism became, in themselves, central stages (and, at times, battlefields) on which rival conceptions of nationalism played out and were contested. Often, especially early in the lives of nationalist movements, this co-optation process involved the masking of particularistic self-interest and egocentrism under a veneer of universal humanitarian virtue. Political leaders have often found that it is difficult to inspire fervent devotion through crass appeals to selfishness alone, and universalism usually tastes better going down than unadulterated chauvinism. The fact that, at least early on, leading nationalist advocates themselves often believed the soaring idealistic rhetoric only intensified the appeal and the effectiveness with which fervor for the national idea penetrated among their followers. By the late nineteenth century, however, a major shift in nationalist discourse had become undeniable. With the certainties provided by pseudoscientific racist platitudes and exposure to the perceived inferiority of colonial "others," European nationalists increasingly dropped the universalist façade and preached more overt forms of exclusionary and aggressive nationalism. The fact that the two catastrophic world wars of the first half of the twentieth century, which were occasioned and sustained largely by nationalist ideology, gave way to a much more peaceful process of European integration in the century's second half was the result of a much sturdier and less artificial pursuit of universalism, embodied in the search for new structures of belonging that transcended nationalist interests. But the successes that many advocates pointed to in having "overcome nationalism" in Europe during the Cold War have been eclipsed in more recent years by a renewal of violent forms of ethnic and exclusionary nationalism and, in the context of the so-called war on terror, by revived internal divisions within Europe over issues of identity. Far from having permanently consigned the politics of exclusion to the dustbin of history, the continent has been plunged into a new era of contestation over the nature and boundaries of national belonging.

* * * *

Having touched briefly on terms such as nation, nationalism, nation-states, and national identity, along with related signifiers like religion and gender, let us now turn to an introductory overview of the development of the field of nationalism studies in recent decades.[15] One of the central debates among scholars has focused on the "when" of nationalism: at what point can we accurately speak of its emergence?[16] Part of this debate revolves, in a sort of chicken-and-egg scenario, around which came first, the nation or the phenomenon of nationalism. The majority view among scholars is the modernist (as opposed to primordialist) approach, which holds that nationalism only really became possible under the conditions of modernity, beginning at the earliest in the eighteenth century. The nationalist ideas and movements that originated in the process of modernization then, in turn, created the reality of nations. To quote the concise summation of Eric Hobsbawm: "For the purposes of analysis, nationalism comes before nations. Nations do not make states and nationalisms but the other way round."[17] For some scholars, like Ernest Gellner, nationalism emerged essentially as a product of deeper structural and material transformations associated with the transition from premodern agrarian society to industrial modernity, which proceeded at different paces and with varying intensity in different locales. This approach allows Gellner and his followers to analyze and compare vastly different temporal and geographic entities within the same framework, from, say, Europe in the early nineteenth century to African and Asian states in the midst of twentieth-century decolonization, so long as the materialist conditions that "produce" nationalism are present.[18] For John Breuilly, it is the coalescence of the centralized bureaucratic state starting in the eighteenth century that is of central importance. Breuilly defines nationalism almost exclusively in terms of the ideas and justifications developed by movements seeking specifically to control the levers of state, and his clear and straightforward political approach has exercised a significant influence.[19]

In contrast, Eric Hobsbawm and Benedict Anderson have placed less emphasis on demonstratively tangible factors like the bureaucratic state, focusing instead on the artificial and constructed nature of modern nationalist discourse. Hobsbawm has pointed to the ways in which nationalist leaders seeking legitimation turned to the "invention of tradition," whereas for Anderson, nations developed as imagined communities within which "the members of even the smallest nation will never know most of their fellow-members, meet them, or even hear of them, yet in the minds of each lives the image of their communion."[20] For many historians who, like myself, accept the artificially constructed nature of the nation and approach nationalism primarily in ideological and cultural terms, it is only in the late eighteenth century that the necessary prerequisites, such as Enlightenment secularization and the concept of popular sovereignty, emerge.[21] But once those concepts emerged, premodern elements often found their way into the visions and programs of modern nationalist movements. In this regard, Anthony D. Smith has pointed effectively to the precarious position of Enlightenment scholars employed or supported by absolutist monarchs in the mid-eighteenth century, who turned to historicism in the hopes of escaping the contradiction between the egalitarian implications of Enlightenment rationality and the unequal structures of the absolutist systems in which they lived and worked.[22] In addition to encouraging the study of archaeology, history, and classical philology, this historicist turn provided the building blocks for forging modern national imagery on the basis of older ethnic identities, incorporating premodern myths and symbols as well. In exploring these connections, Smith pioneered what came to be known as the "ethnosymbolist" approach, which has operated as a sort of bridge between modernists and their primordialist opponents.[23] In this view, the manifestation of nationalism was modern, but the myth–symbol complexes, cultural images, and ethnic identities it built upon were much older.

The primordialist minority itself has argued that the origins of nations and nationalism can be traced in a direct sense to premodern times.[24] Medievalists have for some time asserted that forms of national identity are clearly discernible in the middle ages, particularly in medieval literature, but their findings have made only limited headway among modernists.[25] Susan Reynolds has argued forcefully for the existence of conceptions of nationalism within medieval political structures, although she concedes that there are enough differences between the medieval and modern eras that her modernist counterparts are likely to remain unconvinced.[26] Many in this camp agree that nationalism and national sentiment only became widely influential in the eighteenth century and later, but contend that nations themselves predated these nationalist expressions by centuries. This is essentially the case made by John Armstrong, whose work has traced the development of "nations before nationalism" by examining ethnic identities that stretch back centuries, beginning in nomadic times, and following their elaboration in religious systems (primarily Islam and Christianity) and their institutional development in contexts ranging from city-states to medieval empires, before concluding with the communication systems and linguistic traditions that fed directly into the articulation of modern nations.[27] Armstrong, who is often classified as an ethnosymbolist, has noted that he sees a number of points of agreement between his approach and that of modernists.[28]

Other scholars, such as Azar Gat, Philip Gorski, Adrian Hastings, and Liah Greenfeld, diverge almost entirely from the work of modernists. Azar Gat has recently emerged as perhaps the most widely discussed of these figures.[29] Focusing on early forms of "political ethnicity," Gat argues that the distant roots of nations and nationalist sentiment date to early ethnic kinship networks that prioritized insiders over outsiders due essentially to a dim awareness of genetic overlap. Gat thus concludes that the emotive exclusionary elements seen in most forms of nationalism are in fact grounded in human nature, and that these elements coalesced in political form much earlier than the modern era.[30] Gorski, while critical of what he sees as oversimplified aspects of the primordialist approach, examines developments in the Netherlands in the sixteenth century to argue that a form of identification that can accurately be termed nationalist grew out of Dutch resistance to Habsburg control, with Calvinist theology providing the vessel for both religious defiance and nascent national solidarity. Calvinist clergy and writers disseminated carefully chosen biblical images, especially from the Old Testament, to establish the existence of an ancient "Hebraic nationalism," which they then adapted and applied to an emergent form of Dutch identity.[31] Adrian Hastings, for his part, detects the emergence of nationalism in fourteenth-century England, when a distinct and ethnically exclusive identity, based also in part on Old Testament imagery, was constructed through the establishment of vernacular religious literature.[32] Liah Greenfeld also sees England as the early prototype—"God's firstborn" among nations, as she puts it—with the English Reformation and the consolidation process that followed reinforcing notions of God's covenant with the "chosen" people of (Protestant) England.[33]

In addition to debating the "when" of nationalism, scholars have also argued about the various forms taken by nationalist ideas after their emergence. One of the earliest differentiations, surfacing originally in the work of Hans Kohn, is the distinction between civic and ethnic nationalism. Kohn had experienced personally the dislocations caused by radical nationalist politics, having been born in Prague in 1891 when the Habsburg Empire included more than a dozen competing ethnic and linguistic groups; he then spent considerable time in Russian captivity (during and after the First World War) and in the Palestinian mandate during a period of rising interwar tensions, before ultimately settling in the United States.[34] Kohn distinguished strongly between the "benign" civic nationalism of the West, which he saw as characterized by voluntaristic inclusion, equality, and the protection of individual rights, and the destructive ethnic nationalism of Central and Eastern Europe, which was organic, innate, and largely involuntary, framed by immutable boundaries of identity that largely prevented assimilation. It is not coincidental that Kohn's central work on the topic was conceived when the Nazi brand of racialized nationalism was at its destructive peak.[35] Other categorizations include the contrast between aspirational nationalism, which applies mainly to groups striving for the initial establishment of an independent nation-state, and integral nationalism, which applies typically to existing nation-states and is characterized by internal conformity, radical exclusionary politics, and often some form of expansionist militarism.[36] On the other hand, similarities can be seen between irredentist nationalism, which promotes the restoration and, if necessary, reconquest of territory deemed to have been lost or otherwise taken from the national entity, and pan-nationalism, which often transcends (minor) distinctions between groups and ethnicities perceived to be related, and typically advocates an overarching political or regional union.[37] Many scholars have also been critical of the creation of airtight typologies, and empirical research has begun to show that the stark differentiation between civic and ethnic nationalism often breaks down upon closer examination.[38] Maria Todorova, for instance, has recently proposed a recalibration of these categories to focus instead on a more allusive distinction between "weak" and "strong" forms of national mobilization as a way of understanding the relative mildness or virulence of the ideas and practices thereby produced.[39]

Scholars have also investigated the ways in which nationalist ideas come to penetrate the everyday lives of members of the nation, with "banal" nationalism serving as the most notable expression for this permeation.[40] Religion and gender comprise two of the most important points of intersection at which nationalism and quotidian individual experience meet. Arguing against the idea that European religion experienced only inexorable decline as modernization progressed, Philip Barker's close analysis of Greece, Ireland, and Poland has demonstrated effectively how thoroughly religion can be co-opted and employed in the service of the nation.[41] Nuanced theoretical paradigms regarding the complex relationship between religion and nationalism have been put forward by scholars ranging from Roger Friedland to Rogers Brubaker.[42] Due to its multifaceted nature, scholars have approached the relationship between nationalism and gender on a number of different levels, with studies of individual national contexts being too numerous to mention.[43] Important works by Michele Cohen and George Mosse have explored the intertwining of nationalism and normative visions of masculine comportment.[44] Patrizia Albanese has demonstrated the centrality of women's reproductive capacities to widespread pronatalist imagery peddled by nationalist movements across Europe.[45] Other scholars have emphasized the "ironic" (i.e., blatantly hypocritical) nature of nationalist gender politics, as well as the role played by feminists in attempting to transcend nationalist conceptions of belonging.[46] The permeation of national ideals in everyday life can also be traced in the spheres of music, sport, and visual imagery.[47]

Identity and belonging in premodern Europe

While there is a general scholarly consensus that the nation and nationalism should be seen as modern phenomena, group identities are as old as humanity. Before proceeding to our exploration of nationalism in modern Europe, let us first make a brief accounting of the various forms of political belonging and social cohesion that took shape in earlier centuries.

Occasional references to "nations" and related entities were made in biblical sources and in classical antiquity, usually to construct clear contrasts with those characterized as foreigners, although difficulties of translation require caution in the application of these terms. The Hebrew scriptures used the word *gôyim*, often translated as "nations," to describe separate patterns of linguistic and familial descent: "These are the descendants of Shem according to their families, their languages, their lands, and their nations (*gôyim*). These are the families of Noah's sons, according to their genealogies, in their nations; and from these nations spread upon the earth after the flood."[48] The categorization of humans into nations was also central to the unique covenant formed between God and the descendants of Abraham: "As for me, this is my covenant with you: you shall be the ancestor of a multitude of nations. No longer shall your name be Abram, but your name shall be Abraham, for I have made you the ancestor of a multitude of nations."[49] The biblical concept of nation, as formulated in Genesis, was to become central to later Christian debates over ethnic and linguistic differences in Europe.[50] For the Greek historian Herodotus, writing in the fifth century BCE, cohesive ties based on blood, language, and customs produced what he called a "common Greekness," a distinct *ethnos* that transcended individual identities based on *poleis* (city-states) like Athens or Sparta: "We are one in blood and one in language; the shrines to the gods belong to us all in common, and the sacrifices [are] in common, and there are our habits, bred of a common upbringing."[51] For Plato, Greek identity similarly had ethnic, almost proto-genetic, roots in Greek "stock" (*genos*) and was cultivated in opposition to "barbarian" foreigners.[52] Such ancient distinctions—whether between the Greek *genos* and barbarian aliens or between the chosen Israelites and foreign *gôyim*—were initially challenged on an intellectual level by the emergence of Pauline Christianity before being transformed even more fundamentally, in late antiquity, by patristic interpretations of a new covenantal relationship with God based on the universal salvific intervention of Jesus.[53]

Yet in practice, the universalist Christianizing mission in Europe could only work in concert with, not in place of, tangible communities of language and descent. Beginning in the 1960s with the work of Reinhard

Wenskus and elaborated further by Herwig Wolfram and Walter Pohl, early medievalists pioneered a broad scholarly framework for what is often termed ethnogenesis, arguing that the various barbarian tribes of the late Roman period established traditions and linguistic bonds—albeit *not* built exclusively on common ancestry—that came to form the kernel of new protean "ethnic" entities.[54] Patrick Geary has employed research on ethnogenesis to demonstrate the fundamental fluidity of Germanic tribal identities between the fourth and tenth centuries, striving in the process to debunk the claims of later ethnic nationalists who have often peddled an unscholarly form of ethnogenesis to wrap their chauvinistic appeals in the garb of pseudo-historical archaism. Geary demonstrates convincingly the futility of attempts to locate "nations" in the early middle ages.[55] Ian Wood has argued that a form of "nationality" seems to have emerged among the Burgundians and Franks in the fifth and sixth centuries, but on the basis of birthplace or social rank rather than blood or descent.[56] In the Latin crusader states of Outremer, established in the aftermath of the First Crusade, a similarly mutable form of Frankish identity can be observed, particularly in the writings of Fulcher of Chartes, who used common terms to describe the crusading armies regardless of their vast regional and linguistic diversity, constructing a new shared identity that materialized almost magically upon arrival in the orient:

> He who was a Roman or a Frenchman has in this land been made into a Galilean or a Palestinian. He who was of Reims or Chartes has now become a citizen of Tyre or Antioch. We have already forgotten the places of our birth....Words of different languages have become common property known to each nationality, and mutual faith unites those who are ignorant of their descent.[57]

And once this new identity took shape in the Holy Land, it was grafted onto imagery of the Israelites as a chosen "race" in a similarly creative leap. So while ethnic and racial terminology did indeed emerge within the crusader kingdoms of Outremer, as Alan V. Murray argues, those terms were not based in common biology or ancestry.[58]

The arguments of historians Adrian Hastings and Liah Greenfeld regarding the origins of nationalism in premodern England have already been discussed. John Gillingham, for his part, has contended that a form of distinctly English national sentiment coalesced in the twelfth century, as the descendants of the Norman invaders came to see themselves as English partly through the works of historians like Henry of Huntingdon, author of the *Historia Anglorum*, and partly as a result of the Anglo-Norman invasion of Ireland in the spring of 1169.[59] But in a nuanced study of mutual imagery reflected between England and France in the decades before and after the Hundred Years War, Ardis Butterfield demonstrates convincingly that any attempt to identify a specific "English" nation as distinct from French identity at that point is, at best, a distorted anachronism. The two "familiar enemies" created mutually dependent conceptions of identity and belonging, extending even to the quintessentially English poet Chaucer, who Butterfield places firmly within a broader Francophone context.[60] In perhaps the most thorough study of the formation of English national identity, Krishan Kumar states that it may be possible to trace the most distant roots of that identity back to premodern times, and his account devotes at least some attention to the development of various articulations between the Norman invasion and the early modern era. But he argues forcefully that those premodern elements must be differentiated from modern national identity: "It is not until the late nineteenth century, at the earliest, that we find a clear concern with questions of 'Englishness' and English national identity, let alone any strong expressions of English nationalism."[61]

While scholars like Kumar are firm in their modernist convictions, there is no question that conceptions of belonging in Europe were shaped significantly at a much earlier point by centralizing trends within Western Christendom and in the massive state-building projects that stretched from the late middle ages through the early modern period. For Benedict Anderson, the central prerequisite for the capacity of individuals in the modern era to see themselves as members of imagined national communities was the sense of belonging cultivated in much earlier religious and dynastic structures, which "in their heydays, were taken-for-granted frames of reference, very much as nationality is today." Yet the necessary self-evidence of these systems broke down: "For all of the grandeur and power of the great religiously imagined communities, their unselfconscious coherence waned steadily after the late Middle Ages."[62] One does not have to embrace the determinism of Anderson's conception of modernization and secularization to agree with him on the importance of these broader shifts. In what remains perhaps the best encapsulation of medieval state building and its impact on dynastic loyalties, Joseph Strayer traced the mechanisms through which bureaucratic state structures embodied in impersonal and durable institutions were initially established, achieved widely accepted legitimacy, and ultimately subordinated all other loyalties—whether family, communal, or religious—to the authority of the state.[63] This was, no doubt, an impressive set of achievements. But Strayer was insistent on differentiating the allegiances generated by these developments from nationalism:

Loyalty to the [medieval] state is not the same thing as nationalism; in fact, in some areas nationalism worked against loyalty to existing states. Even in the fortunate countries where nationalism eventually reinforced loyalty to the state, loyalty to the state came first and was a much cooler kind of emotion.... It took four or five centuries for European states to overcome their weaknesses and to bring lukewarm loyalty up to the white heat of nationalism.[64]

Strayer's focus was primarily on Western Europe before the Reformation. But in Central Europe, particularly in the period between the Peace of Augsburg and the Thirty Years War, the politics of state building and dynastic loyalty were further problematized by the reality of religious division. Since the 1980s, scholars have examined the extent to which the "confessionalization" process—that is, the attempt within both Protestant and Catholic regions to consolidate dynastic loyalty and deepen religious identification largely by contrasting their own identity with the opposing confession—impacted the development of a German national identity.

The confessionalization paradigm grew out of dissatisfaction with the conceptual dichotomy between the early sixteenth-century Reformation and the Counter-Reformation of the second half of that century. Seeing the latter term as reactive and ill-fitting, scholars such as Wolfgang Reinhard and Heinz Schilling began to conceptualize the second half of the sixteenth century in less pejorative terms, as a period in which Lutheran, Calvinist, and Catholic leaders began building modern, clearly defined confessional church structures ("confessional" for being based on written doctrinal confessions).[65] As Joel Harrington and Helmut Walser Smith have shown, the paradigm has inspired a large and growing literature, providing insights into the ways in which streamlined religious identities, effected through various forms of "social disciplining," spurred more efficient and modern state-building techniques, while also reinforcing the divisions that delayed German unification well into the nineteenth century.[66] But the impact of religious retrenchment and division was not limited to the arena of state building; it also produced virulent ideologies of difference that underpinned the violence of the Thirty Years War, tearing apart the social fabric of the Holy Roman Empire. A corollary to the confessionalization paradigm in the conflict-ridden German territories can be seen in the work of Anthony Marx, who has argued that religious intolerance in the same era—as manifested particularly in Spain, France, and England—is itself at the heart of the later exclusionary violence that characterized modern nationalism.[67] The intolerant and divisive politics of religion in the seventeenth century were, of course, central targets for disparagement within the Enlightenment project that unfolded throughout Europe in the decades leading up to the French Revolution.

Enlightenment legacies

The Enlightenment emphasis on universalism, rationality, and reason—on elevating the head over the heart and humankind over parochial interests—was framed in direct opposition to the perceived backwardness, superstition, and emotive violence of the preceding era.[68] The literature on the Enlightenment, in all of its intellectual complexity and variety of geographic expression, is too monumental to recount here.[69] And in any event, what concerns us here most centrally are two major outgrowths of the Enlightenment era: the transformative reforms of Enlightened Absolutist Rulers (also known as Enlightened Despots), and the emergence of new conceptualizations of social cohesion and popular sovereignty. Both would have an important impact on the subsequent emergence of nationalism.

On the surface, it would seem that the emotive and irrational thrust of nationalism, along with its prioritizing of the particular over the universal, would indicate that it was entirely unrelated, perhaps diametrically opposed, to enlightened thought. This view has found support in the fact that the Enlightenment and nationalism flourished in different centuries, and in the idea that the parts of Europe where enlightened ideas penetrated least (the central, eastern, and southeastern periphery) became the regions in which the most virulent forms of nationalism flourished; in contrast, the western and northern European bastions of "enlightenment" later exhibited mild and primarily rational forms of Liberal and civic nationalism.[70] But the issue is much more complex. As Michael Mann has shown, the Enlightenment project was central to the creation of the social constellation that produced the earliest nationalist effusions of the French Revolution. By destabilizing the moral basis of the Old Regime and supplying the secular ideological glue that linked the interests of the petit bourgeoisie, the lower clergy, and professional elites, the Enlightenment ultimately fed, rather than retarded, the nascent nationalist aspirations of the Third Estate, particularly on the level of social relations.[71]

But elsewhere in Europe, and on a more structural level, the political institutions fashioned during the seventeenth century by so-called Enlightened Absolutists also created new frameworks within which novel notions of political belonging could be forged, and provided many of the tools with which governments in the nineteenth century would transform and "nationalize" the masses of their populations.[72] Among the German states, Prussian king Frederick the Great and his Austrian counterparts Maria Theresia and Joseph II invested unprecedented sums in the modernization of military and bureaucratic structures, physical infrastructure, and educational and cultural institutions.[73] The longer-term result, particularly in the Prussian case, was the creation of new ways of envisioning social and political solidarity and the forging of what Matthew Levinger has termed "enlightened nationalism."[74] The Swedish king Gustav III, for his part, engaged in an ambitious reform program in pursuit of enlightened rationalization from the early 1770s until his assassination in 1792.[75] The model he provided led Sweden, and with it the rest of Scandinavia, to experience the broader transformations of political and social belonging "in no lesser degree than the rest of the Western world."[76] In Russia, the German princess who, benefiting from the assassination of her husband, ascended to the throne and ruled as Catherine the Great, undertook a similarly ambitious set of rational economic and legal reforms, but with a much greater emphasis on the repressive machinery of state borrowed partly from German sources.[77] To the extent that one can speak of a Russian Enlightenment, it remained the purview of a limited number of intellectuals and elites.[78]

As important as the governmental reforms of Enlightened Absolutists were, the intellectual and cultural developments of the era were even more influential for the emergence of nationalism. The two philosophers who exercised the most significant impact on the development of nationalist ideas were Jean-Jacques Rousseau and Johann Gottfried Herder. While both were products of the Enlightenment era, the ideas they presented transcended and in some ways opposed central aspects of the Enlightenment project. Although neither can be held responsible for the ways in which their writings were later used, the fact remains that many of their posthumous admirers would employ their works to launch frontal attacks on enlightened visions of social belonging and, especially, against the notion of cosmopolitan universality.

Rousseau was born into a middle-class family in Geneva, but was forced to move frequently beginning in his youth and seems always to have longed for the lost stability of his childhood home. Scholars have debated the extent to which his restless itinerancy impacted his conceptions of community and, ultimately, the nation.[79] Rousseau's national thought emerged in rather piecemeal fashion in several major works. In *Discourse on Inequality*, published in 1754, Rousseau envisioned nations (or their equivalents) as having predated the development of political structures, taking shape in the distant state of nature.[80] In his *Essay on the Origin of Languages*, which was written at the time of the *Discourse on Inequality* but was not published until after his death, Rousseau portrayed linguistic and cultural traditions as being rooted in the hard-wired essence of individual nations, conditioned by their various climates and locales. This view was further elaborated in his treatment of Polish identity in *Considerations on the Government of Poland*, which was also published posthumously.[81] But it was, by far, Rousseau's 1762 *Social Contract* that has had the most profound impact on the course of nationalism. The social contract itself was Rousseau's proposed solution to the problem of how to maintain liberty within the context of the necessary obligations that emerge within social aggregations, when people leave the freedoms (and vulnerabilities) of life in the state of nature and come together in search of collective security. As seen in the excerpt below, what is produced in the forging of the social contract is a dynamic force—the "general will"—which serves as the basis for political sovereignty. In the hands of nationalists, the concept of the general will would come to be intertwined with notions of the identity or essence of the nation and would be framed in often conflicted ways, as the source of potential emancipation but also as the disciplinary mechanism for internal coercion.

EXCERPT 1.1

The Social Contract (1762)

Jean-Jacques Rousseau

I suppose men to have reached the point at which the obstacles in the way of their preservation in the state of nature show their power of resistance to be greater than the resources at the disposal of each individual for his maintenance in that state. That primitive condition can then subsist no longer; and the human race would perish unless it changed its manner of existence.

But, as men cannot engender [*give rise to*] new forces, but only unite and direct existing ones, they have no other means of preserving themselves than the formation, by aggregation, of a sum of forces great enough to overcome the resistance. These they have to bring into play by means of a single motive power, and cause to act in concert.

This sum of forces can arise only where several persons come together: but, as the force and liberty of each man are the chief instruments of his self-preservation, how can he pledge them without harming his own interests, and neglecting the care he owes to himself? This difficulty, in its bearing on my present subject, may be stated in the following terms: "The problem is to find a form of association which will defend and protect with the whole common force the person and goods of each associate, and in which each, while uniting himself with all, may still obey himself alone, and remain as free as before." This is the fundamental problem of which the *Social Contract* provides the solution.

The clauses of this contract are so determined by the nature of the act that the slightest modification would make them vain and ineffective; so that, although they have perhaps never been formally set forth, they are everywhere the same and everywhere tacitly admitted and recognized, until, on the violation of the social compact, each regains his original rights and resumes his natural liberty, while losing the conventional liberty in favor of which he renounced it. These clauses, properly understood, may be reduced to one—the total alienation of each associate, together with all his rights, to the whole community; for, in the first place, as each gives himself absolutely, the conditions are the same for all; and, this being so, no one has any interest in making them burdensome to others.

Moreover, the alienation being without reserve, the union is as perfect as it can be, and no associate has anything more to demand: for, if the individuals retained certain rights, as there would be no common superior to decide between them and the public, each, being on one point his own judge, would ask to be so on all; the state of nature would thus continue, and the association would necessarily become inoperative or tyrannical.

Finally, each man, in giving himself to all, gives himself to nobody; and as there is no associate over which he does not acquire the same right as he yields others over himself, he gains an equivalent for everything he loses, and an increase of force for the preservation of what he has. If then we discard from the social compact what is not of its essence, we shall find that it reduces itself to the following terms. *Each of us puts his person and all his power in common under the supreme direction of the general will, and, in our corporate capacity, we receive each member as an indivisible part of the whole.*

[...] In order then that the social compact may not be an empty formula, it tacitly includes the undertaking, which alone can give force to the rest, that whoever refuses to obey the general will shall be compelled to do so by the whole body. This means nothing less than that he will be *forced to be free*; for this is the condition which, by giving each citizen to his country, secures him against all personal dependence. In this lies the key to the working of the political machine; this alone legitimizes civil undertakings, which, without it, would be absurd, tyrannical, and liable to the most frightful abuses.[82]

In addition to the concept of the general will as the source of sovereignty, this passage is most famous for the coercive power it authorizes in dealing with those who do not (or cannot) get in line with the general will. By proposing that people be "forced to be free," Rousseau was trying, perhaps understandably, to protect the viability of the social contract by making the general will inviolable. Exceptions would destroy the rule. But the notion that those who deviate from the essence of the nation can be coerced, disciplined, and perhaps even eliminated was to leave a legacy that, in light of the catastrophic national violence that would be enacted in pursuit of the general will, has marred Rousseau's body of work. Certainly, it has overshadowed the other elements of the *Social Contract*. As Peter Gay put it: "That phrase about forcing men to be free has generated more controversy, more stinging attacks and elaborate apologies, than the rest of the treatise together."[83] While a number of apologists have defended Rousseau against his many critics, Steven Engel has argued persuasively that Rousseau's ideas, in their internal logic, must still be seen as providing the basis for nationalist thought and practice regardless of whether he would have endorsed the actual actions undertaken in the name of the general will.[84] Writing in 1943, in the face of the totalizing racial nationalism employed by the Nazi state, Robert Nisbet stated famously: "More than perhaps any other theorist, Rousseau, by the sheer brilliance of his style, has popularized that view of state and society which underlies totalitarianism and which has indeed made possible the acceptance of the total state in this century."[85]

If scholars have typically treated Rousseau as the father of political nationalism, Johann Gottfried Herder has often been labeled the father of cultural nationalism.[86] As a philosopher, Herder broke with the cool objectivity of his mentor, Immanuel Kant, and espoused an increasingly emotive form of expression, taking up literary criticism and influencing the young Goethe, among others. Herder eventually turned his attention toward linguistics and philology, gaining fame with his *Treatise on the Origin of Human Language* in 1772, which rooted separate linguistic and cultural traditions in the identities of individual nations in ways that loosely paralleled Rousseau's essay on language (although Rousseau's piece was published posthumously in 1782, and Herder was likely unaware of it).[87] Various folk customs, including music, dance, poetry, and dress, were for Herder the external manifestations of an internal organic unity.[88] This organic cultural vision of national identity differed from Rousseau's emphasis on political will.[89] As he traveled within the German territories, Herder was troubled by the fact that enlightened German elites often avoided use of the German vernacular in speech and in writing, aspiring instead to be cosmopolitan citizens of the world. For Herder, this amounted to a fatal betrayal of the natural organic essence of German identity, as embodied in language and custom, and he urged a revival of German literary tradition to create a new organic mode of belonging and sociability, which he labeled the *Publikum*.[90]

But Herder was not just concerned with internal development; he was also fascinated by the vast variety of different cultures in Europe, each of which he viewed as an organic outgrowth of a separate national essence. In several of his works on culture and folklore, including most famously *The Voices of the Peoples*, he compared nations to different types of plants and flowers, all with their unique leaves and blossoms, and all coexisting fruitfully in the "garden of humanity."[91] The differences between the plants were celebrated as contributions to the overall beauty of the garden, in the same way that colorful varieties of flowers are more appealing than monochromatic uniformity. Ultimately, though, Herder's impact on nationalist thought was complicated. On the one hand, his appreciation of cultural diversity could be pointed in the direction of tolerance and understanding. But on the other, his conception of national identity as an organic, immutable essence could (and did) lead others to preach a chauvinistic vision based on blood and biological descent. As it happened, within a century of Herder's death, the harmonious "garden" of peaceful national coexistence would be transformed into a virtual piranha tank.

Europe in the eighteenth century was comprised of a vast variety of state structures and geographical entities, ranging from sprawling multiethnic empires to clearly demarcated kingdoms to tiny fiefdoms and principalities still resembling anachronistic medieval obscurities. One of the largest territorial states in Europe was Poland-Lithuania, which would cease to exist as an independent entity in the 1790s after the last of a series of partitions. The Ottoman Empire controlled huge amounts of land in southeastern Europe, including Greece and most of the Balkan region. The German territories were fragmented into more than 200 individual states

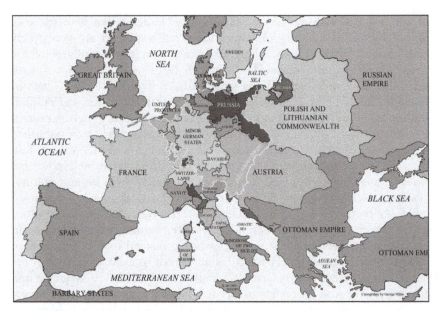

MAP 1.1 Eighteenth-Century Europe. © *George Edward Milne, 2017. Reproduced with permission.*

and principalities. Together they comprised the loose union known as the Holy Roman Empire of the German Nation, whose two most important member states, Prussia and Habsburg Austria, came in many ways to overshadow the empire itself. The Italian lands were divided and, on the level of European politics, comparatively insignificant in the eighteenth century. Scandinavia was dominated partly by Denmark, which included Norway, Iceland, and the duchies of Schleswig and Holstein, and partly by Sweden, which possessed all of Finland and parts of what would later become eastern German territory. In the British Isles, the United Kingdom had been solidified in the Act of Union of 1707 and possessed a rapidly expanding empire, whereas on the continent relatively cohesive kingdoms such as France and Spain had emerged as definable entities. But only Britain had begun to industrialize in any meaningful sense, and the economic, social, and political structures of Europe quickly evolved so dramatically that a person born in 1770 who lived up to 1850 might look back in old age on his early adulthood and have the feeling of observing a different universe. The fact that the pace of change would accelerate even more rapidly in future decades should not blind us to the radical nature of the upheaval Europe was about to experience in the revolutionary and Napoleonic eras.

Finally, in regard to France, where much of that upheaval would begin, significant changes had taken place simultaneous to the modernization and state-building processes underway in other parts of Europe. Louis XIV and his advisors had ushered in a period of bureaucratic and territorial centralization, which was accompanied by a strikingly gaudy visual reinforcement of the majesty of absolutist rule.[92] Aside from the elaborate cultivation of Louis's own personal appearance, the most notable feature of that visual reinforcement was the Palace of Versailles, within which Louis took up residence in 1682, and whose fountains and gardens were designed with specific political symbolism in mind.[93] His successors would continue aspects of the absolutist cult while experimenting with a variety of modernization schemes, some of which failed spectacularly. Perhaps more importantly, there was a growing disjuncture between the world of the Bourbon court and the transformative power of enlightened ideas coursing among educated professional elites. A clash of some sort with the structures of the absolutist state increasingly took on the contours of near-inevitability.[94] It should be noted, however, that the literature on French state building has itself undergone a transformation in definition and perspective. James Collins has argued persuasively for the abandonment of the term "absolutist" in favor of the "monarchical state," because of the indispensable centrality of the court itself, in all its profligacy and intransigence. Collins sees this monarchical state being born around 1630, more than a decade before the young Louis XIV came to the throne and more than two decades before he actually ruled, with the years between 1690 and 1730 as a period of adolescent state maturation. The patterns thus established were, for Collins, already disrupted in 1787, perhaps irrevocably, when the French Assembly of Notables was called in an atmosphere of swirling economic crisis.[95] So the eruption of the French Revolution two years later came initially as the continuation of a new and uncertain chapter that had already been opened in the history of the French state. That revolutionary eruption, against the backdrop of the Assembly of Notables and the convening of the Estates-General that followed, dramatically altered conceptions of political and social belonging and set in motion the dramatic chain of events pursued in the chapter that follows.

2

The French Revolution
and Napoleonic Era, 1789–1814

On January 24, 1789, when the Estates-General of France were formally summoned by royal edict, few could have foreseen the tumultuous events that would unfold over the ensuing twenty-five years, events that would transform not only France but also the geographical and ideological landscape of Europe. Many contemporary observers were indeed convinced of the necessity of a written constitution to mediate between the crown and its subjects, but the now-famous hallmarks of French revolutionary history were virtually unthinkable: the transformation of the Estates-General into the National Assembly, the storming of the Bastille, the manifestation of nationalistic fervor on the battlefield at Valmy, the execution of the king as an "enemy of the people," the infamous Terror initiated in the name of the newly empowered French nation. Nor could anyone have imagined the subsequent emergence of the Napoleonic empire or the colossal impact of its conquests throughout the European continent. What was clear to observers in early 1789 was that France's financial situation was dire and that the revenue shortfall could only be addressed by a convening of the Estates-General, which had not met formally since 1614 and whose archaic constituent orders were famously unequal. The First and Second Estates, representing respectively the clergy and nobility, made up between 1 and 2 percent of the population, but were allocated, at least in theory, two-thirds of the votes within the Estates-General. The other third went to the 98 percent represented by the Third Estate, or commoners, whose members ranged from wealthy merchants and intellectual elites to urban artisans and the rural poor.[1] When the more than 1,500 representatives from across France and its territorial possessions convened in Versailles in May 1789, they arrived with vastly divergent visions of economic policy and political representation. The stage was set for the unfolding of the foundational drama of modern European history, even if the set-designers and actors were themselves unaware of the plot twists that lay ahead.[2]

The causes of the financial crisis stretched back decades. France's catastrophic losses in the Seven Years' War between 1756 and 1763 occasioned both economic pain—with the colossal expense of fighting on two continents exacerbated by France's humiliating loss of territory and natural resources in North America—and a heightened, near-fanatical resentment of the British. When tensions between the British crown and its North American colonies boiled over into armed conflict in 1775, foreign minister Vergennes had advocated intervention on behalf of the rebellious colonists not only in pursuit of revenge against Britain but also as an opportunity to solidify the flagging geopolitical interests of France. Idealistic young nobles like the Marquis de Lafayette, who would later come to play such an important role in the early stages of the French Revolution, raised troops and gathered supplies, often at their own expense, and set sail to serve under George Washington. If the massive cost of French assistance was, in the short term, rewarded by the emotionally satisfying defeat of the British, a further series of devastating financial missteps left France's coffers empty and the prestige of the monarchy in tatters.[3] The politics of financial scandal became a virtual spectator sport in pre-revolutionary France, enhancing the destabilizing effect. Greedy land and currency speculators vied with corrupt government officials as the objects of popular gossip and scorn, and in 1785 the royal family itself was implicated in an embarrassing scandal involving an extravagant diamond necklace, a dishonest and sycophantic churchman (the Cardinal de Rohan), an even more dishonest and sycophantic social climber (the infamous Jeanne de LaMotte), and a misguided prostitute hired to impersonate Queen Marie Antoinette. After the convoluted story played out in the press and in a series of court sessions, the queen's reputation was decimated.[4] Such scandals were complemented by the French government's financially irresponsible scheme to expand and modernize the French navy throughout the 1780s, epitomized perhaps most colorfully by the fantastical attempt to overhaul the naval port at Cherbourg by creating, *ex nihilo*, a chain of nearly one hundred futuristic "barrier islands" consisting of massive conical structures made of wood, each measuring more than 140 feet in diameter and rising more than 60 feet over the water's surface, which were filled with tons of stone and other debris. By December 1789, when the project was finally shelved, relentless waves and voracious wood-eating sea worms had turned the would-be archipelago into a pitiful and horrifically expensive mess.[5] By that date, however, the early stages of the Revolution were already under way.

Revolution, war, and the mobilization of popular nationalism

Against the backdrop of Enlightenment notions of popular sovereignty, with Rousseau's concept of the general will taking center stage, some of the earliest ripples of what would become a wave of revolutionary nationalist sentiment emerged as the decade of the 1780s progressed.[6] In addressing the financial crisis, Louis XVI's advisors hoped to rely on and, if possible, strengthen the tradition of "royal patriotism" that had spread in previous decades among broad segments of the French nobility but was now under increasing duress.[7] In the summer of 1786, Charles Alexandre de Calonne, who guided fiscal policy in his position as Controller General, had put forward an economic reform package based on a new land tax, which ran into staunch opposition from previously exempt elements within the nobility and clergy. In an attempt to gain leverage, Calonne ultimately summoned the Assembly of Notables, itself an archaic entity that had not been convened since the 1620s. In his opening speech on February 22, 1787, he acknowledged the need for the Assembly to be seen as representing not only the interests of the aristocracy but those of the French people, replacing the traditional maxim "As the King wishes it, so be the law" with a fairly sweeping appeal to popular sovereignty: "As the happiness of the people commands, so the King desires."[8] When neither Calonne nor his able successor Loménie de Brienne was able to forge a consensus, pressure from the banking sector and the threat of future loan refusal forced the king and his advisors to consider convening the Estates-General. The decision was finally made, reluctantly, in August 1788, with the official royal summons appearing the following January and elections for representatives to the Estates stretching into the early spring. Among the most striking products of the election season were the petitions of grievance (*cahiers de doléances*) published throughout France, which revealed the growth of a powerful, if still somewhat embryonic, national sensibility.[9] These months also witnessed the publication of two works that helped solidify conceptions of national belonging and established an exclusionary discursive trajectory that was to be pursued with bloody consequences over the ensuing years.

The first, entitled *What Is the Third Estate?*, was written by the ambitious and worldly minded Abbé Emmanuel Sieyès, one of a growing number of secular clergy who sympathized with or overtly supported the commoners of the Third Estate. Sieyès answered the question in his title by arguing that the Third Estate was "everything"—since it produced everything of value in terms of goods and services—and that it constituted in and of itself a "complete nation." Drawing on Rousseau's vision of the general will, Sieyès identified the leaders of the Third Estate as the legitimate arbiters of the nation's prerogatives, as "interpreters of its will and defenders of its interests." The other two Estates, the clergy and the nobility, were nothing more than "burdens upon the nation" who could justifiably—in pursuit of the coercive elements of Rousseau's ideal—be excluded or excised without any damage to the nation or its interests: "It [the Third Estate] is the strong and robust man whose one arm remains enchained. If the privileged order were abolished, the nation would not be something less but something more....Whatever is not the Third Estate may not be regarded as being of the nation."[10] The image of the French nation as an able-bodied man crippled by the dead weight of the privileged orders was to have a lasting impact.[11] But in what way could one envision the dead weight being "abolished"? A powerful potential answer emerges in the second text, *The Last Blow Against Prejudice and Superstition* by Jacques Nicolas Billaud-Varenne, who would later serve alongside Robespierre on the Committee of Public Safety during the Reign of Terror. The *Last Blow* was originally written in 1787 but was not published until early 1789, in slightly reworked form, and the dramatic events of that year served to greatly magnify the missive's impact. Whereas Sieyès had directed the brunt of his ire against the nobility, Billaud-Varenne took aim primarily at the Church, but his advocacy of the cause of the Third Estate was just as sweeping and his imagery just as corporeal. It was also much more violent. Sieyès' robust man in chains appears in the *Last Blow* as a healthy body with a gangrened limb whose only hope for salvation lay in severing the diseased member completely: "However painful an amputation may be, when a member is gangrened it must be sacrificed if we wish to save the body."[12] R.R. Palmer has noted the impact of this imagery: "This fatal metaphor of the gangrened limb spread like a contagion through French politics for five years. It was a commonplace in the Jacobin clubs, and it was the justification for the guillotine."[13]

The major milestones of the Revolution, even in its earliest stages, were thoroughly saturated with self-conscious, if protean, references to the "nation." When the first session of the Estates-General opened on May 5, 1789, the representatives of the Third Estate immediately pushed for a more equitable distribution of power by appealing to the interests of the nation at large. When, under the influence of Sieyès and Honoré Gabriel de Mirabeau, the dissolution of the Estates-General was proclaimed on June 17, it was unthinkable for the successor body to be called anything other than the "National" Assembly.[14] Three days later, when the so-called Tennis Court Oath was proclaimed—pledging the members of the new National Assembly not to disband until they had formulated a constitution—Mirabeau grounded its authority first and foremost on the claim to represent the will of the nation.[15] The constitutional ambitions of the National Assembly were, to be sure, moderate in comparison to the radicalized attitudes that emerged among the urban poor and rural peasantry over the ensuing weeks, but nascent nationalist rhetoric and imagery flowed unpredictably through a broad variety of political groupings in the summer of 1789. When the Parisian mobs stormed the Bastille on July 14, their insurrectionary language explicitly adopted the discourse of the nation, albeit perhaps without fully understanding its implications; it is no coincidence that the citizen militia formed the day before the storming of the Bastille took the name "National Guard" and adopted the tricolor flag as its rallying symbol.[16] It is true that the unruly violence of the Great Fear, the wave of peasant uprisings that swept the French countryside from mid-July to early August, was occasioned more by pecuniary opportunism than national idealism. But the peasants' broader attack on the manorial system directly influenced the members of

FIGURE 2.1 Storming of the Bastille on 14 July 1789 *by Charles Thévenin. Metropolitan Museum of Art/Wikimedia Commons.*

the National Assembly who, on the uncommonly humid evening of August 4, loudly proclaimed amid profuse weeping and streams of sweat the abolition of feudal privilege in the interest of national solidarity.[17] The emotive fervor of that evening, over-idealized as it came to be in French public memory, has throughout the years exercised a decisive influence on nationalist rhetoric and imagery—particularly at moments when nationalists have felt the need to emphasize the power of an inclusive sense of belonging that crosses class boundaries.

The most famous document of the Revolution's early constitutional phase, the Declaration of the Rights of Man and of the Citizen, was promulgated on August 27, incorporating both abstract Enlightenment ideals and more practical principles drawn from the young American experiment in constitutional republicanism. As such, it presents us with an early instantiation of the potent mixture of universalist idealism and particularist self-interest that would come to characterize much nationalist discourse over the next two centuries. The principal author of the Declaration, Lafayette, had been deeply impacted by his experience fighting under Washington in North America, and it was there that he began to link the universal cause of Liberty with both the specific mission of the French nation and a megalomaniacal sense of personal destiny. When Lafayette returned triumphantly to France in 1779, Benjamin Franklin presented him with a ceremonial sword whose inscription, *crescat ut prosim* (let me grow to benefit mankind), can be read as the shrouding of egotism within a hazy gauze of universalist virtue.[18] While it is true that Thomas Jefferson was an important influence on Lafayette, the presence of Rousseau's general will echoes most clearly throughout the entirety of the Declaration—particularly in Article 3 ("The principle of any sovereignty resides essentially in the nation") and Article 6 ("The law is the expression of the General Will").[19]

Over the next two years, the remainder of France's first constitution was assembled piecemeal, in fits and starts, with the composition process overseen by two successive constitutional committees within the Assembly and, finally, by a committee of revisions. It appeared in print in early September 1791 with the Declaration as its preamble, and its passages established new standardized administrative and judicial structures while creating out of the labyrinthine patchwork of feudal properties a new "national" division of France into 83 roughly equal *départements*. While the 1791 Constitution established the legal basis of national sovereignty along the lines of the general will, the democratic structures it created were quite limited in practice. France was to be a constitutional monarchy, with the skeptical Louis XVI still on the throne, and French citizens were divided into "active" and "passive" categories, with full voting rights being restricted to French men over the age of twenty-five who paid a certain amount in taxes. They voted for electors who would, in turn, elect the actual parliamentary representatives, and the number of men eligible to serve as electors and representatives was limited even more severely by higher income requirements. Of a French population that numbered between 25 and 30 million, only slightly more than 4 million were enfranchised, with only a few thousand eligible to serve as electors or representatives.[20] Direct participation in the political life of the nation was to be a rare privilege.

While the legal framework for the political sovereignty of the nation was being cobbled together at a deliberate pace in the Assembly's constitutional committees, a much more emotive sense of French national sentiment had spread rapidly throughout broad segments of the population since the storming of the Bastille. In early October 1789, the National Guard, led by Lafayette, participated in a boisterous popular march on Versailles, forcing the royal family to relocate to the Tuileries Palace in Paris, where they could be kept under closer observation both by militia forces and by the National Assembly, which itself relocated from Versailles to Paris later that month. Passionate public speeches and demonstrations became increasingly regular aspects of everyday life in Paris. New vocabularies of popular engagement were pioneered, and the discourse of the nation was translated increasingly from the realm of abstract theory to the level of personal identity formation in a series of performative mass mobilizations.[21] When, in June 1791, Louis XVI and his immediate family were captured in their attempt to escape Paris in the infamous "Flight to Varennes," they became the objects of widespread derision and scorn.[22] The ill-fated escape attempt also had the effect of undermining the Constitution of 1791 even before its publication that September, since its provisions were predicated on the king's support for constitutional monarchy, support that was now undeniably lacking.

The prime catalyst for the widespread mobilization and eventual crystallization of national sentiment throughout France was the long-running military conflict that developed between France and the monarchies of Europe. In August 1791, the Prussian King Friedrich Wilhelm II and the Austrian Emperor Leopold II responded to the capture of the royal family at Varennes by issuing the Declaration of Pillnitz, which committed Prussia and Austria to military intervention in France if either the lives of the royal family or the institution of monarchy were threatened.[23] When war against Austria was declared in April 1792, with Prussia joining the conflict soon after, popular enthusiasm for a glorious victory far outpaced French military preparedness. The early stages of what became known as the First Coalition War did not go well for France. By late July, Prussian troops had defeated the French decisively at Verdun and were advancing further into French territory, when the Prussian commander, the Duke of Brunswick, issued his famous manifesto, threatening that his troops would "take unforgettable vengeance on Paris" if the royal family were harmed.[24] The result inside Paris was initial panic followed by erratic mobilization in a series of violent episodes undertaken in self-appointed defense of the nation. Most notably, on August 9–10, the local National Guard led a popular uprising to occupy the Tuileries Palace, forcing the king and his family to seek shelter in the meeting rooms of the Assembly.[25] Although their lives were saved, at least for the moment, the institution of the monarchy was abolished categorically a few weeks later. Any doubts as to the rapidly radicalizing trajectory of the Revolution were erased in the so-called September Massacres, which featured rabid crowds storming the prisons of Paris, claiming to act in defense of the nation to prevent imprisoned royalists from escaping and aiding the enemy. More than 1,000 prisoners were summarily executed in a series of purgative collective rituals of violence overseen by improvised tribunals of ad hoc judges and executioners.[26] This euphoric violence on the home front was matched, and perhaps exceeded in symbolic terms, by the battlefield performance of impassioned French citizen-soldiers. An important military turning point, and a significant moment in the broader history of nationalism, was the French victory at Valmy on September 20, 1792.

The Battle of Valmy has been immortalized in numerous paintings and works of literature. It pitted the young and ill-trained French Army, commanded by François Kellermann and Charles Dumouriez, against a battle-tested array of forces commanded by the Duke of Brunswick, consisting primarily of Prussian, Austrian, and Hessian troops, but with further support provided by the Army of Condé, which drew into its ranks émigré French royalists fighting to restore the absolute monarchy. Facing dark skies, intermittent torrential rain, and muddy terrain, the French revolutionary army succeeded in repelling the advance of Brunswick's more experienced forces via a mixture of luck, bravado, and nationalist enthusiasm. According to the overwrought imagery of later accounts, the decisive symbolic moment emerged when, during a brief lull in the battle, Kellermann turned toward his troops, waived his hat, and shouted "Vive la nation!" That rallying cry was repeated in successive waves up and down the French lines, even as entire units began belting out the newly composed *Marseillaise*, whose refrain echoed across the battlefield.[27] Opposing Prussian troops responded to the thundering chorus with bewilderment and uncertainty before beating a hasty and ultimately devastating retreat.[28] The events at Valmy did not, as it turns out, signify a broader French triumph or an end to the war. But the intoxicating orgy of nationalistic fervor unleashed that day provided the Revolution with its greatest measure of national legitimacy to date and its most lasting and potent set of triumphant symbols. The significance of Valmy in the broader history of European nationalism was perhaps even greater. The famous writer Goethe, who witnessed the battle, was being only slightly hyperbolic when he later recalled telling those with him: "Here, today, a new epoch of world history has begun, and you can say that you were present."[29]

Importantly, the victory at Valmy also created the space within which the revolutionary experiment in Paris could continue to unfold along its rapidly accelerating course. On the day following the battle, the new parliamentary body that had been elected weeks earlier under an expanded suffrage opened, changing its name from the Assembly to the National Convention. Its members were markedly more radical than had been the representatives of the Assembly, with the most notable extremist force within the new Convention being the Jacobin Club. The Jacobins took their name from the former Dominican monastery of St. Jacques, where the club held its first meetings, and their most prominent members included the physician-journalist Jean Paul Marat and the lawyers Georges-Jacques Danton, Jacques Pierre Brissot, and Maximilien Robespierre. As their numbers grew, the Jacobins were themselves increasingly divided internally between a somewhat more moderate faction, known as the Girondists and led by Brissot, and a much more radically extremist faction known as the "Mountain" and led by Robespierre.[30] While claiming loudly to espouse such humanitarian and universalist ideals as Reason and Liberty—as trumpeted in the December 1792 proclamation that France, under Jacobin leadership, would come to the aid of all European peoples oppressed by monarchical tyranny—a defining hallmark of Jacobin thought was an obsessive, often pathologically paranoid, brand of national chauvinism.[31] This emotive fervor united both Jacobin factions and saturated the rhythms of their everyday existence, extending even to their interpersonal greetings, their daily vocabulary, and their clothing.[32]

Initially, the Girondists under Brissot had exercised primary influence within the National Convention, but the ambitious Robespierre and his supporters within the Mountain searched eagerly for a path to power. The debate over the fate of Louis XVI provided Robespierre with an opportunity to demonstrate his persuasive skills and, it was hoped, to outflank his rival

Brissot. The king had been under effective house arrest since his attempt to flee Paris in June 1791 and, following the storming of the Tuileries in August 1792, he had been incarcerated in the Temple Fortress awaiting trial for treason. When the trial officially opened in December, Brissot and the Girondists advocated keeping Louis XVI alive, if for no other reason than that he could serve as a potentially valuable hostage. But on December 3, 1792, Robespierre, in one of his most famous speeches, appealed to the inviolability of the nation as clear justification for the king's execution, while also invoking the coercive aspects of Rousseau's general will.[33]

EXCERPT 2.1

Speech of December 3, 1792

Maximilien Robespierre

The Assembly has been unwittingly led far from the true question. There is no question here of a trial. Louis is not an accused person; you are not judges—you are, you can be, only statesmen and representatives of the nation. You have no sentence to render for or against a man, but a measure of public safety to take, an act of national providence to exercise. [...]

When a nation has been forced to have recourse to the right of insurrection, it returns to a state of nature with regard to the tyrant. How can that tyrant invoke the social pact? He has annihilated it. The nation can still preserve it, if it thinks it well, for that which concerns the relations of citizens among themselves; but the effect of tyranny and insurrection is to entirely sever relations with the tyrant; it is to place them reciprocally in a state of war. [...] The peoples do not judge as do judiciary courts: they do not pronounce sentence, they launch the thunderbolt; they do not condemn kings, they plunge them into nothingness; and this justice is worth far more than that of tribunals.

[...] Yes, the death penalty is generally a crime, and for that reason only, according to the indestructible principles of nature, to be justified in the case where it is necessary for the safety of individuals or the social body. So the public safety never makes use of it against ordinary offences, because society can always prevent these by other means, and can render the guilty incapable of injuring it. But with a King dethroned in the midst of a Revolution which is nothing less than cemented by the laws, a King whose name alone brings the scourge of war upon the agitated nation, neither prison nor exile can render his existence indifferent to the public welfare; and this cruel exception to the ordinary laws avowed by justice can be imputed only to the nature of his crimes. I pronounce this fatal truth with regret—but Louis must die because the nation must live.[34]

Robespierre and the radicals carried the day, and Louis XVI was duly delivered to the guillotine and beheaded on January 21, 1793.[35] This was not simply a purgative event of symbolic import. In a very real sense, for Robespierre and the growing tide of revolutionary nationalists, the nation was liberated—indeed redeemed in an almost metaphysical manner—by this violent act of removal. The traditional announcement upon the death of a French monarch ("The king is dead, long live the king!") was on this day supplanted by the frenzied cry "*Vive la nation!*" as the king's bloody head was held up for the crowd to ogle. As Adam Zamoyski has noted: "The message was unequivocal. The nation had replaced the king as the sovereign and therefore as the validating element in the state."[36] It would seem that Billaud-Varenne's "gangrened limb" had indeed been severed, but as future events would demonstrate, the wound would not heal easily.

In his quest for power, Robespierre began looking increasingly to the unruly mobs of urban poor in Paris—the so-called *sans-culottes* ("without breeches") who wore workmen's trousers rather than the knee breeches of the elites—as both a malleable mass ripe for political manipulation and as a valuable source of street-level muscle. Robespierre also assumed a central position on the Committee of Public Safety, which was formed in the spring of 1793 as a state surveillance agency with wide-ranging authority, and he proceeded to use the new tools at his disposal to remove obstacles to his power, while striving to foment popular nationalism to an unprecedented degree. Thus, in the summer of 1793 he orchestrated the arrest of his chief rival Brissot, along with nearly thirty of Brissot's moderate Jacobin supporters, while pushing through, in concert with fellow Committee member Lazare-Nicolas Carnot, a sweeping mass military mobilization—a *levée en masse*—which drafted all single French men aged 18–25 into national military service, regardless of regional or social background. Although it took until October for Brissot and his compatriots to be tried and executed, the *levée en masse* exercised an almost immediate positive impact on the French conduct of the war, with nearly one million new recruits taking to the field within the first six months.[37] Also, in a longer-term perspective, the imperative of universal military service helped spread identification with the nation through broad segments of society, acting as a collective rite of passage.

From the summer of 1793 until the summer of 1794, revolutionary France experienced the infamous Reign of Terror, in which tens of thousands of French citizens were executed under the authority of the Committee of Public Safety and its revolutionary tribunals. Scholars have engaged in extensive debates over the causes and significance of the Terror, with historians such as Simon Schama, Eli Sagan, and Adam Zamoyski seeing a godless and essentially demonic collectivistic impulse at the heart of the bloodshed,[38] while more sympathetic interpreters like Patrice Higonnet and Slavoj Zizek have attempted to salvage positive elements of Jacobin ideology from beneath the mass detritus of state-sponsored carnage.[39] Other scholars, such as Timothy Tackett and Marisa Linton, have taken somewhat more balanced narrative approaches.[40] Robespierre's stated purpose in imposing the Terror was to create and maintain a "republic of virtue," which would champion universalistic and humanistic ideals throughout the world for the betterment of mankind. In a more practical and parochial sense, terror was seen as necessary not only to overcome the resistance of oppressive Old Regime structures but to serve as a perpetual purifier of the nation. It was during the Terror that the triumphalist rhetoric of national greatness reached its most fevered pitch, with France being celebrated as a nation of destiny bound for inevitable glory. But in reality, the bombast of that discourse masked a deep-seated insecurity that the young nation was fragile and vulnerable, necessitating constant vigilance and an obsessive paranoia toward perceived internal and external threats.[41] There was, of course, no shortage of these threats to be found.

The victims of the Terror included a broad spectrum of perceived subversive elements and "enemies of the nation." The royalist uprising in the Vendée, in northwest France, had provided justification for a brutal crackdown starting already in the spring of 1793, with the so-called infernal columns (*colonnes infernales*) mobilized under General Louis Marie Turreau in October engaging in widespread civilian massacres and racking up a death toll that reached perhaps 40,000 by the summer of 1794.[42] Recalcitrant clergy were also targeted for extermination, with the mass drownings of priests in the Loire River between October 1793 and February 1794 serving as perhaps the most infamous illustrations.[43] But it was the guillotine that stood as the most visible (and lethal) symbol of state-sponsored violence during the Terror. Statistically, the largest proportion of its victims were farmers, peasants, and shopkeepers convicted by revolutionary tribunals for placing selfish interest over the interests of the nation—typically via hoarding, draft evasion, or desertion—but significant numbers of nobles and family members of royalist emigrés were also targeted in successive purgative waves. The condemned were often carted in ritualized processions through the streets of Paris on the way to face the "national razor," as the guillotine quickly became known.[44] Famously, as vigilance turned increasingly to paranoia, the Revolution began obsessively to devour its own supporters. Early champions of revolutionary egalitarianism like the so-called *Enragés* (the Enraged), who mobilized mass urban "sections" and helped Robespierre bring down Brissot and the Girondists in early June 1793, came under increasing suspicion.[45] Their most notable leader, Jacques Roux, delivered a fiery manifesto before the National Convention on June 25, 1793, attacking parasitical financial speculators alternately as "vampires," "bloodsuckers," and "assassins of the nation," and claiming that widespread executions among the wealthy were imperative in order to "save the fatherland."[46] But within a few weeks, Roux himself was arrested on suspicion of having treasonous foreign contacts and was brutally interrogated and imprisoned for several months. While Roux managed to commit suicide in jail before being led to the guillotine in February 1794, the beheading of his influential *enragé* collaborator, Jacques Hébert, was turned into a major public spectacle.[47] The April 1794 trial and execution of former Jacobin leaders Camille Desmoulins, who had been a childhood friend of Robespierre, and Georges Danton, who had served alongside Robespierre on the Committee of Public Safety, were pitched as events of even greater national significance.[48]

The excesses of the Terror led directly, if not quite inevitably, to the fall of Robespierre and the Committee of Public Safety in the summer of 1794. When Robespierre refused to moderate the Terror despite tangible improvements in security both internally and externally, moderates within the National Convention moved quickly to depose him in what became known as the Thermidorian Reaction. On July 26, 1794, the ninth of Thermidor on the Revolutionary calendar, Robespierre was shouted down in the Convention while preparing to announce another wave of purges, and a measure was hastily passed ordering his arrest and that of several dozen of his closest supporters. After apparently attempting (and failing) to commit suicide in custody that night by shooting himself in the face—the bullet ripped away part of his jaw but left him alive—he was paraded the next day through throngs of jeering onlookers to the guillotine on the Place de la Revolution where, after having his facial bandage painfully torn away by the executioner, he was guillotined.[49]

It took some time after the death of Robespierre for the proverbial dust to settle. Periodic violence continued over the next year or so in the form of the White Terror—reprisals directed at those who had participated in Robespierre's bloody reign—and an especially poor harvest in 1795 led to further unrest and periodic bread riots.[50] A new constitution was published in 1795, creating a bicameral legislature and authorizing the formation of a five-person executive body known as the Directory.[51] Despite the fact that some sense of domestic normalcy began to return, and although French military forces continued to experience a fair amount of success, the Directory was broadly unpopular. It was particularly unsatisfying for those who had tasted the heady brew of nationalist fervor and longed to see it mobilized again. In 1799 Abbe Sieyès, who ten years earlier had so effectively captured nascent nationalist sentiment in his pamphlet *What Is the Third Estate?*, used his position as one of the five Directors to maneuver into power the figure who would exercise a monumental influence on France, the rest of Europe, and the history of nationalism: Napoleon Bonaparte.

Before proceeding to the Napoleonic era, a brief consideration of the interplay between French revolutionary nationalism and two other central markers of identity—religion and gender—is in order. The religious landscape of the Old Regime was dominated by the Gallican Church, which provided France with an important measure of social cohesion despite internal tensions occasioned by the Jansenist movement and secular challenges presented by enlightened *philosophes*. It is true that by the 1780s the Church was facing a severe shortage in priestly vocations, with the ranks of the clergy dipping to approximately 170,000 (or 0.6 percent of the population). But the Church and its ancillary institutions still directly owned some 10 percent of the land throughout France while exercising less direct control over a much larger territory through the collection of the tithe.[52] Even in the capital Paris, the Church controlled fully one-quarter of all property in 1789.[53] The search within the National Assembly for quick financial fixes placed the Church clearly in the cross-hairs. Following the abolition of the ecclesiastical tithe in August 1789, Church holdings fell victim to successive waves of confiscation in the name of national renewal. The language of the resolution passed by the Assembly on November 2, 1789, was particularly sweeping: all the property of the Church was to be "placed at the disposal of the nation."[54] The Civil Constitution of the Clergy, promulgated in July 1790, demanded that French priests declare loyalty first and foremost to the nation, and the subsequent requirement that priests swear an oath in support of the constitution divided the French clergy in roughly equal portions between "juring" and "non-juring" or refractory priests.[55] The perceived antinational stance of the latter, particularly in Paris, made them subject to consistent harassment and persecution.

The political ascendancy of the Jacobins brought with it a wide-ranging campaign of dechristianization. The nation replaced the Church as the organizing principle behind the new revolutionary calendar, in which religious holidays and saints' days were abolished, and streets and places named for Christian saints gave way to new appellations venerating national heroes.[56] Dechristianization should not, however, be seen as a fundamentally atheistic project, nor did it signify the abandonment of the search for transcendence. It was in distinct opposition to the radical revolutionary atheism of Jacques Hébert and others that Robespierre proposed perhaps his most ambitious project: the elevation of the nation, veiled in the noble attire of humanist universalism, to a position of divine supremacy. The Cult of the Supreme Being, as it was called, was announced in the spring of 1794 as the basis for a new state religion that would, it was hoped, provide increased social cohesion and imbue the new France with a cosmic sense of mission.[57] In keeping with Rousseau's emphasis on popular festivity, the Cult was inaugurated by a grandiose open-air ceremony on the Champ de Mars on June 8, 1794, the Festival of the Supreme Being, which was intended to serve as the model for future weekly festivals throughout France. Planned and choreographed by the painter and "pageant master" of the revolution Jacques-Louis David, the Festival's aim was to foster a powerful sense of performative belonging that would lift participants out of their mundane daily existence and transport them to a sublime plane of collective transcendence.[58] David's intricate plan called for events to begin that morning at 5 a.m., with citizens organizing themselves into gender-specific age groups—each group with a different prescribed mode of uniform attire—and then, following an artillery salvo at 8 a.m., processing in unison past a "large body of musicians" to the main gathering area, on which a huge artificial mountain had been built.

FIGURE 2.2 Festival of the Supreme Being *by Pierre-Antoine Demachy.*
Carnavalet Museum, Paris/Wikimedia Commons.

Robespierre delivered an impassioned sermon in which he fused the
cause of France with the broader fate of humanity, skillfully adorning
nationalist fervor with the emblems of universal idealism. The synthesis was
striking on a number of levels. Preparations for the event had been designed
to celebrate the broader virtues of Freedom, with houses being decked out
in the "beloved colors of Liberty" which, of course, happened to consist of
nothing other than the blue, white, and red of the French tricolor. Atop the
artificial mountain was the "Tree of Liberty," whose universal symbolism
was paired with (and, in fact, dwarfed by) the giant "Altar of the Nation,"
with the surrounding landscaped terrain identified as the "National
Garden." Robespierre's address was designed to "honor Nature's Creator"
and venerate the "Liberty and Virtue [that] issued together from the breast
of the Supreme Being," while condemning the "oppressors of the human
race" and presiding over a bizarre symbolic ritual in which the "monster
Atheism" was destroyed. While these elements claimed to speak to universal
human callings, the central formulation used by Robespierre in addressing
those assembled framed the Festival first in nationalist, then in political,
terms: "Frenchmen, Republicans, it is up to you to cleanse the earth..."[59]
The Supreme Being can, in fact, be seen in many ways as a manifestation
of the purported greatness of the French nation itself. Not long before,
Robespierre had made this equation explicit, rendering the French nation
as the modern corollary to the great gods of the ancient Greeks: "You are,
among the nations, what Hercules was amongst the heroes....Nature has
made you sturdy and powerful; your strength matches your virtue and your
cause is that of the gods themselves."[60]

It is worth noting that one of the last waves of anti-Christian persecution before the fall of Robespierre featured a group of Carmelite nuns who famously sang as they were led to the guillotine on July 17, 1794.[61] Their fate connects in interesting ways with the broader fate of women during the Revolution. Rousseau, the model for so many revolutionaries, had been opposed to women's participation in the public sphere, relegating them to the private domain of domesticity and virtuous child-rearing.[62] The Declaration of Rights of Man and Citizen was, despite its soaring emancipatory imagery, clear in its gendered exclusivity, and the Constitution of 1791 did nothing to enfranchise women (although, it should be noted, its limited franchise also excluded a majority of French men). The gulf between rhetoric and reality did not go unnoticed. Perhaps most famously, on the eve of the promulgation of the 1791 Constitution, Olympe de Gouges published her "Declaration of the Rights of Woman and the Female Citizen," which appealed directly to nationalist sentiment in mocking the revolutionary hypocrisy that kept French women in a subordinate position. The preamble framed the entire document in national terms, beginning: "Mothers, daughters, sisters, and representatives of the nation demand to be constituted into a national assembly." Article Three provided a particularly sweeping characterization of women's centrality to the nation—"The principle of sovereignty rests essentially with the nation, which is nothing but the union of man and woman"—while Article Sixteen proceeded to critique the forthcoming constitution as a violation of national solidarity: "The constitution is null if the majority of individuals comprising the nation have not cooperated in drafting it."[63] De Gouges' manifesto not only fell on deaf ears among early revolutionary moderates. Having run afoul of Robespierre and his allies, she was sent to the guillotine in November 1793.[64]

While excluded from official channels of political participation, the active agency of women was an indispensable component of the Revolution's broader mobilization of national sentiment. On October 5, 1789, it was Parisian women who, fueled by anger over high bread prices and offended by reports of a gluttonous banquet sponsored by Marie Antoinette a few days earlier, stormed the Hôtel de Ville in Paris before staging a dramatic march to Versailles, where they helped force the relocation of the royal family to the Tuileries Palace. The participation of Lafayette and the National Guard in the march came not as an instigating force, but as a hasty response to the unexpectedly powerful mobilization of women from below.[65] In describing the self-identification of women with the nationalist cause and the impact of female activism on the evolution of revolutionary national discourse, Dominque Godineau has characterized French women in the early 1790s as "guardians of the nation."[66] On a more official level, women did make some modest gains in these years—such as limited divorce and inheritance rights—although most of these were eventually abandoned with the adoption in 1804 of the Code Napoleon.

Whereas religious identity in the French revolutionary context was typically framed as an impediment to national solidarity, gendered imagery was, though fraught with contradictions, often successfully co-opted and woven into the fabric of nationalist mobilization. It is strangely fitting that the exclusion of women from parliamentary politics proceeded alongside the compensatory proliferation of the idealized feminine image of Marianne, who was proclaimed the national symbol of France in September 1792, the same month as the Battle of Valmy.[67]

Napoleonic exports

Napoleon's establishment of power in France set the stage for his campaigns of conquest throughout Europe, under cover of which many of the principles of the Revolution—not least the idea of the nation—were exported across the continent. In certain ways, Napoleon's central influence on the spread of nationalism seems contradictory. The coup that initially brought him to power in 1799 was widely seen as marking the end of the French Revolution, and with it potentially the end of the heyday of political and military mobilization in the name of the nation. His 1804 self-coronation as hereditary emperor constituted a violation of the principle that the nation alone, embodied in the general will, was the source of sovereignty. Furthermore, although on occasion Napoleon did attempt to foment nationalist sentiment among other European peoples, the overarching goal of his conquests was to establish a continental empire, not a Europe of free and independent nation-states. Much of the nationalist wave that swept Europe during the era was formulated in opposition to Napoleonic military and occupation policies. That did not, of course, make the wave any less powerful.

Napoleon himself represented a tangle of contradictions, particularly in regard to conceptions of national identity. He was born in 1769 on the island of Corsica, which belonged to France but whose population was comprised primarily of Italian-speakers. Napoleon's parents were descended from Tuscan nobility, and Napoleon himself spoke French with a pronounced accent his entire life.[68] One of the earliest expressions of his messianic ambition was his childhood fantasy of leading the glorious liberation of Corsica from French control. That his megalomania was ultimately directed in the service of France, rather than against it, had less to do with the decision to send him as a boy to elite French military academies—where he was bullied for his short physical stature and mocked for his foreign accent—than with the careerist opportunities that eventually presented themselves to him. After graduating early from the *École militaire* in Paris in 1785, at age 16, he was commissioned as a junior officer in the French artillery, while maintaining a fervent desire for Corsican independence from France. In May 1789, as the Estates-General were beginning deliberations amid swirling winds of nascent nationalist idealism, Napoleon eagerly appropriated the discourse of the nation in the service of his island homeland, writing to a fellow Corsican patriot: "As the nation was perishing, I was born. Thirty thousand Frenchmen were vomited on to our [Corsican] shores, drowning the throne of liberty in waves of blood....Slavery was the price of our submission. Crushed by the triple yoke of the soldier, the lawmaker, and the tax inspector, our compatriots live despised."[69]

Showing himself to be unusually adept at opportunistic manipulation, however, Napoleon maneuvered himself through the various radicalizing phases of the Revolution, ultimately embracing the Jacobin cause and aligning himself with Robespierre's younger brother Augustin.[70] In September 1793, as the Terror was still in its early stages, the twenty-four-year-old Napoleon was rewarded for his connections and given command of French republican forces in the siege of Toulon, fighting against royalists supported by the English and Spanish. In the course of the successful siege, Napoleon received not only a leg wound, which burnished his heroic image, but also promotion to the rank of general. He also came to the attention of Paul Barras, one of the leaders of the Thermidorian Reaction, who after the fall of Robespierre employed Napoleon's military skills in the service of the Directory and brought the ambitious young general increasingly into the spotlight of public celebrity.[71] Having crushed a royalist uprising on the streets of Paris in October 1795—in the so-called Battle of 13 Vendémiaire—Napoleon continued his ascent, leading French forces in northern Italy to a series of striking victories before suffering his first substantial setbacks in a series of defeats to the British in Egypt.[72] It is a further testament to Napoleon's opportunistic skill that he escaped the Egyptian disaster with his reputation largely unscathed, returning to France in the fall of 1799 and stepping smoothly into a ready-made coup orchestrated that November by Sieyès and others, who schemed to replace the Directory with a more streamlined form of governance.

The "Coup of 18 Brumaire," as it became known, established the successor system to the Directory—the Consulate, which governed France for the next several years—and Napoleon's initial title within the new government was simply that of First Consul. Once in this position, however, he moved quickly to expand and consolidate his power, presiding over the writing of a new constitution and instituting financial reforms that helped balance the budget while also distributing the tax burden somewhat more equitably.[73] These economic reforms were matched in the realm of legal theory by the construction of the Code Napoleon which, after some four years of elaborate drafting, was published in March 1804.[74] While essentially a nonreligious Catholic himself, Napoleon was intent on building bridges with the Church in France. In December 1799, he issued two edicts that returned to the Church significant amounts of property that had not yet been sold off, and in July 1801 he signed a symbolically important Concordat with Rome. Perhaps most notably, the Concordat reinforced the primacy of national imperatives over religious identity, but did so skillfully and with a reassuring nod to traditional Catholics, proclaiming that "Catholicism is the religion of the majority of the French" while explicitly stopping short of declaring Catholicism the state religion.[75] While Pope Pius VII was present at the ceremony at which Napoleon was crowned emperor in December 1804, it was Napoleon himself who performed the ostentatious coronation. The image of the newly minted imperial dictator was marketed and sold to the French people as the glorious embodiment of the nation. While cultivating an external aura of invincibility, internal structures of coercion and surveillance were established to purify and police the nation, and freedoms of speech and the press were increasingly curtailed. Having consolidated his base of power, Napoleon could claim to be the guardian of the Revolution's legacy at home, even as he prepared to spread many of its ideals throughout the European continent via military conquest.

Building on the model of national conscription pioneered more than a decade earlier, Napoleon assembled one of the premier fighting forces in European history, christening it the *Grand Armée* and fueling its ranks with equal measures of nationalist fervor and masculinist bravado, as Michael Hughes has shown.[76] Following a brief and uneasy period of peace in the aftermath of the treaties of Lunéville (February 1801) and Amiens (March 1802), hostilities between France and much of Europe were resumed in 1803 and would continue for more than a decade. One of the central early causes of renewed fighting was the establishment and nature of French rule in Italy, which the British and Austrians saw as a destabilizing force in Europe. French control of northern and central Italian territories dated back to the campaigns of 1796 and 1797, which at the time had afforded the up-and-coming Napoleon with a significant boost in popular publicity.[77] The next several years witnessed the proliferation throughout the region of Jacobin-style clubs, in which an emotional form of republican nationalism was cultivated among idealistic young Italians, even as the French occupying forces under the Directory looked at these clubs with increasing suspicion. In 1802, when Napoleon established the so-called Italian Republic, he named himself President and continued to foment nationalist sentiment by creating an Italian National Guard, while also instituting reforms modeled on French Revolutionary practice.[78] Following Napoleon's imperial coronation, the republican façade in Italy was dropped entirely with the 1805 establishment of the Kingdom of Italy—composed of northern and eastern territories, along with parts of the Dalmatian coast—which Napoleon nominally ruled as "King," although governance lay largely in the hands of his stepson Eugène de Beauharnais, who served as viceroy. The military of the Kingdom of Italy was incorporated into Napoleon's *Grande Armée* and participated in several key Napoleonic battles over the ensuing years.[79]

Other Italian territories were progressively folded into the Napoleonic system as well, beginning with the annexation of the Republic of Liguoria in the summer of 1805, and continuing the next year with the conquest of the southern half of the Italian peninsula and Sicily, which were given, under the rubric of the Kingdom of Naples, first to Napoleon's brother

Joseph to rule and then to his brother-in-law Joachim Murat.[80] Napoleonic forces invaded the Papal States in 1808 and occupied Rome starting in 1809.[81] While traditionalists saw little but aggression and exploitation in Napoleonic policies, younger Italians increasingly embraced the discourse of the nation as the vehicle for a revival of Italy's historic greatness. Ultimately, French control of Italy was to be short-lived, collapsing first with Napoleon's defeat and initial exile in 1814 and ending completely with the October 1815 execution of Murat. But the powerful dream of unification and national rebirth—the roots of the so-called *Risorgimento*—would have been unthinkable without the ideas and movements that coursed through Italy in the Napoleonic era.[82]

After having been placed by his brother on the throne of the Kingdom of Naples in 1806, Joseph Bonaparte was transferred by Napoleon two years later to the Iberian Peninsula and proclaimed the new King of Spain. Earlier, under King Charles IV, Spain had allied itself with Napoleonic France, but ever-increasing numbers of French forces on Spanish soil, combined with growing economic problems, sparked widespread unrest and led to a coup in March 1808, which forced Charles IV to abdicate in favor of his son Ferdinand VII. Napoleon seized the opportunity to expand his power and, refusing to recognize Ferdinand, proceeded to install his brother Joseph on the throne, initiating a brutal period of French occupation and Spanish resistance that lasted until 1814. It was in opposition to Napoleonic oppression that a heroic narrative of Spanish national independence emerged, beginning with the heavily mythologized uprising of May 2, 1808, which was followed the next day by reprisal executions. The martyrs of the third of May, captured memorably in one of Goya's most famous paintings, were elevated to a position of national sainthood. As the conflict spread, British troops joined with the indigenous opposition to fight against French forces (and a minority of pro-Napoleonic Spanish elites) in what became known as the Peninsular War, devolving quickly into a messy quagmire characterized by bloody guerrilla warfare.[83] The revived brand of Spanish nationalist sentiment fostered during the Peninsular War was married in interesting ways to Catholic identity, as shown in an insightful recent study by Scott Eastman, and then exported to Spanish holdings in the Americas.[84] Importantly, idealized visions of heroic Spanish resistance served as inspiration for aspiring nationalists oppressed by Napoleonic expansion elsewhere in Europe.

In the Scandinavian states, the impact of the Napoleonic system, and the French revolutionary era before it, was varied. In the late eighteenth century, the two dominant regional powers—both absolutist monarchies— were Sweden, which included all of Finland and parts of what is now eastern Germany, and Denmark, which included Norway, Iceland, and the duchies of Schleswig and Holstein. On the eve of the French Revolution, in 1788, the Danish crown had initiated a wide-ranging agrarian reform program that was implemented gradually over the next two decades, ultimately

Denmark + France against Sweden + co.

leading to the abolition of serfdom and an increased measure of popular dynastic loyalty.[85] Danish sympathy for the French revolutionary cause was somewhat surprisingly visible, particularly among governing elites who, as self-professed (albeit selective) advocates of Enlightenment, saw themselves in strange ways as kindred spirits with French reformers. In 1793, a group of Copenhagen merchants organized a celebration in honor of the French Jacobins, which included the donning of cockades and the singing of the Marseillaise. Pro-Jacobin sentiments were also fairly widespread at the time among university students, who formed the Copenhagen Jacobin Club.[86] On a more official level, during the Napoleonic wars, Danish participation was intermittent but almost exclusively on the side of France. In 1801, the British navy attacked and defeated the Danish fleet in the Battle of Copenhagen, before eventually destroying the fleet entirely in the aftermath of the brutally destructive bombardment of Copenhagen in 1807.[87] Starting in 1809, under the new king Frederick VI, Denmark fought a series of successful battles against Sweden, which had aligned itself with Britain and the broader anti-Napoleonic coalition.[88]

In Sweden, the absolutist monarchy under Gustav III had already begun to reframe its public face by fusing dynastic and Enlightenment imagery in the 1770s and 1780s.[89] During the French revolutionary and Napoleonic eras, Sweden was consistently on the side of France's opponents. In the context of the 1809 Swedish defeat to Denmark and Russia, which at the time was temporarily aligned with Napoleon, Gustav IV was forced to summon Sweden's archaic parliamentary estates, known as the *Riksdag*, which preceded his ouster in a coup led by military elites. Under his successor, Charles XIII, Swedish politics over the next several years were dominated by wide-ranging reform plans fueled in part by French-inspired nationalist ideals among the growing middle classes, who proposed a reformation of the Riksdag and the adoption of a bicameral parliament. Ultimately, however, Liberal and nationalist idealism waned, and Sweden went on to become one of the last European countries to abandon its archaic estates system several decades later.[90]

The British Isles witnessed a significant amount of activism at the time of the French Revolution, with much of it continuing on into the Napoleonic era. Beginning in the 1790s, as the Jacobins were emerging in France, Irish patriots and displaced religious dissenters from England formed armed militias of "Volunteers," and in July 1792 celebrated the third anniversary of Bastille Day on the streets of Belfast, joined by some of the most influential early exponents of literary romanticism in Ireland.[91] As Britain entered the war against France, Irish Jacobins began calling for national independence and the formation of an Irish Republic. With the creation of the United Irishmen in 1791, nascent ideals of Irish national solidarity overcame even religious divisions, as leading Protestant dissenters joined forces with Catholics to launch the movement that culminated in the Irish Rebellion of 1798, which Ian Haywood has described as a particularly dramatic instance of "bloody romanticism."[92] The rebellion was crushed by the British military and the insurgents were executed in massive numbers that rivaled the Reign of Terror in France, with estimates ranging from 30,000 to 100,000—all the more striking since the Irish population was but a fraction of the population of France.[93] An abortive uprising led by Robert Emmet in 1803 was similarly stamped out, but Emmet's last words before his hanging would resonate in Irish nationalist discourse for more than a century: "When my country takes her place among the nations of the earth, then, and not till then, let my epitaph be written."[94] Although the United Irishmen were effectively dissolved in the aftermath of Emmet's execution, due in part to the emergence of sectarian differences, the group continued to influence the radical wing of the nationalist movement, associated most notably with Irish Republicanism.

As was the case in Ireland, the early romantic literary revival in Scotland—particularly associated with Robert Burns—fed into a nascent form of Scottish nationalist mobilization in the 1790s.[95] Partially under the influence of the United Irishmen, a Society of United Scotsmen was formed, idealizing French Jacobin imagery and calling for a republican form of Scottish independence.[96] Following the imposition of a new British conscription law in 1797, the Scotsmen launched an abortive uprising, which mobilized romantic imagery to an unprecedented extent but was ultimately crushed.[97] However, one of their leading members, Thomas Muir, traveled to France in 1798 and met with Talleyrand in an (ultimately unsuccessful) attempt to gain material and military support for a continued uprising.[98] When Muir died in early 1799 while in hiding in France, the nationalistic cult of his heroic martyrdom began. After the launching of the Napoleonic project in that same year, attitudes in Scotland grew increasingly anti-French, with Napoleon's ultimate defeat at Waterloo forming a central element in the accelerating nationalistic mythology.[99]

In political and military terms, the British government was the most consistent enemy of Napoleonic France in all of Europe in these years, having been the first among the European powers to resume hostilities in 1803 and continuing to fight across numerous theaters until Napoleon's final defeat.[100] Against the backdrop of the very real threat of French invasion—Napoleon had gathered a massive force at Bolougne, on the coast of the English Channel—the stunning British naval victory over the French and (pro-Napoleonic) Spanish fleets at Trafalgar in October 1805 cemented the image of Lord Nelson, the battle's most famous fatality, as perhaps the quintessential paragon of English national virtue.[101] The threat of invasion also sharpened and deepened popular mockery of Napoleon—the hated "Boney" whose unseemly ambitions were portrayed as laughably out of step with his diminutive physical stature—which in turn helped define perceptions of British national character in reverse.[102] Trafalgar also forced Napoleon to focus his primary energies on the continent rather than on the seas.[103]

And so it was that the German-speaking territories bore the brunt of Napoleon's continental assault, being transformed as a result perhaps more thoroughly than anywhere else in Europe. As the central power within the Holy Roman Empire of the German Nation—a "nation" that existed only in the vaguest of symbolic terms—Austria's geopolitical position was precarious and its military largely outdated. Having been technically at peace with France since signing the Treaty of Lunéville in early 1801, Austria responded to Napoleon's founding of the Kingdom of Italy in March 1805 by joining with Britain and Russia in a new anti-Napoleonic coalition. By that fall, though, Austrian forces had suffered a series of devastating defeats in the prolonged Ulm Campaign, and Vienna itself was occupied by Napoleonic troops. This set the stage for the Battle of Austerlitz, widely considered Napoleon's most stunning victory, which was fought on December 2, 1805—one year to the day after Napoleon's glorious self-coronation as French emperor.[104] A combined Austrian and Russian force was routed by the *Grande Armée* in such decisive fashion that Austria was forced to sign a humiliating peace in the form of the Treaty of Pressburg.[105] The coalition, at least for the time being, collapsed.

The resumption of fighting the next year was presaged by two significant developments within the German-speaking lands. In July 1806, the Confederation of the Rhine (*Rheinbund*) was created as a Napoleonic satellite entity, consisting initially of sixteen German states—by 1808, the number had swelled to thirty-five—and further underscoring the hopelessly divided nature of Central European dynastic and territorial politics.[106] Since these states had been members of the Holy Roman Empire, whose viability was now essentially null, the emperor Francis II was forced in August 1806 to officially dissolve the Empire, bringing to an ignominious end the sprawling structure that had been a conspicuous, if amorphous and ever-shifting, feature of the map of Europe for nearly a millennium.[107] Under Napoleonic influence, the states within the Confederation of the Rhine underwent a series of modernizing reform projects, ranging from the imposition of the Code Napoleon to the secularization of Church property to, in the case of Bavaria, the adoption of a constitution in 1808.[108] In the whirl of chaotic events, it was impossible to predict when—or if—a unified German nation-state might emerge out of the rubble of the collapsed Empire. Divisions and competing agendas within the Empire had certainly provided no consensus as to what could or should define an overarching sense of German national identity.[109] In light of the incorporation of so many German states into the *Rheinbund*, and with Austria largely on the sidelines until 1809, it fell to Prussia to pick up the mantle of German resistance against Napoleon.

When Prussia declared war on France as part of a new coalition in August 1806, citing the Napoleonic occupation of Hanover as partial cause, it was prepared to go it alone. In many ways, there was no other option. The British had initiated a naval blockade in May 1806 and, in the short term, Britain's main contribution to the anti-Napoleonic coalition would take the form of economic warfare, not overt military engagement.[110] The other major coalition partner, Russia, was similarly unprepared to mobilize militarily in the short term. After several weeks of jockeying and brinksmanship, on October 14, 1806, the Prussians engaged Napoleonic forces in the battles of Jena and Auerstedt. The results were famously disastrous for Prussia. Not only were Prussian troops defeated soundly on the battlefield by numerically smaller contingents of the *Grande Armée*—with nearly 200,000 Prussians either dead, wounded, or captured—but Napoleon pushed on to Berlin and occupied the city in late October before forcing Prussia into a painful peace. The humiliation ran deep and was not without consequence for the future of Prussia and the course of German nationalism.[111] It was against the backdrop of French-occupied Berlin that the Prussian philosopher Johann Gottlieb Fichte delivered his famous *Addresses to the German Nation*, calling for revenge against France while also offering an impassioned plea for national unification. In the Fourteenth Address, excerpted below, Fichte's approach manifested several features seen in earlier nationalist appeals—particularly the cloaking of national self-interest in the mantle of universalism—while revealing some of the fault lines that would plague nationalists' attempts to define "Germanness" over the coming decades.

EXCERPT 2.2

Addresses to the German Nation

Johann Gottlieb Fichte

In the addresses which I conclude today, I have spoken aloud to you first of all, but I have had in view the whole German nation, and my intention has been to gather round me, in the room in which you are bodily present, everyone in the domain of the German language who is able to understand me. If I have succeeded in throwing into any heart which has beaten here in front of me a spark which will continue to glow there and to influence its life, it is not my intention that these hearts should remain apart and lonely; I want to gather to them from over the whole of our common soil men of similar sentiments and resolutions, and to link them together, so that at this central point a single, continuous, and unceasing flame of patriotic disposition may be kindled, which will spread over the whole soil of the Fatherland to its utmost boundaries.

These addresses have not been meant for the entertainment of indolent ears and eyes in the present age; on the contrary, I want to know once for all, and everyone of like disposition shall know it with me, whether there is anyone besides ourselves whose way of thinking is akin to ours. Every German who still believes himself to be a member of a nation, who thinks highly and nobly of that nation, hopes for it, ventures, endures, and suffers for it, shall at last have the uncertainty of his belief removed; he shall see clearly whether he is right or is only a fool and a dreamer; from now on he shall either pursue his way with the glad consciousness of certainty, or else firmly and vigorously renounce a Fatherland here below, and find in the heavenly one his only consolation. To them, not as individuals in our everyday limited life, but as representatives of the nation, and so through their ears to the whole nation, these addresses make this appeal:

Centuries have come and gone since you were last convoked as you are today; in such numbers; in a cause so great, so urgent and of such concern to all and everyone; so entirely as a nation and as Germans. Never again will the offer come to you in this way. If you now take no heed and withdraw into yourselves, if you again let these addresses go by you as if they were meant merely to tickle your ears, or if you regard them as something strange and fabulous, then no human being will ever take you into account again. Hearken now at last; reflect now at last. Go not from your place this time at least without first making a firm resolution; and let everyone who hears my voice make this resolution by himself and for himself, just as if he were alone and had to do everything alone. If very many individuals think in this way, there will soon be formed a large community which will be fused into a single close-connected force. But if, on the contrary, each one, leaving himself out, puts his hope in the rest and leaves the matter to others, then there will be no others, and all together will remain as they were before. Make it on the spot, this resolution.

To all you Germans, whatever position you may occupy in society, these addresses solemnly appeal; let every one of you who can think, think first of all about the subject here suggested, and let each do for it what lies nearest to him individually in the position he occupies.[112]

On the one hand, Fichte employed inclusive elements of Rousseau's general will, cultivating a powerful sense of belonging by basing his vision of the social contract on a fundamental equality that would cross lines of social division. In defining who would constitute those Germans to whom he was appealing, Fichte's sweeping appeal claimed to build on the inclusive foundation of common language and culture, enhanced by a strong voluntaristic faith. At the same time, it must be said, exclusionary seeds were sown that would later be cultivated by nationalists with much narrower visions of German identity. Fichte went on in later sections to call for Germans to resist Napoleon's empire, the "Rome of today," by drawing inspiration from their forebears' successful conquest of the western Roman Empire in the fifth century. But he also placed special emphasis on the heroism of Luther's battle against the Roman Catholic Church— the "holy war for the freedom of belief and of religion"—in terms that hinted at the possible exclusion of German-speaking Catholics who would otherwise fit within Fichte's more open linguistic appeal. Similarly, Fichte's initial linguistic definition of Germanness would seem to offer no basis for the exclusion of German Jews.[113] But multiple references in several of the *Addresses* to "race" and to "German stock," while not to be equated with later pseudoscientific racial terminology, do represent potential exceptions to the "inclusive" rule. Fichte's dream of the German nation being "fused into a single close-connected force" could easily, as it turns out, be used to justify coercive violence as part of the fusion process.[114] Furthermore, Fichte continued the trend of marrying nationalism to cosmic universalism, ultimately linking the imperative of German national unification with the broader destiny of mankind in terms reminiscent of Robespierre: "If you perish in this your essential nature, then there perishes together with you every hope of the whole human race for salvation from the depths of its miseries.... There is, therefore, no way out; if you go under, all humanity goes under with you, without hope of any future restoration."[115]

Fichte's sweeping emotional appeal was complemented on a more sober level by major governing reforms in Prussia designed to redress the internal deficiencies that had contributed to the disasters of Jena and Auerstedt. Generally associated with Prussian ministers Karl vom Stein and Karl August von Hardenberg, the reform program was launched in October 1807 with the abolition of feudalism, and ensuing years witnessed a major overhaul of municipal self-governance, the strengthening of administrative and ministerial responsibility, a wide-ranging economic liberalization package, and the creation of new educational structures such as the University of Berlin, which was inaugurated with much fanfare in October 1810.[116] A sweeping set of military reforms was initiated under Gerhard von Scharnhorst and August von Gneisenau which included the introduction of compulsory military service, the creation of a new Prussian Ministry of War, and the opening up of the officer corps to merit-based promotion.[117] Drawing on a combination of eighteenth-century theories of rationalization and the legacy of revolutionary nationalist mobilization in France, the broader Prussian reform program aimed ultimately to increase efficiency while forging what Matthew Levinger has termed a sense of "enlightened nationalism."[118]

In comparison to Prussia, the growth of German nationalist sentiment and the pace of official reform in Austria was, on the whole, slow and rather muted.[119] On a popular level, to be sure, a number of idealized patriotic heroes emerged in 1809, when Austria resumed hostilities against the Napoleonic forces. The most notable figure was Andreas Hofer, who owned a tavern in the Austrian Tyrol and rose to lead anti-Napoleonic volunteers to a series of victories before being captured and executed in early 1810.[120] The adventurous nature of Hofer's improbable successes, combined with his perceived courage in the face of execution, made his story ready-made for posthumous mythologizing, and countless poems, novels, and plays were written to commemorate him as a heroic martyr figure.[121] But the provincial nature of his uprising and the mixed ethnicity of his Tyrolean homeland ultimately limited Hofer's usefulness in the eyes of later German nationalists.

As the Napoleonic tide surged eastward in Europe, the idea of the nation was adapted, adopted, and resisted in interesting ways, as seen particularly in the cases of Hungary and Poland. In ethnically diverse Hungary, under Austrian control, early Enlightenment-inspired visions of national independence had been paired with calls for Magyar linguistic dominance, and were championed primarily by the nobility throughout the 1780s.[122] Much of the energy driving noble activism stemmed from opposition to the heavy-handed Germanizing policies of the Austrian emperor Joseph II.[123] In 1794, middle-class Hungarian Jacobins modeling their activism after the Jacobins in France commandeered the discourse of the nation in their attempt to establish an independent Hungarian Republic. Their leading figure was Ignác Martinovics, a former Franciscan who became a fanatical follower of Rousseau, and his execution in May 1795 marked the effective end of the Jacobin-nationalist threat.[124] Over the coming years, nationalist activists in Hungary—whether from noble or bourgeois backgrounds—were remarkably quiescent and supportive of Leopold and Francis II, conditioned in part by those rulers' reversal of many of Joseph II's anti-Magyar policies. In 1809, when Napoleon offered Hungary an opportunity for independence from Austria, his overtures were sharply rebuffed.[125] Throughout the period, Hungarian troops fought consistently, and more or less reliably, against Napoleon as part of the Austrian army.[126]

In the Polish territories, on the other hand, Napoleon appeared to many as a glorious force for national liberation and renewal. Historical memory in Poland was a particularly bitter enterprise, as the "golden age" of the Polish-Lithuanian Commonwealth in the seventeenth century was progressively eclipsed, first by the reduction of the Commonwealth to the status of a Russian lackey state, and then by a series of three partitions between 1772 and 1795, at which point Poland ceased to exist as an identifiable geographic entity.[127] Ideas of national renewal thus circulated in tandem with the reality of decline. In 1788, as plans were being set in place for the convening of the Estates-General in France, the Great Sejm (also known as the "Four Years' Parliament") began its deliberations in Warsaw. Drawing inspiration and ideas from events in France, its most significant achievement was the construction of a new constitution, Europe's first, which was promulgated on May 3, 1791.[128] Important parts of the constitution were written by Ignacy Potocki, the so-called Polish Lafayette, and the infusion of French-style Liberal and nationalist ideals was a central justification for the 1792 Russian invasion of Warsaw, which Catherine the Great labeled a "brazier of Jacobinism."[129] That invasion brought about the second of the three partitions, in 1793, with a repressive crackdown being launched against nationalists and "Jacobins," including Potocki, who sought refuge in Saxony, and Tadeusz Kościuszko, who briefly joined Potocki in Leipzig before relocating to Paris to seek official French support for a planned Polish national uprising.

EXCERPT 2.3

Polish Constitution, May 3, 1791

Preamble

Persuaded that our common fate depends entirely upon the establishing and rendering perfect a national constitution; convinced by a long train of experience of many defects in our government, and willing to profit by the present circumstances of Europe, and by the favourable moment which has restored us to ourselves; free from the disgraceful shackles of foreign influence; prizing more than life, and every personal consideration, the political existence, external independence, and internal liberty of the nation, whose care is entrusted to us; desirous, moreover, to deserve the blessing and gratitude, not only of our contemporaries, but also of future generations; for the sake of the public good, for securing our liberty, and maintaining our kingdom and our possessions; in order to exert our natural rights with zeal and firmness, *we do solemnly establish the present Constitution*, which we declare wholly inviolable in every part, till such period as shall be prescribed by law, when the nation, if it should think fit, and deem it necessary, may alter by its express will such articles therein as shall be found inadequate. And this present Constitution shall be the standard of all laws and statutes for the future Diets.[130]

As a young noble, Kościuszko had initially moved to Paris twenty-five years earlier to study painting and military engineering before eventually sailing with French forces to North America in 1776, ultimately playing a significant role in the American colonists' successful military effort. When he finally returned to the Polish-Lithuanian Commonwealth in 1784, he increasingly sided with Liberal activists and supported the constitution produced by the Great Sejm, although he found it generally too moderate. Traveling back to Paris after the 1792 Russian invasion, Kościuszko remained there for more than a year and drank even more deeply from the cup of Jacobin-oriented nationalism.[131] The "Act of National Insurrection," which Kościuszko proclaimed from Krakow in March 1794, was to be the opening salvo of a glorious war of national liberation. In reality, it inaugurated what turned out to be only a short-lived, ill-planned, and poorly funded uprising. Help from France was not forthcoming and, at that point, most likely would have made little difference. Kościuszko was captured by the Russians that fall and, after a year of further deliberations, in October 1795 Polish territory was finally partitioned into oblivion between the Russians, Austrians, and Prussians.

Polish emigres who had fled to Paris, however, proceeded to establish connections with Napoleon on the eve of his rise to power. In 1797, Napoleon approved the creation of the Polish Legions, led by Jan Henryk Dabrowski, who fought alongside the French in Lombardy and went on to play a major role over the next decade in campaigns in Italy and the German lands.[132] Kościuszko, for his part, had been released from Russian captivity in 1796 and, after briefly emigrating to the United States, returned to France and offered his services to Napoleon in late 1799. Their personalities and political visions did not mesh.[133] While Kościuszko retired to the French countryside, Napoleon continued to forge his image as the messiah of aspiring nations, and his decisive conquests over the Austrians and Prussians were particularly satisfying to Poles still seething over the pain of partition. For Polish nationalists, however, by far the most significant achievement of the Napoleonic era was the creation of the Duchy of Warsaw in the summer of 1807. While only of limited geographic scope and only nominally independent—as a Napoleonic satellite state, it was placed in personal union with the allied Kingdom of Saxony—the Duchy became the screen onto which the hopes and dreams of frustrated Polish nationalists could be projected.[134] To some it appeared the first step toward an expanded Polish Kingdom and a restoration of the monarchy; to others it seemed to presage a future independent Polish Republic, within which the abortive constitutional tradition would be revived. But to more cynical observers, the skeptical Kościuszko prominent among them, Napoleon was merely an opportunist whose support for the Polish national cause was instrumental at best. Nonetheless, the Army of the Duchy of Warsaw, which grew out of the Polish Legions and was commanded by Józef Poniatowski, became a key component of the Napoleonic military coalition, winning a series of victories against Austria in 1809 before participating centrally in Napoleon's disastrous 1812 invasion of Russia. Perhaps more importantly, the memory of the passions aroused during the Napoleonic era would echo for more than a century.

The invasion of Russia, of course, was the first major step in Napoleon's ultimate fall. Under Catherine the Great, Russian responses to the French Revolution and the initial mobilization of nationalist sentiment had been overwhelmingly negative.[135] The radicalization of the Revolution caused Catherine herself to abandon many of the enlightened Western ideals she had earlier championed, and the "Jacobin" features of the Polish constitution of 1791 led directly to her decision to invade the Polish-Lithuanian Commonwealth in 1792.[136] When the youthful Alexander I assumed the throne in 1801, he was for a brief time favorably disposed toward Napoleon, influenced in part by his childhood tutor, Frédéric-César de La Harpe.[137] However, as La Harpe progressively soured on the authoritarian Napoleon, and as new geopolitical imperatives began to emerge, Alexander became a resolute opponent of Napoleon and joined Britain and Austria in the third anti-Napoleonic coalition in 1805. Beginning with the humiliating defeat at Austerlitz in December 1805 and continuing through the disastrous Battle of Friedland in June 1807, Russia's poor military performance forced Alexander to sign the Treaty of Tilsit with Napoleon.[138] For the next three years, Russia was an uncomfortable ally of France, aiding Napoleonic forces in campaigns against Austria in 1809, while looking to enhance Russian influence in Eastern Europe.[139] The nascent Franco-Russian alliance ultimately collapsed as a result of conflicting visions for the future of Poland and, secondarily, Alexander's unwillingness to support Napoleon's anti-British economic system. In the greatest miscalculation of his career, Napoleon responded with the decision to invade Russia.[140]

At the time of the invasion in June 1812, the *Grande Armée* numbered more than 650,000 soldiers from a wide variety of territories under Napoleonic control.[141] While French troops made up the largest portion of the invading force, the second largest contingent was comprised of Poles from the Army of the Duchy of Warsaw who believed they were fighting an early battle on the road to national independence. The Russians, for their part, saw the engagement as the "Great Patriotic War," with Alexander pitching the conflict in cosmic terms, speaking explicitly of an apocalyptic "holy war" in defense of the Russian nation, rooted in Orthodox Christianity, in the face of the godless Napoleonic hordes.[142] Early on, the Napoleonic force made rapid progress, winning several minor battles throughout the summer, as Russian troops pulled further and further back, avoiding large direct confrontations and engaging in a scorched earth policy to deprive the invaders of the ability to live off the land.[143] When Napoleon reached Moscow in September, it had largely been evacuated, and the infamous fire that ensued and raged for nearly four days destroyed some three-quarters of the city.[144] Short on supplies, and with winter fast approaching, Napoleon made the fateful decision to withdraw from Moscow in mid-October, and it was on the retreat that his tired, hungry, ill-clad, and often sick soldiers were routed by Russian troops employing guerrilla tactics.[145] By the time Napoleon's forces made it out of Russian territory in December, they had suffered well more than 400,000 casualties, with perhaps 100,000 more in captivity.[146] It was an unmitigated disaster.

While Napoleon managed to make it to Paris, where he attempted to regroup, the Russian campaign had demonstrated his vulnerability and many of his unwilling "allies" began jumping ship. It was on Christmas Day 1812, redolent with images of birth and rebirth, that Prussia under Ludwig Yorck von Wartenburg officially repudiated its unwanted alliance with France.[147] A new, much more extensive, anti-Napoleonic coalition formed, and in October 1813 at the Battle of Leipzig—also known as the "Battle of the Nations"— Napoleon was defeated by the combined forces of Prussia, Austria, Russia, and Sweden, with more limited support from Britain and Bavaria, the latter of which had formally seceded from the Napoleonic Confederation of the Rhine only days before the battle.[148] A German "national uprising" against Napoleon had been called, and the fighting in October 1813 was especially notable in that it witnessed soldiers on both sides fighting with impassioned nationalist fervor. As the tide turned increasingly against Napoleon both militarily and in terms of popular sentiment, he was driven back into France

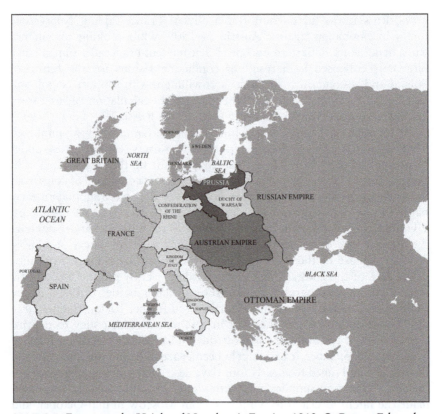

MAP 2.1 Europe at the Height of Napoleonic Empire, 1812. © *George Edward Milne, 2017. Reproduced with permission.*

and coalition forces entered Paris in late March 1814. Napoleon was forced to abdicate a week later, and was exiled initially to the island of Elba in the Mediterranean. Polish nationalists who had continued to support Napoleon until very late in the game were, not surprisingly, disillusioned, their dreams of national independence put on hold indefinitely.

For the major European powers, however, plans for an international summit to be held in Vienna in September 1814 offered an opportunity not only to sort out the political and geographical landscape of Europe after two and a half decades of almost constant upheaval, but also to address the powerful forces of nationalism and liberalism that had been unleashed during those years.

3

Restoration, Romanticism, and Emancipatory Impulses, 1815–1850

When the European powers convened at the Congress of Vienna, it appeared that the threat that had begun with the French Revolution and continued through the Napoleonic era had at last been eliminated. The time seemed right to draw up a provisional balance sheet of the preceding twenty-five years. For Klemens von Metternich, the Austrian chief minister who served effectively as host of the Congress, the lessons of recent history were clear. The revolutionary idea of the nation had enflamed popular passions and led fallible humans to elevate themselves to a position of collective divinity, upsetting the natural order both politically and socially, and leading in the process to unprecedented bloodshed and chaos. Authority, discipline, and legitimacy were the imperatives of the day.[1] For Lord Castlereagh, who as foreign secretary represented Great Britain in Vienna, the primary sin of the preceding era had been its brutally chaotic instability and the attendant disruptions it wrought upon British global interests. While Castlereagh was ultimately unable to overcome the disruptions of his own chaotic mental instability—descending into a fog of erratic paranoia before committing suicide by slitting his throat with a pen knife in 1822—the system he helped design at Vienna should be credited for providing part of the framework for a stable balance of power over the coming decades.[2] France, for its part, was represented at Vienna by Talleyrand, the politically elastic former Bishop of Autun whose dramatic personal odyssey through the various stages of the French Revolution, which he helped initiate, was eclipsed only by his even more contorted maneuverings during the Napoleonic era. By 1814 he, like many others, had come to believe that France's future greatness lay in the restoration of the Bourbon monarchy.[3] The broader restoration program that emanated from Vienna, along with the principles of authoritarian order and dynastic legitimacy that underpinned it, are examined in the chapter that follows, as are the disruptive challenges posed by Liberals and nationalists across Europe who drew inspiration not only from French revolutionary and Napoleonic ideals but also, increasingly, from the emotive force of romanticism. As will be seen, the formation of national independence movements and the revolutionary upsurge that swept through much of the continent in the late 1840s demonstrate both the dynamic potency and the practical limitations of Liberal nationalist mobilization.

The other major powers present in Vienna, Prussia, and Russia, were represented both by ministerial statesmen—the diplomatic counterparts of Metternich, Castlereagh, and Talleyrand—and by the monarchical rulers themselves. The Prussian king Friedrich Wilhelm III took somewhat of a back seat to his chief ministers, Karl August von Hardenberg and Wilhelm von Humboldt. Tsar Alexander I, however, emerged as one of the most striking characters in Vienna, often overshadowing his highly skilled foreign minister Karl Nesselrode.[4] Alexander had recently come under the mystical spell of a religious prophetess named Juliane von Krüdener, who claimed to be guided by a divine "voice" and who exerted a strong influence on Alexander's advocacy of the Holy Alliance forged in Vienna between the Christian monarchs of Russia, Prussia, and Austria.[5] As Alexander's religious predilections became increasingly bizarre, they engendered bemusement among his counterparts at Vienna, with Metternich, the self-styled realist, growing particularly concerned. On one occasion, when Metternich joined Alexander for an evening dinner, Juliane von Krüdener was present at the table, along with an empty fourth chair. When Metternich asked if another guest would be joining them, Alexander replied earnestly that the extra place had been set for Jesus.[6] On a more substantive level, Krüdener's influence was at least partly responsible for imbuing Alexander's sense of Russian national destiny with a cosmic element. In one of her most widely read works, published in French during the proceedings in Vienna, she portrayed the victory of the "Russian nation" over Napoleon, whom she labeled the Antichrist, as the glorious first chapter in an unfolding narrative of global religious renewal, as "the introduction to the [story of the] Universe … and as a living preface to this sacred history that must lead to universal regeneration."[7] As it happened, though, the Antichrist, who had not yet been permanently dispatched, managed to reemerge briefly for one final stand, diverting international attention away from the Congress of Vienna before it had reached its conclusion.

Having been exiled to the island of Elba following his defeat in the spring of 1814, Napoleon was guarded only lightly there and allowed to maintain many of the gaudy trappings of imperial rule, including a sycophantic entourage. Members of the miniature court he assembled in his villa on Elba engaged in elaborate ceremonials clad in uniforms of Napoleon's own design, but the hollowed-out symbolism was little more than a pitiful reminder of the lost grandeur of the figure who, only a few years earlier, had been seen by millions as the embodiment of French national greatness. In late February 1815, however, as deliberations in Vienna were continuing, Napoleon orchestrated an escape from the island and returned to France to launch the brief revival of his power often referred to as the Hundred Days, drawing heavily on volunteer troops known as *fédérés*.[8] By late May, when the forces supporting him had reached nearly 150,000, Napoleon was faced with a new oppositional military coalition, headed by the British under Wellington and the Prussians under Blücher. The decisive engagement was, of course, the Battle of Waterloo on June 18, 1815, in which Napoleon's forces were defeated soundly.[9] Not only had the Napoleonic mystique faded to non-existence on the battlefield, but Napoleon himself presented an increasingly wretched figure, bloated from weight gain and unable to ride on horseback for more than a few minutes due to painful hemorrhoids.[10] *yikes* Although his forces continued fighting for another two weeks in the broader Waterloo campaign, Napoleon himself left the front for Paris on 19 June and, with Prussian and British forces in hot pursuit, was forced to tender his final abdication three days later.[11] Rather than surrender immediately, however, Napoleon spent the next several weeks attempting to flee the continent—he considered, among other things, sailing to the United States—but on July 15, 1815 he ultimately turned himself in to British forces at the port of Rochefort. After brief deliberations, the British decided to exile Napoleon to the remote island of St. Helena, whose location in the South Atlantic made the prospect of a renewed escape attempt extremely unlikely.[12] Napoleon would remain on St. Helena until his death in 1821.

Back in Vienna, the remaking of Europe continued apace, concluding a few days before the Battle of Waterloo. The list of the Congress's achievements was long, even if many of the new state structures it created were fragile or short-lived. In France, the European powers legitimized the Bourbon restoration, in which the brother of Louis XVI, the former Count of Provence, was called to the French throne and installed as King Louis XVIII. His troubled reign would last barely a decade, and his successor Charles X would himself be swept from power after only six years on the throne. Another of Vienna's creations, the United Kingdom of the Netherlands, would survive intact only until 1830, when the regions that became Belgium gained their independence. Division and foreign rule were reinforced in Italy, with Austrian domination providing the foil against which the leaders of the *Risorgimento* would mobilize, and the system created in 1815 was dissolved entirely in the course of Italian unification in the late 1850s and early 1860s. The German Confederation (*Deutscher Bund*) created at Vienna would have only a slightly longer shelf life. Replacing the more than 300 principalities of the Holy Roman Empire of the German Nation with some thirty-nine member states, the *Bund* would survive fifty-one years before being dissolved in the aftermath of a civil war between its two most powerful states. The restoration of the Bourbon monarchy in Spain brought Ferdinand VII back to the throne, and though the monarchy itself would survive into the twentieth century, it suffered periodic dissolution and was perpetually under duress. The Poles, among the biggest losers in the Vienna settlement, had their hopes for national independence crushed, with the partitioning powers of the previous century—Russia, Austria, and Prussia—regaining significant amounts of Polish territory. Most notably, the Napoleonic Duchy of Warsaw was dissolved, and a new rump state, known as the Congress Kingdom of Poland, was created as a Russian satellite. The Polish self-image as the persecuted "Christ of nations" was reinforced at Vienna and would continue to gain currency for more than a century.[13]

On an ideological level, the two most dangerous threats identified by the conservative post-Napoleonic establishment were the intertwined forces of liberalism and nationalism. Although the "liberal" camp was broad and riven with internal divisions, what generally united Liberals in the early nineteenth century was an inclination toward increased freedoms, both in an economic and political sense, involving some form of citizens' participation in their own governance.[14] It would prove difficult for European Liberals to establish any modicum of consensus on exactly how these freedoms should be defined, let alone how much real influence the people should have in the governing process. But the Liberal threat appeared magnified when combined with the potent dynamism of popular nationalism. In addition to identifying the people, or nation, as the source of political sovereignty, many Liberals envisioned a future Europe within which independent, self-governing nation-states would replace the messy and seemingly arbitrary patchwork of state structures that issued from the Congress of Vienna.

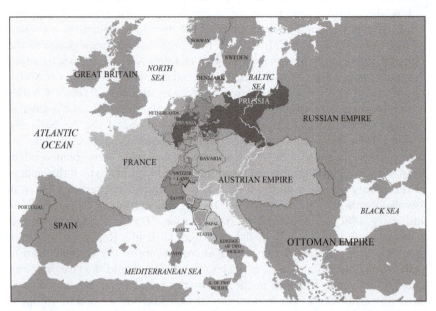

MAP 3.1 Europe in 1815. © *George Edward Milne, 2017. Reproduced with permission.*

The dangers posed by liberalism and nationalism were particularly acute from the Austrian perspective, as the Habsburg Empire contained more than a dozen separate linguistic and ethnic groups, each of which could, if sufficiently stoked by nationalist agitators, make the case for independence to the detriment of the empire's German ruling minority.

Overall, while the Vienna settlement should be credited with establishing a stable and relatively peaceful balance of power for several decades, its principal flaw was the attempt to crush Liberal dreams and national aspirations without providing any corresponding ideal that could unify and inspire. As will be seen, attempts of Restoration-era regimes to foster traditional dynastic loyalty, often with little consideration for issues of national identity, were largely unsuccessful in arousing political passions or cohesive notions of belonging.

Restoration Europe and the politics of dynastic loyalty

The phrase "Restoration" was used in 1816 by the reactionary Swiss political theorist Karl Ludwig von Haller to describe the return of Europe to prerevolutionary, and in his view more proper, conceptions of the state and governance.[15] The term circulated widely and came to characterize the broader conservative system created at Vienna, although the designation "Concert of Europe" was also used commonly in official diplomatic communications.[16] A brief tour of the map of Restoration-era Europe allows us to examine the political structures that constituted this system, along with some of the background developments that preceded it and a few of the challenges to its authority that emerged after 1815. In Europe's major monarchies, these years witnessed various official attempts to foster territorial and dynastic loyalties and to mobilize them in the service of bureaucratic modernization and state-building, often in explicit opposition to the intertwined ideals of liberalism and nationalism.

At the northern periphery of Europe were the Scandinavian states. The Danish crown had aligned itself with Napoleon and, while Copenhagen suffered some privations as a result of British attacks, in 1809 the Danes experienced a series of victories against rival Sweden, which had aligned itself with the anti-Napoleonic coalition. But by 1814, bankrupted by war and disillusioned for having backed the losing side, the Danish king Frederick VI was forced to accept the independence of Norway, which then entered a personal union with Sweden.[17] In ensuing years Frederick engaged in a number of attempts to fuse "Danishness" and dynastic loyalty via artistic patronage, mixing royal and historicist imagery in equal measures. Perhaps most famously, in 1819 he commissioned the neoclassical sculptor Bertel Thorvaldsen to design external iconography for the rebuilding of the Copenhagen Cathedral, which had been destroyed in the 1807 British bombardment and whose restoration was to symbolize a renewed sense of idealized Danish identity. Although Thorvaldsen spent much of his subsequent career in Rome, his work was imitated widely in public sculpture throughout Denmark, and his cool classicism offered a contrast to later romanticist motifs. When he returned permanently from Rome in the late 1830s, he was feted as a cultural icon, with a museum dedicated entirely to his work being constructed on one of Copenhagen's most exclusive pieces of real estate, directly next to the Christiansborg Palace.[18]

In Sweden, which had sided consistently with anti-Napoleonic forces, dynastic politics were made somewhat messy when, in 1818, the French military officer Jean-Baptiste Bernadotte, who more than a decade earlier had been appointed by Napoleon as one of the eighteen Marshals of the French Empire, assumed the throne after the royal line died out with Charles XIII. Taking the name Charles XIV John, he ruled Sweden (and Norway) with a significant degree of popular support until his death in 1844, presiding over decades of relative peace and economic expansion.[19] As a Frenchman ruling in Scandinavia, he serves as an interesting, and somewhat rare, illustration of the ways in which dynastic loyalty—in this case, attached to an entirely new dynasty—could be successfully forged and maintained in the Restoration era over and above issues of national identity.

A move to Western Europe brings us to an examination of the long-established powers of Britain, France, and Spain. In Britain, gradualist conceptions of social and political change conditioned official formulations of nationalism and dynastic legitimacy in the Restoration era. As Linda Colley and others have argued, a fairly stable sense of British national identity had attached itself to the Stuart dynasty, straddling the 1707 Act of Union with Scotland and strengthened by equal measures of Protestant hegemony and anti-French sentiment, which was, in turn, reinforced by the geographic isolation of the British isles from the continent.[20] During the Napoleonic era, potential Jacobin plots and a variety of other perceived subversive threats were dealt with mercilessly. After 1815, popular opposition to official government policy was fueled largely by economic hardship, as seen in the rioting that followed the passage of the 1815 Corn Laws, which greatly increased food prices, and in the August 1819 Peterloo demonstration in Manchester, which ended in the shooting deaths of more than a dozen protesters and the wounding of several hundred more.[21] In the aftermath of the Peterloo Massacre, as it came to be known, parliament passed the Six Acts, which severely restricted freedom of speech and assembly. Over the ensuing decades, however, support for moderate Liberal principles continued to coalesce gradually, and the Corn Laws were ultimately repealed in 1846.[22] With the formation of a new Whig government under Lord Grey in 1830, the issue of parliamentary reform gained broader backing, culminating in the so-called Great Reform Bill of 1832.[23] Unlike elsewhere in Europe, moderate forms of economic and political liberalism emanating from the government came to be incorporated increasingly into official expressions of British national identity, helping constitute what Jonathan Parry has called the "politics of patriotism."[24]

In France, Louis XVIII attempted to steer a cautious course in his ten years on the throne. He had fled France in June 1791, at the time of his brother's infamous Flight to Varennes, and spent the next two decades on the move as an itinerant exile. Upon his initial return to France as the new ruler in 1814, he appeared comically out-of-date in his insistence on wearing his favorite blue tailcoat, knee breeches, and powdered wig, while being chauffeured in an ornate carriage driven by elaborately clad footmen.[25] One of his earliest acts was to issue the constitutional Charter of June 1814, which maintained some of the Liberal gains of the revolutionary era while reinforcing traditional royal prerogatives. The Charter created a bicameral legislature, consisting of the Chamber of Deputies and the Chamber of Peers, while continuing to limit freedom of speech and declaring Roman Catholicism the state religion of France.[26] The Church was envisioned as a key component in forging an orderly sense of dynastic loyalty among the French populace, in contrast to the unruly popular emotion that had fueled earlier nationalist mobilization. As the near-perfect antithesis to Napoleon's heroic charisma, however, the dour and unpopular king found himself increasingly in a sort of political no-man's land, opposed on the one hand by French Liberals and those who still harbored sympathies for Napoleon, while on the other hand fighting against "ultras," royalist nobles who had returned from exile and attempted to regain their lost property and privileges.[27] Attempts to establish himself as the unifying symbol of French identity were weakened by his poorly concealed lack of commitment to the new restoration state; tellingly, the king refused to transfer his private assets to France, leaving them on deposit with English banking houses.[28] When Louis XVIII died in 1824, his brother and successor, Charles X, staged a famously ornate coronation ceremony at Reims, attempting to regenerate dynastic loyalty within the French populace by returning to the trappings of medieval pomp and circumstance.[29] He would, of course, be driven from power six years later in the July Revolution of 1830.

In Spain, the newly restored Ferdinand VII attempted to rule largely through autocratic repression, and his reign was plagued by chronic instability. Upon his return to the throne in 1814, one of his first acts was to repeal the Constitution of 1812, which had been adopted by the parliamentary *Cortes* during the later phases of the Peninsular War. In the place of conceptions of emancipatory nationalism and popular sovereignty that had been promulgated by Liberals in the Cortes, Ferdinand pitched himself—ultimately unsuccessfully—as the dynastic embodiment of Spanish identity. The weakness of his position was reinforced when, in January 1820, a military coup forced Ferdinand not only to reinstitute the Constitution of 1812 but also to submit himself to virtual imprisonment for nearly three years, the so-called *Trienio Liberal*.[30] The brief period of Liberal rule ended in 1823 when French troops—ordered by Louis XVIII and authorized by the international Congress of Verona—invaded Spain to restore dynastic legitimacy. The French forces invoked the medieval image of Saint Louis as the symbol of common Catholic identity and as an antidote to the perceived dangers of modern Liberal and nationalist ideals.[31] This re-restoration of Ferdinand led to a brutal period of repression. When he died in 1833, his wife Maria ruled as regent on behalf of their daughter Isabella who, not yet three years old at the time of her father's death, was next in the line of succession. In response, Ferdinand's brother Don Carlos, who had been passed over, emerged as the central figure in what became known as the Carlist Revolt, a violent conflict over dynastic legitimacy that was accelerated by regional tensions in the Basque regions and Catalonia. Its first phase ended with Carlos's exile in 1839.[32] The young Isabella assumed power in her own right in 1843 and survived another Carlist uprising in Catalonia a few years later, eventually reigning for several decades before ultimately being deposed as a result of the Spanish "Glorious Revolution" that began in 1868.[33]

In central and southern Europe, the majority of territories were either disjointed and splintered or ruled by foreign powers. Among the loosely aligned member states of the German Confederation, the structures of governance varied. In Austria, the emperor Francis insisted on a continuation of absolutist rule, rejecting all calls for a constitution out of hand. In the states of Bavaria, Baden, and Württemberg, constitutional trajectories that had been set in motion during the Napoleonic era were extended, whereas in Prussia, king Frederick William III made vague constitutional promises that were left unfulfilled.[34] Despite these differences, throughout the Confederation ruling figures strove to cultivate narrow dynastic loyalties among their respective populations, typically in opposition to overarching appeals for national unification and political liberalization. In Austria, intellectuals like Joseph von Hormayr turned to the writing of popular history to emphasize the virtues and achievements of the Habsburgs, articulating a distinctly Austrian dynastic identity that was connected to but separate from the other German territories.[35] Elsewhere, governing elites employed a strategy often described as the "invention of tradition." In Prussia, this involved a massive building program in Berlin, led by architect Karl Friedrich Schinkel and characterized by monumental neoclassical structures, which, it was hoped, would lend the sense of weighty tradition and permanence that was sorely lacking in the upstart Prussia.[36] In Bavaria, a similar neoclassical building boom occurred, as king Ludwig I's goal of making Munich into "Athens on the Isar"—and thereby fashioning a new sense of historical continuity and legitimacy—was largely achieved by his chief architect Leo von Klenze.[37] Additionally, since its territory had been dramatically expanded at the Congress of Vienna, Bavaria now possessed large numbers of new Bavarians who had never before had a connection with the Wittelsbach crown. To foster unity and a greater sense of dynastic historical identification, local festivals were either revived or created anew. The most striking manifestation of this invention of tradition was Oktoberfest, which began as a one-time wedding celebration on the occasion of Ludwig's marriage in 1810, but was revived several years later and marketed subsequently as the quintessential symbol of Bavarian identity.[38] Ludwig also attempted to marry dynastic politics with broader romantic and national visions, as seen in the famous Walhalla monument outside Regensburg, which was constructed between 1830 and 1842 and whose central hall immortalized a pantheon of German cultural icons.[39] Despite such opportunistic references to broader German solidarity, which were visible in smaller German states as well, it was against this patchwork of dynastic and territorial identities that the oppositional drive for German national unification was ultimately launched.

Further south, on the Italian peninsula and in the Balkans, foreign domination remained the order of the day. At the Congress of Vienna, Austria had been given outright possession of the northern Italian territories of Lombardy and Venetia, while exercising substantial, albeit less direct, control over the restored Grand Duchy of Tuscany, the Duchies of Parma and Modena, and the Kingdom of the Two Sicilies in the south.[40] The Papal States, governed by the pope, and the Kingdom of Piedmont-Sardinia, ruled by the House of Savoy, were the only Italian territories that were accorded at least nominal independence. In the Balkan regions, including Greece, the Ottoman Empire had exercised control since the fifteenth century. Ottoman rule tended to be decentralized and Orthodox Christian communities in the Balkans were thus accorded a measure of local autonomy, although as non-Muslims they were subjected to various discriminatory measures.[41] Military setbacks against Austria and Russia, in separate wars that concluded in the early 1790s, had weakened Ottoman control of the Balkans and set the stage for the next century's increasingly powerful challenges to the Sultan's authority. The earliest of these challenges, launched by the Serbs in 1804, played out largely against the backdrop of older religious identities—with appeals for Orthodox Serbian mobilization being answered by Turkish calls for Muslim jihad—rather than deriving its motivation from French revolutionary nationalism or romanticism.[42] In that sense, the initial Serbian uprising differed somewhat from the subsequent drive for Greek independence, which is discussed in greater detail later in this chapter.

At the eastern extreme of Europe was Russia, the most autocratic of all European states in this period. Alexander I, whose religious eccentricities had raised eyebrows in Vienna and elsewhere, demonstrated at least a modicum of flexibility in regard to certain national groups on the margins of the Russian empire. In 1809, Russia had gained Finland from Sweden, and the Finns were subsequently allowed a degree of autonomy, as were the Baltic possessions of Lithuania, Estonia, and Latvia. In Russia proper, Alexander paid little more than lip service to a number of proposed political reform projects, continuing to focus primarily on the marriage of Christian tradition and Russian identity. Behind the scenes, however, a number of secret societies had begun to proliferate in which potentially dangerous political reform ideals circulated. Chief among these was the "Union of Salvation" club, which was formed in 1816 to advocate secretly for political modernization. As a reflection of its attempt to ground popular sovereignty in the discourse of the nation, the group eventually changed its name to the "Society of True and Loyal Sons of the Fatherland" and played a central role in the lead up to the famous Decembrist Revolt.[43] That revolt materialized in the aftermath of Alexander I's death in December 1825, as a coterie of military officers, many of them members of secret societies, opposed the succession to the throne of Alexander's brother Nicholas I in the hopes of pushing through modernizing reforms. The most notable conspirator was Pavel Pestel, a well-traveled Liberal ideologue whose family traced its origins to German Lutheran stock.[44] Despite the subsequent attention it received, the uprising itself was quite limited in scope and its political impact in the short term was negligible.[45] Pestel and three other Decembrist leaders were executed in 1826, more than 100 were exiled to Siberia, and Nicholas remained firmly in power for the next three decades.[46] In those years, the primary hallmark of Nicholas's reign was the articulation of a state-sponsored vision of Russian national identity.[47] It was Nicholas's minister of education, Sergey Uvarov, who was primarily responsible for the tripartite formulation that served as the memorable catchphrase of the program: "Orthodoxy, Autocracy, Nationality."[48] The Orthodox component emphasized the important stabilizing role to be played by the Russian church, whereas the reference to autocracy reflected the fact that political liberalism continued to be viewed as an unhealthy foreign disease. The principle of nationality would not be extended to the Poles, as seen in the merciless crushing of their nationalist aspirations in the early 1830s.

Importantly, though, in Poland as elsewhere, challenges to the dynastic legitimacy of Restoration governments did emerge and were framed increasingly in Liberal and nationalist terms, driven forward by the affective power of romanticism.

Romanticism and the disruptive force of national belonging

As a broad set of cultural and intellectual currents, romanticism reached its heyday in Europe roughly between 1815 and 1850, although its roots date from the late eighteenth century and the timing of its subsequent impact was varied in different geographic contexts and cultural fields.[49] Defined in part by the contrasts it presented with earlier normative ideals and intellectual currents—particularly enlightened rationalism and the tradition of classicism in the arts—romanticism emphasized intense emotion and individual experience over the cold calculus of reason. In the place of emotional restraint and externalized propriety, romanticism idealized unruly passions and the eccentricities of internal "authenticity." Against the backdrop of the elegance and urbanity of classical antiquity, romantic figures counterposed the gaudy colors of the Middle Ages and the wild, untamed majesty of the natural world. Enlightenment images of society as a harmonious, well-ordered machine were supplanted by appeals to bold individual activism and heroic struggle. Importantly, however, romantic figures also longed for an overarching, almost metaphysical unity of the individual and the collective.[50] Politically, this orientation could be deployed in the service of tradition and reaction, as a powerful antidote to the dangers ushered in by the French Revolution. This was certainly the case with early French romantics like Chateaubriand, whose 1802 treatise *Genius of Christianity* idealized medieval Catholicism and the society of orders it underpinned, while simultaneously inspiring a generation of romantic writers to embrace the virtues of monarchical legitimacy.[51] Similarly, the apolitical internality of many early British romantics helped direct a potentially powerful counter-cultural current into politically pliant channels, while also on occasion fostering what Anne Frey has termed a statist form of "bureaucratic nationalism."[52] Increasingly, however, the aesthetic values and heroic imagery cultivated by romantic figures came to fuel explicitly disruptive nationalist movements, contributing centrally to revolutionary uprisings across Europe by the late 1840s.[53] The romantic longing for a totalizing unity between the individual and the collective most frequently identified the nation as the legitimate repository and primary object of those longings.

We see this union of romantic emotion and disruptive nationalist activism emerging first on the peripheries of the British Isles. From a very early point, literary romanticism in Ireland was deeply implicated in questions of national identity and belonging.[54] As influential as the earlier bardic tradition was to the flourishing of the late eighteenth-century Irish literary revival, romantic poetry was intricately intertwined with the presentist imperatives of nascent anti-British nationalist mobilization.[55] The towering Irish political figure in the early nineteenth century—in pushing for self-governance and Catholic emancipation within the context of Romantic idealism—was the lawyer and political activist Daniel O'Connell.[56] One of his initial supporters, the publicist Feargus O'Connor, fashioned together ideals of Irish nationalism and political reform within the Chartist movement, which both O'Connell and O'Connor helped launch in the late 1830s.[57] O'Connor eventually broke with more moderate Chartist activists, who advocated a milder form of "moral force" over the physical intimidation favored by O'Connor. His growing radicalism was matched and perhaps surpassed by James Bronterre O'Brien, who attempted to balance the proto-socialism of the French radical Babeuf with a Jacobin-inspired brand of Irish nationalism.[58] O'Connor and Bronterre suffered increasing health problems—both physical and, in the case of O'Connor, mental—and their influence declined greatly after 1848. But the patterns they established and the ideas they set in motion would have wide-ranging effects in the decades that followed.

The romantic literary movement in Scotland was already fairly well established by the late eighteenth century, with the works of Robert Burns, many of them in the Scots language, constituting perhaps the most notable manifestations.[59] As noted in the previous chapter, the death of Thomas Muir in 1799 had launched a nationalistic cult of heroic martyrdom. Stretching throughout the early decades of the nineteenth century, Muir's messianic image remained a central staple of Scottish romantic poetry, and when the famous Political Martyrs' Monument was erected in Edinburgh in 1844, embodying the romantic aesthetic in full bloom, Muir was commemorated as the first of the five "holy" martyrs who had sacrificed themselves for the cause of the Scottish nation.[60] Culturally, the hugely popular romantic novels of Walter Scott, particularly *Waverley* (1814), *Rob Roy* (1817), and *Ivanhoe* (1820), helped forge a distinct historical sense of Scottish national identity.[61] But as conceptions of British "nationality" proved increasingly adaptable, calls for Scottish independence remained rather muted. In contrast to other seemingly similar cases throughout Europe, romantic nationalism in Scotland was not inextricably linked with the cause of political liberation. In part, this can be seen as the result of a lack of success in linking nationalist ideals with working-class identity, despite the notable efforts of Scottish Chartists in the early 1840s.[62] Overall, an examination of Scottish identity serves as a useful reminder that nationalism—even powerfully emotive romantic nationalism—cannot be interpreted entirely through the lens of the achievement of political autonomy.[63]

In Scandinavia, the most notable intertwining of romanticism, liberalism, and nationalism was manifested in Norway, which had been ruled by Denmark starting in the sixteenth century before being ceded to Sweden in the Treaty of Kiel, signed in January 1814. Working behind the scenes in an attempt to forestall Swedish control of Norway, prince Christian Frederik, heir to the Danish crown, lent his unofficial support to a Norwegian uprising whose twin goals were independence and constitutional governance. Under threat of a Swedish invasion, elections were held in February 1814 for a constituent assembly, which convened in April on an estate in Eidsvoll, some 70 kilometers north of Christiania (present-day Oslo), producing the Norwegian Constitution of May 17, 1814.[64] Although Swedish forces invaded that summer, crushing the bid for independence and forcibly bringing Norway into submission under the Swedish crown, the Norwegians were accorded a degree of autonomy, with the 1814 Constitution and their own parliament remaining intact. At the same time, public expressions of Norwegian nationalism, which circulated with increasing urgency throughout the 1820s in a romantic popular revival of folklore and customs, were deemed subversive and outlawed.[65] In 1828, the Swedish king Charles XIV John banned all Norwegian Constitution Day celebrations, but the following year, on May 17, 1829, extensive commemorative activities were nonetheless staged on the central market square in Christiania. The result was a severe government crackdown and subsequent uprising known as the *Torgslaget* (Market Battle), whose symbolic significance has been compared to the Boston Tea Party.[66] One of the central instigators was the young student poet Henrik Wergeland, who went on to a career as perhaps the most influential representative of literary romanticism in Norway, eventually being celebrated as a heroic national icon upon the achievement of full Norwegian independence in 1905.[67] In addition to his involvement in the 1829 *Torgslaget*, it was, more than anything else, his striking public advocacy of the July 1830 revolution in France that cemented his early fame. After making a personal pilgrimage to Paris in 1831, his return to Norway and his championing of romantic nationalism generated significant publicity and stimulated an interest in his works that continued unbroken for decades.[68]

The July Revolution in France played out against the backdrop of the repressive policies of Charles X, who assumed the throne upon the death of his older brother Louis XVIII in 1824 and proceeded to stage a gaudy coronation ceremony at Reims that was saturated with medieval pageantry. In 1789, during the initial stages of the French Revolution, Charles's intransigent attitude toward the (comparatively moderate) demands of the Third Estate had made him one of the royal court's staunchest hardliners, and that anti-reform intransigence was resumed upon his accession to the throne. Importantly, however, the absolutist tenor of his coronation was not merely a supportive nod in the direction of the reactionary ultras. The ceremony also exercised a strong appeal for French romantics whose imaginations found inspiration in royalist medievalism, as demonstrated in part by Rossini's famous ode to the coronation, *Il viaggio a Reims* (The Journey to Reims), which premiered in Paris in June 1825.[69]

It should be noted that the political actors who paved the way for the revolution of 1830 in France did not frame their activism primarily in terms of hazy romanticism or the obscure sentimentalism of secret societies—as elsewhere in Europe—but claimed first and foremost to be clear-sighted realists in pursuit of the principles of constitutional legitimacy, as enshrined in the 1814 Charter. Following Charles's imposition in 1829 of a new government dominated almost entirely by ultras, with the arch-reactionary Jules de Polignac as new chief minister, the Liberal opposition in parliament grew more vociferous. In response, Charles dissolved parliament in March 1830 and, when new elections brought resounding gains for the Liberals, Charles and Polignac chose the route of further repression, issuing the infamous July Ordinances, which announced yet another dissolution of parliament and the imposition of strict censorship laws.[70] The revolutionary street fighting that ensued between July 27 and 29, 1830—replete with iconic images of barricades and tricolor flags—brought about the demise of the restored Bourbon monarchy at the cost of between 1,000 and 2,000 lives.[71] The ramrod inflexibility of Charles X was to be replaced by the pragmatism of the Duke of Orléans, who now assumed the throne as the "citizen king" Louis Philippe. The elderly revolutionary veteran Lafayette was summoned

FIGURE 3.1 Charles X *by Henry Bone. Metropolitan Museum of Art/Wikimedia Commons.*

from retirement to make a public appearance in Paris alongside the new king in an attempt to lend legitimacy and a sense of continuity to the new post-Restoration system.[72] But before the contours of that fledgling system had even begun to emerge, the July Revolution sent shock waves throughout much of Europe, beginning with the southern regions of France's northern neighbor, the Kingdom of the Netherlands, where activists utilized the unrest in Paris as a pretext to mobilize for Belgian national independence.

Among the territorial revisions instituted by the Congress of Vienna was the transfer of the lands formerly known as the Austrian Netherlands to the Dutch crown. Within the newly expanded United Kingdom of the Netherlands, these primarily Catholic territories, which included speakers of both Dutch and French, had very little connection to the Protestant ruling house of Orange-Nassau. King William I's initial attempts to build dynastic loyalty within the new territories focused especially on the forging of a common literary identity that would, it was hoped, create new cohesive traditions and smooth the tensions between the northern and southern parts of his kingdom.[73] The success of these efforts was limited, and William I turned increasingly to a policy of restricting French language rights and reducing the public influence of the Catholic Church, which angered Dutch- and French-speaking Catholics equally. Secular advocates of political liberalism in the south were also increasingly irritated by William's autocratic governing style. By the late 1820s, a rather strange alliance of conservative Catholics and disaffected Liberals had emerged, with both sides eager to mobilize popular disaffection to further their own goals, which converged and crystallized around the ideal of independence. Resentments escalated in the summer of 1830 and, as news of the revolution in France spread, an uprising erupted in Brussels, setting in motion a chain of events that led, surprisingly quickly, to a new internationally recognized independent Belgian state.

The immediate catalyst of the Belgian Revolution was the performance on August 25, 1830, of Daniel Auber's romantic opera *La Muette di Portici* (The Mute Girl of Portici), which told the story of a heroic seventeenth-century revolt in Naples against Spain.[74] During the singing of the opera's centerpiece "Amour Sacre de la Patrie" (Sacred Love of the Fatherland)— performed that night by both the romantic lead Adolphe Nourrit, best known as Rossini's favored tenor, and the composer Daniel Auber himself— the crowd in the National Theater grew increasingly frenzied and began to spill out into the streets, joining a rising tide of demonstrators that managed, throughout the night, to seize central government buildings across Brussels. Advised by his two sons, William I was initially reluctant to use military force to quell the uprising. When a compromise solution proved elusive, however, bloody clashes ensued in Brussels between royalist forces and insurgents, spreading throughout the city from 23 to 26 September and ending with William's troops being forced to retreat. A provisional government was established, issuing the Belgian Declaration of Independence on 4 October and announcing elections for a new National Congress, which convened the following month. Although William and the Dutch authorities refused to recognize Belgian autonomy, an international conference met in London in December, officially recognizing the legitimacy of the new Belgian state.[75] The ensuing weeks witnessed widespread demonstrations of Belgian solidarity, led in part by Catholic priests, while parliamentarians and jurists worked to construct a constitution, which was published in February 1831. After the German prince Leopold of Saxe-Coburg agreed in June 1831 to assume the Belgian crown as King Leopold I, Dutch forces loyal to William I began massing for a military invasion, leading in August to the brief conflict known as the "Ten Days' Campaign." French intervention led to the defeat of the Dutch invasion and William was forced to reconcile himself to the lasting reality of Belgian statehood, although he waited until 1839 to make that recognition official.[76]

The successful drive for Belgian independence is significant on a number of levels. First, it demonstrates the potential of romantic imagery to spark not only vague sentimentality but concerted, real-world action. The emotive power of the romantic opera performance that launched the revolution was matched, and in some ways surpassed, by the self-styled heroic champions of Belgian romanticism who emerged in its wake. Hendrik Conscience, whose 1838 novel *The Lion of Flanders* became one of the most influential romantic epics of its era, provides only the most notable example of this intertwining of romanticism and national idealism.[77] Second, in the pluralistic nature of its constituent parts—with French-speaking Walloons and Dutch-speaking Flemings uniting under a common banner—Belgian identity offers a striking illustration of the potential for federalistic conceptions of nationhood and statehood to overcome cultural, linguistic, and ethnic divisions.[78] As a result, the case of Belgium has often been cited as an early manifestation of civic, as opposed to ethnic, nationalism.[79] One scholar has gone so far as to characterize Belgium as a "nation that failed to be ethnic."[80] Finally, in its timing, the Belgian case invites comparisons with near-contemporary movements for national independence and unification elsewhere in Europe, most notably in the Italian territories, the German states, Poland, and Greece. As will be seen, it would take the Italians and Germans decades to achieve national unification, whereas the Greeks succeeded in gaining their independence from the Ottoman Empire only shortly after the successful Belgian Revolution, benefiting, as did the Belgians, from international intervention. For the Poles, independence would have to wait until the next century.

On the Italian peninsula, which was dominated by Austria following the Congress of Vienna, a particularly striking mixture of romanticism and aspirational nationalism emerged under the banner of *Risorgimento*, or "rebirth."[81] A number of Italian activists were drawn to the model of European secret societies, such as the Freemasons, which had spread rapidly throughout the eighteenth century. Initially, the most significant of these were the Carbonari, a clandestine brotherhood utilizing coal-burning imagery that combined Enlightenment idealism and vague dreams of universal fraternity and political emancipation with radical anti-Habsburg sentiment. In July 1820, the Carbonari led a major uprising in Naples, forcing King Ferdinand I to agree to the formulation of a constitution. While the constitution never materialized and the uprising was crushed brutally by Austrian military forces in early 1821, the Naples episode inspired similar revolutionary activities elsewhere on the peninsula. In March 1821, far to the north in the Kingdom of Piedmont-Sardinia, the Carbonari orchestrated an insurrection that also resulted in the king, Victor Emmanuel I, giving promises of a constitution. That revolt was suppressed by Habsburg troops in less than a month.[82] Many Carbonari leaders were forced into exile or jailed, but the organization continued to develop underground.

Inspired by the July 1830 revolution in France, the Carbonari emerged again that year to incite an insurrectionary wave that spread throughout the Italian territories. Revolutionary uprisings in Parma and the Papal States experienced brief success in late 1830 and early 1831. In Modena, the Carbonari leader Ciro Menotti plotted a revolution with the tacit support of Modena's Duke Francis IV, who entertained ideas of placing himself at the forefront of a national unification movement. When the revolt was launched in February 1831, Francis IV performed an infamous about-face, having Menotti arrested and eventually hanged, while attempting to destroy all evidence of his own earlier involvement.[83] Menotti went on to become one of the central martyr figures in the nationalist mythology of the Risorgimento, but in the short term Austrian troops were able to squash the various revolts in the spring of 1831 and the dynastic status quo was maintained.[84]

In the months that followed Giuseppe Mazzini, who had been among the most idealistic Carbonari members, founded an even more radical secret society, Young Italy, which committed itself entirely to the overthrow of the patchwork of Austrian-backed dynastic entities and the creation of a unified Italian republic, embracing the cause of revolutionary nationalism more explicitly than had the Carbonari.[85] One of the youthful adventurers drawn to Young Italy in its earliest years was Giuseppe Garibaldi. As a seaman first class in the Piedmontese Navy, Garibaldi participated in an abortive uprising in Genoa in early 1834, organized by Young Italy but undermined from within by government agents, and the failure of the revolt turned Garibaldi into a celebrated fugitive.[86] His self-congratulatory memoirs recall, in almost excessive detail, his heroic exploits while on the run from reactionary authorities over the ensuing months.[87] He made his initial escape from Genoa by hiding in a fruit shop, whose female owner was apparently so taken by his dashing gallantry that she hid him, disguised him as a farmer, and then led him safely out of the city. During his subsequent flight to France, Garibaldi proceeded to hike across the Alps near Sestri, before swimming across the treacherous River Var and eventually evading monarchist agents by jumping out of a window, while his less athletic pursuers "preferred going down the long way via the staircase." Ever the romantic, Garibaldi was perhaps most proud of the manner in which he won the admiration of an innkeeper near Marseille, who had discovered Garibaldi's fugitive identity and planned, with the assistance of nearly a dozen burly patrons, to turn him over to the authorities. Remembering the lyrics of one of France's leading romantic hymnists, Pierre Beranger, Garibaldi broke into song and swept along all who were in the pub on a tide of brotherly harmony. Responding to the romantic intensity of Beranger's verses, and "perhaps the pleasant manner in which I sang," his would-be captors quickly became his devotees, staying up all night to drink and sing with him, before helping him along his way the following morning.[88] Despite the inescapably hyperbolic nature of Garibaldi's account, it communicates some of the sense of adventure and romantic zeal that characterized the drive for Italian national unification in these early years. As marked men, both Mazzini and Garibaldi would be forced to remain abroad for more than a decade, before returning to resume their activism during the revolutionary turbulence of 1848.

Within the German Confederation, the intertwining of romanticism, Liberal emancipatory ideals, and visions of national solidarity also created a potent ideological mix that challenged dynastic loyalties and helped transform the discourse of the nation from the ethereal realm of coffee-house elites to a palpable political force embodied in social practices and voluntary associations. George Mosse famously characterized this process, in which romantic imagery played a key role, as the "nationalization of the masses."[89] In the aftermath of the devastating losses to Napoleonic forces at Jena and Auerstedt in 1806, several rabidly anti-French clubs were established on the basis of broad and somewhat protean visions of German national identity. The *Tugendbund* (League of Virtue), a secret society founded in Königsberg, attracted a number of would-be romantic folk heroes, including Wilhelm von Dörnberg, who in April 1809 led an abortive uprising against French occupation in Kassel, motivated, it was said, not by particularistic Prussian interests but "by the purest love and enthusiasm for Germany and the German nationality."[90] The gymnastics movement established in 1811 by Friedrich Ludwig Jahn, venerated by his followers as the *Turnvater* ("gymnastics father"), brought together young German men to engage in stringent physical and moral training in an atmosphere saturated with nationalistic fervor—preparing youthful bodies and minds for revenge against France, which was achieved in part through the gymnasts' legendary engagement as volunteers in the 1813 Battle of the Nations.[91] Similarly, the student fraternities (*Burschenschaften*), founded shortly thereafter by young veterans returning to their university studies, quickly became incubators of ritualized nationalistic camaraderie, fueled, in the words of Jonathan Sperber, both by the "romantic politics of personalized, emotional commitment" and "a quasi-religious devotion to the nation."[92]

The powerful combination of romantic aesthetics, emotive nationalism, and religious-oriented fervor was demonstrated clearly in the October 1817 Wartburg Festival, staged by gymnasts' groups and student fraternities in joint commemoration of the 300th anniversary of Luther's launching of the Reformation and the fourth anniversary of the victory over Napoleon in the Battle of the Nations. Participants engaged in torchlight parades, the singing of both patriotic and explicitly Christian hymns, and other celebratory rituals of national belonging, such as the elaborate book-burning ceremony in which "un-German" works were consigned to the flames in a symbolic act of collective purgation.[93] The disruptive potential of such events recalled the emotive politics of the revolutionary era and deeply concerned the ministers of the German Confederation. When, two years later, a crazed fraternity member named Karl Sand assassinated the reactionary playwright August von Kotzebue—who in many ways symbolized conservative opposition to nationalism and liberalism—it provided Metternich and his colleagues with a pretext for broad repressive measures. Following a ministerial summit in the resort town of Carlsbad, the so-called "Carlsbad Decrees" were promulgated in September 1819, imposing strict limits on freedoms of speech, press, and assembly, and banning student fraternities, whose subversive Liberal and nationalistic ideals were seen as dangerous toxins.

The German case offers a particularly striking illustration of radicalizing tendencies within early nineteenth-century nationalist thought. On the ideological level, romantic themes increasingly infused conceptions of German nationalism, largely in the sense of the organic cultural nationalism advocated by Herder, but with Herder's inclusive "garden of humanity" given a much sharper chauvinistic edge. Josef Görres, one of the most energetic exponents of literary romanticism early in his career, constructed striking images of German identity as an exclusivistic community based on blood.[94] In 1813 Görres wrote:

> In itself every nationality is a completely closed and rounded whole; a common tie of blood relationship unites all its members.... This instinctive urge that binds all members into a whole is the law of nature which takes precedence over all artificial contracts. The voice of nature in ourselves warns us and points to the chasm between us and the alien.[95]

An even more influential representative of German romanticism, Ernst Moritz Arndt, drew inspiration from the Roman historian Tacitus, whose *Germania* had praised the insular vigor of the first-century Germanic tribes who "realized how important it was for their future greatness and majesty that they preserved the purity of their blood and resembled only themselves."[96] Upon the promulgation of the Carlsbad Decrees, Arndt was labeled a subversive threat for the emotive extremism of his nationalist effusions and in 1819 was dismissed from his teaching post at the University of Bonn.[97]

The spread of such radicalized imagery, however, could not easily be stemmed by legal measures; in fact, throughout the decade of the 1820s romantic nationalist sentiments took on increasingly powerful religious-oriented contours. In May 1832, nearly 30,000 nationalist and Liberal activists gathered near the town of Neustadt in southwestern Germany, engaging in a veritable orgy of religio-romantic fervor amid the picturesque ruins of Hambach castle. Participants of the Hambach Festival, as it came to be known, attended impassioned nationalist speeches, sang the chauvinistic hymns of Arndt while marching in torchlight processions, venerated "liberty trees" in the mode of the French revolutionary Jacobins and, perhaps most notably, called for the dissolution of the sovereign states of the German Confederation in favor of overarching national unification.[98] In describing the radicalization of nationalist imagery at Hambach, particularly in comparison to the Wartburg Festival fifteen years earlier, George Mosse has argued that the activists of 1832 largely abandoned the Christian elements still visible in 1817, constructing a decidedly secular and potentially revolutionary "national liturgy" in the face of the repressive structures of the German Confederation.[99]

In addition to carrying the black-red-gold flag of aspirational German unity, a number of Hambach participants also carried the flag of Poland in solidarity with their Polish counterparts whose national uprising had been crushed by Russian military force, the previous year. The failure of the Polish independence drive is often cited as a cautionary tale of missed opportunity and misfortune—especially when compared to successful independence movements in Belgium, discussed earlier, and Greece, to be discussed shortly.

Following the establishment of the Congress Kingdom of Poland in 1815, Alexander I had given the Poles a measure of autonomy, allowing the continuation of the parliamentary *Sejm* and tolerating the creation of a constitution. Nicholas I, who came to the throne after Alexander's death in 1824, engaged in more overtly repressive measures. At the same time, a generation of young Polish writers came of age, embracing romanticism as a vehicle for both their literary ambitions and their dreams of national independence.[100] The dominant figure among them was Adam Mickiewicz, who was born in 1798 and created a literary sensation with the appearance in 1822 of his *Ballads and Romances*, leading immediately to comparisons with Walter Scott.[101] Due to his membership as a student in a secret society known as the Philomaths, he was imprisoned in 1824 for several years and then exiled abroad, where he continued to write. Other members of this emerging generation were Seweryn Goszczyński, born in 1801 and author of the Byron-inspired Gothic romance *The Castle of Kaniów* (1828), and Maurycy Mochnacki, born in 1803, whose father had participated proudly in the Kościuszko Uprising of 1794. Mochnacki became not only an influential literary critic and exponent of romanticism in the 1820s, but also one of Warsaw's leading romantic pianists, idealized especially by the young Chopin during his teenage years.[102] Somewhat younger was Juliusz Słowacki, born in 1809 but destined to become perhaps Poland's most influential, or at least perhaps its "angriest," romantic lyricist.[103] In the aftermath of the July 1830 revolution in France, these figures, and thousands of others similarly fueled by the dynamic mixture of romanticism and nationalism, joined eagerly in the bid for Polish independence.

The November Uprising, as the Polish revolution came to be known, was inspired in part by Mickiewicz's 1828 epic poem *Konrad Wallenrod*, which idealized a fourteenth-century pagan from Poland-Lithuania who was forced to convert to Christianity by the Teutonic Knights. Wallenrod's ultimate return to his pagan roots was portrayed as a heroic act of rebellion against foreign interference, and his self-sacrificial suicide at the poem's end served as a "call to arms" for revolutionary action, enflaming the romantic imaginations of countless Polish youths eager to sacrifice themselves, if need be, for the Polish nation.[104] The revolt itself began on November 29, 1830, when cadets from the military training school in Warsaw, led by the young officer Piotr Wysocki, marched against the Belvedere Palace, the residence of the Russian Grand Duke Konstantin, who had overseen Poland as viceroy for more than a decade. Konstantin quickly took flight, and a provisional Polish government was formed under Adam Czartoryski, who initially tried to mediate between the insurgents and Russian authorities.[105] Driven forward by the so-called "Patriotic Club" surrounding the aforementioned Mochnacki, radicals in Warsaw refused any form of negotiation and appealed directly to Polish soldiers, who joined the revolutionary movement in large numbers. In early December, Mochnacki and several other radicals joined the provisional government, and the *Sejm* was convened to proclaim a national uprising against Russia. This was followed in January by an official renunciation of Russian rule.

Tsar Nicholas responded swiftly, mobilizing Russian forces and launching an invasion that began in early February. Polish troops were hastily raised and often poorly trained, and were overmatched both numerically and in terms of equipment. By late summer Warsaw was encircled, and Polish forces could only hold out until early October before surrendering. Sympathy for the Polish cause had been fairly widespread throughout Europe—and would increase in subsequent years, as seen among the Hambach demonstrators in 1832—but there was never any realistic expectation of substantial international intervention. Revolutionary leaders who were unable to flee were arrested, executed in large numbers, and exiled in even larger numbers (up to 80,000 were sent into Siberian captivity), while the *Sejm* was forcibly disbanded, universities closed down, and the dream of Polish independence placed on hold for the foreseeable future. The anguish caused by the initial thwarting of that dream would lead Adam Mickiewicz to paint Poland once again as the messianic "martyr" nation of Europe.[106] It is also worth noting that, just as Mickiewicz's romantic *Wallenrod* helped inspire the revolution, its powerful imagery was also central to subsequent commemorations, providing the basis for one of Chopin's most emotive *Ballades*, which was composed explicitly as a "narrative of national martyrdom."[107] The emotive force of his lyricism is amply illustrated in the following excerpt.

EXCERPT 3.1

To a Polish Mother (1831)

Adam Mickiewicz

O Polish mother, if the radiant eyes
Of genius kindle in thy darling's face, ~~spark of creation,~~
If even in his childish aspect rise ~~non-independent~~ ~~seeds of nation~~
The pride and honour of his ancient race; ~~nationalist calling to ethnic unity~~

If, turning from his playmates' joyous throng,
He runs to find the bard and hear his lays, ~~leaving the crowd of countries~~
If with bowed head he listens to the song
Of ancient glory and departed days: ~~the past as a glorious time~~ ~~establishing new nationalism~~

O Polish mother, ill must be his part!
Before the Mother of Our Sorrows kneel,
Gaze on the sword that cleaves her living heart – ~~Poland as martyr~~
Such is the craven blow thy breast shall feel! ~~cowardly~~

Though people, powers, and schisms a truce declare, ~~speaks to historical complexity~~
And though the whole wide world in peace may bloom,
In battle—without glory—must he share; ~~long-suffering~~
In martyrdom, with an eternal tomb.[108]

The movement for Greek national independence came against the backdrop of earlier challenges to Ottoman rule, beginning most notably with the Serbian uprising of 1804, which had been fueled largely by competing visions of religious identity—Orthodox Christians fighting an emancipatory crusade versus Muslim Turks in pursuit of defensive jihad.[109] In contrast, the Greek uprising was not framed primarily as a drive for confessional liberation and mere political independence, but as a transformative revival of the Greek nation, drawing both on the Enlightenment idealization of classical antiquity and on the dynamic force of early nineteenth-century romanticism.[110] As the first major war for independence to succeed since the American Revolution, the uprising drew the attention of huge numbers of Europeans up to its culmination in 1832. Unlike the Polish case, the major powers of Europe ultimately intervened on behalf of the Greek insurgents, and the episode came to serve as an idealized model for a number of later national revolutions.

The immediate roots of the uprising lay in the Greek diaspora that stretched throughout much of eastern and southeastern Europe. The widely recognized intellectual father of the revolution was Rigas Velestinlis, editor of a Greek-language newspaper in Vienna at the time of the French Revolution. In the 1790s, Rigas penned a Greek adaptation of the *Declaration of*

Rights of Man and Citizen, as well as a draft constitution for his vision of an independent Greek Republic and a revolutionary anthem, the *Thourios*, which became the Greek equivalent of the *Marseillaise*.[111] In 1798, as a result of clandestine contacts he established with French military figures, he was arrested by Austrian authorities and killed while in custody, apparently by strangulation.[112] As news of his heroic "martyrdom" spread through Greek communities, the impact of his writings was magnified greatly. Also central to the early development of Greek independence ideals was Adamantios Korais, a classical philologist who experienced the French Revolution firsthand as an émigré scholar in Paris. Initially inspired by the idea of replicating the unifying impact of French revolutionary nationalism back home in Greece, Korais became increasingly disillusioned with the violent excesses of the Jacobins and ultimately advocated a dramatic leap back in time to the values of the Periclean age in Athens, which he viewed as a healthier model for emancipated Greek identity.[113] While lacking the emotive appeal of Rigas's martyrdom, Korais's extensive writings on the linguistic and legal structures of classical antiquity and on the theoretical underpinnings of constitutional law helped imbue, by the sheer magnitude of their scope, the Greek nationalist movement with substance and scholarly prestige.[114]

EXCERPT 3.2

Report on the Present State of Civilization in Greece (1803)

Adamantios Korais

In the middle of the last century the Greeks constituted a miserable nation who suffered the most horrible oppression and experienced the nefarious effects of a long period of slavery. There yet remained in the nation's midst a very small number of schools in which a very small number of Greeks acquired only the most superficial knowledge of the Greek language. The rest of the nation was condemned to the crassest ignorance and to the reading of books, acquaintance with which is worse than non-acquaintance. [...]

Greeks, hitherto stricken, raise their heads in proportion as their oppressors' arrogance abates and their despotism becomes somewhat mitigated. This is the veritable period of Greek awakening. Minds, emerging from their lethargy, are amazed to observe this deplorable state; and that same national vanity which had hitherto prevented them from seeing it, now increases their amazement and irritation. For the first time the nation surveys the hideous spectacle of its ignorance and trembles in measuring with the eye the distance separating it from its ancestors' glory. This painful discovery, however, does not precipitate the Greeks into despair: *We are the descendants of the Greeks*, they implicitly told themselves, *we must either try to again become worthy of this name, or we must not bear it.*[115]

In 1814, in the Russian port city of Odessa, émigré Greek merchants and commercial elites founded a secret society known as the *Filiki Eteria* (Friendly Society), which was organized initially on the model of a small masonic lodge but quickly expanded to include branches throughout much of southeastern Europe. As the society grew, the absence of a unified ideology became clear, although throughout its expanding underground networks there was common agreement on the goal of Greek independence from Ottoman control. With the election in April 1820 of Alexander Ypsilantis as head of the society, its efforts became increasingly streamlined into clandestine militarized channels. Ypsilantis had served as a cavalry officer in the Russian military during the Napoleonic Wars, famously losing his right arm fighting against Napoleon in the 1813 Battle of Dresden.[116] The opportunity for the *Filiki Eteria* to launch a broad-based uprising emerged in the summer of 1820 as the result of a growing military conflict between Ali Pasha, the ambitious Ottoman administrator who oversaw much of the empire's Greek territory, and the Sultan Mahmud II.[117] As the conflict escalated into a virtual civil war throughout the winter of 1820–1821, Ypsilantis massed troops in southern Russia in the hopes of exploiting any gains that might be made by Ali Pasha's forces while, if possible, spurring the Russians under Alexander I to intervene. Whereas Ali Pasha's troops failed miserably on the battlefield, resulting in his capture in February 1821, the bigger blow to Ypsilantis's plans came that same month in the form of Alexander I's flat refusal to offer any support. The fate of the planned uprising was rescued in legendary fashion, however, when on March 25, 1821, the Bishop of Patras consecrated the flag of revolution before it was raised above the walls of the monastery at Agia Lavra, providing a central rallying symbol and signaling the start of armed insurrection throughout the Peloponnesian peninsula.[118]

In the initial months of brutal fighting, Greek forces were able to make considerable gains on the peninsula, but the leaders of the uprising—still smarting from the cold indifference of Russia—recognized that continued success was dependent on support from the other major powers of Europe. At the outbreak of the revolution, Petrobey Mavromichalis had issued an impassioned plea for assistance, pointing to the noble legacy of classical Greece:

We invoke therefore the aid of all civilized nations of Europe, that we may the more promptly attain to the goal of a just and sacred enterprise, reconquer our rights, and regenerate our unfortunate people. Greece, our mother, was the lamp that illuminated you; on this ground she reckons on your philanthropy. Arms, money, and counsel are what she expects from you. [119]

Like Russia, however, the other European states had been hesitant to respond. A national assembly was convened at Epidaurus, and in early 1822 the first Greek constitution of the modern era was published. By codifying their bid for independence in constitutional form, and by forming a new national government on its basis, Greek leaders hoped to force the Great Powers to engage directly in diplomatic relations. The fledgling government was, however, wracked with dissension and lacked legitimacy. A second assembly was convened in April 1823, with Petrobey being elected as president, but the internal tensions escalated and European assistance continued to prove elusive. Even more problematically, by late 1823 the Greek gains made in the early stages of the conflict were being rolled back increasingly by Ottoman forces.

What transpired next sheds light on the immense power of the union of nationalism and romanticism. Just as the Greek cause seemed to be faltering, it came to be enveloped in a glorious haze of romantic idealism that spread throughout much of Europe. Young enthusiasts whose sympathies had been aroused by romantic evocations of Greek culture began traveling to Greece in increasing numbers to aid the independence fighters. Most famously, the British romantic poet Lord Byron arrived in Greece in December 1823 and emerged as the rallying icon of these international volunteer forces, who came to be known collectively as the Philhellenes.[120] In addition to using his poetic skills to raise international awareness (and money) for the Greek cause, Byron briefly assumed command of a small military unit in early 1824, despite a complete lack of military training.[121] Falling ill with what was initially identified as rheumatic fever, however, Byron's health declined rapidly in the space of a few weeks, and on April 19, 1824, he died near Missolonghi at the age of thirty-six. William Parry, one of the men under Byron's military command, was present at his deathbed, and Parry's account of his idol's final illness—citing as causes of death both Byron's selfless overcommitment to the mission and the inept attempts of doctors to combat the fever via unsanitary bleeding techniques—shaped subsequent perceptions.[122] Byron's death did as much to publicize the Greek cause as his actions had done, but the tide of the war continued to flow in favor of the Sultan and his forces.

In the end, when Greek success did eventually materialize, it was the result of official (albeit severely belated) intervention on the part of the Concert of Europe, spurred somewhat surprisingly by the Russians. Assuming the crown after the December 1825 death of his brother Alexander I, who had demonstrated so little sympathy for the Greek cause, Nicholas I faced a domestic challenge in the form of the Decembrist Revolt and was eager to deflect attention and expand Russian influence abroad, primarily at the expense of the Ottomans.[123] The British, in turn, signed a joint agreement with the Russians in April 1826, opting for intervention largely in the hope of preventing potential Russian expansion from upsetting the European balance of power. France under Charles X joined the anti-Ottoman coalition in July 1827. Militarily, the decisive victory of the coalition came fairly quickly, in October 1827, when Ottoman forces were crushed on an epic level at the Battle of Novarino.[124] While the final outcome was never in

FIGURE 3.2 Lord Byron on His Deathbed *by Joseph Denis Odevaere.*
Groeningemuseum/Wikimedia Commons.

serious doubt after Novarino, the conflict dragged on for several more years,
as hawkish advisors in the court of the Sultan pressed for the continuation
of hostilities regardless of the cost.

Divisions also continued among Greek leaders. Following the convening
of a third national assembly, which produced the Constitution of 1827,
it was hoped that newly elected president Ioannis Kapodistrias, who had
extensive experience in the Russian diplomatic service, would succeed as
a stabilizing force. Although he managed to push through basic military
and bureaucratic reforms, his harshly autocratic style sparked almost
constant opposition, as seen most notably in the public outrage over his
imprisonment of Petrobey in 1831. Even before his assassination by vengeful
members of Petrobey's family later that year, Kapodistrias was forced to
admit that a stable Greek state could only be achieved by full reliance on the
administrative expertise of the Great Powers, whose goal was the creation of
a Greek monarchy that could be integrated easily into the European order.[125]
As a result of the Treaty of London signed by Britain, Russia, and France in
May 1832, the Greek crown was offered to Otto, son of the Bavarian king
Ludwig I, who accepted and thus became the ruler of the first independent
Greek nation-state in history.[126] Ironically, Otto soon embarked on a series
of wide-ranging construction projects in Athens, refashioning the modern
Greek capital along the lines of his father Ludwig's ongoing architectural
transformation of Munich, which was itself being refashioned on the model

of classical Athens.[127] As Peter Jelavich has noted, this constituted a kind of "tyranny of Greece over Germany" in reverse.[128]

Overall, the linkage of romanticism and nationalism proved a dynamic and potentially destabilizing factor. As the decade of the 1830s progressed, Europe witnessed growing economic prosperity in a number of sectors, fueled in part by rising levels of industrialization and the early spread of railroads. But agricultural production, still the dominant sector of the economy, remained unpredictable and precarious. The subsequent decade was characterized by poor harvests—on a disastrous level in 1843 and then again between 1845 and 1847—leading to a radicalization of the tensions that continued to simmer beneath the surface of the traditionalist status quo. When these tensions boiled over into wide-ranging revolutionary activism across Europe in early 1848, the dramatic interweaving of political liberalism and romantic nationalism would lead hopeful commentators to refer to the period as the "Springtime of the Nations."

The revolutionary wave of 1848–1849

As in 1789, and again in 1830, the revolutionary wave of 1848 began in France, at least in its most substantive form. The citizen-king Louis Philippe, who assumed power after the July Revolution, had attempted to demonstrate the contrast between himself and his predecessor by staging a discreet and modest coronation ceremony in the Chamber of Deputies, pledging his support for the 1814 Charter and positioning himself as a unifying figure.[129] But Liberals and radicals were soon disillusioned with the new king and, especially, with the extent of continuity he allowed with the restoration era. The corrupt former ministers of Charles X—including the widely vilified Polignac—had been placed on trial, to be sure, but they were saved from harsh sentences by Louis Philippe, leading to a groundswell of bitter discontent visible especially in the Parisian satirical press.[130] Following the funeral of the republican military hero Jean Maximilien Lamarque in June 1832, renewed revolutionary violence had broken out in Paris, and nearly 800 were killed in fighting in the streets and on the barricades. While all too often overlooked in surveys of the era, it is this uprising that is immortalized in Victor Hugo's *Les Misérables*.[131] As the decade progressed, the government of François Guizot, who had earlier been a much more vociferous Liberal, pursued a course of cautious moderation. Periodic radical uprisings, such as that led by Auguste Blanqui's proto-communistic "Society of the Seasons" in 1839, were suppressed rather easily.[132] Challenges were also launched from the political right, with self-proclaimed Bourbon "legitimists" refusing to recognize the July Monarchy, while Bonapartists aligned with Napoleon's nephew Louis-Napoleon undertook abortive uprisings in Strasbourg in 1836 and Boulogne in 1840.[133] Throughout the 1840s, as economic hardship worsened, French society was increasingly polarized.

Following their defeat in the 1846 elections, oppositional Liberals turned more and more to extra-parliamentary gatherings as vehicles for political mobilization. Among the most popular of these gatherings were ones that, perhaps not surprisingly, involved food and drink. The related movement for political reform thus became known as the "banquet campaign."[134] When Guizot's government prohibited a well-publicized banquet scheduled for February 22, 1848, crowds in Paris took to the streets. Tensions escalated greatly the following day, when more than fifty demonstrators were shot by government troops, leading not only to Guizot's forced resignation but also, surprisingly swiftly, to the abdication of Louis Philippe, who fled to Britain. A provisional government was formed, announcing on February 25, 1848, the abolition of the monarchy and the establishment of the Second Republic under the presidency of the romantic poet Alphonse de Lamartine.[135]

As news of the February Revolution reverberated throughout Europe over the subsequent weeks and months, the provisional government in Paris struggled to rise above the pervasive factionalism that grew up as a result, among other things, of new land taxes that were levied to pay for job creation programs organized through National Workshops. As oppositional forces coalesced in traditionalist rural areas, elections in April also reflected gains for conservatives and moderates. In May, radical workers stormed the Assembly, attempting to form a new government and thereby breathe new life into the revolution, but were suppressed by the National Guard. The following month, in what became known as the "June Days," tens of thousands of workers took to the streets and barricades to fight a bloody urban battle for three days, before ultimately succumbing to the superior force of government troops commanded by General Eugène Cauvignac.[136] With the agents of change increasingly divided politically between moderates, Liberals, and radicals, and socially between the bourgeoisie, artisans, and workers, the forces of moderation and conservative order were able to reassert themselves. The constitution of November 1848 provided for the basic structures of the fledgling Second Republic, and elections for President were held in December. Napoleon's nephew, Louis-Napoleon, scored a major victory for the Bonapartist movement by decisively defeating General Cauvignac and several lesser-known candidates.[137] While it would take until 1851 for Louis-Napoleon to dismantle the Second Republic in favor of an imperial dictatorship, over which he would preside for two decades as Napoleon III, the trappings of authoritarianism were already visible in December 1848 in his adoption of the title Prince-President and in the refashioning of his palatial residence as a virtual royal court.[138]

In the smaller countries of Western Europe, the revolutionary wave emanating from France impacted existing political structures in different ways. In neighboring Belgium, the revolutionary repercussions of 1848 were ultimately much milder than had been the case in 1830. This outcome can be seen as surprising on a number of levels. First, the Belgian economy had experienced massive dislocations in the 1840s, as technological modernization, particularly in the textile and steel industries, produced large numbers of unemployed workers. Second, Belgian politics remained deeply divided, as seen in the continued acrimony between conservative Catholics and secularized Protestant Liberals. In August 1847, the Liberal Charles Rogier formed a new government, which also bore signs of the continuing linguistic division between Dutch-speaking Flemings and French-speaking Walloons. Rogier had been a member of the first Belgian provisional government in 1830 and had stated famously that the goal of his administration was to "destroy the Flemish language"; ironically yet fittingly, when Rogier later survived a pistol duel with his rival Charles Gendebien, he was shot, of all places, in the tongue.[139] Finally, in addition to economic disruption and internal division, starting in early 1845 Brussels was also home to the future paragon of revolutionary activism, Karl Marx, who was joined there a few months later by his collaborator Friedrich Engels.[140] Marx's time in Brussels ended with his expulsion by Belgian police in early March 1848, in the immediate aftermath of the publication of the *Communist Manifesto*. By that point, the revolution in France had already progressed significantly, and several days had passed since Louis Philippe's flight from Paris. Despite initially offering his own abdication on February 26, 1848, Leopold I remained on the throne throughout the crisis and Rogier's government was at least marginally successful in weathering the storm.[141] The most significant challenge came at the end of March, when increasing numbers of Belgian workers who had been abroad, many of them in Paris, returned home with the goal of inciting revolutionary upheaval. A group of several thousand armed insurgents, calling themselves the "Belgian Legion," engaged in pitched battles with government troops on 26 and 29 March before being put down.[142] Ultimately, in light of the violence of the June Days in Paris, many Belgians opted to drop their longstanding social and political antagonisms in favor of a program of broad consensus, which was reaffirmed in elections that summer.[143] Divisions did not disappear entirely, of course, but the system of constitutional monarchy emerged, somewhat surprisingly, strengthened.[144]

In Switzerland, whose cantonal system remained divided between Protestant and Catholic regions, conflict had actually begun the previous year. Liberals and radicals from the wealthier and more urbanized Protestant cantons had called for the seizure of Catholic Church property and the banning of the Jesuits, inciting seven largely rural and alpine Catholic cantons to form the secessionist *Sonderbund* (Separate Confederation). This led in November 1847 to a largely bloodless civil war, known as the *Sonderbundskrieg*, in which the numerically superior Swiss Confederation troops were able to put down the secession in less than a month.[145] The conservative governments in the Catholic separatist cantons were replaced with the Liberals, and plans for a reformation of the entire cantonal system were set in motion. As revolutionary chaos was coursing through much of Europe in the spring and summer of 1848, the Swiss reform project proceeded fairly smoothly. By September, a new constitution had been published, replacing the traditional autonomy of the cantons with a unified, federal state.[146] As had been the case in Belgium, Swiss governing structures were ultimately able to transcend linguistic and religious divisions, although as Oliver Zimmer has noted, the pluralistic nature of the Swiss polity would ensure that Switzerland remained a "contested nation."[147]

In Northern Europe and Scandinavia, revolutionary activity in 1848 was similarly varied. Whereas England was largely untouched by widespread revolutionary disruption, Ireland experienced a dramatic, if ill-fated, rebellion. The mid-1840s had been catastrophic for many Irish citizens, as the potato blight that destroyed the country's central food staple led inexorably to the Great Famine. Relations with the British crown were greatly strained, as anger spread over the perceived indifference of London to the plight of starving children.[148] Furthermore, due to the lack of success of Daniel O'Connell's Repeal Association, whose goal had been to overturn peacefully the Act of Union (which had absorbed Ireland into Britain in 1801), more radical activists came increasingly to the fore to agitate for the twin ideals of national independence and republicanism. Many of these were associated with the Young Ireland movement, which had been founded in Dublin in the late 1830s as a rough corollary to Mazzini's Young Italy. Its organ was the aptly named periodical *The Nation*, and its leading early figure was the romantic poet Thomas Davis, whose anthem "A Nation Once Again" ensured his lasting fame.[149]

EXCERPT 3.3

A Nation Once Again

Thomas Osborne Davis

When boyhood's fire was in my blood,
I read of ancient free men
For Greece and Rome who bravely stood,
Three hundred men and three men.
And then I prayed I yet might see
Our fetters rent in twain;
And Ireland, long a province,
Be a nation once again!

And from that time, through wildest woe,
That hope has shown a far light;
Nor could love's brightest summer glow,
Outshine that solemn starlight;
It seemed to watch above my head
In forum, field, and fane,

Its angel voice sang round my bed,
"A nation once again!"

It whispered, too, that "freedom's ark
And service high and holy,
would be profan'd by feelings dark
And passions vain or lowly;
For freedom comes from God's right hand,
And needs a godly train;
And righteous men must make our land
A nation once again."

So, as I grew from boy to man
I bent me to that bidding –
My spirit of each selfish plan
And cruel passion ridding;
For, thus I hoped some day to aid –
Oh! can *such* hope be vain? –
When my dear country should be made
A nation once again.[150]

After Davis fell ill and died suddenly in September 1845, other members of Young Ireland who had previously been skeptical toward O'Connell's Repeal Association broke away entirely. In their eyes O'Connell's moderation amounted to a virtual betrayal of the national cause. Under the leadership of William Smith O'Brien, who had taken over as head of Young Ireland after the death of Davis, the much more radical Irish Confederation was founded in early 1847.[151] Inspired by the events of February 1848 in France, and fueled in part by continued despair over the potato famine, the "Young Irelander Revolt" was launched in the summer of 1848.[152] O'Brien and several compatriots had traveled to Paris in early June, finding the city, in O'Brien's words, "in a state of absolute intoxication from excitement," with romantic aesthetics embodied in massive armed processions and the proliferation of liberty trees.[153] Having returned to Ireland before the bloody June Days in Paris, O'Brien and the Young Ireland movement decided to strike the following month, mobilizing secret weapons caches and erecting barricades in several towns and cities throughout the south. The rebellion's most famous episode took place on 29 July in the form of a shootout between police forces, who had taken hostages inside a widow's farmhouse in Ballingarry, and insurgents in the surrounding fields. Police reinforcements eventually arrived and the hostage situation resolved with only one fatality, as rebel forces backed down.[154] Over the next few days the broader revolt was also quelled, with the ringleaders being arrested and sentenced to death for treason. Those sentences were eventually suspended in favor of transportation, primarily to Van Diemen's Land, where O'Brien spent the next several years.[155] While the Young Irelander revolt produced no immediate gains, and a frustratingly small number of heroic martyr figures, it was yet another chapter in the developing Irish narrative of national independence.[156]

In Norway, in the aftermath of the May 1829 *Torgslaget* (Market Battle), the yearly Constitution Day festivities continued as a vehicle for protean national idealism, although the harsh anti-Swedish tenor was softened considerably over the following decade. By the early 1840s, as the effects of industrialization spread, a convergence emerged between workers' activism and elements of what Oscar Falnes has called "national romanticism."[157] One of the central figures in this development was Marcus Thrane, who in the late 1830s had studied in France before returning in 1840 to the University of Christiania. After a brief career in teaching, Thrane settled on politically active journalism as the preferred outlet for his energies. When the February 1848 revolution broke out in France, Thrane published a radical article in the *Morgenbladet*, Norway's leading newspaper, in which he idealized the French revolutionary cause and called for massive political reforms, including the imposition of universal suffrage.[158] From March 10 to 12, 1848, there were unruly demonstrations outside the offices of the *Morgenbladet*, as thousands of revolutionary supporters and their opponents clashed over differing conceptions of political and national solidarity. The famous Norwegian violinist Ole Bull, living in Paris, presented the interim French president Lamartine with a Norwegian flag as a sign of romantic national solidarity.[159] Following his missive in the *Morgenbladet*, Thrane was made editor of the *Drammens Adresse*, a newspaper in the growing industrial city of Drammen, which Thrane transformed into the most politically radical publication in Norway. In December 1848, he founded the Drammen workers' union, and worked with missionary zeal to establish other labor unions, most notably in Christiania in March 1849. The revolutionary activism of Thrane's followers resulted in his eventual arrest and imprisonment for four years, after which time he ultimately emigrated to the United States.[160] While he is mostly remembered as a proto-socialistic internationalist and a mild precursor of Norway's later labor movement, in 1848 he was very much a product of the Liberal and nationalistic wave that swept Europe.[161]

In Sweden, Jean-Baptiste Bernadotte, who ruled for more than two decades as king Charles XIV John, died in March 1844 and was succeeded by his son Oscar I. During the later stages of his father's reign Oscar had been widely suspected of harboring Liberal sympathies, leaving many optimists disappointed with the cautious moderation he pursued upon taking the throne. Though only in his mid-forties at the time, and with no visible gray hair, Oscar nonetheless seemed perpetually aged, embracing stability and predictability—and, it should be noted, the outdated Estates system—to such an extent that the boring quiescence of Swedish politics became the butt of jokes. The playwright August Strindberg, born in Stockholm during the early years of Oscar's reign, felt pity for the plight of the neighboring Norwegians under the Swedish union, calling Norway "a young and healthy country chained to a rotten and decrepit one."[162] The relative calm was broken briefly in the aftermath of the February Revolution, in what became known as the *Marsoroligheterna* (March Disturbances), which began with a Parisian-style political banquet on March 18, 1848. Crowds of protesters took to the streets outside the Stockholm hotel where the banquet was held, demanding political reform and the abolition of the archaic Estates. While the crowd was dispersed more or less peacefully that evening, deadly rioting ensued on the following day, with government troops killing some thirty demonstrators.[163] The revolutionary enterprise, which could have spiraled into further violence, was moderated fairly quickly by figures like André Oscar Wallenberg, a Liberal naval officer whose conciliatory diplomacy in certain ways foreshadowed that of his great-grandson, the diplomat Raoul Wallenberg, who would rescue thousands of Jews during the Holocaust.[164] Wallenberg played a central role in the Reform Society of Stockholm starting in March 1848, before cofounding the moderate Liberal newspaper *Bore* later in the year. *Bore*, which in Swedish refers to the freshness of the north wind, became the mouthpiece of so-called Harmony Liberalism, the tame centrist channel into which much reformist zeal was directed over the subsequent decade.[165] The cautious course pursued in Sweden in 1848 was partly responsible for the fact that it took nearly twenty more years for the archaic Estates system to be transformed into the representative bicameral Riksdag.[166]

In absolutist Denmark, the pace of change was more rapid. King Christian VIII, who had come to the throne in 1839, died suddenly in late January 1848, leaving his son and successor, Frederik VII, little time to acclimate himself to the rhythms of governance before facing the wave of revolutionary activism emanating from France. The Danish National Liberal Party, which had been founded in 1842, had long sought an opportunity to push for constitutional reform and the abolition of the absolutist system. When the party staged a massive demonstration on March 21, 1848, in which more than 15,000 Danes marched on Christiansborg Palace, King Frederik not only agreed to an immediate audience with the Liberal leadership but astonished them with the news that he was willing to suspend all sitting government ministers. A provisional government was formed the next day, dominated by moderate Liberals and reform-oriented conservatives, and the era of absolutist rule in Denmark was effectively brought to a close in the course of less than two days. The constitution that was published the following June established a greatly expanded suffrage, a bicameral parliament known as the *Rigsdagen*, and a fairly broad set of personal and civil liberties.

For all of its internal conciliatory harmony, however, the Danish experience of 1848 was shaped externally by a much sharper nationalist inflection than was seen elsewhere in Northern Europe. The duchies of Schleswig and

Holstein, which were part of the Danish kingdom but whose populations included a majority of Germans, became flashpoints for competing national identities. In 1815, Holstein, the southernmost duchy, had been accorded membership in the German Confederation, while remaining under the Danish crown. The fact that Schleswig was not included in the German Confederation was seen as problematic in light of the "indissoluble union" established exclusively between Schleswig and Holstein in the 1460 Treaty of Ribe.[167] As romantic nationalist ideas spread in the early decades of the nineteenth century, Germans in both territories grew increasingly agitated.[168] In mid-March 1848, as revolution swept through the individual German states, representatives from the two duchies had demanded approval to secede from Denmark and to enter the German Confederation as the joint state of Schleswig-Holstein, in order to participate in early deliberations over German national unification. When the new Danish government was formed on March 22, 1848, however, the king and the National Liberals in Copenhagen insisted on maintaining firm possession of Schleswig.[169] In response, German nationalists revolted and formed a provisional government in Kiel, resulting in the lengthy military conflict known as the First Schleswig War. Although Prussia and Sweden aided the German nationalists, who held out for more than two years, by early 1851 Danish forces, strengthened by anti-Prussian international sentiment, ultimately prevailed.[170] Both duchies, which Martin Klatt has aptly termed "mobile regions," remained in personal union with the Danish crown until the Second Schleswig War in the 1860s.[171]

Within the German Confederation, revolutionary activism was dramatic, but also often fragmented and decentralized. On the eve of 1848, confessional division continued to limit the horizons of many advocates of national unification. Protestants, even if secularized, tended to see Prussia as the agent of national destiny, whereas most Catholics looked to Austria and the Habsburgs for leadership. In 1840, with the death of the Prussian king Friedrich Wilhelm III and the accession of Friedrich Wilhelm IV, the hopes of Liberals and nationalists had been raised by the cryptic ruminations of the new ruler, who encouraged the completion of the Cologne Cathedral as an exercise in romantic medievalism.[172] The fact that his political vision was fundamentally anti-constitutional was often overlooked. Liberals and radicals in the Austrian camp turned increasingly to voluntary associations, such as the Juridical-Political Reading Club in Vienna, as venues for oppositional activism.[173] It was difficult to know what to make of the Austrian ruler Ferdinand I, who came to the throne in 1835; he was mentally unstable, and his most famous statement—"I am the emperor, and I want dumplings!"—became a sort of catchphrase for the monarchical debilities of the era.[174] Complicating matters further was the fact that the linkage between liberalism and nationalism was contorted in the Habsburg lands, as Hungarians, Czechs, Poles, and a host of other ethnic entities eyed their opportunity for national liberation, but with social and cultural visions that were often contradictory. Hungarian nationalists pushed for greater

Magyarization, moving to replace Latin with Hungarian, and thereby angered national and linguistic minorities scattered throughout the region, particularly Romanians in Transylvania.[175] In early 1846, Polish nobles and nationalist intellectuals in Austrian Galicia rose up in anticipation of a planned uprising throughout the entirety of partitioned Poland, but were famously crushed by counterrevolutionary peasants fighting in defense of the Habsburg system (and with support from Austrian authorities) in an episode known as the "Galician Massacres."[176] The behavior of the Polish peasants demonstrates, if nothing else, the continued ability of dynastic loyalties to overcome nationalist challenges, especially when self-appointed nationalist leaders failed, as was the case in Galicia, to address the varied social identities and traditionalist concerns of the agrarian countryside.[177]

The earliest sizable demonstrations within the German Confederation took place in the southwestern state of Baden, led by Friedrich Hecker and Gustav Struve. In Bavaria, King Ludwig I faced the revolutionary tide of 1848 with his credibility already severely undermined by a scandalous extramarital relationship with an exotic dancer calling herself Lola Montez (in reality, she was an Irish charlatan named Eliza Gilbert).[178] By the time Lola was chased out of Munich in February 1848 by angry mobs of morally outraged citizens, the damage to Ludwig's reputation was irreparable. When French-inspired revolutionary demonstrations spread to Munich in mid-March, Ludwig was compelled to abdicate, becoming the only European monarch, other than Louis Philippe, to be forced off the throne in the early stages of the revolution. It is important to note, however, that the proponents of change were deeply divided, and Ludwig's son and successor Maximilian II was able, after making initial concessions, to restore much of the conservative status quo. That general pattern was reflected throughout many of the smaller and mid-sized German states, as initial revolutionary openings closed under the weight of existing political divisions. In the two largest states, Austria and Prussia, the course of the revolution was shaped to a much greater degree by conflicting nationalist ideals.

In the Habsburg domains, mass demonstrations began in Vienna on March 13, 1848, with violent crowds forcing the resignation of Metternich, the Austrian chief minister, who was forced to flee to England. Despite initial efforts by the dim-witted Ferdinand and his remaining advisors to stem the revolutionary tide, in May 1848 the court was forced to relocate from Vienna to Innsbruck. On and off for several months, the city of Vienna was effectively in the hands of a divided lot of radicals and moderates, students and workers, and middle-class professionals.[179] Imperial military forces launched a successful strike to retake Vienna in October, with several thousands killed in street fighting and hundreds more being forced into exile. The next month, Ferdinand was convinced by his advisors to abdicate the throne, allowing for an orderly transition of power to his eighteen-year-old nephew Franz Joseph, who would proceed to rule Austria well into the twentieth century. But the pursuit of order in the Habsburg lands was complicated by a series of nationalist uprisings whose leaders hoped to use the revolutionary caesura as an opportunity to establish national independence. Czech nationalists in Bohemia and Moravia, with the Liberal historian Frantisek Polacký foremost among them, led a series of largely peaceful demonstrations in Prague between March and May 1848.[180] But violence erupted on 12 June, as imperial troops commanded by Prince Alfred Windischgrätz confronted a large crowd of student demonstrators, touching off five days of intense street fighting within the city. Windischgrätz's wife was killed in the initial stages of the conflict, but by 17 June the insurgent forces had been crushed in what became the first major victory of the militant counterrevolution.[181] The Hungarian uprising had begun in early March 1848 with a famous speech by Lajos Kossuth, which fueled a series of demonstrations and led to the formation of a new Hungarian government with enhanced autonomy.[182] Upon taking the throne in November, Franz Joseph quickly disavowed all previous concessions and Austrian military might eventually crushed the fledgling Hungarian government, which also faced armed opposition from Croats, Romanians, and Slovaks who themselves sought to exploit the upheaval to achieve their own goals of independence.[183]

In Prussia, the earliest major revolutionary agitation came not from nationalists, but from the internationalist, proto-communist left in the form of mass demonstrations in early March 1848 led by the radical physician Andreas Gottschalk in Cologne, part of the Prussian Rhineland.[184] In Berlin, Friedrich Wilhelm IV made initial conciliatory gestures, but unrest boiled over in the demonstrations of 18 March, in which more than 300 civilians were killed.[185] Over the next few days, the king continued to make concessions—transferring authority from the palace guard to a citizens' militia, wearing the gold-red-black armband of Liberal nationalists in public, and delivering a speech in which he seemed to endorse the project of national unification, announcing that "Prussia dissolves into Germany."[186] But a new crisis quickly emerged in the East, as Polish nationalists launched a revolt in Prussian Poland, led by Ludwik Mierosławski.[187] His supporters fought against Prussian forces for more than a month, but by early May they had been overpowered and scattered. For the Prussian radical Wilhelm Jordan, the brutal suppression of the Poles was justified by the need among Germans to "awaken a healthy national egotism, without which no people can grow into a nation."[188] Liberal nationalists in Prussia increasingly linked the perceived superiority of the German nation with the drive to unify the German states under specifically Prussian leadership.

These ideas played out publicly in the energetic debates of the Frankfurt Parliament, which convened for much of the revolutionary period. Beginning its deliberations in the Frankfurt *Paulskirche* in May 1848, the approximately 800 delegates from throughout the German Confederation attempted to iron out a plan for German unification and to construct a consensus form of government enshrined in a constitution. Ultimately, the political divisions between the parliamentarians—who ranged from radicals to moderate Liberals to conservative constitutional monarchists—undermined attempts to forge compromise, and the incompatible egos of Prussia and Austria further destabilized the proceedings and resulted in insoluble gridlock.[189] By the time the Prussian king Friedrich Wilhelm IV officially refused the crown of a unified constitutional monarchy in March 1849, thus dashing all hope of a broad-based solution, the main question remaining was what specific form the postrevolutionary settlement would take. It was the 1850 Treaty of Olmütz that ultimately reconstituted the structures of the German Confederation and ushered in a new era of continued dynastic rule. What had begun with much optimism in the early stages of revolutionary upheaval proved to be a failure on virtually every level.

There are important lessons to be taken from the revolutionary experiences of the German states. First, the divisions among the proponents of change illustrate the tremendous logistical challenges of nation-building in the face of fundamentally incompatible visions of social and political belonging. These divisions would continue to impact Germany's political development long after unification was achieved.[190] Secondly, the public nature of Wilhelm Jordan's aforementioned call for "healthy national egotism" illuminates the continued abandonment of the façade of universalist humanitarian virtue often maintained by nationalist spokesmen. Exclusivistic chauvinism was becoming the increasingly visible glue of national belonging. Finally, the failure of the Frankfurt Parliament meant that when German unification was achieved more than two decades later, it would be through a fatefully divergent process. Rather than resulting from a broad-based movement of the people, unification would be forged through authoritarianism and militarism, setting Germany (and Europe) on a fundamentally different trajectory.

The impact of the 1848 revolutionary wave was also dramatic in the Italian territories, where not a single state had a constitutional government in the early 1840s. Organizations like the Congress of Italian Scientists, which met yearly and drew together scholars from across the Italian peninsula, had served as fronts for Liberal and nationalist mobilization transcending the boundaries of the individual dynastic states.[191] Against the backdrop of Austrian domination, only the Kingdom of Piedmont-Sardinia maintained any measurable independence. In January 1848, insurgents in the Sicilian capital of Palermo rose up and seized control of the island, setting the stage for the more substantive upheaval that emerged further to the north in subsequent months. In Austrian-controlled Lombardy, the so-called "Five Days of Milan" began on March 18, 1848, with nationalist activists led by Carlo Cattaneo clashing with Austrian forces commanded by General Joseph Radetzky.[192] Although some 500 insurgents were killed in the fighting, Radetzky's troops were forced to retreat and regroup, even as rebels in neighboring Venetia decided to launch their own bid for independence from Austrian control.[193] Carlo Alberto, the king of Piedmont-Sardinia, intervened militarily on the side of the insurgents in late March, fueled by equal measures of opportunism and sincere anti-Austrian sentiment.[194] After a series of humiliating defeats, however, Carlo Alberto was forced to sue for peace in August 1848, before reversing himself once again and resuming hostilities against Austria in the spring of 1849. Following the Battle of Novara, Carlo Alberto was forced, in even greater humiliation, to admit defeat and to abdicate the throne in favor of his son Victor Emmanuel II.[195] Lacking strong military backing, the insurgents in Lombardy and Venetia were unable to hold out and both territories remained in Austrian control.

Meanwhile, events in Rome developed dramatically. Pope Pius IX, who had ascended the papal throne in 1846, initiated a series of Liberal reforms in the spring of 1848, only to swing dramatically in a counterrevolutionary direction following the assassination of one of his chief ministers in November. When Pius abandoned Rome for the safety of the fortress at Gaeta the next month, revolutionary forces began a dramatic political experiment in the Eternal City. Mazzini returned from exile and, throughout the spring and summer of 1849, presided over the construction of a Roman Republic, with Garibaldi also returning to organize military defenses.[196] Viewing the Republic as an early step in the realization of Mazzini's dream of national unification within a republican framework, the fledgling government pushed through reforms including the declaration of religious freedom (granting full emancipation to the relatively small number of Jews living in Rome) and the establishment of a public welfare system to benefit Rome's poor. The Roman Republic was dismantled in July 1849, when French troops conquered the city and returned it to papal control despite Garibaldi's creative efforts at defense, and both Mazzini and Garibaldi were forced back into exile.[197] Even if it had not been defeated militarily, the Republic would almost certainly have collapsed from within. Mazzini's economic redistribution policies had led to runaway inflation, and the political structures of the fledgling republican system were riven with dissension. Even if it was not entirely apparent at the time, though, an important symbolic step had been taken toward national unification, embodied in new conceptualizations of social and political belonging.[198]

* * * *

Taken in sum, the events of 1848 and 1849 not only reveal the potential power of the linkage of Liberal nationalism and romantic idealism, but also the massive obstacles that lay in the way of overarching political transformation. As will be seen in the chapter that follows, however, the German and Italian territories in particular would witness dramatic national unification drives in the context of rapid economic modernization.

4

Industrialization, Ideological Radicalization, and Imperialism, 1850–1890

On January 11, 1850, at a meeting of the Royal Commission in London, concrete plans were made for the convening of the world's first Great Exhibition, an international gathering designed to showcase the latest achievements in scientific and technological progress around the globe, but framed explicitly within the context of individual nations and states. The Commission undertook a massive fundraising campaign, primarily through private subscriptions, and oversaw the construction of the Crystal Palace, which was to house the exhibition.[1] The Crystal Palace design, a futuristic fusion of iron and glass, was the brainchild of Joseph Paxton, who had made his career through the construction of greenhouses and conservatories, and Charles Fox, a railway engineer. Thus, the structure itself brought together a number of tangible symbols at the heart of British self-perception: pastoral verdancy, industrial dynamism, and innovative entrepreneurialism.[2] When the exhibition opened in May 1851, it quickly developed into "a forum for discussions of British national identity in the broadest sense."[3] Its scope was broad, including exhibits from some fifty countries—in addition to all British colonies and possessions—and it was visited by more than six million patrons over its five-month run. Like Britain, the participating countries used the spaces of the exhibition to frame the modernity of their own national identities as compellingly and cohesively as possible.[4] As Geoffrey Cantor has shown, however, the event was not only the occasion for positive self-presentation; it also provided a stage on which religious identities could be displayed and contested, with exhibits from Catholic countries coming in for heavy doses of scorn from the largely Protestant English public.[5] Ultimately, the exhibition brought to the fore two central themes that will be pursued in this chapter: the transformative power of scientific and technological modernization, and the mutually exclusive visions of national superiority that would resonate through Europe over the ensuing decades. Both of these elements underpinned the sprawling imperialist projects that dominated the second half of the nineteenth century, bringing massive changes to the internal and external dynamics of new and existing nation-states.

The decades that followed the dramatic political revolutions of 1848 were characterized by even more wide-ranging revolutions in production and manufacturing. While Britain's industrial revolution began at least a century earlier, throughout much of the European continent, it was the middle third of the nineteenth century in particular that manifested the most dramatic productive expansion ever seen.[6] New sources of power proliferated, with earlier steam engine technology being supplemented by the compound engine around 1850 and then the turbine engine by the 1880s. Coal, the central fuel source of the steam engine, was mined with increasing efficiency in these decades, whereas fledgling technologies requiring rubber, oil, and other petroleum products initiated a massive competition for new sources of raw material. Heavy industry was transformed by advances in steel production, particularly the Bessemer process pioneered in the mid-1850s, and transportation was revolutionized by improvements in shipbuilding and in railway and locomotive production. Engineering concerns worked with municipal and state authorities increasingly to undertake massive infrastructure modernization projects, such as bridges, dams, canals, and irrigation systems. Agricultural production was further enhanced by new chemical fertilizers. Communication technologies also expanded greatly as the telegraph, which had been developed in earlier decades, spread throughout Europe. The first underwater cable was laid across the English Channel in 1851, followed by the first transatlantic cable in the 1860s. The telephone and typewriter first came into use in the 1870s, as did the first high-speed rotary printing presses, which greatly accelerated the dissemination of news and other information. Against the backdrop of these technological innovations, new forms of large-scale manufacturing were pioneered, and massive numbers of Europeans were drawn from the countryside into existing cities and new, rapidly expanding urban agglomerations.[7]

The processes of industrialization and urbanization in Europe are typically linked, for good reason, with the growth of class consciousness. The transformative impact of these processes, however, also fundamentally shaped nation-building projects and conceptions of national identity.[8] Urbanization spawned not only working-class misery, child labor, and Dickensian squalor. It also produced new and larger communities of bourgeois elites and educated professionals, many of whom emerged as mouthpieces for nationalist ideologies. The progression of industrialization was often uneven, generating stark disparities in wealth and resources, along with corresponding resentments, both within individual societies and between industrializing nation-states. Although nationalist discourse would come increasingly to embrace wistful rural metaphors of blood and soil by the early twentieth century, in the decades after 1850, the symbolic universe of nationalist thought was more often characterized by visions of industrial might as manifestations of national strength and vitality. With the enshrining of manufacturing power as the perceived pinnacle of human achievement came an increased embrace of power politics among nationalist figures, as the earlier idealistic and ethereal linkage between romanticism and nationalism gave way to a more hardened real-world emphasis.

Industrialization and nation-building: The cases of Italy and Germany

The list of the 1851 London exhibition's participants was missing two entities without which it would be nearly impossible, only a few decades later, to imagine the map of Europe: Italy and Germany. Several of the Italian kingdoms were represented individually—with Piedmont-Sardinia generating the most attention—but the German states were identified under the less-than-inspiring banner of the "Zollverein," the customs union dominated by Prussia.[9] Both Italy and Germany would, of course, go on to provide the most notable examples of national unification and nation-building in Europe in the second half of the nineteenth century.[10] The individual cases of Piedmont-Sardinia and Prussia demonstrate effectively the ways in which technological development, industrial dynamism, and economic modernization could propel one state to the forefront of a successful national unification drive.

Italian unification

Starting in the 1840s, a prescient observer could have noted three possible paths for Italian national unification.[11] The least likely, at least in retrospect, was the one for which many traditional Italian Catholics had longed for centuries: a unified Italy bound together by religious identity and governed in some fashion by the pope. A leading figure in this trajectory was the priest and publicist Vincenzo Gioberti, who as a young cleric was influenced by Mazzini and was chased out of his native Piedmont in the early 1830s because of a dispute with the Jesuits over his reputed ties to secret societies. After spending more than a decade in an extended scholarly exile in Paris and Brussels, Gioberti turned increasingly away from radical republicanism and embraced the idea that a strong moral and political authority was necessary to achieve unification for Italy while maintaining an ideal combination of independence, external stability, and internal liberty. He ultimately settled on the papacy as the best vehicle for this authority. His most influential work, published in 1843 and bearing the telling title *The Civil and Moral Primacy of the Italians*, argued that the restoration of Italy's historical supremacy was only waiting for the proper framework, and he proposed an Italian federation linked under the presidency of the pope.[12] Initially, though, his plan lacked one absolutely essential ingredient: a pontiff who would be both willing and able to assume this role. The current pope, Gregory XVI, was an arch-reactionary who had greatly increased religious and political persecution in the early 1830s; collectively he and his two predecessors, Leo XII and Pius VIII, were known derisively as the "zealots."[13] The situation changed dramatically, however, upon the election in June 1846 of Pope Pius IX, who demonstrated remarkably open attitudes toward modernity and liberalism in his earliest years. Within a month after his election, he announced an amnesty of political prisoners and exiles, a hugely significant move that contrasted sharply with his predecessors' repressive policies, leading suddenly to an unprecedented wave of papal hero-worship. As a contemporary noted of the July 1846 amnesty celebrations in Rome: "A vast crowd assembled in the Colosseum and at the Capitol and marched in procession, with wax candles and singing joyful songs, to the Monte Cavallo, to return thanks to their chief and beg his benediction. Since the fall of the last of the Tribunes, there had been no such day in Rome."[14] In the ensuing months, Pius IX proceeded to issue a new press law that allowed (a limited number of) Liberal and nationalist works to be published, in addition to updating transportation and communications infrastructure throughout the Papal States and appointing a semi-parliamentary consultative body. It seemed to many that "Gioberti's pope" had indeed arrived.[15]

The year 1848 was to bring Pius IX's early Liberal period to a dramatic end. In March, during the initial spread of revolutionary activism throughout Europe, he had moved proactively to proclaim a constitution for the Papal States, known as the "Fundamental Statute."[16] A bicameral legislative body was established and a constitutional ministry under Cardinal Giacomo Antonelli was formed.[17] Unsure how best to respond to the anti-Austrian uprisings in Lombardy and Venetia that spring, Pius IX watched somewhat passively as demonstrations in Rome gained in intensity throughout the summer and into the fall. The breaking point for the pope came in November 1848, when a protester attacked and killed one of his chief ministers, Pellegrino Rossi, stabbing him in the neck as he sat in his carriage in front of the papal chancellery.[18] Pius was forced to flee Rome to the port city of Gaeta, and the ensuing months brought an almost complete change in his political orientation, as he watched the rise and fall of the short-lived Roman Republic from afar. Upon his return to Rome in April 1850, absolutist rule was reestablished in the form of a new government under Antonelli, and Pius spent his subsequent years, until his death in 1878, as an increasingly harsh critic of both Liberal democracy and national unification.[19]

The second potential path to Italian unity can be identified as the radical-republican trajectory, which seemed briefly, during the early phases of the Roman Republic in 1849, to be in the ascendant. Many of the early advocates of the *Risorgimento* had, like Mazzini, combined the goals of national unification and republican politics with strong doses of romantic imagery. Some, like the poet Ugo Foscolo, had died before the broad contours of the republican dream had even become plausible, while others, like Alessandro Manzoni, had eventually abandoned their republican roots, embracing various forms of conservative traditionalism. Mazzini and Garibaldi, however, had kept the republican faith while in exile, and both returned to play key roles in the Roman Republic of 1849. Following its collapse, both were forced back into exile—Mazzini primarily in England, Garibaldi primarily in the United States—and both continued to bide their time, awaiting another moment of opportunity. Mazzini in particular continued to write prolifically. Perhaps his most influential work, which he began in 1844 but did not complete until the late 1850s, was *Duties of Man*.[20] The book was an impassioned plea for republican-oriented national unification, aimed specifically at the Italian working classes but couched inexorably in the discourse of universalism and virtue. Mazzini claimed that the most pressing duty of each individual was to Humanity—"you are men before you are citizens or fathers"—but maintained that the nation was a divinely inspired mandate: "God gave you this means when he gave you a Country, when, like a wise overseer of labor who distributes the different parts of the work according to the capacity of the workmen, he divided Humanity into distinct groups upon the face of our globe, and thus planted the seeds of nations."[21] While the pursuit of a sort of cosmic universalism was the ultimate goal for Mazzini, Italians could only achieve this if they put their own house in order first, unifying and creating a national government in Rome. The costs of failing in this historic mission were high: "Without Country you have neither name, token, voice, nor rights, nor admission as brothers into the fellowship of the Peoples. You are the bastards of Humanity." In one of the book's most telling passages, excerpted below, Mazzini roots the concept of the nation, suitably cloaked in cosmopolitan virtue and saturated with heroic martyr imagery, in the powerful sense of belonging at the heart of ancient religious systems.

EXCERPT 4.1

The Duties of Man

Giuseppe Mazzini

A people—Greek, Pole, Italian or Circassian, raises the flag of Country and independence, and combats, conquers, or dies to defend it. What is it that causes your hearts to beat at the news of those battles, that makes them swell with joy at their victories, and sink with sorrow at their defeats? A man—it may be a foreigner, in some remote corner of the world—arises, and amidst the universal silence, gives utterance to certain ideas which he believes to be True, and maintains them throughout persecution, and in chains; or dies upon the scaffold, and denies them not. Wherefore do you honor that man, and call him saint and martyr? Why do you respect, and teach your children to respect his memory?...Is it that there is in your heart a voice that cries unto you: "Those men of two thousand years ago, those populations now fighting afar off, that martyr for an idea for which you would not die, are your brothers; brothers not only in community of origin and of nature, but of labor and aim."...Those populations consecrate with their blood an idea of national liberty, for which you too would combat. That martyr proclaimed by his death that man is bound to sacrifice all things, and, if need be, life itself, for that which he believes to be Truth. What matters it that he, and all of those who thus seal their faith with their blood, cut short their individual progress on Earth? God will provide for them elsewhere....

How great is the distance between this faith, which thrills within our souls, and which will be the basis of the morality of the coming Epoch, from the faith that was the basis of the morality of the generations of what we term antiquity! And how intimate is the connection between the idea we form of the Divine Government, and that we form of our own duties!

The first men *felt* God, but without comprehending or even seeking to comprehend Him in His Law. They felt him in His power, not in His love. They conceived a confused idea of some sort of relation between Him and their own individuality, but nothing beyond this. Able to withdraw themselves but little from the sphere of visible objects, they sought to incarnate Him in one of these; in the tree they had seen struck by the thunderbolt, the rock beside which they had raised their tent, the animal which first presented itself before them. This was the worship which in the history of Religions is termed *Fetishism*.

In those days men comprehended nothing beyond the *Family*, the reproduction in a certain form, of their own individuality: all beyond the family circle were strangers, or more often enemies: to aid themselves and their families was to them the sole foundation of morality.

In later days the idea of God was enlarged. From visible objects men timidly raised their thoughts to abstractions; they learned to generalize. God was no longer regarded as the Protector of the family alone, but of the association of many families, of the cities, of the peoples. Thus to *fetishism* succeeded *polytheism*, the worship of many Gods. The sphere of action of morality was also enlarged. Men recognized the existence of more extended duties than those due to the family alone; they strove for the advancement of the people, of the *Nation*.[22]

As passionate as Mazzini's blending of nationalist fervor and republican idealism was, its appeal faded somewhat as his generation aged. By the 1850s, many of his former supporters—including Garibaldi—were turning increasingly to the third potential path to unification, which essentially prevailed in the end: that of constitutional monarchy under the leadership of Piedmont-Sardinia and the House of Savoy.[23] The central figures in this trajectory were King Victor Emmanuel II and Camillo di Cavour. Victor Emmanuel had come to the throne upon the abdication of his father, Carlo Alberto, in March 1849. He maintained the constitution his father had granted during the revolution, and in 1852 he made the fortuitous decision to appoint Cavour, who would become the dominant political figure in the unification process, as prime minister. Cavour was born into a Piedmontese noble family that had close Napoleonic connections during his youth. He was trained at the military academy in Turin and was commissioned in the engineer corps of the Piedmontese army, but was by all accounts unhappy with the drudgery and drill of military life. Having eagerly devoured Liberal political philosophy on his own—especially the works of Jeremy Bentham— he expressed public support for the 1830 July Revolution in France and thus came into conflict with his military superiors, who transferred him to a remote mountain garrison. In response, Cavour requested and was granted an honorable discharge in 1831, with poor eyesight as the official justification.[24] Returning to his family estate and immersing himself in local politics, Cavour proceeded to embrace a pragmatic form of Liberal nationalism, albeit overwhelmingly focused on Piedmontese interests and very narrow in its conception of the franchise, which differentiated him sharply from the radical republicanism of his bitter rival Mazzini. In 1847, he founded the famous newspaper *Il Risorgimento* in Turin and, through his advocacy of moderate constitutionalism, brought himself increasingly into the political spotlight on the eve of the 1848 revolution.[25] While largely critical of the conservatism of Carlo Alberto, Cavour energetically embraced the accession to the throne of Victor Emmanuel, who returned the adulation by appointing Cavour to a series of ministerial posts, culminating in that of prime minister in 1852.

Cavour had proven himself an innovator in the management of his family's estate starting in the 1830s—he was, for example, an early adopter of new chemical fertilizing techniques—and this inventiveness continued to characterize his policies as prime minister.[26] Cavour viewed finance and management as his personal areas of expertise, and once in office he moved quickly to liberalize Piedmont's economic structures, reducing barriers to trade, creating a new central bank to provide credit for industrial development, and stimulating the spread of railroad technology.[27] Other measures included major investment in university education and applied research and development, including the beginnings of the Piedmontese armaments industry, along with large infrastructure modernization projects such as the Cavour Canal near Novara.[28] As a result, throughout the 1850s, Piedmont increasingly separated itself from the rest of the Italian territories in terms of higher education and literacy rates and, especially, in its rapidly expanding industrial and manufacturing might, although recent scholars have rightly argued against making overly sweeping contrasts between

FIGURE 4.1 Portrait of Camillo Benso, Conte di Cavour *by A. Masutti.*
Wikimedia Commons.

northern modernization and southern backwardness.[29] Industrialization
took off in the Italian territories rather later than elsewhere in Europe, as
was also the case in contemporary Germany, but under the leadership of
Cavour, Piedmont's production and manufacturing base expanded rapidly,

offering a stark contrast to regions under Habsburg control.[30] As Lucy Riall has noted, "for Cavour nationalism seemed to offer a significant opportunity for endorsing the economic development of northern Italy independently of Austria."[31]

However, against the backdrop of industrial growth, Cavour's political vision initially remained focused on expanding the diplomatic prestige and political interests of Piedmont-Sardinia on the European stage. It is unclear how sincerely Cavour, who knew much more about England and France than about Naples or Sicily, supported the unification of all Italian territories under the Piedmontese crown.[32] Certainly it was a secondary concern during his early years in office. An important opportunity for Cavour's vision of Piedmontese aggrandizement, however, presented itself in the form of the Crimean War, which ultimately set in motion events that helped make Italian unification a reality. In October 1853, the Ottoman Empire went to war against Russia in a dispute that originally stemmed from the treatment of Orthodox Christians in Ottoman-controlled southeastern Europe.[33] Motivated in part by concerns that a decisive Russian victory over the increasingly decrepit Ottoman military might threaten lucrative trade routes in the eastern Mediterranean, Britain and France joined the conflict on the side of the Ottomans in March 1854.[34] After months of deliberation, Cavour agreed to enter the war alongside Britain and France, although by the time Piedmont began mobilization in January 1855, many of the war's most significant campaigns were over. Nonetheless, the contribution of more than 10,000 troops, and their central participation in the pivotal Battle of the Tchernaya, enabled Piedmont-Sardinia to partake of the spoils of victory over Russia, at least symbolically.[35] At the peace congress in Paris that concluded the conflict in March 1856, Cavour was given a prime place at the conference table alongside the leaders of the other Great Powers. International observers noted that a new European player had arrived on the scene, and Cavour's goal of attracting international support for an expansion of Piedmontese interests had been largely achieved.[36] Fittingly, the peace conference was convened just weeks after the conclusion of the *Exposition Universelle*, which Paris hosted as the successor to the 1851 Great Exhibition in London. Piedmont's impressive exhibit within the exposition's Palace of Industry on the Champs-Élysées reinforced the intertwining of the kingdom's growing industrial power and international stature. In 1858, the Piedmontese capital Turin would itself host the Exposition of Industrial Production as a triumphant symbol of the city's emerging significance.[37]

By that point, the march toward Italian unification had already progressed considerably, whether initially desired by Cavour or not. Relations with Napoleon III had warmed since the Paris conference, and in a (now famous) secret meeting with Cavour in July 1858 the French emperor pledged his support for the expansion of Piedmontese control in northern Italy, particularly in Lombardy and Venetia, at the expense of Austria.[38] Both Cavour and Napoleon wanted war with Austria, for their own separate reasons, but neither wanted to seem the aggressor. So they agreed to utilize a flimsy pretext relating to Austrian control of the Duchy of Modena, and thereby to manufacture the conflict one scholar has termed "a carefully planned accident."[39] Following months of brinksmanship, in which Piedmontese troops undertook menacing maneuvers near the border with Austrian-controlled Lombardy, Austria was provoked into declaring war in April 1859. Upholding his agreement with Cavour, Napoleon III brought France into the conflict against Austria. Garibaldi also returned and pledged his support for the Piedmontese crown, mobilizing a fierce fighting force of Alpine guerrillas.[40] The month of June witnessed two terribly bloody battles in Lombardy, at Magenta and Solferino, which were both covered extensively by press correspondents and photographers, thereby raising international awareness of the appalling plight of battlefield wounded.[41] The battles were most costly to the Austrians, but rather than push further against them, Napoleon III abruptly called for peace talks, which left Cavour feeling abandoned and betrayed. In the ensuing Treaty of Villafranca, Piedmont-Sardinia gained control of Lombardy, while eventually ceding Nice and Savoy to the French in return for their support. Austria retained control of Venetia.[42]

The following year, 1860, witnessed the unification of most of the other Italian territories under the leadership of Piedmont-Sardinia. In March, several of the smaller states—most notably Parma, Tuscany, and Romagna—held plebiscites and voted to annex themselves voluntarily to Piedmont.[43] This left the only major separate states in Italy as Piedmont-Sardinia, Venetia (still controlled by Austria), the Papal States, and the Kingdom of the Two Sicilies. In April, small rebellions were launched in the Sicilian towns of Palermo and Messina against the Bourbon monarch Francis II, providing an opportunity the next month for Garibaldi to invade southern Italy with the famous force of red-shirted volunteers known as "The Thousand."[44] Garibaldi's image as a heroic national icon was burnished by the success of this campaign, which brought the entirety of the southern peninsula under the control of Piedmont-Sardinia by November.[45] At the same time, Garibaldi dreamed of invading Rome, displacing the pope, and proclaiming a unified Italy under Piedmontese leadership from within the Eternal City. Wary of the geopolitical implications of such an undertaking, not to mention the moral outrage that would be caused among religious Catholics in Italy, Cavour engaged in a colossal struggle to dissuade Garibaldi from this move, and was finally able to prevail.[46] Although this meant that Rome, along with Venetia, remained unincorporated for the time being, a unified Italian nation-state was proclaimed to much fanfare in March 1861, with Victor Emmanuel II as king and Cavour as prime minister. Cavour would die of an illness less than three months after the kingdom's proclamation, and Mazzini remained perpetually dissatisfied with the monarchical system. It would take until 1866 and 1870, respectively, for Venetia and Rome to come into the fold, but the cornerstone had been laid for a new and deeply conflicted

MAP 4.1 Italian Peninsula before Unification. © *George Edward Milne, 2017. Reproduced with permission.*

era of national identity.[47] In the famous (albeit possibly apocryphal) words of the nationalist Massimo D'Azeglio: "We have made Italy; now we have to make Italians."[48]

German unification

The movement for German national unification invites inevitable comparisons with the Italian case. In both Italy and Germany, the processes of industrialization and unification occurred very late by comparative standards; in both cases, the unification drive was spearheaded by the region's most industrially dynamic state; both were shaped decisively by military conflict; and both nation-states went on in the twentieth century to produce totalitarian dictatorships in the form of the Fascist and Nazi regimes. While these similarities should not be taken too far, historians have rightly attempted to make sense of the nature and longer-term meaning of these parallel projects.[49]

Although it was dominated by the competition between Austria and Prussia, the German unification drive originally materialized, like the Italian case, along three potential trajectories. The most marginal of these, except perhaps to its advocates, was often identified with the "Third Germany"; it centered on the attempt by several of the smaller and mid-sized states within the German Confederation to counterbalance the binary Austro-Prussian rivalry, creating a sort of tripartite equilibrium.[50] While supported by a fair number of officials and bureaucrats from states like Baden, Württemberg, Hesse, and Saxony, this idea was championed most vigorously by the Bavarian monarchs—Ludwig I before 1848, and his son Maximilian II thereafter. Maximilian spent tremendous sums in the 1850s in an attempt to lure academic, literary, and artistic luminaries to Munich, a cultural and moral project he viewed as an essential corollary to Bavaria's emergence as the leading force among the non-Prussian and non-Austrian states:

> Because nature and history have made Bavaria the third power in Germany, it is duty-bound to stand at the head of the second- and third-class German states and of south Germany in general; to raise the prestige of Germany internally and internationally; and to light the way for Germany in matters of the Good, the Beautiful, and the Modern, so to speak, as a central point of crystallization.[51]

While Maximilian's broader cultural program has typically been viewed as a success, the inevitable failure of the political aspects of his vision would leave the southern German states, which had large Catholic populations, in a difficult position during the peak of the struggle for supremacy between Austria and Prussia starting in the mid-1860s.[52]

The second potential path to German unification can be identified as the *grossdeutsch* (Greater German) option. Centering on the inclusion of Austria, the state with the most traditional claim to power under the Holy Roman Empire and within the German Confederation in the Metternich era, this option was the one many earlier observers would have found most likely to succeed. After assuming the throne in the context of revolutionary turbulence, Franz Joseph had hoped that a strong central state, ruled along neo-absolutist principles, would be the best guarantor of Habsburg interests. But the deep ethnic and nationalist divisions that had boiled to the surface in 1848 could not simply be wiped away by traditionalism and bureaucratic measures, despite the fact that Franz Joseph's earliest chief minister, the arch-reactionary Felix zu Schwarzenberg, seemed determined to try.[53] Despite pushing through reforms that centralized governing structures and streamlined bureaucratic processes, Schwarzenberg and his successors were unable to stimulate and modernize Austrian industry to a degree that would allow it to keep pace with the rapid industrialization of Prussia.[54] It was in some ways unavoidable that the sprawling Habsburg lands continued to be characterized to a surprising degree by residual forms of premodern proto-industrialization.[55] Austria's relatively weak economic position within the German Confederation was exacerbated by its continued position outside of the *Zollverein*, the Prussian-dominated customs union that had been founded originally in the 1830s and by the 1850s included every German member state except Austria.[56] While historians have cautioned against drawing too many direct parallels between this form of economic unification under Prussian leadership and the subsequent political unification process, it is impossible not to recognize the importance of industrialization and economic development in giving Prussia a growing advantage in its rivalry with Austria.[57] Furthermore, the intertwining of industrialization and nationalism was extremely complicated in Austria, due to its multinational nature, and the relative economic backwardness that resulted would prove to have decisive consequences in the struggle for supremacy with Prussia. As Herbert Matis has noted:

In most European countries, both the struggle for a bourgeois-liberal constitutional state and the collective social phenomenon of nationalism were closely bound up with the socio-economic structural change which took place in the wake of the process of industrialization and which, in turn, provided the modernization process with additional impetus. In the Austrian dynastic and multinational state, however, nationalism in particular, with its centrifugal tendencies, had a corrosive and destabilizing effect.[58]

Tensions were particularly difficult between the Habsburg crown and its Hungarian subjects. In February 1853, while on an evening stroll, Franz Joseph was attacked by a knife-wielding Hungarian nationalist who stabbed him in the throat. The emperor was badly wounded but survived due partly to the nearly impenetrable starch of his uniform collar and partly to the swift actions of one of the officers walking with him. The assassination attempt served to endear Franz Joseph, who was still only twenty-three at the time, to his German-speaking populace, and a fundraising campaign was mobilized to build a commemorative church on the site of the attack, resulting in the imposing neo-Gothic *Votivkirche* (Votive Church) that still adorns Vienna's Ringstrasse.[59] But the process whereby Franz Joseph became a potent symbol of Austrian identity did not result merely from popular responses to chance events like the 1853 assassination attempt. Elaborate and carefully planned imperial celebrations were staged with regularity throughout the Habsburg domains to foster dynastic patriotism and to reinforce the imperatives of neo-absolutist *Herrschaft* (lordship), to use the favored term of Franz Joseph's advisors.[60] In promoting visions of Austrian dominance, advocates of the Greater German solution pointed to the established tradition of Habsburg preeminence in affairs of state, as well as to the rapid maturation of the young emperor. But challenges from Austria's non-German holdings and continuing internal political tensions siphoned much of the attention and energies of Franz Joseph and his advisors. The 1859 war against France and Piedmont-Sardinia over the territories of Lombardy and Venetia was a damaging defeat for Austria, despite the eagerness of Napoleon III to bring the conflict to a speedy conclusion. The political situation was further complicated by the almost unanimously negative response to the "October Diploma," a conservative constitutional decree issued by Franz Joseph in October 1860, which managed to anger virtually all of the empire's major political constituencies, from the traditional aristocracy to moderate Liberals to oppositional nationalists in the Hungarian and Czech lands. Franz Joseph was forced to issue yet another constitutional document several months later—the "February Patent" of 1861—which officially established the *Reichsrat* as a bicameral parliament, with a lower house to be elected by a very narrow franchise. Because German-speaking interests were strongly advantaged within the *Reichsrat*, Hungarian leaders refused to accept the Patent, and in 1865 Franz Joseph was forced to suspend it entirely.[61] By that point, of course, the rivalry between Austria and Prussia was rapidly coming to a head, and civil war between the two was only a year away.

The third path to unification, known as the *kleindeutsch* (Smaller German) solution, was predicated on Prussian leadership and, in most of its incarnations, on the simultaneous exclusion of Austria and its multiethnic empire. Fueled in large part by Prussian military-industrial dynamism, it was the option that eventually prevailed.[62] While the key figure was clearly Otto von Bismarck, who is typically portrayed as the German Cavour but with a harder edge, the immediate roots of Prussian-dominated unification lay in the ascension of Wilhelm I to the throne of Prussia. Wilhelm's brother and predecessor Friedrich Wilhelm IV survived a stroke in 1857, but his mental abilities were severely diminished and in 1858 Wilhelm assumed power, first as regent and then, after his brother's death in 1861, as king. Wilhelm was exceedingly reserved, but his mental universe had been shaped almost entirely by the culture of Prussian militarism, and his first major project as king was to initiate a massive expansion and modernization of the Prussian military. When Liberals within the Prussian parliament refused to authorize his military budget, a constitutional crisis ensued. Wilhelm's solution to the impasse was to appoint as his new minister-president Otto von Bismarck, a career Prussian diplomat whose anti-parliamentary attitudes were well known.[63] In one of his most famous speeches Bismarck stated that the great issues of the day would never be settled by parliamentary discussions, but rather by "iron and blood"—by which he meant that great men of destiny, like himself, knew how to get things done by cannon and warfare, if necessary.[64] Despite the Liberal opposition in parliament, Bismarck pushed through the military expansion—which included the extension of mandatory military service by a year and the creation of several new infantry divisions and cavalry regiments—in violation of the constitution, relying on the support of the Prussian bureaucracy, which allocated the funds without parliamentary support. The machiavellian *Realpolitik* for which Bismarck became well known was already on full display in this episode, setting the stage for the unification drive that ensued.[65] John Breuilly has argued against viewing Prussian unification as a foregone conclusion, and his detailed research on the unification process has also demonstrated convincingly that Bismarck was in many ways out of step with his contemporaries.[66] But subsequent triumphalist accounts by Prussian historians would paint a picture of the unification process as an inevitability driven forward by the genius and skill of Bismarck.

The backbone of that triumphalist narrative was the string of military victories Prussia achieved in the so-called "wars of unification" against Denmark, Austria, and France. The first of those, also known as the Second Schleswig War, developed after the Danish king Frederik VII died in 1863 without leaving a legitimate heir.[67] As a result Christian IX, who was married to the niece of Frederik but was himself from a different noble house, took the throne and signed the November Constitution, which created a reformed parliament within which Schleswig, with its mixed German-Danish population, would be incorporated.[68] The response within the German Confederation was mixed, but Prussia and Austria, working together, mobilized and quickly defeated Denmark in 1864, placing both Schleswig and Holstein under, respectively, Prussian and Austrian administration.[69] In the aftermath of that conflict, tensions continued to simmer between Prussia and Austria over the administration of the two duchies, with Bismarck looking eagerly for an opportunity to engage Austria militarily in a conflict he believed would finally cement Prussian domination among the German states.[70] Initially, Wilhelm I was hesitant to mobilize against Austria— concerned over the moral implications of Germans fighting Germans and, perhaps more importantly, fearful of international opinion—but in the end, Bismarck's machinations won the day. And in the civil war with Austria that ensued, Prussian forces won the military conflict even more decisively. Lasting only seven weeks in the summer of 1866, the Austro-Prussian War was a lopsided affair, capped by the humiliating Austrian defeat in the Battle of Königgrätz, which potentially opened the way for Prussia to take Vienna. Whereas Wilhelm had been hesitant to go to war in the first place, after Königgrätz he was eager to push on triumphantly to the Austrian capital.[71] But Bismarck, ever the strategist, instead called for peace talks, citing the need for Austria as a potential ally in the future. Although in the peace that followed, the main territorial concession forced upon Franz Joseph was the ceding of Venetia to the new Italian state, the more significant requirement was that Austria leave the German Confederation and agree, essentially, not to interfere with the process of unifying the other German states under Prussian leadership. The following year Austria formalized the Compromise

FIGURE 4.2 Battle of Königgrätz *by Georg Bleibtreu. Deutsches Historisches Museum/Wikimedia Commons.*

of 1867, known as the *Ausgleich*, which elevated Hungary to a privileged position within the new Dual Monarchy that was created.[72] For the next five decades, Austria-Hungary was to develop independent of Germany, although it would not be long before the two powers reemerged as the closest of allies.[73]

Within the German territories, the most significant structural development after the Austro-Prussian War was the creation of the North German Confederation, an amalgamation of twenty-two German states under Prussian leadership. It came on the heels of the so-called Indemnity Bill passed by the Prussian parliament in September 1866, in which the formerly oppositional Liberals agreed to retroactively legalize the four military budgets—between 1862 and 1866—that had been pushed through unconstitutionally. Many Liberal leaders were obsessed with the ideal of national unification, and had begun to countenance the thought that Bismarck, the arch-reactionary, might in fact be the agent of destiny called to accomplish that task. As an increasingly large contingent moved in Bismarck's direction, the Liberal faction was splintered, with the Indemnity Bill serving as the touchstone of debate. The North German Confederation formulated its constitution in 1867 on the basis of universal manhood suffrage, further creating the impression of democratic consensus, which Bismarck was willing to tolerate in the interest of co-opting the Liberals in pursuit of his broader aims.[74] When combined with the Liberals' acquiescence in the Indemnity Bill, historians have often pointed to this period as a decisive failure in the history of German democratic politics, with Liberal principle collapsing feebly before the irresistible pull of national destiny.[75]

With internal political consolidation progressing within the North German Confederation, the primary outstanding question was what would happen with the southern German states, such as Baden, Württemberg, and Bavaria, which had significant Catholic populations and had, in the case of Bavaria, sent support to Austria in the conflict with Prussia.[76] As it happened, a combination of renewed war enthusiasm and mild forms of political bribery were sufficient to get those states off the proverbial fence and aligned with the Prussian-dominated unification process. The war enthusiasm was, of course, directed against France. When a member of the Prussian Hohenzollern family was put forward as a candidate for the vacant throne of Spain in 1870, Bismarck seized on the issue as a way of provoking Napoleon III to war.[77] Having altered a telegram from Wilhelm II to create a sharp incendiary tone, Bismarck leaked the telegram to the press and waited for Napoleon's response. As hoped, the offended French emperor declared war on Prussia in the summer of 1870, and the result for France was a defeat perhaps even more humiliating than the one suffered by Austria four years earlier.[78] After the catastrophic Battle of Sedan, which occasioned the infamous capitulation of Napoleon III in the presence of Bismarck, chaos reigned in France. Prussian forces had shelled Paris mercilessly, and in March 1871 a revolutionary Paris Commune was established, which held out until late May against the forces of the new Third Republic that had been founded after the capitulation of Napoleon.[79] By that point, however, the new German Empire had been triumphantly proclaimed—in a lavish ceremony staged on January 18, 1871 in the Hall of Mirrors at Versailles—with the Prussian King Wilhelm I taking the title of first German Kaiser.[80] Territorially, the new Germany gained the regions of Alsace and Lorraine, which was accompanied by a large war indemnity, and the Kingdom of Italy, which had been the beneficiary of the French transfer of troops out of Rome in 1870 to face the Prussian threat, was finally able to incorporate Rome into the fledgling Italian state. Internally, the southern German states were essentially bribed with major concessions; Bavaria and Württemberg allowed to keep their own military and postal systems, and Bavaria was allowed to maintain, perhaps as importantly, the right to tax its own beer. In the longer term, the fact that the new German Empire was proclaimed explicitly in the context of the humiliation of France would lead to a fatal cycle of mutual hatred and aggression lasting decades.

Having sketched out the broad contours of the Italian and German unification drives, let us turn briefly to some of the ways in which new forms of national belonging were woven together with other signifiers of identity. In both Italy and Germany after unification, we see religion, gender, and nation being intertwined in interesting and complicated ways. In Germany, once unity had been achieved on the map, Bismarck's chief focus turned to internal consolidation through the practice of "negative integration," or the demonization of a targeted minority in the interest of solidifying the majority.[81] Given the exclusion of Catholic Austria from the new German Empire, Catholics now comprised a one-third minority of the population, being concentrated primarily on the peripheries of Prussia—in the Polish

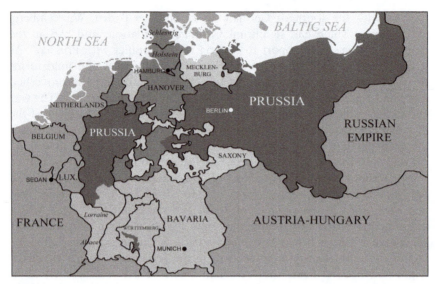

MAP 4.2 German Empire, 1871. © *George Edward Milne, 2017. Reproduced with permission.*

borderlands to the east and in the Rhineland to the west—as well as in Alsace and the south, particularly Bavaria. With the 1870 declaration of Papal Infallibility coinciding with the establishment of the Catholic Center Party on the eve of the first post-unification elections, the specter of Roman interference in German politics provided Bismarck and his Liberal nationalist backers with a useful pretext under which to launch the so-called *Kulturkampf* (Cultural Struggle), a policy of state-sponsored discrimination that lasted nearly a decade.[82] Church freedoms were curtailed severely, particularly in the "pulpit paragraph" of December 1871, which prohibited priests from making even potentially controversial political statements; in the anti-Jesuit legislation of July 1872, which banned all Jesuit activity on German soil; and in the May Laws of 1873, which established tight state controls over the training and discipline of the clergy.[83] The ensuing policy of civil disobedience pursued by the German bishops led to widespread clerical arrests and incarcerations, leaving many bishoprics without pastoral guidance for months and, in some cases, years. The legal measures associated with the Kulturkampf were accompanied by less official, but still quite painful, acts of discrimination. Catholics were dramatically underrepresented in the German civil service and professions. They were also labeled as politically unreliable and insufficiently nationalistic, being accused of having split loyalty between Rome and Berlin due to their religious attachment to the pope.[84]

   In addition to the legal and political aspects of the Kulturkampf, it is important to note the extent to which specifically gendered ideals were mobilized in the pursuit of religious-oriented national consolidation.

Catholics were widely mocked in the Protestant and nationalist press as childish and excessively feminized, due in large part to the public visibility of Marian veneration and the emotive forms of piety that had come to the fore in the religious revival that swept through German-speaking Catholic territories in the decades leading up to unification.[85] David Blackbourn has traced in detail the hyperbolic responses of secular Liberals and Protestants to the proliferation of Marian apparition sites throughout Germany.[86] As Michael Gross has shown, exaggerated tales were circulated about the alleged unseemly activities taking place in the shadows of Catholic monasteries, and images of Catholic backwardness were portrayed as dangerous impediments to German modernization and economic strength.[87] Ultimately, however, the Kulturkampf failed either to unify Germany's Protestant majority or to neutralize the impact of Catholicism in German politics, and following the death of Pope Pius IX in 1878, Bismarck was forced to pursue a much more conciliatory course toward German Catholics during the pontificate of Leo XIII.[88] Having been galvanized by persecution during its first decade of existence, the Catholic Center Party went on to play a central role in German politics for decades.[89] The failure of the Kulturkampf meant that, beginning in the late 1870s, German socialists became the primary targets of "negative integration"; the Social Democratic Party was outlawed in 1878 and remained illegal until early 1890. In the end, religious identity did not fade into insignificance in the face of nationalizing policies. Rather, as Helmut Walser Smith and Lisa Zwicker have shown, religion in Germany became a new field on which rival conceptions of national identity played out and were contested.[90]

In Italy, Massimo D'Azeglio's appeal for internal national consolidation—to "make Italians" now that Italy had been made—was pursued in a variety of ways, not least among women. The feminist activist Anna Maria Mozzoni wrote in 1864 that all attempts to achieve Italian greatness would fail without the active participation of women: "Humanity and the nation, civilization and morality, need women on their side."[91] In public political discussions, the family became a widespread model for social and political belonging. Debates in the 1870s over the introduction of divorce rights became arenas within which male-oriented visions of nation building, constructed on the inviolability of the traditional family and the indissolubility of marriage, clashed with opposing emancipatory ideals.[92] Such hot button issues attracted the attention of feminists elsewhere, especially in Britain, where women had already established a firm tradition of participation in public discourse over the British system and its colonial holdings.[93] The publicity generated by John Stuart Mill's 1861 treatise *The Subjection of Women*, which fused appeals for political and sexual emancipation, helped fuel the interest of Victorian radicals in emancipatory causes throughout Europe. Many of them had idealized Italian figures such as Mazzini and Garibaldi, and pursued the cause of internal liberation in post-unification Italy with almost missionary zeal.[94] A particularly interesting manifestation of this zeal can be seen in the circle surrounding the feminist periodical *Englishwoman's Review*, who envisioned themselves as portents of a new type of holistic nation building, one that utilized the gifts of both men and women, and which forged forms of belonging that would transcend, it was hoped, the particular interests of individual nation-states. The drive to integrate and modernize the south of Italy offered them a cause and a well-defined field in which to work.[95] A number of women associated with the *Review* were initially active in building schools near Naples and, as Maura O'Connor has shown, they expanded their activities in the 1870s to include "civilizing" endeavors designed to lift southern Italian women out of their "semioriental mode of life" and make them orderly, dignified, and modern citizens.[96] Secularized Protestant ideals of respectability were intricately intertwined with this civilizing mission. As George Mosse has shown more generally, the second half of the nineteenth century witnessed the linkage of nationalism with stringent differentiations between respectable normality and deviant transgression, forged in part in Victorian England but with broad impact throughout Europe.[97]

Ideological radicalization and pan-nationalist fervor

The industrialization process not only transformed productive regimes throughout Europe, but also initiated massive social upheavals, demographic dislocations, and new challenges to notions of respectability. Migrations from the countryside to the city resulted in urban overcrowding and a host of related problems. Newly industrialized areas not only lacked educational and police services, but often even the rudiments of sanitation and health care infrastructure. Crime and delinquency grew, a plethora of moral and sexual disorders proliferated, and the spread of cholera and dysentery devastated entire communities. When conditions were appalling enough to be reported widely, thereby shocking middle-class sensibilities, private movements for social reform and moral hygiene were initiated and bureaucratic authorities and state agencies were moved to action. But these often lumbering responses were initially inadequate in addressing actual circumstances. The infamous 1858 London episode known as the "Great Stink," in which unprecedented amounts of human sewage, animal carcasses, and industrial waste lining the banks of the Thames rotted with lethal pungency in the summer heat, led the next year to the first comprehensive sewage reform project in Britain under the engineer Joseph Bazalgette.[98] But it took until 1875 for the Public Health Act to be passed, and many years after that for the term "sanitation" to be even marginally plausible in describing many British industrial conurbations. In Paris, the modernization and expansion of sewage systems was included in 1855 as part of Haussmann's famous demolition and renovation program, but the sewage network itself remained incomplete and partially unusable more than two decades later. In 1880, the system was still so inadequate that Paris famously experienced its own unforgettable "Great Stink" summer.[99] In the German territories, the earliest sewage system was designed and implemented in Hamburg by the British engineer William Lindley in the 1840s and 1850s. But as late as the early 1890s, the city was devastated by a water-borne cholera outbreak that took the lives of nearly 10,000 residents.[100] While tangible hygienic reforms and infrastructure improvements took decades to materialize, and then only imperfectly, what coalesced much more quickly were metaphorical appropriations of the discourse of hygiene, cleanliness, and purity. These intersected with and were reinforced by two central "intellectual" currents—Social Darwinism, consisting of the social misappropriation of Darwin's theory of natural selection, and the clumsy racial ruminations of Gobineau—which, in turn, exercised a significant radicalizing impact on concepts of nationalism and national belonging.

Among the more notable cultural trends in the second half of the nineteenth century was the popularization of scientific thought in virtually all regions of Europe.[101] As new discoveries explained ever more natural phenomena without reliance on the miraculous or metaphysical, and as public lecturers and popular pamphleteers spread awareness of these discoveries, growing numbers of Europeans increasingly embraced an almost religious faith in the verities of science.[102] At the same time, "scientific" fads of questionable veracity proliferated rapidly, often making use of the latest technological gadgetry, as seen in the boost given to spiritualists and ghost hunters by the spread of photographic equipment. On a deeper and more pernicious level, ideological systems claiming scientific justification for exclusionary social and racial visions also took deep root. Whereas the work of Charles Darwin represented the single most significant step forward in understanding the evolution and diversity of biological life on earth, his ideas were among the first to be popularized and, through misappropriation by his self-appointed devotees, were often bastardized beyond recognition. Darwin himself was an exceedingly cautious scholar, and his *Origin of Species*, which appeared in 1859, limited itself to the realm of scientific observation. While he was not the first to advance the ideas of biological evolution and natural selection, he was the first to unite them in an overarching explanatory paradigm. For Darwin, all life on earth was in a perpetual struggle for existence, with some organisms surviving and some forever perishing based on their ability to adapt to their environments. Those best able to reproduce and defend themselves would essentially be selected "naturally" for survival—rather than originating as the exclusive hand-made creations of God—and thus the diversity of biological life on earth could be seen as the product of natural selection over great expanses of time.

For all of Darwin's fastidiousness, his popularizers emerged quickly and almost none of them shared his scholarly caution. Already in 1860, Thomas Huxley was referring publicly to "Darwinism" as a set of scientific principles with broad applicability beyond the realm of biological inquiry, although it should be noted that the phrase "Social Darwinism" did not come into currency until the 1870s.[103] In 1864, the political theorist Herbert Spencer coined the phrase "survival of the fittest" in his *Principles of Biology* which, despite its title, was primarily an economic and political treatise.[104] In the hands of Spencer and others, concepts of "fitness" and "unfitness" were useful in explaining (or explaining away) morally troubling social and political inequalities. The poor, it could be argued, were in that condition because they were deficient, or unfit, in some significant sense—whether through lack of intelligence and personal industry or through laziness and insufficient moral fiber. The privileged could sleep untroubled since their elevated position was merely evidence of their inborn superiority. Social Darwinism provided justification for laissez faire economics in Britain and elsewhere, helping fuel opposition to welfare programs designed to aid the poor and weak by labeling such endeavors an affront to nature. To look ahead somewhat, Darwin's cousin Francis Galton built on these ideas to propose human breeding programs, coining the phrase "eugenics" in 1883 and impacting a variety of twentieth-century schemes to spruce up the human gene pool. In Germany, the zoologist Ernst Haeckel, author of the 1899 bestseller *Die Welträtsel* (The World Riddle), would attempt to translate Social Darwinism into the realm of policy, stating famously that "politics is merely applied biology" and arguing for the necessity of state-sponsored negative eugenic programs, such as forced sterilization and euthanasia.

In the shorter term, though, Social Darwinism quickly transcended domestic discussions of "fitness" and "unfitness" within individual societies. The concept also fueled competitive rivalries between larger social groupings and, especially, between nation-states. If Herder's work, discussed in Chapter 1, portrayed nations coexisting peacefully like different species of plants in the garden of humanity,[105] Social Darwinist thought would help transform that peaceful garden into a roiling piranha tank. Just as some species in the natural world survive and some go extinct, the Darwinian nationalist saw nations on the world stage in the same light—perpetually locked with other nations in a zero sum struggle for survival. While the impact of these ideas on imperialist antagonisms became apparent in the later decades of the nineteenth century, already in the 1860s, they exercised a significant influence on nascent concepts of race and "racial fitness." At the annual meeting of the London Anthropological Society in March 1864, Alfred Russell Wallace applied Darwin's concept of natural selection directly to the question of how human races originated and, especially, how their varying qualities and characteristics should be understood. As seen in the following excerpt, he argued that natural selection was indeed central to the evolution of a physically superior race of Europeans, but concluded that environmental and geographical factors were perhaps even more important than natural selection in forging European intellectual and moral superiority.

EXCERPT 4.2

The Origin of Human Races and the Antiquity of Man Deduced from the Theory of Natural Selection (1864)

Alfred Russell Wallace

From the time, therefore, when social and sympathetic feelings came into active operation, and the intellectual and moral faculties became fairly developed, man would cease to be influenced by "natural selection" in his physical form and structure; as an animal he would remain almost stationary; the changes of the surrounding universe would cease to have upon him that powerful modifying effect which it exercises over other parts of the organic world. But from the moment that his body became stationary, his mind would become subject to those very influences from which his body had escaped; every slight variation in his mental and moral nature which should enable him better to guard against adverse circumstances, and combine for mutual comfort and protection, would be preserved and accumulated; the better and higher specimens of our race would therefore increase and spread, the lower and more brutal would give way and successively die out, and that rapid advancement of mental organisation would occur, which has raised the very lowest races of man so far above the brutes (although differing so little from some of them in physical structure), and, in conjunction with scarcely perceptible modifications of form, has developed the wonderful intellect of the Germanic races.

But from the time when this mental and moral advance commenced, and man's physical character became fixed and immutable, a new series of causes would come into action, and take part in his mental growth. The diverse aspects of nature would now make themselves felt, and profoundly influence the character of the primitive man.

When the power that had hitherto modified the body transferred its action to the mind, then races would advance and become improved merely by the harsh discipline of a sterile soil and inclement seasons. Under their influence, a hardier, a more provident, and a more social race would be developed than in those regions where the earth produces a perennial supply of vegetable food, and where neither foresight nor ingenuity are required to prepare for the rigours of winter. And is it not the fact that in all ages, and in every quarter of the globe, the inhabitants of temperate have been superior to those of tropical countries? All the great invasions and displacements of races have been from North to South, rather than the reverse; and we have no record of there ever having existed, any more than there exists today, a solitary instance of an indigenous intertropical civilisation. The Mexican civilisation and government came from the

North, and, as well as the Peruvian, was established, not in the rich tropical plains, but no the lofty and sterile plateaux of the Andes. The religion and civilisation of Ceylon were introduced from North India; the successive conquerors of the Indian peninsula came from the North-west, and it was the bold and adventurous tribes of the North that overran and infused new life into Southern Europe.

It is the same great law of "*the preservation of favoured races in the struggle for life*," which leads to the inevitable extinction of all those low and mentally undeveloped populations with which Europeans have come into contact. The red Indian in North America and in Brazil; the Tasmanian, Australian, and New Zealander in the southern hemisphere, die out, not from any one special cause, but from the inevitable effects of an unequal mental and physical struggle. The intellectual and moral, as well as the physical qualities of the European are superior; the same powers and capacities which have made him rise in a few centuries from the condition of the wandering savage with a scanty and stationary population to his present state of culture and advancement, with a greater average longevity, a greater average strength, and a capacity of more rapid increase, enable him when in contact with the savage man, to conquer in the struggle for existence, and to increase at his expense, just as the more favourable increase at the expense of the less favourable varieties in the animal and vegetable kingdoms, just as the weeds of Europe overrun North America and Australia, extinguishing native productions by the inherent vigour of their organisation, and by their greater capacity for existence and multiplication.

If these views are correct; if in proportion as man's social, moral and intellectual faculties became developed, his physical structure would cease to be affected by the operation of "natural selection," we have a most important clue to the origin of races. For it will follow, that those striking and constant peculiarities which mark the great divisions of mankind, could not have been produced and rendered permanent after the action of this power had become transferred from physical to mental variations. They must, therefore, have existed since the very infancy of the race; they must have originated at a period when man was gregarious, but scarcely social, with a mind perceptive but not reflective, ere any sense of *right* or feelings of *sympathy* had been developed in him.[106]

Outside the realm of Social Darwinism, but developing essentially in tandem, were a variety of other "scientific" justifications for concepts of racial superiority. The ideas of the French diplomat and novelist Arthur de Gobineau were among the most influential of these.[107] Gobineau was born near Paris shortly after the Bourbon restoration and grew up in a royalist household. His father had more or less illegitimately commandeered a title of nobility for the family, and Gobineau carried throughout his life both the proud appellation "Comte" and a firm conviction in the innate superiority of the nobility over commoners.[108] Gobineau's aristocratic obsessions, which were sharpened by the threat of revolutionary mobs in 1848, fed directly into his racial theories, as did his growing phobias regarding industrialization and urbanization. His most influential work, *An Essay on the Inequality of the Human Races*, was published in multiple volumes between 1853 and 1855, proposing a tripartite division of human races based largely on skin color.[109] The "white" race was portrayed as the pinnacle of human intelligence and beauty, and as the source of all creativity in virtually every realm of technological and cultural achievement. Within this category, he further differentiated between the superior "Aryans," or paler northern Europeans, and the other populations of Europe. The second-tier "yellow" races, which Gobineau rooted in Asia, the Near East, and parts of the Mediterranean basin, were able to mimic many of the achievements of the white race, but were largely incapable of creativity and independent innovation. At the low end, Gobineau depicted the "black" races, among whom he counted not only Africans but other undeveloped indigenous and aboriginal peoples, as perhaps possessing physical strength but lacking the intelligence, work ethic, and emotional stamina to even borrow effectively from the achievements of the Aryans.[110] To the extent that history seemed to demonstrate impressive cultural and technological accomplishments among non-whites, these were explained away as the result of racial miscegenation. And it was on that latter point that Gobineau's radical pessimism became most visible; he envisioned a future Europe within which racial intermarriage had destroyed all individual genius and beauty.[111]

Despite the fact that Gobineau himself was not particularly antisemitic, his work influenced future racial theorists and nationalists who would come to identify the Jews as the most pernicious racial threat of all. The danger of debasing the Aryan racial stock was particularly acute because the light skin color of many Jews made it easier to assimilate and intermarry with Europeans.[112] By the time Gobineau penned his racist screed, traditional Christian antisemitism had existed for nearly two millennia, producing horrific outbreaks of persecution and subjecting the Jews of Europe to centuries of social and political ostracism.[113] But this Christian bigotry, which condemned the Jews for their rejection of Jesus as the messiah and their (perceived) responsibility for his crucifixion, could be alleviated by Jewish conversion, either voluntary or coerced. In the eyes of the Christian antisemite, Jews ceased to be Jewish when they abandoned their religious identity. But under the influence of Gobineau's ideas, in combination with Social Darwinistic impulses, antisemitic ideas underwent a major transformation beginning in the mid-nineteenth century.[114] The result was a potent new form of racial prejudice that could not be "solved" by a change in theology or religious ideals. Against the backdrop of the dislocations and resentments engendered by industrialization and economic modernization, preexisting

praised or boasted about

associations of the Jews with finance and capital were supplemented by racial categories. As official Jewish emancipation spread in these decades—with Britain giving full rights to the Jews in 1858, followed by newly unified Italy in 1861, Austria-Hungary in 1867, and Germany in 1871—new and more compelling justifications for anti-Jewish prejudice were sought.[115] Racial antisemitism was particularly appealing because it was not couched primarily in backward, medieval superstition, but in the vaunted objectivity of "scientific" modernity. Older stereotypes and grotesque caricatures of perceived Jewish physical and cultural characteristics continued, to be sure, and it is important to note that the most significant outbreak of mass violence against the Jews in these decades—the Russian pogroms of the early 1880s—was driven primarily by premodern prejudice.[116] But the lethality of twentieth-century antisemitism is only conceivable in a mental universe constituted by "modern" racial antisemitism.

The radicalizing impact of Social Darwinism and racial thought will be discussed in the context of nationalism and imperialism later in this chapter. But racial thought also fostered and gave sharper contours to broader conceptions of identity and belonging, fueling preexisting attachments that can best be described as pan-nationalist. Good examples are provided on the peripheries of Europe, in the Scandinavism of Denmark, Norway, and Sweden, and in the pan-Slavism of eastern and southeastern Europe. Scandinavism developed as an intertwined set of political and cultural ideals between the 1840s and 1860s, with Danish literary and artistic figures as the most energetic initial advocates. The Danish children's author Hans Christian Andersen published his famous poem "We Are One People, We Are Called Scandinavians" in 1840, although it had been conceived originally several years earlier during a Christmas celebration in Rome with other displaced Danes, including the sculptor Bertel Thorvaldsen.[117] The pastor and poet N.F.S. Grundtvig collected and published a wide variety of Norse poems and epics to demonstrate the existence of a racially inflected Nordic "soul," and in the mid-1840s, he pioneered Europe's first experiments in continuing adult education, known as folk high schools, which were saturated with romantic imagery and which preached an idealized version of Nordic union.[118] In 1844, Niels Høyen, professor at the Royal Academy of Fine Arts in Copenhagen, delivered a programmatic lecture entitled "On the Conditions for the Creation of a Scandinavian National Art," in which he employed proto-racial nationalist discourse in the service of a broader Scandinavian identity.[119]

original or early

Scholars in other disciplines began weaving together Scandinavism and "scientific" racial thought. The Danish anatomist Anders Retzius created the "cephalic index" in the 1840s as a way of measuring cranial shape and brain capacity. By the mid-1850s, he had expanded his field of inquiry to the whole of humanity, separating human races into two broad groupings: the short-skulled brachycephalics and the long-skulled dolichocephalics.[120] This index would become the most widely used tool for racial theorists to claim the objective superiority of the Nordic race. Jens Worsaae, perhaps Denmark's foremost archaeologist, used his excavations in the late 1840s and early 1850s to argue for a common Nordic racial identity distinct from the Germans to the south.[121] As the field of anthropology developed and expanded between the 1850s and the 1880s, Scandinavian scholars played a key role in extrapolating from a variety of ethnographic, linguistic, anatomical, and archaeological sources coherent "ethnic identity narratives," as Richard McMahon has demonstrated.[122]

Politically, Scandinavism reached its peak in the 1850s. When Denmark went to war against Prussia in the First Schleswig War of 1848, the ideal of Scandinavism seemed on the verge of broad mobilization. Norwegians and Swedes formed a joint expeditionary force to fight on the side of the Danes, but the conflict was lost before the force could be fully mobilized. The Danish defeat did, however, increase desires for closer cooperation among the Scandinavian states as a counterbalance to the growing power of Prussia. In subsequent years, the ideal of Scandinavism was also accelerated by industrialization and the modernization of communications systems. As telegraph technology spread in the 1850s, fledgling European news agencies came to treat the "Nordic region" as its own distinct entity.[123] Viggo Rothe, the secretary of the Danish Federation of Industry, proposed a common Scandinavian customs union on the model of the Prussian-dominated *Zollverein* within the German Confederation.[124] By the early 1860s, as Italian unification was capturing attention across Europe, advocates of Scandinavian union became increasingly optimistic, championed in part by Norwegians. In 1861, Christiana University (the present-day University of Oslo) held its fiftieth anniversary celebration as a hopeful expression of "Scandinavian solidarity."[125] But when Swedish and Norwegian troops failed to come to the aid of Denmark during the Second Schleswig War with Prussia in 1864, it became increasingly clear that the prospects for any real Scandinavian union would likely remain illusory. The idea of a pan-Nordic identity would reemerge in the twentieth century, but under quite different circumstances.

In eastern and southeastern Europe, the phenomenon of pan-Slavism spread rapidly between the 1850s and 1870s. Within the Austrian empire alone there were millions of Slavic peoples—Czechs, Poles, Slovaks, Ruthenians (Ukrainians), Slovenes, Serbs, and Croats—who saw themselves as linguistically and culturally distinct not only from the German-speaking Austrians but also from the Hungarian Magyars, whose linguistic lineage derived from the separate Finno-Ugric line.[126] The first pan-Slavic Congress had been held in Prague in June 1848, with more than 300 delegates pledging solidarity against the oppression of the Germans and Hungarians within the empire.[127] While that initial gathering did not produce lasting results, the concept of pan-Slavic unity continued to develop, especially after 1867 when the Austrian *Ausgleich* elevated the position of Hungarians within the Dual Monarchy and did nothing to address the demands of the Slavs. In the Balkans, the south Slavic peoples included Slovenes, Croats, Bosnians, Serbs, Macedonians, Montenegrins, and Bulgarians, who were spread out across territory controlled primarily by the Ottomans. As the result of a series of revolts starting in 1804, Serbia gained an important measure of autonomy within the Ottoman Empire in 1835, and went on to serve as the chief repository of pan-Slavic unification ideals. Over the ensuing decades, Serb identity continued to be framed by oppositional imagery—resistance against foreign rule—with the 1389 Serbian defeat against the Turks in the Battle of Kosovo echoing loudly nearly five centuries later.[128] Miloš Obilić, who had assassinated the Sultan Murad on the day of the battle before being captured and beheaded himself, was revived as a central martyr of the nation.[129] By the 1850s, this martyr imagery was shifting from the realm of religious iconography to an increasingly race-inflected symbology. The celebrated epic poem *The Mountain Wreath*, published by the poet and prince-bishop Njegoš in 1847, emphasized themes of death and sacrifice in opposing Turkish influence and was initially shaped by the religious tenor of the immediate context in which it appeared; the same year had witnessed the publication the vernacular translation of the New Testament by Vuk Karadžić.[130] In subsequent decades, however, Balkan martyr ballads and national sagas were increasingly constructed along racial-oriented lines.

EXCERPT 4.3

The Mountain Wreath (1847)

Njegoš

What is Bosnia and half of Albania?
They're your brothers of the same parentage.
United all, there's enough work for all!
Your destiny is to bear the cross
of the fierce fight against brothers and foes!
The wreath's heavy, but the fruit is so sweet!
Without death there is no resurrection.
Under a shroud of glory I see you
and our nation's honour resurrected.
I also see the altar turned eastward
and a fragrant incense burning on it.
Die in glory, if die indeed you must!
Wounded honour inspires courageous hearts;
those hearts cannot tolerate such illness.
The altar by pagans desecrated
will once again receive the grace of God.[131]

The largest of all the Slavic populations, the Russians, saw themselves in many ways as protectors of their Balkan Slavic cousins, providing part of the context out of which the Crimean War emerged.[132] As the Ottoman Empire continued to limp along, the 1850s and 1860s brought partial autonomy for Montenegro and Romania; the latter's linguistic descent from the Romance family of languages gave it a separate identity from the Slavic Bulgarians to its south and the Hungarian Magyars to its north and west. Throughout the 1860s, individual nationalist aspirations continued to gain traction alongside broader pan-Slavic visions, culminating in a series of uprisings in the 1870s that collectively became known as the Balkan Crisis. In the summer of 1875, a fairly limited revolt was launched in Herzegovina against Ottoman control, which was followed in April of the next year by a more extensive uprising among the Bulgarians.[133] When the Principalities of Serbia and Montenegro joined the conflict in June 1876, a full-fledged military conflict ensued. Due in part to the poor preparation of Serbian and Montenegrin troops, the imperial forces of the Ottomans managed to prevail, and the uprisings were essentially extinguished. Or so it seemed. In April 1877, Russia declared war on the Ottomans, motivated partly by the ill-treatment of Serbs and Montenegrins and partly by the longer-term desire to reverse some of the losses from the conclusion of the Crimean War more than two decades earlier.[134] After months of fighting characterized by siege warfare and heavy civilian casualties, the Russians succeeded in largely driving the Ottoman forces out of the Balkans.[135] The Sultan was forced to surrender in early 1878. In the ensuing Treaty of San Stefano, Serbia and Montenegro were granted territorial expansions and their previous autonomy was transformed into full sovereignty. Of more concern to the Great Powers was the fact that the treaty also established an independent Principality of Bulgaria, which many feared might increase Russian influence excessively and upset the delicate balance of power in the region. So an international conference was convened in Berlin in the summer of 1878, creating a new settlement that revised the San Stefano Treaty. The independent sovereignty of Serbia, Montenegro, and Romania was affirmed, but the Principality of Bulgaria had a significant portion of its territory returned to the Ottomans, and its original independent status was scaled back to mere political autonomy under the nominal authority of the Ottoman Empire.[136] Additionally, Bosnia and Herzegovina became de facto possessions of the Austro-Hungarian Empire.[137]

The messy patchwork of Balkan territories, state structures, and ethno-linguistic identities would continue over the ensuing decades to provide the potential for dangerous destabilization on the southeastern periphery of Europe.

National identity and the imperialist project

The intertwining of Social Darwinist assumptions and racial thought can be seen clearly in the colossal imperialist project launched by European powers in the second half of the nineteenth century. While the motivating factors behind imperialist expansion were varied—ranging from capitalist economic interests to Christian missionary impulses—the desire for enhanced national prestige was an almost universal driving force.[138] Imperialism also served to sharpen nationalist thought in potentially contradictory ways, reinforcing common perceptions of shared European "superiority" on the one hand, while on the other giving ambitious European nation-states an expansive stage on which to engage in deadly competition with each other.[139] As had also been the case on the European continent in the Napoleonic era, overseas imperial expansion frequently engendered oppositional nationalist movements in conquered and occupied territories.

The first wave of European imperialism in the fifteenth and sixteenth centuries had differed significantly from the "new" imperialism that began in the mid-nineteenth century. As early Portuguese and Spanish explorers had ceded primacy to the Dutch and British, the major engines of imperial expansion became elaborate private corporations and joint stock companies, such as the British East India Company founded in 1600 or the rival United East India Company established by the Dutch in 1602.[140] The home metropole typically maintained a measure of involvement, to be sure, but these private enterprises wielded tremendous independent power, establishing their own trade routes, maintaining their own military and defense forces, and acting in many ways as sovereign mini-states.[141] As competition patterns changed and as these companies struggled to remain profitable, European states increasingly stepped in to assume more direct control. On the Indian subcontinent, British hegemony was exercised through "company rule," as the exploitive dominance of the East India Company was termed, until the famous Sepoy Mutiny of 1857–1858.[142] In the aftermath of the rebellion, parliament dissolved the Company's charter and transferred its governing authority to the British crown, thereby creating the Raj system that lasted for nearly a century.[143] As a result of this more direct control, the British project in India became no longer an economic enterprise of prime interest to financial backers, but a national mission. India became a screen onto which conceptions of British identity could be projected, with the Sepoy mutiny as a key opening chapter in this new narrative.[144] As Ralph Crane and Radhika Mohanram have argued, the mutiny became the cornerstone of a compelling mythology of British "masculinity forged under siege."[145] And as Steven Patterson has noted of the "changed moral tone of British rule in India after the mutiny," an almost limitless set of possibilities emerged over the subsequent decades for the fashioning of quintessentially British notions of honor and masculine virtue—forged on the imperial periphery but consumed with zeal on the domestic scene.[146]

By the early nineteenth century, France had lost virtually all of the overseas colonial holdings it had gained in the first wave of European expansion. A new upsurge of French colonial activity began with the conquest of Algeria in 1830. In the mid-1850s, the French diplomat and land speculator Ferdinand de Lesseps began consultations with Said Pasha, the viceroy who administered Egypt on behalf of the Ottoman Sultan, about the possibility of opening a trade route between the Mediterranean and the Red Sea. The end result was the creation of the Suez Canal, which was opened in November 1869 to great fanfare in an elaborate ceremony attended by international dignitaries, including Eugenie, the wife of French emperor Napoleon III.[147] As French imperial expansion grew during the "scramble for Africa" over the ensuing decades, manifestations of racial superiority kept pace, fueled in part by the popularity of Gobineau's ideas and the expansion of racial anthropology in French academic circles.[148] Throughout the 1880s, Liberal nationalists like Jules Ferry made sweeping public statements about the right and "civilizing duty" of the "superior races" to dominate the "inferior races" in Africa.[149]

EXCERPT 4.4

Speech Before the French Chamber of Deputies, March 28, 1884

Jules Ferry

The policy of colonial expansion is a political and economic system ... that can be connected to three sets of ideas: economic ideas; the most far-reaching ideas of civilization; and ideas of a political and patriotic sort.

In the area of economics, I am placing before you, with the support of some statistics, the considerations that justify the policy of colonial expansion, as seen from the perspective of a need, felt more and more urgently by the industrialized population of Europe and especially the people of our rich and hardworking country of France: the need for outlets [for exports]. Is this a fantasy? Is this a concern [that can wait] for the future? Or is this not a pressing need, one may say a crying need, of our industrial population? I merely express in a general way what each one of you can see for himself in the various parts of France. Yes, what our major industries [textiles, etc.], irrevocably steered by the treaties of 1860 into exports, lack more and more are outlets. Why? Because next door Germany is setting up trade barriers; because across the ocean the United States of America have become protectionists, and extreme protectionists at that; because not only are these great markets ... shrinking, becoming more and more difficult of access, but these great states are beginning to pour into our own markets products not seen there before. This is true not only for our agriculture, which has been so sorely tried … and for which competition is no longer limited to the circle of large European states…. Today, as you know, competition, the law of supply and demand, freedom of trade, the effects of speculation, all radiate in a circle that reaches to the ends of the earth…. That is a great complication, a great economic difficulty; … an extremely serious problem. It is so serious, gentlemen, so acute, that the least informed persons must already glimpse, foresee, and take precautions against the time when the great South American market that has, in a manner of speaking, belonged to us forever will be disputed and perhaps taken away from us by North American products. Nothing is more serious; there can be no graver social problem; and these matters are linked intimately to colonial policy.

Gentlemen, we must speak more loudly and more honestly! We must say openly that indeed the higher races have a right over the lower races …. I repeat, that the superior races have a right because they have a duty. They have the duty to civilize the inferior races …. In the history of earlier centuries these duties, gentlemen, have often been misunderstood; and certainly when the Spanish soldiers and explorers introduced slavery into Central America, they did not fulfill their duty as men of a higher race …. But, in our time, I maintain that European nations acquit themselves with generosity, with grandeur, and with sincerity of this superior civilizing duty.[150]

Whereas Britain and France were the leading European colonial powers up through the 1880s, in that decade they were challenged by other ambitious European nation-states eager for their "place in the sun." The most aggressive of these, Germany, would not engage fully in the colonial scramble until after the dismissal of Bismarck in 1890, although as Matthew Fitzpatrick has shown, there were rising voices among Liberal and nationalist elites advocating expansionism before then.[151] In Italy, following a bungled bid to seize Tunisia in 1879, desires for a colonial empire continued to grow, and in the following decade Italians established a growing foothold in the Horn of Africa.[152] But two subsequent attempts to take Ethiopia failed, and Italian colonial ambitions would continue to overreach Italian military and administrative capacities for decades.

One of the most notable additions to Europe's colonial holdings in Africa was the Congo Free State, a personal fiefdom established by Belgian king Leopold II in the 1880s. Before he came to the throne in 1865, Leopold had been envious of earlier Dutch colonial successes, and began eyeing the uncultivated Congo River basin in central Africa as the site for a colonial enterprise. During the 1870s and early 1880s, he commissioned topographical studies, but his initial plans were blocked by

European powers, until an international conference in Berlin authorized the establishment of the Congo Free State in 1885. The state itself was constituted by a strange amalgamation of royal prerogative and private enterprise. It was a personal holding of Leopold, rather than a responsibility of the Belgian treasury, so both the funding and the profits from the venture were tied directly to the king.[153] The Congo basin was rich in natural resources, enabling Leopold and his administrators to attract to the region a vast assemblage of European schemers and adventurers, who became implicated in a brutal campaign of torture and exploitation against the native population. The majority of official atrocities were undertaken by the private army employed by Leopold, the *Force Publique*, which was led by white Europeans but comprised largely by soldiers and trainees from a variety of African backgrounds.[154] The vast amounts of copper, ivory, and rubber extracted from the Congo Free State greatly enriched Leopold's personal coffers, but international outrage against catastrophic human rights abuses led to calls for the king's private exploitation project to end. It was not until 1908 that the Belgian parliament voted to annex the Congo Free State as an official Belgian colony, but by then the pattern of brutal abuse had been mirrored many times over in other colonial holdings. To the present day, the Belgian case stands as the quintessential manifestation of the potent mixture of industrial modernity, nationalist colonial competition, and European notions of racial superiority.

* * * *

Overall, in taking stock of the massive transformations witnessed between the mid- and late nineteenth century, it should be noted that the phenomena discussed in preceding sections—"scientific" racial thought, imperialism, and pan-nationalism—were interconnected, feeding into each other in intricate ways. In her seminal work *The Origins of Totalitarianism*, published in the immediate aftermath of the Second World War, Hannah Arendt broke new ground in arguing that nineteenth-century continental forms of imperialism gained their potency specifically because they "enthusiastically absorbed the tradition of race-thinking," fostering a variety of "pan-movements [which] have generally been given scant attention in the discussion of imperialism."[155] In the decades since then scholars have fleshed out the nature of these connections on a much more detailed level, with Robert Gerwarth and Stephan Malinowski referring to much of this more recent scholarship under the rubric of "Hannah Arendt's ghosts."[156] Scholars ranging from Shelley Baranowski to Geoff Eley have illuminated key connections between nineteenth-century colonial ambitions and the racial "imaginary" underpinning twentieth-century genocidal projects.[157]

In the short term, however, European power politics in the 1880s were characterized by the establishment of an intricate network of alliances, partly the brainchild of Bismarck, which was designed to maintain a stable balance of power on the continent. As will be seen in the following chapter, the devastating collapse of that balance was preceded and in some ways paralleled by the explosive transition to mass politics within individual European nation-states. Conceptions of national belonging would be dramatically transformed as a result.

5

European Nationalism between Mass Politics, War, and Peace, 1890–1920

As Otto von Bismarck was preparing to enter his third decade at the helm of German politics in early 1890, tensions between the elderly chancellor and the young Kaiser Wilhelm II came to a head. Wilhelm had come to the throne in 1888—the "Year of the Three Kaisers"—after the deaths of his grandfather Wilhelm I in March and his father Friedrich III in June. Friedrich III had been notably well-educated, Liberal, and cosmopolitan in outlook, which deeply concerned Bismarck, whose relationship with Wilhelm I had afforded him a virtually free hand in domestic and foreign policy over the years. Friedrich's death from laryngeal cancer after only ninety-nine days on the throne thus came as a sort of reprieve from what Bismarck feared would be the implementation of a Liberal "German Gladstone ministry."[1] The alternative, which emerged in the form of the 29-year-old Wilhelm II, turned out to be utterly catastrophic. The young Wilhelm, who was bedeviled by a chaotic tangle of complexes and neuroses, combined many of the least flattering stereotypes of Teutonic bluster with an almost complete lack of compensatory strengths. He was unreflective, vain, superficial, and deeply insecure, a pompous blowhard in ill-fitting military garb who, as a contemporary satirist noted, "insisted on being the stag at every hunt, the bride at every wedding, and the corpse at every funeral."[2] His bombastic theatricality was, in many ways, emblematic of the broader shift away from traditional Prussian austerity and discipline, toward a gaudy state-sponsored egocentrism that would come to demand Germany's "place in the sun." In his first eighteen months on the throne, Wilhelm had coexisted uneasily with Bismarck, but his desire to pitch himself as the "people's Kaiser"—believing his charismatic personality to be an irresistible force that would compel the German working classes to rally behind him—brought with it the decision, against Bismarck's advice, to allow Germany's anti-Socialist legislation to

FIGURE 5.1 Otto von Bismarck *by John McLure Hamilton. Wikimedia Commons.*

lapse. In the power struggle that ensued, Bismarck tendered his resignation on March 18, 1890. Accepting it with enthusiasm, Wilhelm II brought about the end of a seminal era in both German politics and European diplomacy.

Although not entirely clear at the time, Bismarck's departure coincided with an important broader shift in nationalist ideology and discourse. The traditional, state-based realism of Bismarck and Cavour came quickly to appear as if from a different world, as unruly dynamic forces were mobilized in anticipation of the dawning new century. In the place of predictable ministerial diplomacy and cabinet resolutions, radical nationalist pressure groups and extra-parliamentary lobby organizations proliferated. Innovative trends in mass media, marketing, and advertising transformed individual and collective processes of identity formation, with major implications for the articulation of national identity. On the heels of the overseas imperialist projects described in the last chapter, the intertwined forces of radical mass nationalism and racism were manifested on the internal domestic stage to varying degrees throughout virtually the entirety of Europe.[3]

The advent of mass politics and varieties of exclusionary nationalism

The period beginning around 1890 witnessed the high point of the "nationalization" of the masses, the culmination of longer-term processes that transformed the discourse of the nation from the preserve of educated elites to the central animating force in the lives of millions of everyday Europeans. In established nation-states, this process was often initiated by state actors themselves, who implemented mandatory national schooling (with an appropriate emphasis on national history, geography, and language), built national infrastructure, and forged solidarity through broad national programs such as compulsory military service. As Eric Hobsbawm has noted: "These interventions became so universal and so routinized in 'modern' states that a family would have to live in some very inaccessible place if some member or other were not to come into regular contact with the national state and its agents: through the postman, the policeman or gendarme, and eventually through the schoolteacher."[4] Eugen Weber's account of the transformation of "peasants into Frenchmen," in which pluralistic rural identities gave way to nationalized and streamlined conceptions of France, remains among the most influential studies of this type of project in the decades before the First World War.[5] But rather than merely supplanting regional identities, the nationalization process often absorbed and co-opted local folk customs and traditions in making the concept of the nation more tangible, as shown in the work of Celia Applegate and Alon Confino on regionalism in the German Empire.[6] As Caroline Ford has demonstrated in her study of provincial Brittany, the forging of national identity was not so much a straightforward top-down imposition as a complex process of negotiation, integrating, and mediating even particularistic forms of religious attachment.[7]

To understand the transition to mass politics in post-Bismarckian Germany, along with its impact on nationalist mobilization, a brief bit of background on the preceding years is necessary. In the aftermath of the Kulturkampf, the late 1870s witnessed the emergence of an aggressive new form of political antisemitism in Germany. The term antisemitism itself was coined in 1879 by the publicist Wilhelm Marr in the context of the organized political agitation of the Protestant pastor Adolf Stoecker in Berlin.[8] Stoecker had been a chaplain during the Franco-Prussian War before receiving the post of imperial *Hofprediger* (Court Preacher) in 1874. Three years later, he took over leadership of an urban mission in Berlin, which combined charitable work among the city's industrial poor with an evangelistic outreach program.[9] It was in this capacity that Stoecker became convinced of the need not only to Christianize but also to nationalize German industrial workers, who were in danger of being led astray by the godless materialist promises of Marxist agitators. Stoecker saw the Jews as the architects of both international finance capitalism and its opposition, Marxist internationalism. To address the problem politically, Stoecker founded the Christian Social Party in early 1878, which committed itself to representing workers' interests, both spiritual and material, while combatting the influence of "international Jewry."[10] In 1880, the party submitted a famous petition to the Kaiser requesting that the immigration of foreign

Jews into Germany be stopped and that the Jews be excluded from holding public office and government positions. The petition failed, but achieved significant publicity. Early the next year, Stoecker appeared at a number of mass rallies attended by thousands and framed primarily around economic antisemitism, with lecture titles such as "Artisanship Past and Present" and "Compulsory Accident Insurance" being intermingled with his standard stump speech on "The Jewish Question."[11] Stoecker's party experienced a brief period of relevance in the 1880s, before going into steep decline and eventually dissolving entirely, with many of its former members migrating into the German Conservative Party. As Richard Levy has demonstrated, the fate of the Christian Social Party is indicative of the striking failure of political antisemitism in Imperial Germany more generally.[12]

Outside the realm of party politics, however, a broader nationalist mobilization was launched in the post-Bismarckian era, with increasingly racialized overtones.[13] In 1891, the pan-German League was founded as an extra-parliamentary pressure group to represent the interests of "Germandom" around the world—but especially in Central Europe.[14] The League grew in membership among German elites during the 1890s and collaborated with Austrian pan-Germans to launch the so-called *Los von Rom* (Away from Rome) movement around 1900.[15] This was pitched as a religious missionary endeavor, to convert German and Austrian Catholics away from Rome and to the Protestant faith, but the driving impulse was without question nationalistic. Antisemitic from its inception, by the early twentieth century, the League peddled an increasingly radical racialized form of antisemitism and an aggressive vision of colonial expansion overseas. The pan-Germans also advocated fiercely anti-Polish policies in the eastern borderlands, as did the Society for Eastern Marches (*Ostmarkenverein*), which was founded in 1894 to advocate for Germanization in Polish regions.[16] The years around 1900 also witnessed the growth of other mass lobby groups advocating nationalistic authoritarianism and militarism. The Naval League was founded in 1898 to push for the first naval bill under consideration in the Reichstag at that point.[17] The primary force behind it was the Naval Secretary Alfred von Tirpitz, who made it his personal mission to outfit Germany—a largely landlocked country—with a fighting fleet to rival that of Britain, an endeavor that pleased Wilhelm II, who was intensely envious of the British Navy.[18] The League grew quickly and was credited with helping build momentum for the passage not only of the 1898 naval expansion bill but also a similar bill in 1900. Another product of nationalist radicalization in the prewar years was the German Army League, which grew quickly into one of the largest popular pressure groups in Germany, advocating successfully for massive army expansion legislation in 1912 and 1913.[19]

In neighboring Austria, the pan-German movement experienced rapid growth in the 1890s largely as a result of the activism of Georg von Schönerer. Pan-German advocates in the Austrian empire felt themselves disadvantaged by the Habsburgs' multinational dynastic obligations and longed for union with Germany. Many of them came either from Protestant or secularized backgrounds, or converted from Catholicism, as had Schönerer.[20] When the Austrian minister-president Kasimir Badeni proposed new language laws in 1897 that called for civil servants in Habsburg Bohemia to conduct business in both German and Czech, pan-German nationalists cried foul, arguing that Czechs, who grew up learning German in school, would now have a clear advantage as potential government workers over Germans, most of whom could not speak a word of Czech.[21] The uproar over the Badeni Decrees was just one aspect of a running narrative of tension between Germans and Czechs in Bohemia, characterized by Gary Cohen as the "politics of ethnic survival."[22] The Austrian pan-Germans were also staunchly antisemitic, and even when Schönerer's political career declined precipitously—due in part to his massive ego and inability to collaborate—the antisemitic torch was carried by a wide range of racist movements throughout the Habsburg lands, fueled specifically by the rise of mass politics.[23]

Perhaps the most notable example of this mass antisemitic political mobilization was provided by the Christian Social movement under Karl Lueger. With their roots dating to the late 1890s, the Austrian Christian Socials first came to national prominence with the election of the staunchly antisemitic Lueger as mayor of Vienna in 1896, although it took more than a year of wrangling with the Badeni administration before the election was officially recognized. John Boyer has referred to the Christian Social ascent as the "antisemitic conquest of Vienna," and that language is not exaggerated.[24] Lueger, an inveterate populist, went on to launch a major modernization of Vienna's public works services, ranging from water supply to gas and electric utilities to urban beautification schemes, enjoying huge popularity among the Viennese populace as a result.[25] His antisemitic fulminations, which for many observers were the most notable components of his public persona, made him into an icon for the young Hitler, who lived in Vienna during the last years before Lueger's death in 1910.[26]

Although their significance would not be recognized fully until the rise of Hitler's National Socialist Party in the early 1930s, indigenous movements espousing "national socialism" took shape independently within the fin-de-siècle Habsburg domains. The first political party to officially use the name was the National Social Party founded in 1898 among Czechs in Bohemia. While that party remained fairly marginal, ultimately changing its name to the Czech Socialist Party in 1918, it did attempt to fuse working-class socialist concerns with fierce national sentiment, articulated against the German hegemony of the Habsburg crown.[27] Among German-speakers in industrial areas in Bohemia, a separate form of national socialism was pioneered by the German Workers Party founded in 1904. Though the party vehemently promoted German nationalist interests within the empire, at its inception, it was not particularly racist, and even its nationalism was couched primarily in economic terms—advocating for the nationalization of industry and calling for harmonious cooperation between rural laborers, artisans, and industrial workers.[28] By the eve of the First World War, however, the party had fully embraced the radical racism and imperialism of the pan-German movement.

Further east, the first significant mass nationalist movement within the Russian Empire, the antisemitic Union of Russian People, was founded in 1905. Its leading figure, Alexander Dubrovin, was a physician by trade who abandoned medicine for politics around 1900, emerging as a major figure on the authoritarian right during the abortive revolution launched by left Liberals in 1905.[29] The Union's ideology was somewhat muddled and inconsistent, combining traditional monarchism and dogmatic Orthodox Christianity with a populist appeal to the masses and an increasingly racialized form of antisemitism. Much of the group's public imagery hearkened directly back to the tripartite set of themes emphasized by Tsar Nicholas I and his education minister Sergey Uvarov decades earlier: Orthodoxy Autocracy, Nationality. But the self-consciously modern elements of the movement have led some scholars to classify it as an early Russian form of fascism.[30] The organizational structure and style of the Union were particularly striking. Formed into local paramilitary militia groups known as "Black Hundreds," members engaged in street violence and intimidation, disseminated racist propaganda, and incited violent pogroms against the Jews.[31] The Union and Black Hundred activists were also at the center of one of Imperial Russia's most infamous antisemitic blood libel cases: that of Menahem Mendel Beilis in Kiev. In the summer of 1911, Beilis was arrested and charged with the murder of a Ukrainian boy, which was identified by government "experts" as a case of ritual slaughter. In the two years between his arrest and his 1913 trial, in which he was acquitted, Beilis was pilloried by antisemitic journalists affiliated with the Union, who also launched vicious attacks against Russian Jews more generally.[32]

France also experienced an explosion of radical nationalist mobilization in the decades surrounding the fin-de-siècle. In the aftermath of their humiliating defeat in the Franco-Prussian War, many French nationalists had viewed the politics of the Third Republic with skepticism. In 1882, the anti-republican League of Patriots was founded as an extra-parliamentary pressure group, borrowing heavily from Jacobin imagery but employing it in the service of a far-right authoritarian vision devoid of even the slightest pretense to universalism or humanitarianism.[33] Its major founding figure was the poet and playwright Paul Déroulède, who had fought against and was taken prisoner by the Prussians in 1870, and who committed the rest of his life to the twin goals of revenge against Germany and the achievement of a rather ill-defined conception of French national greatness.[34] The League was contemptuous of parliamentary democracy, but appealed explicitly to the masses, advocating a populist vision of charismatic meritocracy under authoritarian leadership. This orientation provided an important point of commonality with the Boulangist movement that emerged in the mid-1880s.

General Georges Boulanger had become the object of a striking form of hero-worship after the Franco-Prussian War, as disaffected nationalists who idealized his military service were joined in their adulation by establishment political figures impressed with his leadership skills. In early 1886, he was appointed Minister of War.[35] When Boulanger was sacked in the spring of 1887, his outraged devotees gathered into a loosely organized political movement to defend his honor and to agitate for an authoritarian nationalist transformation of the republican system. Fueled by the support of the League of Patriots, the Boulangist movement pioneered novel forms of mass propaganda and agitation, which have been seen as among the most significant steps in the development of mass politics within the Third Republic.[36] The movement also appealed to many dissatisfied revolutionaries on the left.[37] In the course of 1888 and 1889, Boulangist candidates performed remarkably well in a string of elections, creating the impression that Boulanger might be on the verge of staging a coup to revise the constitution and overhaul the Republic. While much of the strength of the movement lay in the rural countryside, urban artisans and shopkeepers were mobilized with surprising speed.[38] In the spring of 1889, however, the most energetic Boulangist opponent, interior minister Ernest Constans, announced a crackdown on the movement and issued a warrant for Boulanger's arrest on suspicion of treason. To the surprise of many of his followers, the general responded by fleeing the country.[39] While many continued to long for his messianic return, Boulanger himself descended into a fog of despair after the death of his longtime mistress. In September 1891, without having returned to France, Boulanger committed suicide at her gravesite in Brussels. While this officially ended the Boulangist movement, the transition to mass politics proceeded in the ensuing years along radicalized and increasingly racialized lines.

Among the new organizations that originated in the context of the Boulangist movement was the National Antisemitic League of France, which was founded in 1889 by the journalist Edouard Drumont, whose 1886 missive *La France juive* (Jewish France) had become a rallying point for racist nationalists.[40] After a few years of energetic activity in the early 1890s, the National Antisemitic League began to fade and Drumont largely retreated from public life, relocating to Brussels. But new life was breathed into the movement by the infamous Dreyfus Affair, which brought Drumont back into the limelight. The affair itself began in 1894 with the conviction for treason of Alfred Dreyfus, a French military officer of Jewish descent, who was sentenced to life imprisonment on Devil's Island in French Guiana. When new evidence emerged in 1896 exonerating Dreyfus and implicating another officer, Walsin Esterhazy, the military leadership initially launched a cover up, then hastily organized a trial in which Esterhazy was quietly acquitted.[41] Dreyfus's conviction and sentence stood. At that point, his cause was taken up in the public sphere by journalists and a variety of cultural figures, such as the novelist Emile Zola, who published his famous pro-Dreyfus missive *J'accuse!* (I Accuse!) in 1898 as an indictment of government and military corruption.[42] French society became polarized between "Dreyfusards" like Zola and "Anti-Dreyfusards" like Drumont, who accused Zola of subversion and viewed Dreyfus's Jewishness as an affront to French national identity. The affair came to symbolize a broad set of cultural and political divisions—between antisemites and philosemites, between nationalists and cosmopolitans, between authoritarians and republicans, between traditional Catholics and secularists, between the advocates of order and the advocates of truth.[43] A new trial for Dreyfus was held in the summer of 1899 and he was once again convicted, but this time of a lesser charge and with recognition of extenuating circumstances. Doubts about the evidence continued and public opinion remained enflamed, necessitating a compromise that allowed the military to save face: Dreyfus would accept guilt and then be pardoned by the French president. While his coerced admission allowed him to avoid a return to Devil's Island, his supporters continued to maintain his innocence and ultimately prevailed. In 1906 Dreyfus received full exoneration, his military ranks were restored and, as a bizarre sort of compensation, he was made a knight in the Legion of Honor. He went on to serve in the French army during the First World War and survived to witness, in old age, the 1933 appointment of Hitler as chancellor in neighboring Germany.[44]

Of the numerous radical nationalist organizations that emerged from within the Anti-Dreyfusard camp, the most significant and lasting was *Action Française*, which combined virulent antisemitism with equal doses

FIGURE 5.2 Zola Faces the Mob *by Henry de Groux. Maison d'Émile Zola/ Wikimedia Commons.*

of neo-monarchism and militarism. Drumont's National Antisemitic League had begun to splinter after Dreyfus's pardon in 1899, and many of its members who searched for a new ideological home were drawn to Action Française, which had been founded the previous year by the philosophy teacher Henri Vaugeois and the journalist Maurice Pujo.[45] They were soon joined by Charles Maurras, who became the chief antisemitic ideologist and driving force within the organization over the next three decades. Maurras was both a royalist and a Catholic, although, it must be said, he was rather heretical in both regards. His royalism was of a vague metaphysical nature, envisioning the French nation as an organic entity with the monarchy (or the idea of the monarchy) serving as the head. His Catholicism was utilitarian and practical, idealizing the hierarchical organizational structure of the Church while remaining generally indifferent about theology and religious practice. The fact that Maurras was eventually excommunicated by Rome did not, however, prevent his ideas from finding broad acceptance among conservative Catholics in France.[46] Under the leadership of Maurras, *Action Française* emerged as the most innovative radical national force on the French political scene. It acquired its own newspaper, edited by Maurras, and it pioneered new propagandistic media techniques. Its publications were sold on the street by uniformed youths who also served as a de facto private militia, engaging in frequent street violence with opponents. The group has been categorized by some historians, most notably Ernst Nolte, as the first fascist movement in Europe, predating the Union of Russian People by several years.[47] Others, like Zeev Sternhell, acknowledge the movement's significance, but see it as perhaps less important in the prehistory of fascism than the revolutionary syndicalism of Georges Sorel.[48] What is clear is that *Action Française* managed to bridge ideological differences between nineteenth-century traditionalists—Catholics, monarchists, landowning elites—and forward-looking revolutionary racists and nationalists. By spiritualizing the monarchist idea, while tying it to the youthful vitality of the nation-as-organism, the movement provided a blueprint for how radical nationalist ideology could be adaptively mobilized across social and political boundaries.

Another example of ideological bridge-building within the context of mass politics was the evolution of a French form of "national socialism."[49] The novelist and Anti-Dreyfusard politician Maurice Barrès popularized the term "socialist nationalism" during an election campaign in 1898 and went on to emphasize in his literary works, which he termed "novels of national energy," a collectivist form of national belonging that brought together Darwinist pseudoscience, racial antisemitism, and a wistful nostalgia for premodern society rooted in the French soil.[50] Similar ideas were at play in the activism of Pierre Biétry, who in 1902 founded a radically nationalistic trade union movement known as *Les Jaunes* (the Yellows), in explicit contrast to the "red," or internationalistic, workers' organizations spreading through France at the time. In 1903, Biétry founded a political offshoot, the

French National Socialist Party, which embraced radical antisemitism as a central component of its anti-Marxist platform. While the National Socialist Party was rather short-lived, the trade union movement expanded rapidly and inspired a number of imitators in other parts of the world.[51]

Among the journalists sent to cover the Dreyfus Affair in France was Theodor Herzl, a correspondent for the Viennese daily *Neue freie Presse*. Herzl was raised in an assimilated Jewish family in Pest (now the eastern part of Budapest), whose parents were German-speakers and loyal subjects of the Habsburg crown. In his early years, Herzl himself embraced an idealized vision of German *Kultur*, and after completing his law degree at the University of Vienna in 1884, he embarked on a career in journalism. While covering the Dreyfus Affair in Paris, Herzl was shocked by the depth of antisemitism expressed and gradually became convinced that Jewish assimilation would never become a reality.[52] The best Jews could hope for was to be tolerated in good times, but vilified and persecuted (or worse) in times of crisis. In 1896, he published his most famous work, *The Jewish State*, which borrowed heavily from European nationalist thinkers to argue for Jewish identity as a distinct form of national identity. The only solution to the Jews' precarious position within European society, he argued, was the creation of a national homeland, an independent Jewish state.

EXCERPT 5.1

A Jewish State (1896)

Theodor Herzl

The idea which I have developed in this pamphlet is a very old one: it is the restoration of the Jewish State. The world resounds with outcries against the Jews, and these outcries have awakened the slumbering idea. [...] Everything depends on our propelling force. And what is our propelling force? The misery of the Jews. Who would venture to deny its existence? [...] Am I stating what is not yet the case? Am I before my time? Are the sufferings of the Jews not yet grave enough? We shall see. Now it depends on the Jews to make of this either a political pamphlet or a political romance. If the present generation is too dull to understand it rightly, a future, a finer, and a better generation will arise to understand it. The Jews wish for a State—they shall have it, and they shall earn it for themselves. [...]

I believe that I understand Anti-Semitism, which is really a highly complex movement. I consider it from a Jewish standpoint, yet without fear or hatred. [...] I think the Jewish question is no more a social than a religious one, notwithstanding that it sometimes takes these and other forms. It is a national question, which can only be solved by making it a political world-question to be discussed and controlled by the civilized nations of the world in council.

We are a people—one people. We have honestly endeavored everywhere to merge ourselves in the social life of surrounding communities and to preserve the faith of our fathers. We are not permitted to do so. In vain are we loyal patriots, our loyalty in some places running to extremes; in vain do we make the same sacrifices of life and property as our fellow citizens; in vain do we strive to increase the fame of our native land in science and art, or her wealth by trade and commerce. In countries where we have lived for centuries we are still cried down as strangers, and often by those whose ancestors were not yet domiciled in the land where Jews had already had experience of suffering. The majority may decide which are the strangers; for this, as indeed every point which arises in the relations between nations, is a question of might.[53]

Following the publication of the *Jewish State*, the rise of the antisemitic Christian Social Party under Karl Lueger, the newly elected mayor of Vienna, forced Herzl's ideas to take firmer shape. He became the acknowledged leader of the fledgling Zionist movement, which manifested many of the hallmarks of nationalist ideology.[54] In August 1897, he convened and chaired the First Zionist Congress in Basel, Switzerland, which elected Herzl president, and he began lobbying opinion leaders and heads of state to gain support for the idea of a Jewish homeland. In the fall of 1898, Herzl famously gained a personal audience with Kaiser Wilhelm II during the latter's state visit to Jerusalem, then under Ottoman control.[55] In May 1901 and again in June 1902, he traveled to meet with the Ottoman Sultan to attempt to gain funding and possible territorial concessions, but was ultimately unsuccessful. At the time of his death in 1904, Herzl had been unable to achieve tangible progress toward the homeland dream, but his articulation of Jewish identity as national identity would have a major impact on Jewish responses to future persecution at the hand of European nationalists.

The dawning era of mass politics in Europe also witnessed an upswing in national separatist activism, as seen for example on the Iberian Peninsula in the movements for Basque and Catalan independence. These often exhibited fewer overtly exclusionary elements than the cases just discussed, although forms of antisemitism and xenophobia could be detected in many of their leading figures. Basque separatism was fueled in part by pride in the Basque language, which developed largely in isolated "purity" and is one of the oldest languages in Europe.[56] In the aftermath of the unifications of Italy and Germany, Basque nationalists attempted an armed bid for independence in the 1870s, which failed. As industrialization spread, increasing numbers of non-Basque workers began relocating to Basque cities like Bilbao, leading Sabino Arana to found the Basque Nationalist Party in 1895 to represent new and explicitly racialized visions of Basque identity, in contrast to the earlier emphasis on linguistic purity.[57] Those exclusionary visions would be alternately disavowed and embraced by Basque nationalists in subsequent decades. The region of Catalonia, located south and east of Basque country in the Pyrenees, had long viewed itself as separate from the surrounding regions and identities. Like the Basques, Catalan-speakers traced their linguistic and cultural heritage back centuries, but the Catalan language itself had suffered consistent repression from the unification of the Spanish crown under Ferdinand and Isabella up through the eighteenth century.[58] The first codifications of Catalan as a modern literary language began during the romantic revival known as the *Renaixença* in the 1830s, which was effectively launched when Carles Aribau published his famous vernacular *Ode to the Fatherland* in 1833.[59] Following an unsuccessful bid for independence in the 1870s, Catalan nationalists founded the League of Catalonia in 1885, submitted numerous petitions to the Spanish crown seeking varying measures of autonomy and recognition and worked to flesh out concrete myths and symbols to define Catalan identity.[60] A major landmark was achieved in 1906, when Enric Prat de la Riba published *The Catalan Nationality*, which provided a philosophical and political blueprint for the continued cultivation of Catalan distinctiveness. Prat de la Riba borrowed extensively from German ideas, arguing that the central unifying element of Catalan identity was a unique *Volksgeist*, or national spirit.[61]

Lest it be thought that fin-de-siécle nationalist mobilization occurred only on the political Right and among disgruntled separatists, it should be noted that a number of Liberal and republican movements advocated for more democratic and inclusive visions of national belonging.[62] The work of Karen Offen on French feminists and Kevin Repp on German social reformers has demonstrated that these conceptions of the nation were often infused by humanitarian impulses and progressive optimism.[63] As will be seen in the next chapter, however, that progressive optimism would come to be seen by many in the aftermath of the First World War as hopelessly naïve.

Toward war: Political sleepwalking or biological necessity?

Recent years have witnessed the production of a large number of works on the origins of the First World War, both leading up to and following the 100th anniversary of the outbreak of the conflict. Perhaps the most widely discussed among these—and certainly the most readable—is Christopher

Clark's *Sleepwalkers*, which brilliantly weaves together the broader context of prewar Great Power politics with the actions of individuals and state actors.[64] Clark places developments in the Balkans at the heart of the story long before the fateful summer of 1914. Serbian military and intelligence forces, which were central to the bloody 1903 assassination of the Serbian King Aleksandar and his wife Draga, established a pattern of conspiratorial activism that was ultimately directed against Austrian influence in the Balkans. Among the key figures was Dragutin Dimitrijević (better known by his nickname "Apis"), and the Black Hand network of pan-Slavic revolutionaries over which he presided—including Gavrilo Princip, who undertook the 1914 assassination of Archduke Franz Ferdinand that set in motion the events leading to war. Against the backdrop of an international alliance system that had ossified into two opposing camps, Clark sees the decisions of European statesmen in the summer of 1914 unfolding as a form of political somnambulism, with the chief protagonists essentially unaware of (and initially unconcerned about) the vast and irrevocable repercussions of their actions. But Clark also demonstrates that the decision-making hierarchies of the various states produced leaders who appeared to be in a position to respond decisively, but who in fact lacked the tools and authority to act competently and responsibly under any circumstance. So the search for blame must remain largely elusive. While Clark has come in for some mild criticism for his sympathetic portrayal of Austria-Hungary and the lack of a prosecutorial tone when dealing with Germany, his emphasis on the destabilizing influence of the Serbs offers a useful corrective and ultimately has the benefit of focusing more attention on the role of Russia, Serbia's pan-Slavic cousin.[65]

The roots of the movement that led to the assassination of King Aleksandar in 1903 date back nearly a century to the dynastic rivalry between the Obrenović and Karadjordjević families. The initial Serb uprising against the Ottomans in 1804 had been spearheaded by the progenitor of the Karadjordjević line, Djordje Petrović (known as "Kara Djordje," or Black George, from which the dynasty derived its name). But when the next Serb uprising was launched in 1815, it was led by Miloš Obrenović, who managed to establish the semiautonomous Principality of Serbia within the Ottoman Empire and have himself crowned prince. Kara Djordje, who had been abroad in exile, returned to Serbia in 1817 and was assassinated by Obrenović agents. So while his supporters continued to venerate Kara Djordje as the founding father (and martyr) of Serbia, it was the Obrenvović line that ruled the principality for its first two and a half decades. But dynastic control was to swing back and forth between the two rival families. In 1842, the son of Kara Djordje, Aleksandar, came to power after a revolt forced his predecessor, Mihailo Obrenović, into exile. When internal tensions eventually forced Aleksandar Karadjordjević to abdicate in late 1858, however, Mihailo was able to return and resume his reign. He was, in turn, assassinated in 1868, but power was passed surprisingly smoothly to Mihailo's son, Milan Obrenović, who ruled for more than two decades. It was Milan who was on the throne when Serbia gained its sovereignty in 1878, making him the first king of independent Serbia. When Milan stepped down in 1889, it was in favor of his young son, Aleksandar Obrenović, who went on in 1900 to marry Draga Mašin. On June 11, 1903, when the royal couple was brutally assassinated in their bedchamber, it came as the result of a well-planned conspiracy from within the Serbian military, led by "Apis" Dimitrijević.[66] The coup brought to the throne the rival Petar Karadjordjević, who would rule Serbia as King Petar I for nearly two decades.

The military and security personnel under Apis who had carried out the hit on Aleksandar and Draga continued their conspiratorial activism after 1903, but with the overthrow of Austrian control in the Balkans as the chief objective. It will be recalled that Austria-Hungary had gained de facto possession of Bosnia and Herzegovina at the 1878 Conference of Berlin. In 1908, Austrian authorities made the radical move to overtly annex those territories, making them full constituent parts of the Austro-Hungarian Empire. The Bosnian capital Sarajevo thus continued as a Habsburg provincial outpost, but in a more direct and official administrative sense after 1908.[67] Bosnian Serbs under Austrian control longed increasingly for independent Serbia to play the role of Prussia or Piedmont in leading a glorious pan-Slavic unification drive.[68] Against that backdrop, in 1911 Serbian military officers, Apis chief among them, founded the secret Black Hand organization, which also took the name "Unification or Death." While its clandestine nature meant that the Black Hand could not emerge publicly as a mass political organization, its membership grew rapidly underground, and its members established branches throughout the Balkan region, including (especially) Sarajevo.[69]

In Germany, the year 1911 witnessed the publication of one of the best-selling books of the immediate prewar period, *Germany and the Next War* by Friedrich von Bernhardi. As a young officer in the Franco-Prussian War in 1870, Bernhardi was reputed to have been the first Prussian to ride victoriously through the Arc de Triomphe in Paris.[70] Bernhardi was appointed head of the historical section of the German General Staff beginning in the late 1890s, serving alongside General Alfred von Schlieffen, whose famous plan for military mobilization became the German blueprint for the opening phase of the war in 1914. When Bernhardi's *Next War* was published in 1911, it was embraced by the pan-German League as an effective manifestation of its radical nationalist ideas; the league's leadership also hoped it was an indication of official government approval for its expansionist vision.[71] The text itself, excerpted below, not only glorified war but portrayed it in Darwinistic terms as a "biological necessity" between nation-states.

EXCERPT 5.2

Germany and the Next War (1911)

Friedrich von Bernhardi

Since 1795, when Immanuel Kant published in his old age his treatise on "Perpetual Peace," many have considered it an established fact that war is the destruction of all good and the origin of all evil. In spite of all that history teaches, no conviction is felt that the struggle between Nations is inevitable, and the growth of civilization is credited with a power to which war must yield. But, undisturbed by such human theories and the change of times, war has again and again marched from country to country with the clash of arms, and has proved its destructive as well as creative and purifying power. It has not succeeded in teaching mankind what its real nature is. Long periods of war, far from convincing men of the necessity of war, have, on the contrary, always revived the wish to exclude war, where possible, from the political intercourse of nations.

This wish and this hope are widely disseminated even today. The maintenance of peace is lauded as the only goal at which statesmanship should aim. This unqualified desire for peace has obtained in our days a quite peculiar power over men's spirits. This aspiration finds its public expression in peace leagues and peace congresses; the Press of every country and of every party opens its columns to it. The current in this direction is, indeed, so strong that the majority of Governments profess—outwardly, at any rate—that the necessity of maintaining peace is the real aim of their policy; while when a war breaks out the aggressor is universally stigmatized, and all Governments exert themselves, partly in reality, partly in pretense, to extinguish the conflagration. [...]

This desire for peace has rendered most civilized nations anemic, and marks a decay of spirit and political courage such as has often been shown by a race of Epigoni. "It has always been," Heinrich von Treitschke tells us, "the weary, spiritless, and exhausted ages which have played with the dream of perpetual peace." [...]

This aspiration is directly antagonistic to the great universal laws which rule all life. War is a *biological necessity* of the first importance, a regulative element in the life of mankind which cannot be dispensed with, since without it an unhealthy development will follow, which excludes every advancement of the race, and therefore all real civilization. "War is the father of all things" (Heraclitus). The sages of antiquity long before Darwin recognized this.

The struggle for existence is, in the life of Nature, the basis of all healthy development. All existing things show themselves to be the result of contesting forces. So in the life of man the struggle is not merely the destructive, but the life-giving principle.... There can be no doubt on this point. The nation is made up of individuals, the state of communities. The motive which influences each member is prominent in the whole body. It is a persistent struggle for possessions, power, and sovereignty, which primarily governs the relations of one nation to another, and right is respected so far only as it is compatible with advantage. So long as there are men who have human feelings and aspirations, so long as there are nations who strive for an enlarged sphere of activity, so long will conflicting interests come into being and occasions for making war arise.[72]

The glorification of war as a healthy inevitability was also manifested to varying degrees in Italy and France. In Italy, the years after unification were characterized by a growing sense of disillusion in broad segments of society. The *Risorgimento* had succeeded on a political and geographic level, but the anticipated greatness of Italy had largely failed to materialize. As embittered Italians spoke increasingly of a "missing revolution," cultural avant-gardists began to step forward as prophets of a new era of radical artistic and national renewal. In Florence, the literary group surrounding Guiseppe Prezzolini and Giovanni Papini founded the modernist periodicals *Leonardo* in 1907 and *La Voce* in 1908, which both idealized regenerative violence as a form of secular religion. Prezzolini in particular praised violent conflict as a purgative act of individualistic self-discovery and identity construction: "To separate oneself, to cultivate solitude, to love war, these are the aims of every person who wants to feel himself profoundly. Violence is, then, a moral cure, an exercise that strengthens a categorical imperative for those who love themselves."[73] Even more striking was the idealization of violence and war within the Futurist movement, which claimed to break completely with the past and to fully embrace twentieth-century modernity. Its founding moment is typically dated to the 1909 publication of the "Manifesto of Futurism" by Filippo Marinetti, and the movement grew rapidly over the next few years, especially in the industrialized north of Italy.[74] In many ways, Italian futurism developed as a kind of mass nationalist movement, as a parallel to organizations like Enrico Corradini's Italian Nationalist Association, founded in 1910.[75] As Stanley Payne has noted, its virulent nationalism was what set Italian futurism apart from modernists elsewhere in Europe:

Unlike the artistic avant-garde in some other countries, Italian Futurists were not mere individualists but ardent nationalists. To them, Italy was historically the land of genius, and the great new 'third Italy' (after Rome and the Renaissance) should be led by a new elite of 'young geniuses' (like, they thought, themselves) who would carry it to war, empire, and new national greatness.[76]

Futurist artwork glorified technology, machinery, and especially speed, idealizing the latest advances in the automotive, aviation, and munitions industries, whereas futurist poetry and fiction championed a brutalist style, featuring themes of conquest and destruction.[77] Marinetti's manifesto was explicit in its evocation of war: "We want to exalt movements of aggression, feverish sleeplessness, the forced march, the perilous leap, the slap and the blow with the fist.... We want to glorify war, the only cure for the world."[78]

Parallel trends were visible in prewar France, especially within the avant-garde circles surrounding Georges Sorel and Georges Valois.[79] Charles Péguy, who had begun his writing career as a socialist sympathizer, abandoned internationalism and embraced nationalist self-sacrifice as a spiritual ideal, which was also fueled by his gradual adoption of a vague yet passionate Catholic faith. His death in the first weeks of war in 1914 made his writings into virtual scriptures for young French nationalists.[80] Universities and student organizations had already in the preceding years manifested expressions of longing for war in the service of national apotheosis.[81] The journalists Henri Massis and Alfred de Tarde undertook an early form of "public opinion" survey among students in Paris, publishing their results in 1912 under the pseudonym Agathon.

EXCERPT 5.3

The Young People of Today (1912)

Henri Massis and Alfred de Tarde

How energetically are the young people of today raising themselves up on the morose foundation of the previous generation! We are struck first by their confidence in themselves. They have banished doubt. ... Simply put, what characterizes their attitude is the *taste for action.*

The sentiment which underlies all these youthful attitudes, which unanimously accords with the deepest tendencies in their thought, is that of patriotic faith. That they are possessed of this sentiment is unequivocal and undeniable. Optimism, that state of mind which defines the attitude of these young people, manifests itself from the outset in the confidence which they place in the future of France. There they find their first motive for acting, the one which determines and directs all their activity. [...]

How many times in the last two years have we heard this repeated: "Better war than this eternal waiting!" There is no bitterness in this avowal, but rather a secret hope.

War! The word has taken on a sudden glamour. It is a youthful word, wholly new, adorned with that seduction which the eternal bellicose instinct has revived in the hearts of men. These young men impute to it all the beauty with which they are in love and of which they have been deprived by ordinary life. Above all, war, in their eyes, is the occasion for the most noble of human virtues, those which they exalt above all others: energy, mastery, and sacrifice for a cause which transcends ourselves.[82]

By 1912, it had been nearly a century since all of Europe had been immersed in conflict during the Napoleonic era. Subsequent wars had been limited either geographically or temporally. So it must be remembered that the bellicose attitudes of Bernhardi and the Parisian students were both conceived and expressed within circumstances devoid of the sobering context that the ensuing years would create. As those years would demonstrate, however, faith in the nation provided no protection for the ferocity of modern technological warfare.

Storms of steel and nationalist euphorias

One of Bismarck's most-quoted statements was made when, late in life, he was asked his opinion on the likely cause of the next major conflict to emerge in Europe. Famously, Bismarck replied: "Some damned silly thing in the Balkans."[83] While Bismarck's political instincts were far from infallible, history was soon to prove him right on this count. Tensions had escalated in the aftermath of Austria-Hungary's annexation of Bosnia and Herzegovina in 1908. But when actual military conflict emerged in the Balkans four years later, it was in the context of the continued deterioration of Ottoman control in southeastern Europe. In the First Balkan War, which lasted from the fall of 1912 to the spring of 1913, a coalition of Serbia and Bulgaria, both of which had gained independence in 1878, went to war against the Ottoman Empire, with support from Greece and Montenegro. The result was a stunning disaster for the Ottomans, who lost virtually all of their remaining European holdings.[84] In the May 1913 Treaty of London that officially concluded the conflict, however, Serbian ambitions were frustrated by the decisions of the Great Power representatives at the peace conference. Partly as a result of Austria's desire to thwart the expansion of Serbian influence in the region, an independent Albania was established.[85] Bulgaria, which gained a limited amount of territory, was also dissatisfied with the London settlement, and in the summer of 1913 hostilities resumed in what became known as the Second Balkan War, this time between the former allies (principally Bulgaria fighting against Serbia and Greece). Bulgarian forces were quickly overwhelmed, and in the ensuing Treaty of Bucharest, Bulgaria was forced to cede to Serbia much of the territory it had gained in London.[86] Beyond the details of the geographic reshuffling, the most significant outcome of the Balkan Wars was the strengthening of Serbia's role as the leading force in the region and as the focal point of pan-Slavic longing for an independent and unified Balkan state. By the summer of 1914, those longings had reached a fevered pitch.

But events in the Balkans only account for the war's origins in an immediate sense, even if one extends those origins back to the 1903 assassination of the Serbian King Aleksandar. On a broader level, the First World War was the culmination of many of the trajectories discussed in earlier chapters: dynamic industrialization, technological modernization, imperialist swagger, and radicalizing nationalism. The conflict was to become the first "total war" in modern history, as the belligerent nation-states transformed their economies, refashioned social and gender relations, and mobilized millions of individuals on an unprecedented scale—soldiers and officers, to be sure, but also women, the elderly, and children on the home front. If the Thirty Years War of the seventeenth century was occasioned largely by religious division, albeit with a significant amount of geopolitical calculation mixed in, the First World War was justified and sustained primarily by nationalist fervor. It ushered in an era often referred to as a second Thirty Years War (plus one, of course, since it ran from 1914–1945), which fundamentally transformed the material and mental landscape of Europe. As Hannah Arendt noted after the Second World War:

> It is almost impossible even now to describe what actually happened in Europe on August 4, 1914. The days before and the days after the First World War are separated not like the end and the beginning of a new period, but like the day before and the day after an explosion. Yet this figure of speech is as inaccurate as are all others, because the quiet of sorrow which settles down after a catastrophe has never come to pass. The first explosion seems to have touched off a chain reaction in which we have been caught ever since and which nobody seems to be able to stop.[87]

The proverbial fuse that ignited the explosion of which Arendt wrote was, of course, the assassination of the Austrian archduke Franz Ferdinand on July 28, 1914. He and his wife Sophie were on a tour of the Habsburg provinces and made a state visit to the Bosnian capital Sarajevo, where a cadre of student members of "Young Bosnia," a pan-Slavic group with ties to the larger Black Hand organization, had organized an assassination plot. Following a state reception, the couple rode in an open limousine through the streets of the city, despite the fact that authorities knew that a plot of some nature was afoot. After a confusing detour along the driving route, the limousine came to a stop directly in front of the nineteen-year-old Gavrilo Princip, one of the Young Bosnia plotters, who stepped forward and shot Franz Ferdinand and Sophie at point blank range.[88] The archduke, who had been next in line for the throne, advocated a form of Slav autonomy within the empire which, if implemented, might have diminished the groundswell of disaffection the activists of Young Bosnia and the Black Hand hoped to instrumentalize to bring about full pan-Slavic union under Serbian domination.[89] So the choice to kill Franz Ferdinand was not simply symbolic. The Serb military conspirator Dragutin "Apis" Dimitrijević had helped orchestrate the plot, along with agents within the security services, but the exact nature and extent of Serbian government involvement remains disputed.

The assassination might have remained merely a localized tragedy, but the Austrian foreign minister Leopold von Berchtold decided to use the occasion to push for punitive measures against Serbia in the ultimate hope of strengthening Austria's position in the Balkans.[90] In early July, Wilhelm II and officials within the German foreign ministry informed Berchtold that Germany would offer full military support to Austria should its harsh response to Serbia lead to war (this assurance became known as the German "blank check").[91] Bolstered by this support, Austria issued its infamous ultimatum to Serbia on July 23. The ultimatum was essentially designed to be unacceptable to the Serbs—requiring as it did the virtual abrogation of Serbian sovereignty by demanding that the files of its security services be opened to a foreign power—and when Serbian authorities delayed in answering, Austrian troops mobilized. The official declaration of war was delivered on July 28, and Austrian forces began shelling Belgrade the next day. Within the context of the European alliance network, events unfolded quickly in a sort of domino effect, leading to war by the first week of August. Russia, coming to the aid of its Slavic cousin Serbia, mobilized against Austria-Hungary, France announced that it would mobilize in support of its alliance obligations to Russia, and the British remained mysteriously guarded, although foreign secretary Edward Grey did pledge Britain to defend the territorial neutrality of Belgium.[92] The Germans, having pledged support to Austria-Hungary, launched a preemptive invasion of France by going through Belgian territory, forcing Britain's hand.[93] So by August 4, 1914, much of Europe was at war, with Germany and Austria-Hungary facing enemies to the east (Russia), south (Serbia), and west (Britain and France).

In the major cities of the belligerent nation-states, euphoric demonstrations broke out in the first week of August. In Germany in particular, the war seemed to many to be the longed-for opportunity to demonstrate national superiority and virility. The sense of belonging and purpose cultivated in those early August days—when Germans from varying social and political backgrounds joined together on streets, sidewalks, and squares, singing national hymns arm in arm—felt to those who experienced them like the ultimate culmination of the internal unification process that had begun in a geographical sense in 1871.[94] While recent research has shown the limitations of this image of euphoria, especially in rural regions, the memory of those August days, however distorted, came to elicit a powerful sense of

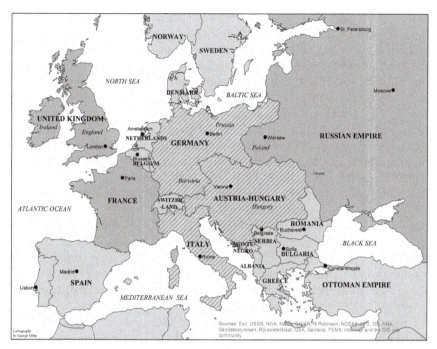

MAP 5.1 Europe in 1914. © *George Edward Milne, 2017. Reproduced with permission.*

longing after the war, when German society seemed so hopelessly divided.[95] In France, the outspoken antimilitarist Jean Jaurès, who had opposed the move toward war, was murdered in a Parisian café on July 31, 1914. The memory of his anti-war message, however, was quickly transformed by the wave of nationalistic war fervor that swept through the French capital in the early days of August. By the time of his public funeral, which was pitched as a unifying event for all Frenchmen on August 4, even Jaurès himself had become a screen onto which a variety of nationalistic sentiments could be projected—sentiments he himself would not have supported. Upon word of mobilization against Germany, cafes and restaurants stayed open late into the night playing endless renditions of the *Marseillaise*, as well as the British and Russian anthems.[96] In London, the Labour leader Keir Hardie organized a large peace demonstration on Trafalgar Square on August 2, but its influence was eclipsed almost entirely by the much more boisterous pro-war rally held in the same location two days later.[97] On virtually all sides, the belligerents expected the war to be glorious and brief, envisioning the masses of soldiers returning home victorious before the end of the year.

The Schlieffen Plan, which the German General Staff had devised to deal with the prospect of a two-front war, was implemented ineptly in many ways. It was predicated on the idea that Russia, while possessing vast manpower and material resources, would take several weeks to fully mobilize, giving the Germans a window of time in which to defeat France before turning to face Russia. The Belgians put up more resistance than had been anticipated, the British Expeditionary Force arrived in France earlier than expected, and the Russians mobilized with surprising speed, engaging the German forces in the Battle of Tannenberg already by late August. The latter battle was a complete disaster for the Russians, however, with the commanding general Samsonov committing suicide in shame on August 30. For Germany the battle was especially significant because it was fought near the site of the 1410 Battle of Tannenberg, in which Polish-Lithuanian forces had defeated the Teutonic Knights, making victory in 1914 a form of (belated) cosmic rectification.[98] The battle also witnessed the emergence of two military leaders who would be central figures both in the German war effort and in German politics after the war—Paul von Hindenburg, the commander of German forces in the east, and his Quartermaster-General Erich Ludendorff.[99] In addition to the heroic imagery surrounding the German victory at Tannenberg, in the west the German forces had advanced to within thirty miles of Paris. Despite the glitches in the Schlieffen Plan's implementation, it seemed that Germany might indeed reach Paris and end the war within its first few weeks. The German advance, however, was slowed and ultimately halted in the First Battle of the Marne between September 5 and 12, in which a massive (albeit possibly fabricated) logistical feat was undertaken as hundreds of Parisian taxis were mobilized to transport soldiers to the front. Regardless of the extent to which the account is true, the German advance was indeed halted, the Renault taxis themselves became known as "Taxis of the Marne," and the French public derived a powerful sense of participatory belonging that paralleled the political truce called across the party spectrum in support of the nation at war.[100] The official name given to this political arrangement, the *union sacrée*, or "sacred union," gives a sense of the sacral nature of national mobilization in 1914.[101]

The First Battle of the Marne, and the so-called race to the sea that followed it, resulted in a stabilized battle front that ultimately ran for more than 400 miles, from northern France to the Swiss border. On either side of the front, opposing troops were forced by the merciless brutality of enemy machine gun batteries to dig underground trenches that developed into vast networks. Trench warfare presented almost unique dangers, both physically and psychologically.[102] Rather than having the chance to demonstrate "masculine" prowess on the battlefield, as many soldiers had anticipated, men were forced to cower in the trenches, hoping that an enemy shell did not fall on them and praying not to be ordered to go "over the top" to storm the opposing trench positions, which required one to proceed through the no-man's-land between the trenches that was often mined, reinforced with barbed wire, and regularly strafed with enemy machine gun fire. Running headlong into that kind of fire was like facing, in Ernst Jünger's famous phrase, a "storm of steel."[103] But life in the trenches during lulls in the fighting was also miserable. The earliest trenches that had been dug through fields in the countryside filled quickly with unsuspecting frogs, field mice, and other critters who hopped or fell into the trenches and were unable to get out and thus seemed constantly to be under foot. The earliest trenches also often had communications cables simply tacked to the walls of the trenches, sliding and falling under foot with the inevitable shifting of dirt and mud (eventually, separate communications trenches were constructed). The trenches also filled with water, forcing soldiers to deal with the painful ulcers, fungal infections, and tissue decay associated with "trench foot." Added to this were the disfiguring wounds and dismembered corpses that became a regular feature of the soldier's visual landscape.[104]

As the stalemate continued throughout 1915 on the western front, the opposing generals continually looked for the elusive breakthrough, and millions of young men were sent to their deaths in this futile search. The death toll in the battles of the Somme and Verdun in 1916 was so catastrophic that most Europeans simply did not possess the mental categories with which to process and make sense of the numbers.[105] War weariness set in on the home front in virtually all combatant countries, as nearly every family in those nations had at least one family member in uniform. As hunger and hardship spread, the national euphoria of 1914 became a distant memory. One way of tracing the discrepancy between idealized visions of national sacrifice and the reality of combat is to examine the writings of soldiers themselves, many of whom had volunteered enthusiastically and full of zeal for the national cause. The case of Rupert Brooke, the English poet, has been studied in particular detail.[106] The German literature professor Philipp Witkop assembled a large collection of war letters from German university students who died in combat, as seen in the excerpts below.

EXCERPT 5.4

German Students' War Letters

Philipp Witkop, editor

WALTER LIMMER, Student of Law, Leipzig

Born August 22nd, 1890, at Thiergarten, near Plauen in Vogtland.
Died September 24th, 1914, of wounds received September 16th, near Chalons-sur-Marne.

Leipzig, August 7th, 1914.

(*In the train*): Our march to the station was a gripping and uplifting experience! Such a march is hallowed by its background of significance and danger. Both those who were leaving and those who remained behind were beset by the same thoughts and feelings. It seemed as if one lived through as much in that hour as ordinarily in months and years. Such enthusiasm! The whole battalion with helmets and tunics decked with flowers—handkerchiefs waving untiringly—cheers on every side—and over and over again the ever fresh and wonderful reassurance from the soldiers: "*fest steht und treu die Wacht am Rhein!*" This hour is one such as seldom strikes in the life of a nation, and it is so marvellous and moving as to be in itself sufficient compensation for many sufferings and sacrifices.

South of Chalons, September 9th, 1914.

This ghastly battle is still raging—for the fourth day! Up till now, like most battles in this war, it has consisted almost entirely of an appalling artillery duel. I am writing this letter in a sort of grave-like hole which I dug for myself in the firing line. The shells are falling so thick today, both before and behind us, that one may regard it as only thanks to the special mercy of God if one comes out of it safe and sound.

Attigny, September 20th, 1914.

My dear, good parents and brothers and sisters—Yes, I can hardly believe it myself, but it's true: I am on my way to you and home. Oh, how happy I am to see a brighter world again, instead of that world of horror! At last I am free from that secret dread which always haunted me, that I should never see you and your world again, for Fate has presented me with the hope that, unless some unforeseen obstacle should arise, I shall look into your dear eyes once more. [Four days later he died of tetanus in the Military Hospital at Luxemburg.]

FRANZ BLUMENFELD, Student of Law, Freiburg

Born September 26th, 1891, at Hamburg.
Killed December 18th, 1914, near Contalmaison.

In the train, September 24th, 1914.

My dear, good, precious Mother, I certainly believe and hope that I shall come back from the war, but just in case I do not I am going to write you a farewell letter. I want you to know that if I am killed, I give my life gladly and willingly. My life has been so beautiful that I could not wish that anything in it had been different. [...]

Then I want to write to you about something else, which, judging from bits in your letters, you haven't quite understood: why I should have volunteered for the war? Of course it was not from any enthusiasm for war in general, nor because I thought it would be a fine thing to kill a great many people or otherwise distinguish myself. On the contrary, I think that war is a very, very evil thing, and I believe that even in this case it might have been averted by a more skillful diplomacy. But, now that it has been declared, I think it is a matter of course that one should feel oneself so much a member of the nation that one must unite one's fate as closely as possible with that of the whole. And even if I were convinced that I could serve my Fatherland and its people better in peace than in war, I should think it just as perverse and impossible to let any such calculations weigh with me at the present moment as it would be for a man going to the assistance of somebody who was drowning, to stop to consider who the drowning man was and whether his own life were not perhaps the more valuable of the two. For what counts is always the readiness to make a sacrifice, not the object for which the sacrifice is made.

This war seems to me, from all that I have heard, to be something so horrible, inhuman, mad, obsolete, and in every way depraving, that I have firmly resolved, if I do come back, to do everything in my power to prevent such a thing from ever happening again in the future...

HELMUT ZSCHUPPE, Student of Philosophy, Leipzig

Born December 29th, 1897, in Vienna.
Killed September 18th, 1917, near Maronviller (La Neuville).

Military Hospital, Rethel, September 10th, 1917.

I have reported fit for service. I am restless. I hate the kitchen table at which I am writing. I lose patience over a book. I should like to push the landscape aside as if it irritated me. I must get to the Front. I must again hear the shells roaring up into the sky and the desolate valley echoing the sound. I must get back to my Company. They are all now very much reduced in strength; and, worn out and over-tired, have to be on guard the whole time in the Front line. I must get back into touch with the enemy. I know far too well what the danger is, but I must live once more in the realm of death...

September 14th, 1917.

Yesterday the Iron Cross of the Second Class was sent to me. The pleasure this gave me was some small compensation. Tomorrow I start back to the Company. Today I am in the Convalescent Section getting ready. Well, and what now? When one thing is over one begins to ask, what next? I wait for what fate may bring; am low-spirited, pale, and love the dusk. It seems as if many sleepless nights had made one ultra-sensitive.

When I was left alone for a few minutes with the Cross, I had quite different thoughts from those that were in my mind before. It seemed as if the Cross were made of shell splinters—black blood congealed on a yellowish dead face with open mouth—bandages encrusted with pus—the strangled cries of hoarse voices—flaccid, gangrened flesh on the stump of a leg.

But all that shall not make me hold back! And I am comforted by the thought of your prayers and your love.[107]

Aside from shifting individual attitudes like those we see in the students' letters, several key broader developments emerged during the middle years of the war that had a decisive impact on European nationalism well into the interwar era. In Turkey, which had entered the war on the side of the Central Powers, a set of genocidal policies against the Armenian minority was implemented starting in 1915.[108] The background to the genocide lies in the 1908 coup launched by the Young Turk movement, which rebelled against the absolutist rule of Sultan Abdul Hamid II, deposing him and launching a modernization program in an attempt to halt the steady deterioration of the Ottoman Empire.[109] Many within the Young Turk movement styled themselves as modern Western-oriented nationalists, and their ideology embraced varying degrees of exclusionary nationalism borrowed in part from European sources.[110] The Armenians, primarily Christian, had lived for centuries in territory that came to straddle the border between Russia and the Ottoman Empire, and their perceived pro-Russian sympathies made them special targets for nationalist persecution once the Turks entered the war against Russia. Beginning in April 1915, brutal deportations of Armenian communities were launched, and over the ensuing three years approximately one million Armenians died as a result of starvation, exposure during death marches, disease, beatings, and mass shootings.[111] The tragedy of the Armenians is generally considered the first modern genocide; in fact, the term "genocide" itself was coined in 1944 by Rafael Lemkin, a Polish-Jewish human rights lawyer who emigrated to the United States in 1941, largely in reference to the fate of the Armenians during the First World War.[112]

In an unrelated yet significant development, on April 26, 1915, just two days after the first Armenian deportations, a secret agreement was arranged between Britain and Italy that paved the way for Italy's entrance into the war on the side of the Entente powers. Italy had been a member of the Triple Alliance with Germany and Austria-Hungary, but had remained neutral since the outbreak of the war, and its entry in 1915 on the opposite side of the ledger was occasioned in part by domestic pressures and, especially, by the desire to gain the irredentist regions of Istria, Trieste, and Dalmatia—Austrian possessions that the British promised to grant Italy in return for its war support.[113] By entering the war in this way, Italy helped the Entente effort by assuming much of the burden of fighting in the south, particularly against Austro-Hungarian forces in the Alps.[114] Importantly, the irredentist aspirations that drew Italy into the war would also shape Italian attitudes after the war, when the British territorial promises suddenly evaporated, leading nationalists (and ultimately fascists) to rail against the illegitimacy of the postwar settlement.

The year 1916 witnessed dramatic developments among Irish nationalists, who used the context of war to stage an uprising for independence. Since the Young Irelander Revolt in 1848, Irish nationalism had proceeded along both political and clandestine channels. Within the former category, the

Home Rule League was founded in 1873 as an alliance of Irish nationalists in the British parliament, advocating for autonomous self-government within (but not outright independence from) the British Empire.[115] By 1880, the dominant figure within the League was Charles Stewart Parnell, and his influence continued after the League changed its name to the Irish Parliamentary Party in 1882.[116] It was Parnell who was largely responsible for the introduction of the First Home Rule Bill in parliament, which was a significant development even though it was defeated.[117] After the death of Parnell in 1891, attempts to get a Home Rule Bill passed in parliament continued, both in 1893 and again between 1911 and 1914, at which point home rule was passed but never implemented due to the interruption of the war.[118] Irish nationalist activism on a clandestine level was considerably more radical. In 1858, the Irish Republican Brotherhood (IRB) was founded as a secretive pressure group with clear militaristic overtones, participating in armed struggles over agrarian land reform in the 1870s and 1880s.[119] In 1883, a related group calling itself the "Irish National Invincibles" famously assassinated the British chief secretary in Ireland, Frederick Cavendish, and his under-secretary Thomas Burke in what became known as the Phoenix Park murders.[120] In 1905, elements from the IRB were central to the founding of the *Sinn Féin* party under Arthur Griffith, which advocated complete republican independence for Ireland.[121] In 1912, in the context of the Third Home Rule debate, unionists in Ulster formed a paramilitary organization, the Ulster Volunteers, in an attempt to prevent the implementation of home rule. In response, activists from the IRB formed the "Irish Volunteers" to fight, if necessary, unionist attempts to block home rule. With the outbreak of the war in the summer of 1914, tensions within the Irish Volunteers came to a head over the issue of participation in the all-volunteer New British Army being mustered by Lord Kitchener, the British war secretary. Moderate nationalists and parliamentarians like John Redmond, the head of the Irish Parliamentary Party that had championed the Third Home Rule Bill, openly advocated for Irish Volunteer forces to join the British forces. When radical elements refused, Redmond organized the National Volunteers, who went on to play an important role in the British war effort.[122] Radicals and militants within the IRB who viewed Redmond's support for Britain as a traitorous act began looking for an opportunity to launch a revolt under cover of war.

The opportunity materialized in early 1916. Roger Casement, an Anglo-Irish diplomat who had compiled an impressive record as a champion of human rights before transforming himself into a revolutionary, began consultations with German agents over the possibility of gaining German military and financial support for an Irish uprising that would, it was hoped, help cripple the British war effort. A small cell within the IRB—led by Patrick Pearse, Tom Clarke, James Connolly, and Seán Mac Diarmada—worked to recruit and organize domestically, while Casement was underground in Germany. On April 21, the Royal Navy intercepted a German steamship disguised as a Norwegian merchant vessel carrying a huge cache of arms for delivery to the rebels, and Roger Casement was captured the same day after having been transported secretly to the British Isles in a German submarine. Nevertheless, Pearse and the other conspirators made the decision to proceed with the planned uprising, which was launched on Easter Monday, April 24, 1916. Rather than attacking military targets, the rebels seized public buildings in Dublin and held out against British forces for six days before ultimately surrendering. The ringleaders were executed and the total death toll from the fighting numbered around 500.[123] More important than the event itself was the role it came to play in Irish national memory. Patrick Pearse's death in particular was portrayed as a salvific act of selflessness on behalf of the nation, an iconic martyrdom driven by idealistic conceptions of "blood sacrifice, redemptive violence, chiliastic expectation, and Irish national identity."[124] The memory of the Rising would echo powerfully throughout the turbulent developments of the early 1920s.

In 1917, the war's international configuration began a new phase with the entrance of the United States and the withdrawal of Russia. Woodrow Wilson had been reelected U.S. president in 1916 on a promise to keep the United States out of the war in Europe, but a rising groundswell of anti-German popular opinion made that position increasingly untenable. The groundswell had been created in large part by disastrous German public relations blunders, including the sinking of the passenger liner *Lusitania* in May 1915 and the interception and publication of the so-called Zimmermann Telegram.[125] The United States entered the war on the side of the Entente in April 1917. The Russian exit from the war was the result of two successive revolutions that same year. The February Revolution (March on the Western calendar) came on the heels of chronic tensions due to the Russian military's poor performance on the battlefield, growing war weariness, and a series of strikes and economic disruptions. Beginning in the capital Petrograd on March 10, the revolution quickly swept Tsar Nicholas and his family from power, confining them to house arrest, while a provisional government was established initially under Georgi Lvov and then, in July, under Alexander Kerensky. Both Lvov and Kerensky kept Russia in the war, whereas Lenin and the Bolsheviks agitated for an end to the war. In October (early November), largely through the organizational skill of Leon Trotsky, the Bolsheviks launched a new revolution and succeeded in taking control of the city of Petrograd and the levers of government, bringing Lenin to power. Lenin's initial position was precarious, and his primary concern was to address food shortages and, most importantly, to take Russia out of the war. Russian troops suspended most of their military activities in mid-December, and in March 1918, the Treaty of Brest-Litovsk, which ceded to Germany a massive amount of territory in eastern Europe and the Baltics, officially ended the war for Russia.

The Russian withdrawal allowed the German military to redirect the bulk of its energies to the western front, in the hope of breaking up the stalemate that had continued since the fall of 1914. The result was the

Spring Offensive, launched in March 1918, in which German forces drove the British and French from their defensive positions across broad portions of the front, gaining the largest amounts of new territory since the stalemate set in. Throughout the spring and into the summer, the German populace was fed a steady diet of propaganda indicating that the end of the war was (finally) imminent, that after all the sacrifice and hardship the German nation was on the verge of a glorious military triumph.[126] In reality, the German advance had outpaced its supply lines, and the taking of British and French positions had actually exercised a strange demoralizing effect on German troops, as they realized how well-provisioned the enemy was in comparison with their own meager supplies. The influence of the United States, which had initially been limited to material provisions, began to be seen on the battlefield. Not only was the German advance halted, but the Entente forces embarked on a string of striking victories in the late summer known as the Hundred Days campaign.[127] By late September 1918, the German military leadership had advised the Kaiser and his ministers of the need to send out provisional peace feelers. The idea was that, since Germany was still controlling significant enemy territory and there were no foreign troops on German soil, a swift transition to peace talks would put Germany in a position of strength. But the Entente powers would only agree to negotiate if fundamental political reforms were initiated, which led to the appointment in early October of a new government under the moderate Max von Baden.[128] Hostilities continued as these initial moves were made, even as many of Germany's military allies melted away.

In late October, German sailors in the northern port city of Kiel mutinied. This led rapidly to a series of similar mutinies among naval and army personnel throughout Germany, as well as massive strikes in German industrial centers. A wave of political revolution advanced steadily through the early days of November, reaching Berlin on November 9, 1918, and forcing Kaiser Wilhelm II, that self-important paragon of bombast, to abdicate meekly, leaving the city in secrecy for exile in the Netherlands. That night a Republic was declared by the Social Democratic politician Philipp Scheidemann, and a provisional government under his colleague Friedrich Ebert was formed. Concerned about the possibility of the situation radicalizing and spinning out of control like the French Revolution, Ebert's primary concern was to stabilize his government. So on November 10, he made a pact with Wilhelm Groener, the general staff officer in charge of military supply and personnel, in which Ebert implicitly agreed to shield the military from revolutionary reform in exchange for military protection. The Ebert-Groener Pact, as it is known, has often been criticized for crippling the revolution from its inception by ensuring that perhaps the most reactionary and intransigent component of state was allowed to continue essentially unaltered by the political waves swirling around it. Even more importantly, though, on the following day—at 11:11 a.m. on November 11—the armistice that halted the fighting was signed in a railway car in the French forest of Compiègne by a German delegation led by the Center Party politician Matthias Erzberger. The war was officially over, and Germany was the acknowledged loser.

Problematically, however, the German people were left angry, disillusioned and, above all, confused by the outcome of the war. They had been told for months earlier in the year that they were on the verge of victory, and the fact that Germany still occupied enemy soil while its own territorial integrity was intact seemed to reinforce that perception. The unacknowledged truth was that German forces had in fact been driven back and defeated in a series of battles in the late summer, that their manpower reserves and morale had been dwindling rapidly, and, ultimately, that the revolutionary chaos on the home front made it impossible for Germany to continue fighting. Germany did indeed lose the war. But the combination of confusion and willful blindness led to the search for alternative explanations, and the myth of the "stab-in-the-back" was born. The myth allowed for the fantasy of German national superiority to remain intact by blaming the war's end on cowardly politicians in Berlin who, manipulated by nefarious (perhaps Jewish) interests behind the scenes, had pulled the plug on the war prematurely, abandoning the valiant military, which had been "undefeated in the field," as the common phrase went.[129] Disillusion and division thus characterized the birth of the democratic system that was to govern Germany for the next fourteen years. Elections to the constituent assembly in Weimar were held in January 1919—the first elections conducted under universal suffrage, with men and women going to the polls—and the Weimar constitution was cobbled together over the next several months. Although the Jewish identity of the chief author of the constitution, Hugo Preuss, would be used by racist nationalists to try to taint the entire document, the constitution itself was remarkably democratic and forward-looking. When it was signed into law on August 11, 1919, by Friedrich Ebert, who assumed the role of the Weimar Republic's first president, it was in many ways overshadowed by the outrage and controversy surrounding the Treaty of Versailles, which had been completed at the Paris Peace Conference only a few weeks earlier.

The new world (dis)order

The Paris Peace Conference convened in the Palace of Versailles on January 18, 1919, almost exactly 130 years after the official call was issued to summon the Estates-General to Versailles in January 1789. The more salient comparison, however, is with the Congress of Vienna, which established both a repressive order opposed to the "modern" forces of nationalism and liberalism and, it must be said, a framework for European stability that lasted decades.[130] The Paris conference and the treaties it produced were intended to create a much different "new world order" following the devastation of continental war: forward-looking and modern, free and democratic, and constructed along the lines of national self-determination.[131]

The result, however, was a catastrophic escalation of instability within an unruly new Europe of fledgling nation-states, redrawn boundaries, and displaced individuals and ethnic minorities. The mess created by the postwar settlement did not make the Second World War inevitable; but it did greatly increase the likelihood that another major conflict would emerge in the near future, as disaffected actors challenged and contested the new arrangement with increasing vehemence. Nationalist ideals would be at the heart of that contestation.

The failures of the Paris proceedings did not result from a lack of imagination. Before the opening of the conference, most expected the intellectual tone to be set by the Fourteen Points promulgated by Woodrow Wilson in January 1918. One year later, however, Wilson's even-handedness seemed to many to be an outdated relic of a bygone era, and the French were insistent on using the peace settlement not only to punish German aggression, but also to ensure that their neighbors to the east were unable to continue the pattern of geopolitical bullying established initially at France's expense in 1870. Although the conference was attended by officials from more than thirty countries, the major players were the United States, Britain, France, and Italy (although Italy was essentially marginalized in practice). The overarching purpose of the conference was to establish treaties with all of the defeated Central Powers, taking the form of the Treaty of Saint-Germain with Austria; the Treaty of Neuilly with Bulgaria; the Treaty of Trianon with newly independent Hungary; and the Treaty of Sèvres with Turkey, which was emerging from the collapsed Ottoman Empire. But the Treaty of Versailles with Germany received the most attention, then as now. The treaty's various clauses and paragraphs can be grouped into four broad themes. In a territorial sense, Germany was stripped of approximately 10 percent of its land and population, including all of its overseas colonies. In provisions that were supposed to be part of a broader disarmament policy across Europe, the German military was reduced significantly, with its submarine fleet and air force being dismantled entirely, with naval equipment and weaponry being scuttled, and with the overall size of the military reduced to a token force of 100,000 men. Morally, the treaty established German responsibility for the massive material and human losses of the war, enshrined in the infamous Article 231, known as the "war guilt" clause.[132] And if Germany could be held responsible morally, it could certainly be held responsible financially, and an initially unspecified amount of monetary reparations was written into the treaty.[133]

A German delegation was present at the conference, but was not consulted or allowed to participate in deliberations. When the treaty was completed in June 1919, the German delegation was simply forced to sign. Outrage in Germany was paralleled, albeit much less emotionally, by a number of international participants in the conference who were skeptical about the impact of the harsh treatment of Germany. The economist John Maynard Keynes, who was present as part of the British delegation, published a best-selling book just weeks after the completion of the treaty entitled *The Economic Consequences of the Peace*, in which he predicted that the Carthaginian nature of Germany's treatment would lead to instability not only in Germany but in all of Europe. Later events were to prove him correct on a number of levels.

* * * *

The war and its aftermath not only transformed the political and geographic landscape of Europe, but had a dramatic impact on ways of conceiving identity, both individual and national, and on broader conceptions of belonging. The reality of the machine gun and the nature of trench warfare, which removed virtually all opportunities for battlefield prowess, led to what a number of observers termed a "crisis of masculinity." Recent scholarship has demonstrated clearly that masculinity cannot be seen as a monolithic entity; at virtually every point, there is some form of contestation between hegemonic and alternative forms of masculine comportment, making it more accurate to speak of "masculinities."[134] While it is also true that masculine identities seem always, in some way, to be in crisis, the immediate postwar years were in fact particularly complicated for European men. Jason Crouthamel has provided a nuanced account of the disillusionment that set in when returning German soldiers, who had experienced new sexual freedoms while in uniform, were forced to deal with the restrictions and norms of civilian life.[135] As Jessica Meyer has shown, disabled war veterans in Britain had particular difficulties transitioning to "domestic masculinity," especially when their injuries prevented them from engaging in the occupations that had helped constitute their public identities before the war.[136] Carol Poore and Heather Perry have documented similar struggles in Germany, as has Deborah Cohen in her comparative study of interwar Britain and Germany.[137] Beyond the challenges of physical injury, large numbers of men were, for the first time, diagnosed with shell shock, whose manifestations ranged from night terrors to sexual dysfunction; it is telling that these symptoms were often referred to as "male hysteria."[138] Of course, no one actually believed that the war had somehow led to male possession of a uterus, but the reference to hysteria (from the Greek root *hysterikos*, or "of the womb"), gives insight into the extent to which the war was seen as having fundamentally altered men and their identities. Ultimately, to understand the extreme articulations of nationalist discourse in the interwar period, which were often pitched in a hyper-masculinistic key, this background must be kept in mind.

The war also occasioned massive shifts in conceptualizing the relationship between individual citizens and the nation-state and its agencies. During the war, state intervention into the lives of citizens reached unprecedented proportions. The war economy established in Germany under Hindenburg and Ludendorff in 1916 is but the most easily identifiable example.[139] In all belligerent countries citizens had their lives uprooted in various ways. The involvement of the home front in the war effort—the central element that made this the first "total war"—brought with it changed political expectations in the postwar years. Millions of Europeans were enfranchised for the first time, especially women, and the new states that were constructed were democracies of some stripe. But as the next chapter illustrates, the search for Liberal democratic forms of belonging in the interwar era was anything but smooth. Many of the new democracies, and some of the older ones as well, were either taken over by authoritarian regimes or voluntarily used their democratic freedoms to vote democracy out of existence.

6

Nationalism and the Politics of Belonging in an Age of Extremes, 1920–1945

The League of Nations held its first deliberations on January 16, 1920, having begun its official life six days earlier when the provisions of the Treaty of Versailles came into force. The League, which ultimately came to include sixty-one member states, lasted for a quarter century and served as the central precursor to the United Nations founded in 1945.[1] Its stated purpose, as outlined in its founding covenant, was global—"to promote international cooperation and to achieve international peace and security"—but its overwhelming focus was on maintaining stability specifically in Europe.[2] In practice, this meant wrestling with the messy nationalist implications of the postwar settlement: what to do about millions of displaced persons and ethnic minorities left unmoored by the collapse of major European empires; how to respond to persistent border challenges occasioned by the creation of new nation-states; and, perhaps most importantly, how to foster forms of belonging built on democratic and inclusive ideals. Although the League had been proposed by Woodrow Wilson as part of his fourteen-point program, the U.S. Senate refused to ratify the organization's covenant in 1919 and the United States ultimately never joined. Within Europe itself, the two most notable absences during the League's earliest years were Germany and the fledgling Soviet Union, the two powers who would come to epitomize the dramatic political polarization of Europe in the years leading up to the Second World War. Caught between the extremes of interwar fascism and communism, the League and its two most influential members, Britain and France, would struggle to maintain a political order based on Liberal parliamentarism and supranational cooperation. It was to be largely a losing battle, at least in the short term. From the perspective of the early 1940s, when the German and Soviet titans began their epic military clash, it seemed that visions of a Liberal polity based on individual rights were destined for conquest at the hand of rival collectivist notions of belonging.

The search for Liberal democratic visions of belonging

A central element of the League's approach to resolving the lingering aftereffects of war was the creation of a High Commission for Refugees, headed by the Norwegian explorer Fridtjof Nansen and charged with a variety of tasks including, initially, the repatriation of prisoners of war. Nansen was in many ways the ideal candidate for this position, and his personal biography is particularly revealing. Following his famous expedition to the North Pole in the 1890s, Nansen had emerged as a central advocate of Norwegian nationalism, pushing for the end of the union with Sweden and using his considerable influence to help convince the Danish prince Carl to take the throne of an independent Norway in 1905.[3] The impassioned independence appeal he published in book form that year garnered worldwide attention and was translated into numerous languages almost immediately upon its appearance.[4] In the ensuing years, Nansen served as a Norwegian diplomat in London and was an energetic supporter of Norwegian neutrality during the First World War. In response to the carnage of war, which he saw as the inevitable outgrowth of exclusionary nationalism, Nansen envisioned a new form of humanitarian belonging within which the interests of individual nation-states would be aligned in the common pursuit of amity and reconciliation.[5] This fit perfectly with the ideals enshrined in the League of Nations covenant. In his first year as the League's high commissioner for refugees, he presided over the return of nearly half a million prisoners from military captivity, and in subsequent years his *Nansenhilfe* (Nansen-Aid) project orchestrated the provision of food and supplies to hundreds of thousands of people displaced by the civil war in Russia. He also established the so-called Nansen passports, providing legal documentation and the ability to travel and establish domicile for thousands of Europeans who had become stateless in the war's aftermath. The initial title for these documents—intergovernmental "identity certificates"—is indicative of the broader goal of Nansen and his supporters to create new forms of identity and belonging on the basis of supranational cooperation.[6]

The Western democracies, which played key roles within the League of Nations, had come through the war with their nation-state infrastructures largely intact, unlike the situation in Central, Eastern, and Southern Europe. A fairly significant number of Western Europeans concluded, like Nansen, that virulent nationalism had been discredited by its association with the mass carnage of war, and gravitated increasingly toward various forms of internationalism and pacifism. Mona Siegel has referred to this process in interwar France as a kind of "moral disarmament."[7] The pacifist movement in France was quite socially diverse, ranging from human rights advocates to more militant "integral" pacifists to radical feminists.[8] Catholic leftists in France also developed a strong pacifist tradition, a spiritual "disarmament of hatred," under the leadership of Marc Sangnier.[9] Belgium gained a worldwide reputation as a leader in international understanding during the interwar years, as the "chosen land of cosmopolitan assemblies."[10] Interwar Britain, for its part, manifested what Martin Ceadel has called "the most interesting and influential pacifist movement in modern times," developing along three central trajectories: humanitarian, religious, and sociopolitical.[11] The leading role played by British pacifists, whom Ceadel labels "semi-detached idealists," was the result, at least in part, of the relative security offered by Britain's geographic isolation from the continent.[12] But at the same time, in Britain and France in particular, the conservative governments that came to the fore in the immediate aftermath of the war continued to cultivate nationalist visions of belonging.

After the war, British Liberal prime minister David Lloyd George, who had come to power in 1916, continued on in that position as head of a coalition government, but it was the conservative majority in the House of Commons that increasingly set the tone. In 1922, Lloyd George was forced out in the context of the Irish civil war, which will be discussed later in this chapter, and he was replaced by Andrew Bonar Law, head of the Conservative Party and one of the chief opponents of Irish home rule. With the exception of the brief Labour interlude in 1924 under Ramsay MacDonald (the first socialist prime minister in Europe), the Conservatives were to hold power throughout the remainder of the decade under Stanley Baldwin. Although MacDonald headed another Labour government starting in 1929, by 1931, he allowed himself to be maneuvered into forming the so-called National Government—a coalition with MacDonald as prime minister but dominated in reality by Baldwin and the Conservatives. When MacDonald stepped down due to health problems in 1935, Baldwin continued on as prime minister until 1937, at which point Neville Chamberlain and then Winston Churchill continued the run of Tory dominance. In May 1924, during his first ministry, Baldwin gave a striking speech to the Royal Society of St. George, in which he rooted his vision of English identity in the pastoral countryside.

EXCERPT 6.1

On England

Stanley Baldwin

The Englishman is all right as long as he is content to be what God made him, an Englishman, but gets into trouble when he tries to be something else. There are chroniclers, or were chronicles, who said it was the aping of the French manners by our English ancestors that made us the prey William the Norman, and led to our defeat at Hastings. Let that be a warning to us not to ape any foreign country. Let us be content to trust and be ourselves. [...] To me, England is the country, and the country is England. And when I ask myself what I mean by England, when I think of England when I am abroad, England comes to me through my various senses—through the ear, through the eye, and through certain imperishable scents. I will tell you what they are, and there may be those among you who feel as I do.

The sounds of England, the tinkle of hammer on anvil in the country smithy, the corncrake on a dewey morning, the sound of the scythe against the whetstone, and the sight of a plough team coming over the brow of a hill, the sight that has been in England since England was a land, and may be seen in England long after the Empire has perished and every works in England has ceased to function, for centuries the one eternal sight of England. The wild anemonies in the woods of April, the last load at night of hay being drawn down a lane as the twilight comes on, when you can scarcely distinguish the figures on the horses as they take it home to the farm, and above all, most subtle, most penetrating and most moving, the smell of wood smoke coming in an autumn evening, or the smell of the scutch fires: that wood smoke that our ancestors, tens of thousands of years ago, must have caught on the air when they were still nomads, and when they were still roaming the forests and the plains of the continent of Europe. These things strike down into the very depths of our nature, and touch chords that go back to the beginning of time and the human race, but they are chords that with every year of our life sound a deeper note in our innermost being. These are things that make England....

It may well be that these traits on which we pride ourselves, which we hope to show and try to show in our lives, may survive—survive among our people so long as they are a people—and I hope and believe this, that just as to-day more than fifteen centuries since the last of those great Roman legionaries left England, we still speak of the Roman character, so perhaps in the ten thousandth century, long after the Empires of this world as we know them have fallen and others have risen and fallen again, the men who are then on this earth may yet speak of those characteristics which we prize as the characteristics of the English, and that long after, maybe, the name of the country has passed away, wherever mean are honourable and upright and persevering, lovers of home, of their brethren, of justice and of humanity, the men in the world of that day may say, 'We still have among us the gifts of that great English race.'[13]

Conservative power in Britain was paralleled in France beginning with the first postwar election in 1919, when rightist elements came together in the Bloc National founded by Georges Clemenceau, Alexandre Millerand, and Paul Deschanel.[14] The members of the Bloc National came from a handful of right-leaning parties, whose members switched ministerial positions like a game of musical chairs. Clemenceau, who had served as prime minister in the later stages of the war and throughout the proceedings of the peace conference in Paris, stepped down in favor of Millerand in early 1920, whereas Deschanel, who succeeded Raymond Poincaré as French president for several months in 1920, descended increasingly into a morass of mental illness and was institutionalized that September before dying the following spring.[15] The nationalist and conservative majority in parliament was fairly secure, leading to its designation as the Chamber of the Blue Horizon, because of the preponderance of veterans' blue uniforms among the deputies.[16] When Raymond Poincaré formed a government in 1922, he turned increasingly to the politics of bellicosity, ordering French troops into Germany to occupy the Ruhr valley region in January 1923 to seize raw materials in place of the reparations not being paid by the government in Berlin.[17] An uproar erupted both internationally and internally over this act of aggression, and Poincaré was forced from power; in 1926, however, he returned to form the National Union ministry that governed France until 1929. In the course of the economic depression that ensued, a rapid succession of statesmen tried their hands at governing, including several on the political left, and French society became increasingly polarized. A near-breaking point was reached in early 1934 in the so-called Stavisky Affair, in which a French-Jewish financier, Alexandre Serge Stavisky, was tried for embezzlement but protected (or at least was perceived as being protected) by the government of Edouard Daladier, before dying in what was ruled a suicide but was shrouded in mystery. In response, the radical right in France mobilized with a vehemence perhaps not seen since the Dreyfus Affair of the 1890s, inciting riots and violent demonstrations that led, in one particularly chaotic demonstration on February 6, 1934, to eleven shooting deaths and, ultimately, the collapse of Daladier's government.[18] Eventually, however, the forces of the Left banded together to form the Popular Front that governed France, primarily under Leon Blum, starting in 1936. But, the polarization continued.

One way historians have traced the search for unifying conceptions of national belonging in the interwar Western democracies has been to examine the commemoration of war dead, with death and the meanings derived from it applied broadly as the glue that would, it was hoped, bind together the living members of the nation.[19] The memory and memorialization of the war brought about what Jay Winter has termed a "return of the sacred," as the nation was elevated to a position of divinity to help ensure that the massive number of deaths in war did not seem utterly meaningless in an increasingly secularized mental universe.[20] The primary vessels through which sublime meaning was bestowed by the nation upon those lost in the war were sacred national myths which, in the words of George Mosse,

> transcended death in war, giving a happy ending to war's drama: those who sacrificed their lives will be resurrected; indeed, they are already among

us. To fulfill this function the myth used the traditional Christian means of consolation, the belief in the death and resurrection of Christ.... The burial and commemoration of the war dead were analogous to the construction of a church for the nation, and the planning of such sacred spaces received much the same kind of attention as that given to the architecture of churches.

In the end, even war itself was redeemed through the discourse of the nation: "War was made sacred, an expression of the general will of the people."[21]

In Britain, these impulses were manifested clearly even before the war ended, as seen in the establishment of the War Graves Commission in 1917.[22] The year 1917 also witnessed the founding of the Imperial War Museum, although it did not open fully to the public until 1920.[23] The museum's initial home was London's Crystal Palace, which some seventy years earlier had witnessed the intense (peaceful) competition between nation-states in the first Great Exhibition; its memorialization of the First World War, however, has been characterized aptly as the commemoration of "man's greatest lunatic folly."[24] For many, even the material culture of war itself came to generate metaphysical meaning, as the objects enshrined in the museum's exhibition spaces took on the contours of "sacred relics."[25] The first Armistice Day celebration began in London on the night of November 10, 1919, and built toward the armistice hour at 11:11 a.m. the following morning; over the ensuing decades, these occasions were widely replicated on the local and neighborhood level and became communal events of religio-national significance.[26] The phenomenon of "battlefield tourism" emerged in these years as a form of holy pilgrimage, while also constituting a kind of commemorative vacation culture.[27] As the interwar period progressed, conceptions of British identity increasingly incorporated gendered imagery, utilizing the iconography of victory in war as a way of envisioning forms of national masculinity—or "unconquerable manhood," to use Gabriel Koureas's term—that transcended internal divisions along class lines.[28] The memory of the war was also employed as a unifying mechanism to reinforce hegemony on the peripheries of the British Empire.[29] In France, the construction of war memorials was similarly widespread, but also riven with tensions over issues ranging from commercial interests to artistic taste.[30] Commemorations were particularly complicated in the French colonies and in contested territories like Alsace, which had been part of the German Empire but reverted to France after the war.[31] In Belgium, the memory of war was refracted through the lens of competing national identities—Flemish and Walloon—in complex and often visually stunning ways.[32]

Overall, among the victorious powers, the state typically played a more central role in organizing national commemorations than in Germany or Austria. In part, this was occasioned by financial constraints in the defeated countries, but the more salient point is that the British and French dead had fought for nation-state structures that continued to exist after the war, whereas in Germany and Austria new (and to a certain degree unwanted) state structures had been produced by the war, leaving private and often oppositional groups to assume a more visible role. In interwar Germany, Nazi ideology even in its earliest stages held that continued fighting against Weimar democracy was necessary to give genuine meaning to those who died in the war. And, that struggle itself would produce more martyrs, whose deaths would, in turn, only attain their true cosmic significance with the ultimate triumph of National Socialism. Taken in sum, the continued existence and legitimacy of the prewar nation-state in the postwar era were at least partially necessary to derive a strong sense of meaning and belonging from state-sponsored commemoration.

In Ireland, the war dead were memorialized in a broad array of commemorative spaces and public monuments.[33] That commemoration was made more complicated by the legacy of the 1916 Easter Rising and by the drive for independence and subsequent civil war that stretched through the early 1920s. Following the failed Rising, Irish national sentiment had continued to simmer, and in the December 1918 election the *Sinn Féin* party, which included many who had taken part in the Rising, managed to win nearly three-quarters of the approximately one hundred Irish seats in the British Parliament.[34] But rather than taking their seats in Westminster, in January 1919, the Irish delegates announced the formation of their own parliament, the Dàil Eirann, whose first act was to adopt an Irish Declaration of Independence, proclaiming Ireland to be an independent Republic.[35] At the same time, the Irish Republican Army, which had grown out of the Irish volunteer movement, began military activities to defend the First Dàil and to protect the development of the fledgling Irish Republic, while also launching guerilla attacks in major cities throughout England.[36] After more than two years of fighting, in what is alternately known as the Irish War of Independence and the Anglo-Irish War, the British government was forced to call for a truce in the summer of 1921, which was followed officially by the Anglo-Irish Treaty of December 1921 that provided for the formation of the independent Irish Free State.[37] The treaty made the new Irish state a dominion of the British crown, whereas the six northeastern counties of Ulster were allowed to exempt themselves entirely, constituting their own separate entity as Northern Ireland and remaining fully incorporated in the United Kingdom.[38] As a result, the treaty occasioned a civil war between supporters of the treaty, such as Michael Collins, and those like Eamon De Valera who felt it represented a betrayal of the national republican ideal.[39] In the course of the civil war, Michael Collins was ambushed and killed in August 1922, and his leadership role among the protreaty forces was taken by Richard Mulcahy, who presided over the ultimate defeat of the republican fighters in the spring of 1923.[40] Eamon De Valera was briefly imprisoned in 1923, but eventually emerged as an essentially unifying figure within Irish politics, founding the Fianna Fáil party in 1926 and being elected President of the Executive Council, the equivalent of prime minister within the Irish

Free State, in 1932.[41] The wounds of the civil war era showed signs of
healing, although the division in the north would continue ominously over
the decades.

Before examining developments in Central and Eastern Europe, let us
first turn our attention southward. In Spain, which remained neutral during
the First World War, political stability had been largely maintained since the
1870s by an elitist Liberal consensus, but during and after the war, traditional
elites struggled to adjust to the changing times, particularly the imperatives
of mass politics. In the early 1920s Barcelona, the primary industrial hub,
was besieged by a series of crises, ranging from labor unrest to separatist
terrorism, and a long-running revolt in Spanish Morocco exercised a further
destabilizing influence. So, in September 1923, King Alfonso XIII appointed
Miguel Primo de Rivera prime minister, but with vastly enhanced powers
to govern by decree. While initially designed to be a temporary (ninety-day)
solution to the immediate crises facing Spain, Primo de Rivera established an
authoritarian quasi-dictatorship that lasted until early 1930, when he was
effectively sacked by Alfonso in the context of the growing global economic
downturn. While Primo de Rivera is generally not regarded an outright
fascist, he had fairly close relations with Mussolini, and his regime provided
a (somewhat problematic) model for later fascist-oriented authoritarians
like Francisco Franco, who would launch the bloody civil war that tore
Spain apart between 1936 and 1939.[42] In neighboring Portugal, where
constitutional governance had been established in the 1830s under the royal
House of Braganza, power rested in the hands of a fairly exclusive political
caste of Liberals and elites until the early twentieth century. In February 1908,
however, King Carlos I and his designated successor, the Duke of Braganza,
were assassinated by republican radicals, and the institution of monarchy
was abolished altogether in the revolution of October 1910, which led to a
new constitution and new structures of governance in the First Portuguese
Republic. But, the fledgling system was wracked by instability both during and
after the First World War, with a series of radical authoritarian movements
gaining ground in the early 1920s. After only sixteen years of existence,
the First Republic was overthrown by a (largely peaceful) military coup on
May 28, 1926, ushering in a period of authoritarianism that would itself be
overtaken by the more overtly fascist-oriented dictatorship established by
António de Oliveira Salazar the following decade.

In the new states of Central and Eastern Europe, the attempt to fuse
national identity and Liberal democratic forms of belonging made significant
progress initially, despite a notable measure of chaos and uncertainty, before
the same rightward drift seen in Spain and Portugal became evident here
as well. Virtually all of the successor states formed out of the lands of the
former Habsburg empire initially lauded the virtues of constitutionalism
and democracy, while also being internally riven by ethnic and national
divisions.[43] The last Habsburg emperor, Karl I, had agreed to withdraw
completely from "every participation in the administration of the state" on

MAP 6.1 The New States of Europe, 1919. © *George Edward Milne, 2017. Reproduced with permission.*

November 11, 1918, the same day the armistice was signed; on the following day, the new (and ultimately short-lived) "Republic of German-Austria" was proclaimed.[44] The republic's founding proclamation offers a striking indication of the hopes for a new form of belonging that would combine democratic ideals with a greater German territorial identity: "German-Austria is a democratic republic. All public authority is derived from the people.... German-Austria is a constituent part of the German Republic."[45] But, unification with Germany was strictly prohibited by the Treaty of Saint Germain, and German-Austria remained little more than a fleeting wish projection. Elections were held in February 1919 for the constituent assembly that produced the constitution of the new state structure, the Republic of Austria, which was published the next year. Despite a degree of postwar territorial chaos, as contested regions were challenged by ethnic minority movements—particularly by Slovenes in Carinthia and Hungarians in Burgenland—the Austrian republic developed fairly stable democratic roots throughout the first fifteen years after the war. The city of Vienna remained largely in the control of the Social Democrats, whereas the Christian Social Party dominated national elections and provided virtually all of the chancellors leading up to the major rightward turn effected by Engelbert Dollfuss's "Austrofascist" takeover in 1934.

The Czech and Slovak territories within the Habsburg empire had not waited for the war's end to proclaim their independence. On October 28, 1918, the *Declaration of Independence of the Czechoslovak Nation* was issued, framing the democratic aspirations of its founding figures—Tomas Masaryk, the first president, chief among them—in terms of a new hybrid national identity alleged to stretch back through history: "We accept and shall adhere to the ideals of modern democracy, as they have been the ideals of our nation for centuries."[46] But the viability of that "nation," whose two state peoples—the Czechs and Slovaks—comprised less than two-thirds of its total population, would ultimately be called into question over the issue of minority rights. The substantial German minority was, at 25 percent, the second largest component of the population, far outpacing the Slovak contingent. In response, German nationalists would bemoan the violation of Wilsonian self-determination, portraying the Sudeten Germans as victims of an unjust postwar settlement in need of complete revision.[47] In the short term, however, optimism regarding the new Czechoslovak experiment reigned supreme. Its foreign publicity machine, which was particularly active in the United States, triumphantly compared the young democracy to the established Western systems it emulated: "Out of the ruins of the German, Austrian and Russian empires a number of new, democratic states are arising. But so far only one has reached the stage where it possesses a properly functioning government as solid, stable, and truly democratic as France, England, or America. The new Czechoslovak republic has justified all the high expectations of its friends."[48] The following excerpt from the speech of President Tomas Masaryk held upon the one-year anniversary of the republic's Declaration of Independence outlined his ideal of tolerance and inclusive national belonging.

EXCERPT 6.2

President Masaryk's Message on First Independence Day

This day ends the series of the memorable days of our revolution and our political victory; it was declared a national holiday and it is thus very appropriate for serious counsels about recent past and near future. Our revolution had a peculiar character. ... It is surely a peculiar revolution—a revolution of work, and thus democratic in the best sense of the word. This revolution secured to us a victory, a great victory. It has often been said that states maintain themselves by the same means by which they came into being. Our republic arose out of battle and work, and by work it will maintain itself; the battle, let us hope, will not be necessary. We have got over this first year peacefully on the whole; physiologists say that the first year of human life is decisive for the life of the individual. Perhaps we may employ this analogy for our state. But of course it is our task not merely to keep our republic alive, but to build it up completely through well-reasoned policies.

[...] In order to accomplish this fully, we must endeavor to get rid of the old language and nationality disputes which endangered Austria-Hungary and finally contributed so much to its downfall. At the Paris Conference the principle of nationality was very largely carried out, but even the new states have national minorities. The development of modern nationality took place side by side with the development of internationalism. As [Russian novelist] Dostoievsky well pointed out, man has not only love for his own nation, but also desire for communion with other nations and for universal union. That is also the sense of the humanitarian program of our national awakeners. Our revolutionary propaganda abroad gained sympathies for our nation by appeal to this program. A truly national policy will not be chauvinistic....

Our policy in this respect will gladly recognize national and language rights of the other nationalities of our republic. We have created the state, and it is thus natural that it will have a special character; that is implied in the very expression of independent state. But in our republic there will be no forcible denationalization.

I hope that the League of Nations will contribute to the strengthening of friendly relations between states and nations. In any case it must be the goal of our politics to further national tolerance; in our republic national minorities will be able to cultivate their nationality without hindrance.[49]

In the lands of the former Habsburg Kingdom of Hungary, a new Hungarian People's Republic was proclaimed on November 16, 1918 under Mihály Károlyi and Dénes Berinkey.[50] But, the relative harmony and stability reflected in the early stages of independent Czechoslovakia were nowhere to be found in the new Hungary. Before the young republican system could get its sea legs, Budapest was seized in a communist coup launched in March 1919 by Bela Kun, whose reign of brutality lasted nearly five months.[51] Hungarian national military forces under Miklós Horthy overthrew the Bela Kun regime in August 1919, and in the White Terror that ensued, reinvigorated forms of Hungarian nationalism were intertwined with rabid antisemitism, as embodied perhaps most infamously in the excesses of the reactionary forces led by Captain Pál Prónay.[52] In March 1920, the Hungarian parliament voted to replace the republic with a constitutional monarchy, but since there was no possibility of return for the deposed Habsburg monarch Karl I, Horthy was installed as Regent, ultimately governing as an authoritarian strongman for more than two decades.[53]

In neighboring Romania, which had been independent since 1878 and had joined the war in 1916 on the side of the Entente powers, the challenges of the immediate postwar years were ushered in by massive geographic enlargement. The territory of Greater Romania, as it was now known, was nearly twice the size of prewar Romania, with large ethnic minorities living in the newly acquired regions of Transylvania, Bukovina, and Bessarabia. The aspirations of these minorities—mainly Hungarians, Germans, and Jews—were largely ignored within the structures of the Romanian state, and various programs aimed at Romanization were instituted. Under Alexandru Averescu, the populist People's Party emerged as a major political force in 1920, and a series of coalition governments comprised of the National Liberals, the People's Party, and the National Peasant Party provided a measure of stability throughout the 1920s.[54] All three parties put forward their own drafts for a new constitution, although the final version adopted in 1923 was essentially the product of the National Liberals, guaranteeing extensive democratic rights for all Romanians for the first time in history. But, literacy rates remained among the lowest in Europe, agricultural reforms were only partially successful, and antimodern antisemitic ideas spread increasingly among peasant groups in the countryside. In university towns, particularly Iaşi, intellectual ferment swept up larger numbers of students and professors, many of whom laid the foundation for the indigenous forms of Romanian fascism that eventually flourished in the 1930s.

In the Balkans, parts of what had been Habsburg territory were incorporated into a new south Slavic union known initially as the Kingdom of Serbs, Croats, and Slovenes, which was proclaimed in early December 1918 under the Serbian King Alexander I. The multiethnic nature of the kingdom made it perpetually, in Vesna Drapac's term, a "state in search of a nation."[55] The 1921 constitution of the new state thus attempted to overcompensate by proclaiming loudly: "There is only one nationality for all the subjects of the Kingdom."[56] But, the difficult balance between broader south Slavic identity and individual ethnic and national visions would continue long after the institution of a monarchical dictatorship under Alexander in 1929, at which point the kingdom's name was changed to Yugoslavia to reflect both a streamlined (i.e., antidemocratic) set of governing structures and a more unified sense of identification. Following Alexander's assassination while on a state visit to France in 1934, some measure of constitutional governance returned, but harmony between its various component identities proved more elusive.[57]

In Bulgaria, which had established universal manhood suffrage at the time of its independence in the late 1870s, defeat in the Second Balkan War of 1913 was followed by an even more extensive defeat as one of the Central Powers in the First World War. In 1919, in the first postwar election, the populist Agrarian Union emerged victorious, enabling its leader Alexandar Stamboliski to govern for a key four year period, during which democratic structures were strengthened and economic development pursued.[58] In June 1923, however, disaffected military figures launched a coup that toppled Stamboliski's government and resulted in his torture and execution.

Although a parliamentary façade was maintained during subsequent years, authoritarian governance was pursued under King Boris by a series of rightists and militarists. To the south, in Greece, preexisting divisions between the king, Constantine I, and the Liberal prime minister Eleftherios Venizelos had been deepened during the First World War. The Germanophile king advocated neutrality, whereas Venizelos urged engagement on the side of the Entente powers. Following a contentious power struggle in which Venizelos prevailed, Greece did enter the war against the Central Powers in June 1917, and conflict continued after the war in the lengthy campaign fought by Greece against Turkish forces between 1919 and 1922 over control of former Ottoman territories. While the nominally democratic structures established in the 1860s (including universal manhood suffrage) continued in principle, Greek domestic politics grew increasingly chaotic, with the military intervening and installing General Theodoros Pangalos as dictator in January 1926.[59] But after only seven months, Pangalos himself was overthrown by those formerly loyal to him, and after the proverbial dust settled, Greece returned to the structures of parliamentary rule. In this sense, the 1926 reinstitution of parliamentarism in Greece ran counter to the broader rightward drift throughout much of Europe.

Further to the north, the new independent state of Poland was carved out of territory that had been part of the German, Austria-Hungarian, and Russian empires. Polish independence had featured centrally as one of Woodrow Wilson's Fourteen Points, but the successful establishment of a stable Polish nation-state was anything but a foregone conclusion. On November 11, 1918, Józef Piłsudski, who had recently been released from German captivity, took command of Polish military forces and proclaimed the creation of an independent state, but its territorial shape and demographic composition was unclear even in the eyes of its founders.[60] While the basic fact of Polish independence was recognized at the Paris Peace Conference in 1919, a series of intense border conflicts ensued between the new Poland and Czechoslovakian, Lithuanian, German, and Soviet forces, until some modicum of geographic stability was established in 1922. At that point, the reality of ethnic diversity was unmistakable, with some thirty percent of the population being comprised of non-Poles, primarily Ukrainians, Lithuanians, Belorussians, Czechs, Germans, and Jews.[61] Piłsudski, who headed a coalition government until late 1922, envisioned a broad regional amalgamation that would include, as had the Polish-Lithuanian Commonwealth, significant numbers of non-Poles. A much narrower vision was advocated by Roman Dmowski, the leader of the National Democracy movement whose development before the First World War was central to the process whereby Polish nationalism, in the words of Brian Porter-Szücs, "learned how to hate." While far from being the inevitable result of radicalizing nationalist discourse, National Democracy did in fact come to represent "a new form of Polish nationalism, one that embraced anti-Semitism, chauvinism, and authoritarianism."[62] Piłsudski briefly retired from politics in 1923, before returning to power in a 1926 coup that established his authoritarian dictatorship, which lasted until his death in 1935.

The three Baltic states of Lithuania, Latvia, and Estonia, which had been part of the Russian Empire, were established as independent republics after the First World War. Lithuania, the furthest to the south, spent much of the war under German occupation, after the German army drove the Russian troops out in 1915. In September 1917, with the tacit approval of German authorities, a conference in Vilnius was convened to discuss Lithuanian autonomy, and an organizational body known as the Council of Lithuania was formed, with Antanas Smetona as chairman.[63] While the majority of Lithuanian nationalists opposed a revival of eighteenth-century structures, which would have included significant Polish and Belarusian elements, many were open to the idea of a constitutional monarchy in some kind of union with the German Kaiser. That had certainly been the goal of the German occupation authorities. But, when the Council promulgated its famous Act of Independence on February 16, 1918, no mention was made of relations with Germany, leading German authorities to respond with (comparatively mild) repressive measures.[64] Following the defeat of Germany in November 1918, however, a new and fully independent Lithuanian government was rapidly proclaimed, although Soviet military forces also advanced rapidly and fought a nine-month war in the attempt to establish a Soviet republic in Lithuania. It would take until 1920 for the peace treaty to be officially finalized, but by the summer of 1919, it was clear that the Soviet effort would fail. Lithuanian independence now took on legitimate meaning; new governmental structures were established and a constituent assembly was organized to draft a constitution, which was completed and published in 1922. By that point, Lithuania had achieved international recognition and, as of September 1921, membership in the League of Nations. Although border conflicts with Poland and Belarus continued to threaten stability in the early 1920s, new conceptions of Lithuanian national belonging were forged alongside optimistic yet unruly discourses of liberation and emancipation, leading some scholars to identify Lithuania as a "rebel nation" from its inception.[65] But, the development of democratic structures lasted only until 1926, when a coup brought Antanas Smetona to power as president; he would govern Lithuania autocratically until 1940.[66]

Events in Latvia and Estonia proceeded along similar lines initially. While neither were under wartime German occupation for as long as Lithuania, both were ceded officially to Germany, along with Lithuania, in the March 1918 Treaty of Brest-Litovsk.[67] Estonia proclaimed its national independence on February 24, 1918, only days after the Lithuanian declaration, and proceeded to fight a successful war against Soviet forces for more than a year. The Treaty of Tartu in February 1920 established the official independence of the Estonian Republic, with a new constitution promulgated that December, followed by membership in the League of Nations in September 1921. As a parliamentary democracy with a unicameral legislature known as the Riigikogu, Estonia developed ideals of national belonging in tandem with the evolution of strikingly inclusive democratic structures. The new Estonian state was particularly notable for its tolerance of ethnic minorities. In many ways early interwar Estonia can be considered an experiment in national "ultra-liberalism," although as David Smith has noted, "ultra-liberal provisions... meant that the political system ultimately proved 'too democratic for its own good' during the interwar period."[68] An authoritarian shift did indeed occur in Estonia, but not until 1934.

In Latvia, German occupation authorities announced in September 1918 plans for a United Baltic Duchy under Adolf Friedrich, the duke of Mecklenburg, which was to include Latvia and part of Estonia. Robert Koehl has characterized this attempt as a "prelude" to Nazi expansionist designs during the Second World War.[69] In any event, German defeat that November nullified those plans, allowing for the convening of an independent Latvian People's Council, which laid the groundwork for democratic elections to a constituent assembly. In December 1918, Latvia began its own successful war against Soviet forces, culminating in the Treaty of Riga in the summer of 1920. In the aftermath of Latvian entrance into the League of Nations, the constitution of 1922 established solid democratic structures, although the multiparty system was riven with internal dissension and ministerial cabinets were shuffled with alarming rapidity. That said, the democratic structures survived until a coup was launched in 1934 by sitting prime minister Kārlis Ulmanis, who dismantled the parliamentary system and maintained dictatorial control until 1940.[70]

The tensions that emerged in the Baltic republics were symptomatic of broader polarizing forces at work in interwar Europe. The earliest moves for independence there had been undertaken against the backdrop of revolutionary developments in Russia that would destroy and, in a convoluted Soviet sense, eventually remake the neighboring imperial hegemon that had so long dominated the Baltic states. The period of Baltic constitutionalism and parliamentary rule in the 1920s paralleled attempts to forge Liberal forms of belonging in the Western democracies. And, the subsequent rightward drift coincided with the spread of fascism and authoritarianism. As will be seen, the interplay between the competing extremes of communism and fascism had a dramatic impact on the conceptualization and expression of nationalist ideals throughout Europe.

Competing utopias: Fascism and communism in the interwar years

In his magisterial reimagining of twentieth-century European history, Mark Mazower argued that of the three major competing ideologies of the first half of the century—Liberal democracy, communism, and fascism—it was the latter that seemed for a time to offer the most compelling response to the challenges of technological and social modernization.[71] Soviet-style communism and Western Liberal democracy, particularly in its Wilsonian idealistic incarnation, had each largely failed by the late 1930s in their pursuit of a utopian future, whereas the fascist right more generally, and Hitler's Nazi vision more specifically, seemed destined for European hegemony. Not only did the far right appear to have the brightest future, but it also grew much more organically from the native soil of Europe than its two main rivals, which were widely seen as foreign impositions: "National Socialism, in particular, fits into the mainstream not only of German but also of European history far more comfortably than most people like to admit."[72] Ultimately, when the German Wehrmacht and the Soviet Red Army clashed epically in what Timothy Snyder has called the "bloodlands" of Eastern Europe, it was much more than a clash of military forces.[73]

Although the establishment of the Horthy regime in Hungary in the spring of 1920 represents the earliest right-wing authoritarian takeover of power in interwar Europe, and while historians like Zeev Sternhell have traced the intellectual origins of fascism to the immediate prewar years, the progenitor of both the term and the phenomenon of fascism was the movement founded by Benito Mussolini in early 1919. After initially embarking on a career as a schoolteacher, Mussolini was drawn increasingly to socialist politics, influenced heavily by Sorel's brand of revolutionary syndicalism but also experimenting eclectically with various combinations of Marxist and nationalist ideas. By the eve of the First World War, he had emerged as one of the rising journalistic stars within the Italian Socialist Party, assuming the editorship of its flagship newspaper *Avanti* in 1913. During the early stages of the war, as the Socialist party supported Italy's continued neutrality, Mussolini came to advocate entrance into the war on the Entente side, motivated partly by a desire to liberate Tyrolean Italians still under the control of Austria-Hungary and partly by a glorious vision of social upheaval and national mobilization he believed the war would unleash. A break with the Socialist party became unavoidable, and the split was to be both bitter and lasting.[74]

Mussolini essentially remade himself as the war progressed. The vague nationalist notions that had accompanied his eccentric brand of socialist fervor were sharpened, and his idealization of amorphous syndicalist calls for violent action-for-action's-sake were hardened into a strict militaristic ethos, albeit with the deed always continuing to take precedence over the idea. He founded a new newspaper, the *Popolo d'Italia*, and in January 1915 established a rudimentary forerunner of the fascist movement, which he called the Fasces of Revolutionary Action after the image of the tightly bound bundles of lictors' rods (*fasces*) that symbolized unity and authority in the ancient Roman Republic. Mussolini's embrace of militarized machismo, which became such a central element of fascist self-presentation, was starkly at odds with his initial shirking of military service and with the underwhelming nature of his war service itself (he was injured in a grenade accident and discharged in the summer of 1917).[75] Returning to the editorship of the *Popolo d'Italia*, Mussolini shared the broad disillusionment felt by many Italians at war's end, when Italy's place among the victors failed to bring with it any of the promised spoils. This sense of disillusionment, which was especially strong among veterans in the north of Italy and was accelerated by postwar economic chaos, provided Mussolini with the fuel needed to launch a political movement, even if he had very few concrete ideas beyond the desire for action.

In March 1919, Mussolini gathered around himself in Milan some 200 activists who formed the backbone of the fascist movement. Initially identifying themselves as *Fasci di combattimento*, or fascist combat squads, these radicals were drawn primarily from the ranks of young veterans and disillusioned former socialists, like Mussolini, and included many who had connections with Filippo Marinetti's futurist movement.[76] The organizational style and public aesthetic of the young movement was striking, combining black-shirted uniforms and stiff-arm salutes with mass rallies and regimented marches, while fostering an internal culture of male bonding saturated with violent machismo.[77] Engaging in street brawls with socialists provided the chief activity for many of the fascist cell groups, and as the economic chaos worsened, the fascist ranks swelled. By December 1920, the movement had attained a membership of some 20,000, but went on to increase tenfold over the next six months, reaching 200,000 members by May 1921. In elections that same month, Mussolini and thirty-seven other fascists won seats in the Italian parliament, and in November 1921, the loosely organized fascist groupings were officially combined into the National Fascist Party, which began developing firmer organizational structures. Over the ensuing year, Mussolini was forced to walk a fine line between continuing the rowdy antisocialist violence of the movement, which made it attractive to many of its members, and maintaining at least the appearance of parliamentary respectability.[78] The latter strategy seemed to bear fruit, as a number of powerful social and political elites—including King Victor Emmanuel III's mother and the Archbishop of Milan—began supporting the fascists as the best hope to defeat the socialists, who were widely blamed for paralyzing the Italian economy. When the socialists led a general strike in August 1922, widespread violence ensued, with at least twelve being killed in brutal street fighting. In response, the government of prime minister Luigi Facta, an old-line moderate Liberal, was increasingly blamed for its inability to keep the social peace and to fix the growing economic crisis.[79] In October 1922, when tens of thousands of Mussolini's blackshirts converged on Rome—peacefully, although carrying billy clubs—the king refused to back the Facta administration and instead, on October 29, invited Mussolini to form a new government. Two days later, on October 31, 1922, Mussolini entered Rome triumphantly at the head of a boisterous victory parade.[80] The so-called March on Rome served as an inspiration to other radical rightists in Europe, including Adolf Hitler, whose political career in the south German state of Bavaria was just beginning to gain momentum.

Once in office, it was unclear exactly how Mussolini planned to govern. He was the head of a multiparty coalition government, within which his fascist party held only four of the thirteen cabinet seats. More seriously, Mussolini was allergic to almost all forms of political theorizing and had spent very little time considering specific policy initiatives. In the excerpt below, which was published several years later, Mussolini looked back on the movement's earliest years and took pride in the fact that fascism had always prized nationalistic action over theory.

EXCERPT 6.3

The Doctrine of Fascism

Benito Mussolini

Fascism was not given out to the wet nurse of a doctrine elaborated beforehand round a table; it was born of a need for action. It was not a party, but in its first two years it was a movement against all parties.

The years preceding the March on Rome were years during which the necessity of action did not tolerate enquiries or complete elaborations of doctrine. Battles were being fought in the cities and villages. There were discussions, but—and this is more sacred and important—there were deaths. People knew how to die. The doctrine—beautiful, well formed, divided into chapters and paragraphs and surrounded by a commentary— might be missing. But there was present something more decisive to supplant it: Faith. [...]

The man of Fascism is an individual who is nation and fatherland, which is a moral law, binding together individuals and the generations into a tradition and a mission, suppressing the instinct for a life enclosed within the brief round of pleasure in order to restore within duty a higher life free from the limits of time and space: a life in which the individual, through the denial of himself, through the sacrifice of his own private interests, through death itself, realizes that completely spiritual existence in which his value as a man lies. [...]

Fascism desires an active man, one engaged in activity with all his energies; it desires a man virilely conscious of the difficulties that exist in action and ready to face them.[81]

Mussolini's first two years in power represented a continuation of parliamentary constitutional rule, but with increasing totalitarian overtones. In December 1922, Mussolini created the Fascist Grand Council, which served as a sort of shadow cabinet, and the following month he established the Voluntary Militia for National Security, built largely on the foundation of private fascist militias and used primarily for intimidation of political opponents. In July 1923, the parliament passed the so-called Acerbo Law, named for its author Giacomo Acerbo, which essentially gutted the Italian constitution's provisions for democratic rule. The law gave any party who garnered more than 25 percent of the vote a two-thirds supermajority in parliament; it was used after the next elections, which took place in April 1924 in an atmosphere of violent intimidation, to give the Fascist Party firm parliamentary control. But several weeks later, in early June, the Acerbo Law's most vocal critic, the socialist parliamentary leader Giacomo Matteotti, disappeared.[82] His body was discovered later that summer, and it was widely suspected that the murder had been commissioned either by Mussolini himself or by someone close to him.[83] Matteotti's socialist colleagues responded by abandoning their parliamentary seats in protest, and Mussolini's administration entered the most severe crisis of its entire existence.[84] Amid swirling rumors and calls for his deposition—calls that were ignored by King Victor Emmanuel III—Mussolini slipped into a deep depression lasting throughout the fall. In December 1924, a delegation of Fascist Party leaders met with Mussolini threatening to push him aside if he did not rouse himself from the doldrums of inactivity.

Mussolini's response came in the form of one of his most famous public addresses, on January 3, 1925, in which he accepted responsibility in a general sense for the atmosphere of crisis that had spread over the preceding months and pledged to exercise firmer control of governance. The speech, which is generally seen as the beginning of Mussolini's actual dictatorial rule, was followed by the arrest of more than one hundred suspected subversives.[85] Over the ensuing years the structures of dictatorial control were erected. In December 1925, Mussolini was made responsible to the king alone, and following a series of assassination attempts the following year, all rival political parties were outlawed, making Italy a one-party state. Non-fascist trade unions were neutralized, corporatist economic structures were introduced, and the press was heavily censored. In 1929, Mussolini signed the Lateran Accords, which established the independence of Vatican City and healed much of the rift that had existed between the secular Italian state and the popes since national unification the previous century.[86] Although Mussolini's totalitarian aspirations never came close to being realized—with the monarchy, church, and military all retaining important elements of independence—the four to five year period that followed the Matteotti crisis represented a significant achievement in dismantling the democratic structures of a major European nation-state.

FIGURE 6.1 Mussolini in 1925. *Wikimedia Commons.*

When Mussolini was at his lowest point, in the summer and fall of 1924, Adolf Hitler was experiencing his own existential political crisis while serving time in a jail cell outside Munich. Mussolini's march on Rome had been one of the central inspirations for Hitler's failed attempt to take control of the Bavarian government by force in November 1923, the so-called Beerhall Putsch, which resulted in his imprisonment. Hitler used that time in part to write the first volume of his political memoir, *Mein Kampf*, in which he placed Mussolini, "the great man beyond the Alps," among the ranks of "the world's great men," especially in comparison to the weakness of Germany's democratic leaders: "What miserable pigmies our sham statesmen in Germany appear by comparison with him. And, how nauseating it is to witness the conceit and effrontery of these nonentities in criticizing a man who is a thousand times greater than them."[87] Important connections exist between Fascism in Italy and National Socialism in Germany, and certain parallels will become evident in the account of Nazi developments that follows here. But the differences between the two movements, particularly in terms of their respective visions of belonging, are also significant. As the initially protean ideology of fascism crystallized into intelligible form under the influence of Giovanni Gentile, one clear point of emphasis was the prioritization of the state over the nation:

> The state is not to be thought of numerically as the sum-total of individuals forming the majority of the nation. And consequently fascism is opposed to democracy, which equates the nation with the majority, lowering it to the level of that majority. Nonetheless it is the purest form of democracy if the nation is conceived, as it should be, qualitatively and not quantitatively, as the most powerful Idea. [...] Not a race, nor a geographically determined region, but as a community historically perpetuating itself, a multitude unified by a single Idea, which is the will to existence and to power: consciousness of itself, Personality. This Higher Personality is truly the nation in so far as it is the state. It is not the nation that generates the State, as according to the old naturalistic concept, which served as the basis of the political theories of the national states of the nineteenth century. Rather the nation is created by the state, which gives to the people, conscious of its own moral unity, a will and therefore an effective existence.[88]

The fascist program represented the state as the creative element that took amorphous and otherwise unintelligible nationalist sentiments and forged them for the first time into the "idea" of the nation. The nation and its "will" (in a Rousseauian sense) only emerge through the agency of the state.[89] For Hitler, in contrast, the state represented a set of external structures whose significance was tied entirely to the cultivation and protection of the racial essence of the nation. An extended discussion in *Mein Kampf* made this distinction clear:

> The state is a means to an end. Its end lies in the preservation and advancement of a community of physically and psychically homogeneous creatures. This preservation itself comprises first of all existence as a race and thereby permits the free development of all the forces dormant in this race.... We must distinguish in the sharpest way between the state

as a vessel and the race as its content. This vessel has meaning only if it can preserve and protect the content; otherwise it is useless. Thus the highest purpose of the *völkisch* [national-racial] state is concern for the preservation of those original racial elements which bestow culture and create the beauty and dignity of a higher mankind. We, as Aryans, can conceive of the state only as the living organism of a nationality which not only assures the preservation of this nationality, but by the development of its spiritual and ideal abilities leads it to the highest freedom.[90]

These divergent approaches to the relationship between the nation and the state help explain one of the central contrasts between fascist and Nazi conceptions of belonging: the place allocated to the Jews within the national collectivity. From its earliest years, Mussolini's fascist movement included a number of prominent Italian Jews; its radical nationalism and advocacy of political violence was not directed primarily into antisemitic channels, at least not until pressure from Nazi Germany in the 1930s eventually led to stepped up persecution.[91] In contrast, the Nazi movement exhibited virulent antisemitism from the very beginning, and Nazi nationalism would remain intricately intertwined with racism until the early 1940s, when it could be argued that the idea of the nation as a central point of reference was essentially swallowed up by the Nazi racial obsession. By placing emphasis on the structural reality of the state as the vehicle for social and political belonging, the fascists felt no compulsion to exclude the Jews; for Hitler and other leading Nazis, however, the organic conception of the nation required a much more stringent internal policing mechanism to establish a firmer sense of belonging. The Jews were not only out of step with the Nazi claim to articulate the general will; they were physically incapable of inclusion and were therefore, according to the central thrust of Rousseauian logic, justifiably and of necessity the targets of coercive state-sponsored violence.

Interestingly, though, the evolution of Hitler's own antisemitism is shrouded in some mystery. There is no doubt whatsoever that Hitler espoused an uncompromising form of exterminatory racial antisemitism, which remained a central component of his worldview up until his suicide in 1945. But, how and when he arrived at that position is much less clear. Hitler was born in 1889 in the Austrian town of Braunau and spent much of his childhood in Linz, where there were virtually no Jews, and he claimed never to have heard of antisemitism as a child. His father was a senior Habsburg customs official whose cosmopolitan outlook led him, in Hitler's words, to view antisemitism as a form of "cultural backwardness."[92] Following the death of his father in 1903, Hitler dropped out of school and eventually moved to Vienna in an attempt to gain admittance to the art academy, for which he was denied on two occasions. Despite these rejections, or perhaps because of them, Hitler's vision of nationalism was often articulated in aesthetic terms.[93] It was shortly thereafter, in Vienna, that Hitler later claimed first to have become a convinced antisemite, although there is good evidence that throughout his time in Vienna, and even after his relocation to Munich in 1913, he maintained close relationships with Jewish figures in artistic circles.[94] It is likely that Hitler's antisemitism was accelerated by his experiences in the First World War, which also decisively shaped his visions of community and belonging.

Hitler was part of a joyous throng that was present on Munich's Odeonsplatz upon the announcement of war mobilization in early August 1914. At that point Hitler was a twenty-five year old failure by any measure, including his own. But as Peter Fritzsche has argued, the inclusive feeling of common purpose and belonging was so overwhelming—for Hitler and millions of others who experienced it—that the summer of 1914 can be seen in many ways as the actual birth moment of the Nazi ideational universe. Once in power the Nazis' radical exclusionary policies would be framed as necessary steps in the restoration of that powerful sense of belonging, which lay buried under layers of subsequent disillusionment.[95] For Hitler personally, his war experience also exposed him to new forms of camaraderie and belonging, although in comparison to his regimental mates Hitler always remained somewhat aloof.[96] In November 1918, when the revolution broke out and the armistice was signed, Hitler was hospitalized after being (temporarily) blinded in a gas attack. After recovering, he remained in the employ of the military and was posted to Munich, where the immediate postwar period was characterized by a series of dramatic political pendulum swings.

The revolutionary wave of November 1918 had swept from power the Bavarian Wittelsbach monarchy, and a provisional government in Munich was established under the former theater critic Kurt Eisner, whose party, the far left Independent Socialists, had little popular support. Following Eisner's assassination after barely one hundred days in power, the spring of 1919 witnessed two brief attempts to erect a Soviet-style dictatorship in Munich, which were, in turn, overthrown by a brutal counterrevolutionary reaction.[97] Bavaria became a haven for right-wing misfits from across Germany who viewed the postwar settlement—both in the form of the Treaty of Versailles and Germany's democratic constitution—as illegitimate foreign impositions designed to strip Germany of its national honor. The Nazi Party was founded in January 1919, initially calling itself the German Workers' Party, and it was still a tiny and insignificant splinter group when Hitler joined eight months later. As Hitler emerged as an increasingly effective propagandistic speaker, the young party gained more and more attention, growing to approximately 20,000 members by early 1923 and to more than 55,000 by the fall of that year.[98] It was at that point that Hitler, wanting to emulate Mussolini's march on Rome, made his failed bid to take power by force in the episode known as the Beerhall Putsch, launched on the night of November 8, 1923.[99] It was a dismal failure, with sixteen of Hitler's supporters being killed in a shootout with police, and the Nazi Party was forcibly disbanded. Hitler and his coconspirators were arrested and tried for treason, but were dealt with in extremely lenient fashion by a sympathetic judiciary. Hitler was sentenced to five years in the state prison at Landsberg, where he wrote the first volume of his memoir *Mein Kampf*, but was released early in December 1924.

Importantly, Hitler then committed himself and his followers to a course of participation within the hated democratic system—planning ultimately to use the structures of democracy to destroy democracy itself—and the banned Nazi Party was allowed to reconstitute itself in February 1925. Hitler also launched a propagandistic campaign to transform the Beerhall Putsch, which had been a miserably planned failure on every level, into the centerpiece of a new form of political religion, which was to characterize the Nazi public aesthetic throughout the duration of the party's existence. The sixteen conspirators killed in the shootout were venerated as "martyrs" of the movement—secular saints, in effect—and one of the swastika flags that had fallen into a pool of blood during the shootout was preserved as the so-called Blood Flag (*Blutfahne*) and was featured as a sacramental relic at future Nazi ceremonies. In the short term, though, the newly refounded Nazi Party had a difficult time gaining any political traction, leading that period to be known as the party's "wilderness years." After garnering a meager 2.6 percent of the vote in the 1928 parliamentary elections, the Nazis were able to capitalize on the world economic crisis that began late the following year. Between 1930 and 1932, the Nazi Party grew to be the largest party in the Reichstag, as three successive traditionalist chancellors attempted to govern without a parliamentary majority—kept in office by the emergency powers granted in the Weimar constitution. After a series of behind the scenes machinations, on January 30, 1933, Hitler was appointed chancellor in a last-gasp attempt to solve the ongoing political and economic crisis in Germany.

When Hitler initially took office he had nothing close to dictatorial power. He owed his position in part to old-line conservatives, who believed that Hitler could be manipulated easily.[100] The Nazis controlled only three of the cabinet seats in Hitler's first administration. But the atmosphere of national security panic that was ushered in by the famous arson attack on the Reichstag in late February 1933 offered Hitler the opportunity to suspend civil liberties and gain a virtual monopoly on public campaigning in the lead up to the next election, scheduled for early March.[101] The Decree for the Protection of the People and the State, known colloquially as the Reichstag Fire Decree, allocated to the government extensive powers for wiretapping and surveillance, authorizing press censorship and suspending protections against illegal search and seizure, while instituting the practice of "protective custody" (*Schutzhaft*), under which potential subversives could be arrested and held indefinitely without charges or evidence being presented against them. The first of the domestic concentration camps, Dachau, was opened hastily to house many of those arrested in the aftermath of the Reichstag fire, including a large number of oppositional political leaders.[102] Even in that atmosphere of intimidation and panic, with their political rivals largely silenced or incarcerated, the Nazis still only received 43.9 percent of the vote in March 1933.[103] But when the new parliament convened later that month in the Kroll Opera House—due to the extensive fire damage to the Reichstag building itself—its first order of business was the passage of the Enabling Act, which provided much of the legal basis for Hitler's dictatorship over the ensuing years.[104] Throughout 1933 and into 1934, the Nazi leadership initiated the process of *Gleichschaltung* (usually translated as "coordination"), which involved the attempt to bring all aspects of German politics and society into line with Nazi ideology. Independent trade unions were dissolved in favor of the Nazi-sponsored German Labor Front, and all non-Nazi political parties either voluntarily disbanded or were forcibly dismantled, with the final hold-out, the Catholic Center Party, going under in July 1933. From that point on, Germany was a one-party state. The civil service and professions were purged of Jews and "politically unreliable" elements, whereas newspapers, publishing outlets, cultural organizations, and the radio, music, and film industries were all brought under the control of the state.

Hitler's political power was further enhanced by two central developments in the summer of 1934. The first, known as the Night of the Long Knives, was a wide-ranging purge of potential threats to Hitler's authority both within the Nazi Party (particularly among the leadership of the paramilitary *Sturmabteilung*, or SA) and within broader conservative circles, claiming the lives of between 80 and 120 victims.[105] The homosexuality of the SA leader Ernst Röhm, which had been widely rumored for some time, was used as partial justification for his swift execution without trial—since the immoral "cancer" of homosexuality necessitated a rapid surgical excision— as was a fictitious coup that Röhm and his accomplices were said to be plotting with support from French sources.[106] The second development was the death on August 2, 1934 of President Hindenburg, which enabled Hitler to combine the two previously separate offices of chancellor and president into the position of *Führer* (leader), and was followed by the institution of the loyalty oath sworn by all military personnel to Hitler personally. By the late summer of 1934, the level of dictatorial control achieved by Hitler was astounding, far outpacing the powers exercised by Mussolini.

The Nazi party rally that was held in Nuremberg the month after Hindenburg's death provides us with an opportunity to discuss the nature of the striking *völkisch* (racist-nationalist) political religiosity cultivated by the Nazis. The Nuremberg rallies were held every September, but the 1934 rally was particularly noteworthy because it was filmed by Leni Riefenstahl as the basis for her most influential film, *Triumph of the Will*, perhaps the most famous propagandistic documentary of all time.[107] Several of the film's most memorable scenes were structured around commemoration of the dead from both the First World War and the Beerhall Putsch shootout, with the continued presence of the dead among the living acting as a source of

constant communion and inspiration. In the ceremony featuring the Labor
Service, a striking liturgical chant is led by a young recruit in an ecstasy of
near-possession, closing with an ode to the fallen: "You are not dead...you
live...in Germany!"[108] Similarly, the massive stadium procession of brown-
shirted SA and blackshirted Schutz-Staffel (SS)men before Hitler's elevated
tribunal, envisioned as a rite of reconciliation in the aftermath of the Röhm
purge, was sealed by the sacramental appearance of the Blood Flag, which
Hitler physically touched to the fabric of each new set of standards being
consecrated at the ceremony.[109] This emphasis on salvation through blood—
not that of Jesus, but the sanctified blood of the Beerhall Putsch martyrs—
was at the heart of a number of other commemorative projects launched by
the Nazis. The architectural refashioning of Munich in the mid-1930s was
particularly striking, consisting of a large monument to the sixteen Nazi
shootout victims that was erected on the Odeonsplatz and a new open-
air shrine complex constructed on the Königsplatz, a few minutes' walk
west. The Königsplatz complex featured two neoclassical Temples of Honor
(*Ehrentempel*), which contained a total of sixteen sarcophagi—eight in each
temple—within which were housed the remains of the martyred putschists,
which had been disinterred and relocated from their respective resting places
by decree of the Führer.[110] School groups and Hitler Youth delegations took
spiritual pilgrimages—in the form of curricular field trips—to the Temples
of Honor, and schoolchildren across Germany had to memorize, in addition
to grammatical rules and multiplication tables, the names of the sixteen
heroes of the nation interred there.

* * * *

As the Nazi regime was consolidating its power in Germany, and as Mussolini
continued to strive toward his vision of a totalitarian social and political order,
the broader process of polarization proceeded rapidly throughout Europe.
In addition to the aforementioned rightward drift toward authoritarianism
in many of the new democracies created after the First World War in
Central and Eastern Europe, overtly fascist-oriented movements grew up in
opposition to the specter of Soviet communism emanating from Moscow.
After several years of civil war and border disputes, the Soviet Union had
emerged in the early 1920s as a new type of multiethnic empire, one whose
ideology claimed to transcend parochial national interests but which, in
practice, fostered ethnic and national attachments when useful, creating a set
of policies Rogers Brubaker has called "institutionalized multinationality."[111]
As Ronald Suny has noted, "Soviet Russia was the first state in history to
create a federal system based on ethnonational units."[112] Yuri Slezkine has
gone so far as to label the Soviet Union a "communal apartment" in which
different national entities constituted individual rooms—separate from
each other, but still incorporated within the whole and, to a degree, sharing
common infrastructure.[113] To continue in the vein of popular metaphors,

Terry Martin has characterized the USSR as an "affirmative action empire" for its utilitarian employment of nationality policy, under both Lenin and Stalin, in building support for the Soviet vision among key regional opinion leaders.[114] Under Lenin, national identification was tolerated (at times, strategically supported) on the level of language and culture, even if this did not take the form of political autonomy. Far from using the Soviet system as a cover for the imposition of Russian chauvinism, Lenin envisioned each of the major Soviet republics—Russia, Ukraine, Belorussia, Armenia, Azerbaijan, and Georgia—as being on an equal footing.[115] After Stalin's full attainment of power in the late 1920s, he initially supported limited forms of linguistic and cultural diversity, but he embarked in the early 1930s on a campaign of repression against the two largest non-Russian nationalities, the Ukrainians, and Belorussians. This coincided with the brutal collectivization of agriculture and produced genocidal results, particularly in the context of the Ukrainian famine of 1932 and 1933.[116] Despite the willingness of Soviet leaders to engage in the politics of ethnicity and nationalism, their acolytes in other parts of Europe strove almost universally to form an internationalist counterweight to the fervent nationalism espoused by fascist-oriented movements. These latter movements, in turn, utilized the threat of communism to portray themselves as indispensable bulwarks against the ideological expansionism of the Soviet Union and its various political satellites. While Mussolini and Hitler remained the most significant fascist dictators, similar figures in Austria, Hungary, Romania, and Spain led fascist-oriented movements whose influence was accelerated by the economic crisis of the 1930s.

In the Austrian First Republic, political activity was dominated, at least on the surface, by the binary opposition of the Christian Social Party and the Social Democrats. But, outside the realm of parliamentary politics, various forms of right radicalism flourished. The most notable right-wing paramilitary organization was the Heimwehr (home guard), which had been founded in 1919 to mobilize against radical leftist forces and which subsequently grew extensively in the Austrian countryside.[117] An indigenous form of Austrian national socialism also developed, building partly on the foundation laid by the prewar German Workers Party in the Sudetenland. By the mid-1920s, however, the movement began to split into two camps, with extreme radicals embracing many of Hitler's ideals, even as the Nazi Party in Germany was struggling for relevance in the midst of the so-called wilderness years. By the early 1930s, as the economic crisis worsened, new radical forces emerged within the established political parties themselves, as seen particularly in the rise of Engelbert Dollfuss within the Christian Social ranks. Coming to power initially as the head of a coalition government in 1932, Dollfuss managed in the spring of 1933 to institute an informal dictatorship built on the support of Christian Socials and the Heimwehr.[118] As political discourse became increasingly polarized and governance increasingly difficult, Dollfuss forged an authoritarian umbrella organization known as the Fatherland Front, which received direct support from Mussolini, who hoped to develop Dollfuss's new regime as a kind of Austrian fascist satellite. However, facing intense internal opposition from the Social Democrats and Austrian Nazi Party, the latter of which reviled Dollfuss for his opposition to plans for union with Germany, the Fatherland Front increasingly courted support from conservative Catholic circles and developed a hybrid form of "clerical fascism" (or Austrofascism).[119] In late June 1934, just days before the Röhm purge in Germany, the Austrian Nazis launched a coup attempt that ultimately failed miserably, although they did succeed in killing Dollfuss.[120] His successor, Kurt Schuschnigg, attempted to forge stability in the ensuing years, moderating some of the excesses of the Heimwehr, which was marginalized within the Fatherland Front before being forcibly dissolved in 1936, while adopting certain fascist-oriented stylistic traits. A new *Sturmkorps* (storm corps) militia was created to replace the outlawed Heimwehr, and their dark blue uniforms and militarized public aesthetic evoked parallels with the Nazi SS, even as Schuschnigg maintained a critical stance toward Nazi ideology.[121] It was Schuschnigg who was at the helm in March 1938, when Germany annexed Austria in the so-called *Anschluss*, with Schuschnigg being replaced by the Austrian Nazi Arthur Seyss-Inquart.[122] The longstanding vision of German-Austrian political belonging was finally established, albeit only through force and intimidation.

In Hungary during Miklós Horthy's long reign as regent, and particularly during the tenure of István Bethlen as prime minister from 1921 to 1931, a fairly traditional form of authoritarian conservatism was maintained. In 1932, a new government was formed by the much more radical Gyula Gömbös, a staunchly antisemitic military officer who idealized Mussolini and Hitler. Once in office, however, Gömbös pursued a more complex path than expected, backing away visibly from some of the more extreme positions he had taken earlier (particularly regarding antisemitism), while forging close economic ties with Germany after Hitler came to power in 1933. After the death of Gömbös in 1936, a similarly complicated trajectory was pursued by his successor, the traditional authoritarian Kálmán Darányi.[123] But behind the scenes, a jumble of radical antisemitic parties proliferated, with the Arrow Cross movement of Ferenc Szálasi emerging as the most significant. Szálasi's movement, which wore green shirts, borrowed explicitly from German Nazi ideology while attempting to pioneer its own idiosyncratic form of "Hungarism."[124] Szálasi envisioned Hungarism to be at the core of a new regional agglomeration that would undo the territorial injustices of the postwar settlement, whose official language would be Magyar and whose leadership would be almost entirely Hungarian, but which would include semiautonomous regions comprised of Slovaks, Slovenes, Croats, and Ruthenians. The ideological principle Szálasi formulated to support this vision was "co-nationalism," but it was underpinned by the unshakeable conviction that the Hungarians were superior in racial terms. Nazi-inspired racial antisemitism festered within the movement well into the years of the

Second World War, although it was only after the deposition of Horthy as regent in 1944 that the Arrow Cross and Szálasi came to power and oversaw the tragic deportation of the Hungarian Jews to Auschwitz.

Romanian politics remained fairly stable for several years following the institution of the constitution of 1923, which had established Romania as a democratically oriented constitutional monarchy under King Ferdinand I.[125] In 1925, in the wake of a series of extramarital scandals, Ferdinand's son and heir Carol had relinquished his right to the crown, declaring his own toddler son Michael as the successor to the throne before moving to Paris to live with one of his numerous illicit partners.[126] When Ferdinand I died in 1927, the crown passed to the young Michael, whose uncle Nicholas (the younger brother of the largely disgraced Carol) assumed power as head of a regency council. In the summer of 1930, however, Carol returned to Romania and was installed on the throne as King Carol II in a fairly low-key coup. Though the democratic constitution remained technically in force under Carol, the structures of democracy were gradually dismantled throughout the ensuing decade. Politically, the most significant development was the rise of the Iron Guard, also known as the Legion of the Archangel Michael, which had been founded among radical intellectuals in the university city of Iaşi by Corneliu Zelea Codreanu in 1927. The Legion has rightly been characterized as a fascist movement, but many of its defining characteristics were idiosyncratic—particularly Codreanu's cultivation of an apocalyptic religio-racial mysticism.[127] In December 1933, the Legion was involved centrally in the assassination of prime minister Ion Duca, and while several top Legionnaires were convicted, Codreanu himself was acquitted and his influence on the radical right grew. Throughout the mid-1930s, a welter of competing radical right organizations jostled for followers, with many of them adopting swastika symbols and overtly fascist-oriented militaristic uniforms. The Legion itself formed so-called death squads and grew rapidly, reaching some 200,000 members by late 1937. Its gruesome initiation rituals—which involved drinking the intermingled blood of fellow members while pledging to kill Jews and other enemies of the movement—reflected the emphasis on apocalyptic antisemitism and mystical violence.[128] King Carol and Romania's narrow political leadership initially responded to the rise of the Legion in various ways, ranging from periodic bans to overt attempts to co-opt its imagery. In February 1938, however, King Carol orchestrated a monarchist coup, promulgating a new constitution, instituting increased repressive measures, and ultimately, in April, having Codreanu arrested, tried, and convicted of subversion. Only a few months into Codreanu's ten-year prison sentence, his successor as leader of the Legion, Horia Sima, initiated a wave of bombings and terrorist attacks. In response, the government executed Codreanu and several other imprisoned Legionnaires on November 30, 1938. Less than two years later, however, the Legion would achieve a measure of revenge, after forging an alliance with the military strongman Ion Antonescu. In September 1940, Antonescu became prime minister and, with the support of the Legion, forced Carol II into exile. It was the Antonescu regime that would preside over the Holocaust in Romania.[129]

On the Iberian Peninsula, Portugal and Spain experienced authoritarian regimes in the 1920s. The Portuguese coup of May 28, 1926, had brought to an end the First Republic, while instituting a military dictatorship whose backing was diffuse and, ultimately, precarious. That regime was, in turn, supplanted by Antonio de Oliveira Salazar, who began as finance minister under the military dictatorship in 1928, was appointed prime minister in 1932, and subsequently instituted his own authoritarian regime, known as the Estado Novo (new state), that governed Portugal according to corporatist economic principles for more than four decades. Early on, Salazar exhibited characteristics some have referred to as fascist-oriented, including the imposition of single-party rule through the National Union. But rather than fostering fascism, Salazar's regime acted as a buffer against it.[130] The most notable form of Portuguese fascism was the National Syndicalist movement of Francisco Rolão Preto, which organized itself into blue-shirted militias and "shock brigades," and experienced particularly dramatic growth in 1933, Salazar's second year as prime minister. In response, Salazar initiated a crackdown against the Blue Shirts, banning their main newspaper and co-opting many of their leaders by bringing them into his administration. In the summer of 1934, he announced the dissolution of the National Syndicalist organization and had Rolão Preto imprisoned. During the Second World War, Salazar maintained Portuguese neutrality while overtly condemning fascism and Nazism.

The experience of Spain exhibited some initial similarities, but ultimately diverged significantly from the Portuguese trajectory. Under the authoritarian government of Primo de Rivera between 1923 and 1930, which engaged in its own aggressive nationalist mobilization, a handful of indigenous fascist-oriented movements had attempted to mobilize but with little lasting success.[131] Following the collapse of Primo de Rivera's regime and the subsequent flight of King Alfonso XIII into exile, the Second Republic was founded in 1931 and for a few years, achieved a measure of stability under a coalition formed by moderate republicans and socialists. Increasingly, however, radical forces on the left grew restless and launched a revolutionary uprising in October 1934 that failed miserably, but did manage to claim more than one thousand lives. Over the next two years, Spanish political culture became polarized to an unprecedented degree, with forces on the right massing their resources for what was viewed as an inevitable clash with the continually radicalizing left. The most dynamic force on the right was the Falange (phalanx) movement founded in 1933 by José Antonio Primo de Rivera, the son of the former dictator, who had died in exile in Paris shortly after his ouster in 1930. Under José Antonio, the Falange initially proclaimed itself overtly fascist and succeeded in uniting a number of disparate radical right organizations, although the movement remained fairly insignificant in numerical terms until 1936.[132] It promulgated a rudimentary political program known as the Twenty-Seven Points in 1934, which espoused central fascist doctrines despite the fact that José Antonio eventually distanced himself from the terminology (albeit not the ideology) of fascism.[133] Following the formation of the far left Popular Front government in February 1936, state authorities initiated a crackdown on the Falange, including the imprisonment of José Antonio in March, and the stage was set for the central conflict of modern Spanish history.

The Spanish Civil War officially began with an orchestrated military uprising primarily in Madrid and Spanish Morocco on June 17, 1936. Whereas rebel military forces were able to take Morocco fairly easily, events in Spain did not proceed as swiftly as the conspirators had planned. Over the ensuing days, government forces maintained control of Spain's major cities, with Barcelona as the major exception, whereas the Nationalists, as the military rebels labeled themselves, gained control of significant portions of the countryside. On July 20, the primary military conspirator, General José Sanjurjo, was killed in a plane crash and leadership was assumed by General Francisco Franco.[134] As fighting continued and intensified throughout the summer and fall, the civil war became internationalized, with Fascist Italy and Nazi Germany lending considerable support to Franco's forces in the form of weapons, supplies, and troops.[135] On the opposite side, so-called International Brigades were formed in defense of the Republic, and large numbers of volunteers from a variety of Western democracies joined the republican cause, although only the Soviet Union sent actual military support.[136] On November 20, 1936, the Falangist leader José Antonio Primo de Rivera, who had been in government custody since March, was executed. The violence continued to escalate, and atrocities were committed on both sides. In April 1937, Franco, who had declared himself dictator the previous October, orchestrated the political fusion of rightist forces into one overarching movement, with the Falange at its core. While Nationalist forces gained control of much of western and northern Spain in the course of 1937 and 1938, they were unable to take Madrid despite repeated attempts. Finally, in March 1939, the capital fell to Franco's forces, who proclaimed victory and launched reprisals against remaining Republican elements, executing tens of thousands. Franco consolidated his dictatorship fairly quickly, and went on to rule Spain for more than three decades.

Importantly, the Spanish Civil War had functioned essentially as a proxy battle between incompatible worldviews in an increasingly polarized Europe. Even the Western democracies that maintained stable political structures witnessed increased internal divisions. Identifiable fascist movements developed in virtually all European countries in the 1930s. In France, early and relatively insignificant fascist movements such as the Young Patriots, founded by Pierre Taittinger in 1924, and Le Faisceau (the Fasces) founded in 1925 by Georges Valois, were ultimately overshadowed by the much more formidable Croix de Feu (Crosses of Fire) movement founded in 1927

FIGURE 6.2 Antifascist caricature of Franco's support from Nazi Germany and Fascist Italy. *Sindicato Professionales Bellas Artes, U.G.T./Wikimedia Commons.*

by military officer François de la Rocque.[137] Having experienced significant growth in the early 1930s, the Croix de Feu was outlawed by France's leftist Popular Front government in 1936, leading to its effective reformation as the French Social Party, which quickly became the fastest growing party in all of France.[138] Perhaps, the most straightforward fascist organization in interwar France was the *Franciste* movement founded by Marcel Bucard in 1933.[139] Whereas Bucard later became a collaborator during the wartime Nazi occupation and was executed for treason in 1946, many early French fascists evolved politically and eventually emerged as anti-Nazi resistance figures.[140] Fascism in Belgium was shaped significantly by Léon Degrelle and his Rexist movement, founded in 1935, which combined authoritarian Catholicism with various fascist economic and stylistic traits.[141] The Rexists emerged as a major force in the 1936 elections, achieving 11.5 percent of the vote, but leveled off thereafter and were in clear decline by the time of the German invasion in 1940, which breathed new life into the movement because of its eagerness to collaborate with the Nazi occupiers.[142] In the Netherlands, the primary fascist manifestation was the National Socialist Movement founded in 1931, which espoused an expansionist foreign policy while adopting, domestically, an Italian-style fascist identity, including the avoidance of antisemitism.[143] In the 1935 regional elections, the Dutch National Socialists gained some eight percent of the entire vote, but by the time of the next national elections, in 1937, the party's level of support had been cut in half. As was the case with the Rexists in Belgium, however, the Dutch National Socialists benefited from the German occupation, remaining the only officially sanctioned political party between 1940 and 1944.[144] In Britain, a good deal of attention has been generated by the British Union of Fascists, founded in 1933 by Sir Oswald Mosley. Much of this attention is due to the charismatic public persona (and elite social connections) of Mosley, since the movement remained virtually insignificant in numerical terms.[145]

In the face of the aggressive foreign policy of Nazi Germany—which annexed Austria in March 1938 and then seized the Sudetenland that September, leading to the ultimate demise of Czechoslovakia—the Western democracies employed a cautious approach generally identified, in a pejorative sense, as appeasement.[146] They did, however, draw a proverbial line in the sand regarding the territorial integrity of Poland, which was widely (and correctly) believed to be the next target of Hitler's expansionism. In response, Hitler and his foreign minister Joachim von Ribbentrop had begun to contemplate the unthinkable: reaching an agreement with the Soviet Union, the ideological polar opposite, to enable Germany's eastward expansion without fear of immediate Soviet intervention.[147] When the Nazi-Soviet Pact was publicized on August 23, 1939, the world was largely stunned. The world would be further stunned by the rapidity and thoroughness of the Nazi conquest of Poland that began on September 1, 1939, launching Europe into its second catastrophic conflict in the past twenty-five years.

Whereas nationalism was at the heart of the justifications for the Second World War, as was the case with the First, the war's conclusion would bring a widespread European effort to transcend the ill-effects of nationalism. That effort would not only play out against the backdrop of the widespread devastation caused by war, but would be shaped fundamentally by the almost incomprehensible genocidal violence unleashed by the Nazis against the Jews and other so-called racial inferiors.

Belonging and genocide: Nation, race, and the cover of war

The broad contours of the early phases of the Second World War are well known. On September 1, 1939, Nazi Germany invaded Poland, using a fictitious border incident as a pretext, while Soviet troops invaded from the east. The fighting was largely over in the space of a few weeks—days, in some parts of Poland—and the world watched with a mixture of fear and amazement at the German *Blitzkrieg* tactics that seemed nearly unstoppable.[148] Britain and France declared war on Germany, having pledged to protect Polish territorial integrity, but neither was able to mobilize before the fall of Poland. During the fall and winter, a state of war existed, but no substantial fighting took place, leading to the popular juxtaposition of the terms Blitzkrieg (lightning war) and Sitzkrieg (sitting war).[149] The following spring brought the German invasion and conquest of Norway and Denmark, which was followed by the seizure of the Netherlands and Belgium, culminating finally in the conquest of France in June 1940. German officials forced the French to sign a humiliating peace in the same railway car in which the Germans had been forced to sign the 1918 armistice; the fact that the car had in the meantime become a treasured museum exhibit merely made the order to move it to the exact spot of the 1918 signing more satisfying for Hitler.[150] When Britain refused to bow out of the war voluntarily, the German Luftwaffe organized a massive bombing campaign that was originally designed to soften up coastal targets in preparation for an invasion of the British Isles. When that plan proved unfeasible, the bombing campaign was maintained and increased, searing the memory of "the Blitz" into the collective psyche of Londoners who had to endure months of steady civilian bombardment stretching well into 1941.[151]

With British resolve proving tenacious—often credited to the perceived inspiration imparted by Winston Churchill's soaring rhetoric—Hitler and his military leadership made the momentous decision to break the Nazi-Soviet Pact and invade the Soviet Union without having knocked Britain out of the war. When the invasion, dubbed Operation Barbarossa, was launched on June 22, 1941, it came as a severe shock to Stalin, who had chosen to ignore significant intelligence warnings.[152] Hitler claimed to have studied

Napoleon's fateful 1812 Russian invasion, which had been derailed as much by weather and terrain as by military developments, and predicted the capture of Moscow before the brutal cold of the Russian winter set in. The early stages of the invasion seemed to confirm Hitler's optimism, as the German advance proceeded rapidly and large numbers of Red Army troops melted away or were captured, including the unprecedented number of more than 500,000 taken prisoner in the September encirclement of Kiev.[153] But, the proverbial clock was ticking and the advance toward Moscow experienced unexpected delays. In October, heavy rains and an early snowfall that melted turned roads to muddy morasses in which vehicles and equipment became mired; then in early November, a freeze set in, hardening the roads, but bringing on such cold temperatures that equipment began to fail, horses began to freeze, and morale among the ill-outfitted German soldiers began to drop. The break in the advance had also given the Soviets time to transfer more than twenty divisions from Siberia to the defense of Moscow. By early December, advance German forces had progressed to the distant outskirts of Moscow, but a massive Soviet counteroffensive was launched on December 5, halting the German advance entirely. Rather than staging a retreat, which had been Napoleon's downfall in 1812, the Wehrmacht forces settled in to ride out the winter in the frozen Russian tundra. The failure to reach Moscow necessitated a major revision of German military plans in the winter of 1941–42.

It was in the context of the shifting fortunes of Operation Barbarossa that the decision to physically eradicate the Jews of Europe was made by the Nazi leadership. Although most scholars agree that the decision was made between October and December of 1941, there is significant debate about its exact timing and specific causation. If the decision was made in October, it was likely undertaken in the euphoria of anticipated victory; if in December, then it was likely occasioned by growing concern and then despair over the failure to reach Moscow.[154] More importantly, at the heart of the Holocaust was not merely the intentional drive to destroy perceived racial enemies under cover of war, but also the corresponding desire to construct new forms of belonging in Nazi-dominated Europe. Thomas Kühne has written insightfully about the relationship between belonging and genocide, noting that Nazis' policy of racial extermination provided much of the glue that bound German society together during the Third Reich; genocide not only destroys, but can also create.[155] The same general principle was visible in many parts of Europe that fell under German control, as indigenous visions of national belonging became intertwined with the extermination of the Jews.

The surviving minutes of the Wannsee Conference, the high-level Nazi meeting held outside Berlin in January 1942, demonstrate clearly that the decision for physical extermination had already been made by that point.[156] While the period between 1939 and 1941 had witnessed the brutal treatment of Jews and other civilians, in the spring of 1942, some 80 percent of the

Jewish victims who would die in the Holocaust were still living.[157] Over the next three years in the killing fields of Ukraine and Belarus and in death factories like Auschwitz and Treblinka, the genocidal plan was implemented with tragic efficiency. While Nazi Germany lost the military conflict, they largely succeeded in winning the "war" against the Jews. As undeniable as is the reality of the Holocaust, it is important to note that the initial processes that led to its realization were tortured and circuitous. To use Karl Schleunes's famous phrase, the road to Auschwitz was "twisted" indeed.[158]

When Hitler came to power in January 1933, the Jews made up less than one percent of the German population. The first few years of the Nazi regime were characterized by forms of discrimination that would be horrific by any normal standard but which, in comparison with what came later, must be considered cautious and somewhat restrained. While the April 1933 boycott of Jewish businesses has received significant attention, less well known is the fact that it was undertaken as a form of compensation, a proverbial bone thrown to Nazi radicals whose random street violence against Jews was reined in by Hitler.[159] This was in no way occasioned by humanitarian concerns, but by the desire to exert rationalized state control over the persecution of the Jews. It is also true that Jews were purged from the German civil service and professions starting in 1933, but even in this, there were initial exceptions made (at the insistence of President Hindenburg) for Jews who had fought for Germany in the First World War.[160] It took until September 1935 for the Nazis to promulgate the Nuremberg Laws, which stripped German Jews of their citizenship and outlawed intermarriage between Jews and Germans—and even then the implementation of the laws was extremely complicated, since it proved difficult to determine with certitude exactly who should be considered Jewish.[161] The later 1930s witnessed increased radicalization with the goal of forced emigration, attempting to make life so miserable for the remaining Jews that they would choose to leave on their own. The November 1938 pogrom known as Kristallnacht, or the Night of Broken Glass, is merely the most notable instance of this stepped up public persecution, which was combined with the Aryanization of Jewish property and a more stringent policy of stripping Jews of their assets before emigration. The issue of emigration was made much more difficult by the unsympathetic immigration laws of numerous countries—including the United States—who were unwilling to take Jewish refugees. Nonetheless, by the summer of 1939, more than half of the Jews who had lived in Germany in 1933 had emigrated.[162] Of those who were left, approximately 165,000 would perish in the Holocaust, meaning that the other approximately 5.8 million Jewish victims came from other European territories that fell under the control of Nazi Germany and its satellites in the course of the war.

So, although the Nazis came into "possession" of a significant number of Jews with the annexation of Austria in 1938, it was the invasion of Poland in September 1939 that changed the equation. Jews made up a significant portion of the Polish population, and in the absence of an overarching plan for the Polish Jews, the Nazis initiated the process of ghettoization—rounding up Jews from throughout towns and villages and concentrating them in closed off areas in major cities. The two largest Polish ghettos, both of which were established in 1940, were Łodz and Warsaw, with the latter swelling to some 400,000 inhabitants at its peak.[163] The ghettoization process was supplemented by mass shootings that targeted Jews and, in larger numbers initially, Polish civilians, officers, and opinion leaders.[164] A territorial solution was sought in the form of the Lublin Reservation plan, according to which Jews would be herded into an enclosed region around the Polish cities of Nisko and Lublin, but the scheme failed due to the massive logistical challenges involved.[165] The conquest of Northern and Western Europe that began in the spring of 1940 brought more Jews into the possession of Nazi Germany and, in the context of the defeat of France, another territorial solution was proposed: the so-called Madagascar plan, which would have required the French to cede control of the island to German authorities for use as an effective holding pen for the Jews under German control. The plan failed in part because Britain maintained control of the seas, making such a massive maritime transfer impossible, but it was discussed at the highest levels of Nazi planning.[166] As significant as the invasion of Poland was in increasing the numbers of Jews under German control, the 1941 invasion of the Soviet Union brought even larger numbers of Jews into the Nazi administrative sphere. Mobile killing squads known as *Einsatzgruppen* (action groups) were deployed behind the rapidly advancing front, shooting Jews, and other civilians. The brutal activities of the Einsatzgruppen were supplemented by mass shootings undertaken by German police forces and other units comprised of indigenous eastern Europeans.[167] In late July 1941, as the German advance into Soviet territory was proceeding rapidly, Reinhard Heydrich, the second most powerful figure behind Heinrich Himmler within the Nazi SS, was given the order to come up with a "total solution" (*Gesamtlösung*) to the Jewish problem. By January 1942, when Heydrich chaired the now-famous Wannsee Conference, the decision had been made to transcend earlier partial solutions like ghettoization, deportation, and shootings, in favor of a "final solution" centered on the construction of death factories in the German-occupied east.

The six generally recognized extermination camps—Auschwitz, Treblinka, Belzec, Sobibor, Majdanek, and Chelmno—were at the heart of a broader network of Nazi camps and installations stretching throughout German-occupied Eastern Europe. While there are organizational and personnel connections between the extermination camps on occupied soil and the concentration camps inside Germany, such as Dachau or Bergen-Belsen, the latter were primarily prisons for political opponents of the Nazis and were largely peripheral to the mass killing of the Holocaust.[168] The three "Operation Reinhard" camps—Belzec, Sobibor, and Treblinka—were opened in the weeks and months after the Wannsee Conference and were designed for the sole purpose of extermination. Of these, Treblinka was the most lethal, achieving a death toll of more than 800,000 in its slightly more than one year of existence.[169] Auschwitz, Chelmno, and Majdanek opened slightly earlier than the Operation Reinhard camps, beginning operations in late 1941. Auschwitz-Birkenau was the largest and most lethal of all the killing centers, with a death toll well over 1 million.[170] The broader Auschwitz complex, of which the Birkenau extermination center was part, encompassed a variety of installations. Victims who were in decent physical condition when they arrived there were often "lucky" enough to be selected for forced labor duty; the ultimate goal would still be extermination, but the Nazis wanted to squeeze every bit of labor value out of the victims before killing them. Those chosen to be worked to death would be subjected to a program of almost complete dehumanization designed to strip them of their humanity, dignity, and even morality, so that when their bodies broke down and were incapable of further labor, they could easily be exterminated as mere human husks. Their identities were erased, with names replaced by tattooed numbers, and their biological functions were reduced to an animal level. Prisoners at Auschwitz were given so few calories per day that it was impossible to survive without stealing from other inmates. So, rather than forging a solidarity of hardship among the prisoners, they were atomized and set against each other in a Darwinian competition for calories. In this sense, Auschwitz represents one logical outcome of the Darwinian nationalism that originated in the previous century. But despite its inescapable brutality, Auschwitz did at least offer the possibility of survival for those, like Primo Levi, whose bodies had not yet broken down by the time the camp was liberated by the Red Army in January 1945.[171] Those sent to Belzec, Sobibor, Treblinka, and Chelmno were typically gassed on their day of arrival.

The Nazi persecution and ultimate extermination of the Jews demonstrates not only the destructive lethality of racialized nationalism, but also its potential as a cohesive agent of belonging. Ordinary Germans were bound more tightly together by their general (if not always specific) knowledge of atrocity and genocide, perhaps not unlike a street gang that is bound together by common criminal complicity.[172] As Götz Aly has demonstrated, German families were enriched by the extensive despoliation of territories under Nazi occupation and thereby became both Hitler's beneficiaries and accomplices.[173] The Nazis also attempted to create a much more powerful sense of internal belonging by replacing social and class distinctions, which had been central to individual identity formation in the pre-Nazi era, with the powerful concept of the racial community. Members of the perceived German race were, regardless of their occupational, educational, or income level, valuable members of the larger biological organism of the German *Volk*.[174] This powerful inclusive appeal was magnified by the stringent reinforcement of the boundaries of the racial community provided by a variety of pseudoscientific justifications. Portraying Hitler as the "physician of the German race," rather than as a traditional politician, Nazi propaganda envisioned a glorious future within which disability and disease would be banished and the health and beauty of the reinvigorated German Volk would flourish. Toward this end, a variety of positive and negative eugenic measures were pursued. Negative eugenics, or the attempt to reduce or eliminate "inferior" elements within the population, included the forced sterilization legislation instituted in July 1933 and the T4 euthanasia program that ran from 1939 to 1941.[175] These programs were not targeted primarily at the Jews or other outsiders, but at the German "gene pool" itself. Positive eugenics, or the attempt to increase the proportion of racially "healthy" members of the nation, included the Nazi cult of motherhood and fertility, as well as the Lebensborn program, which provided maternity services for German women, many of whom were impregnated out of wedlock by SS men, to bring their pregnancies to full term outside of the judgmental eyes of a society not yet ready to fully embrace a post-Christian sense of morality based in blood.[176] Overall, the powerful appeal of racial inclusion could be maintained only if mechanisms of exclusion were instituted.

While the Holocaust was conceived and launched by the Nazi leadership, its implementation relied on a vast amount of support from the variety of peoples who came under the influence or direct control of Nazi Germany during the war. Much of the mass shooting activity in Ukraine, Belarus, and the Baltic territories was undertaken by "Hiwis" (*Hilfswilliger*, or volunteers) drawn from among the populations under occupation. In many cases, these figures relished the opportunity to act on longstanding antisemitic hatreds that had remained buried in peacetime, often initiating atrocities on their own under cover of war.[177] As Jan Gross has documented in excruciating (and somewhat controversial) detail, the Jewish inhabitants who comprised approximately half the population of the Polish town of Jedwabne were massacred in July 1941 not by the German forces who had recently overrun the area, but by their ordinary Polish "neighbors."[178] And as Brian Porter Szücs has shown, a virulently exclusionary form of antisemitism had become a constituent element of Polish national belonging decades before the German invasion.[179]

* * * *

To return briefly to the military course of the war, from the perspective of early 1942, the war was Germany's to win. Despite the halting of its advance toward Moscow the previous December, the Wehrmacht still appeared destined for victory. When the spring thaw brought renewed movement on the eastern front, the main thrust of the German attack was turned southward toward the oil-rich Caucasus region. By the late summer of 1942, the decision was made to engage the Red Army in a massive battle for the city of Stalingrad, which was a tantalizing target not only because of its strategic location on the Volga river but also because it bore Stalin's name. The battle constituted perhaps the most famous example of urban warfare in military history, as fierce fighting in the suburbs and outskirts of the city developed into ferocious combat on a street by street, building by building level. The German Sixth Army under Friedrich Paulus was cut off from support units and encircled in November, leading to two months of brutal attrition until Paulus, acting against Hitler's express orders, surrendered to the Soviets in late January 1943.[180] This disaster of Stalingrad was then followed, in the spring of 1943, by the devastating loss of the German Afrika Korps in Tunisia, which set the stage for the Allied invasion of the island of Sicily in July. As British and American forces moved from Sicily to begin fighting up the boot of Italy, King Victor Emmanuel III, who had appointed Mussolini prime minister in 1922, deposed the fascist leader and took him into custody in late July. This move was followed several weeks later by Italy's official about face, switching sides to align with the Allies.[181] Mussolini, for his part, was freed in a daring rescue mission led by the German SS officer Otto Skorzeny and installed as the head of a northern Italian fascist state that would last until the spring of 1945, when Mussolini was executed by Italian partisans and his body hung upside down in one of Milan's central squares.[182]

For Nazi Germany, the loss of North Africa was followed in July 1943 by a devastating defeat to the Red Army in the Battle of Kursk, which began the inexorable march to drive the Wehrmacht westward across land it had gained in the previous two years. As eastern Europe was being progressively liberated by the Red Army, a new front was opened in the west by the June 1944 Allied invasion of Normandy, which led later that summer to the liberation of France from German control. Despite the brief success of the German offensive in the Ardennes forest in December 1944, known as the Battle of the Bulge, by early 1945, the western Allies had pushed the Germans back and were preparing for the assault on the territory of Germany itself, whose cities had been largely reduced to rubble by Allied bombing campaigns over the previous two years. In effective acknowledgment of the fact that the Red Army had done most of the heavy lifting in defeating the Wehrmacht on the eastern front, the western Allies stopped their advance toward Berlin and allowed the Soviets to take the capital. During the battle for Berlin that raged throughout the spring of 1945, Hitler, the self-proclaimed champion of the German *Volk*, remained almost entirely out of the public eye, holed up with his sycophantic advisors in an extensive bunker system installed beneath the Reich Chancellery in Berlin. A man broken both physically and mentally, Hitler spent his last days divorced from reality, poring over architectural models of the majestic new Berlin he claimed would one day rise from the ashes.[183] His suicide on April 30, 1945, the day after he married his longtime mistress Eva Braun, was both cowardly and anti-climactic. The official German surrender came days later, ending the most destructive chapter in the history of Europe. A very difficult period of reckoning was about to begin.

Globally, the Second World War claimed some sixty million lives. Among its most notable institutional casualties was the League of Nations, whose optimistic creation opened this chapter. The League's ineffectiveness had been undeniable well before the military conflict began. The participants at the Dumbarton Oaks Conference in 1944 had already discussed the creation of a new deliberative structure to replace the League, thus planting the seeds of what became the United Nations.[184] When the final meeting of the League was held in Geneva in April 1946, it was little more than the public funerary display of a body (and a set of ideals) that had died largely unmourned years earlier.

7

The Fate of Nationalism in a Divided Europe, 1945–1989

On the fourth of July 1945, the *New York Times* reported that Harold Denny, one of its most respected correspondents, had died of a heart attack the previous day. Denny had worked for the *Times* for more than twenty years and, after first being posted to Europe in 1934, had covered seemingly all of the major developments that unfolded on the continent. He reported directly on Fascist Italy during the war with Ethiopia in 1936, and later that year was named *Times* correspondent in Moscow, where he made substantial waves, writing a number of influential articles on the Stalinist purges that were, according to his obituary, the "subject of diplomatic protest" and led to the arrest and exile of his personal secretary, who was a Soviet citizen. In 1939, Denny left Moscow for Paris, where he remained until the German invasion of 1940, on which he reported before being evacuated dramatically to Britain in the Miracle of Dunkirk. In 1941, he accompanied British forces to North Africa and was, in November, wounded in an engagement with Rommel's Afrika Korps and captured by German forces near the Halfaya Pass. He was eventually transported to Berlin, where he was held for five weeks in Gestapo custody and "interrogated rigorously," before being shipped to a camp in Italy, from which he was eventually released the following year. In June 1944, he arrived in northern France just ten days after the Normandy landing, and spent the next twelve months following the Allied advance through French territory and into Germany. In June 1945, after witnessing the German capitulation, he returned to the United States and died shortly thereafter in an Iowa hotel room preparing to give a speech at Drake University.[1]

One of Denny's last *Times* contributions had been published in early May, just days before the official German surrender, as he observed local behavior in communities in central Germany that had just come under American and British control. Having taken a tour of the Buchenwald concentration camp, Denny was shaken by the unwillingness of ordinary

Germans to acknowledge the reality of atrocity, and he structured his article around what he termed "the problem of what to do with a people who are morally sick." For Denny, who was unaware of the even greater horrors of the extermination camps in the East, the structures of Nazi oppression revealed a pathology endemic to the German nation itself, one that demanded some form of radical treatment. "Under Hitler Germany has committed the worst horrors history records and has invented new ones on a scale which dwarfs all previous crimes. I say Germany has committed these horrors because the German people as a whole share Hitler's guilt, though already they are hastening to disclaim it." He continued: "What we have here is a gigantic application, with characteristic Teutonic thoroughness, of a deliberately national policy—calculated cruelty, mechanized mass murder." The root of the German pathology was, for Denny, to be found in a national character that was fundamentally diseased, combining moral barbarism with unthinking conformity: "The German's most conspicuous trait, aside perhaps from his plodding industry, is his sheeplike docility, his craving to obey somebody." The moral affliction was so deeply engrained, and the barbarism so fundamental to German identity, that Denny envisioned the only possible solution as a biological one, to be effected through some kind of extended genetic disciplinary mechanism: "Perhaps in time this barbarism can be bred out of them. But if so, it will be a difficult process, lasting for generations."[2] Having covered both the catastrophic Soviet purges and the twisted racial fantasies of the Nazis, in the end Denny could apparently do no better than to reach for the same sort of eugenic prescriptions that lay at the heart of the Nazi racial obsession itself.

Harold Denny was far from alone in struggling to come to grips with the nature and extent of Nazi atrocities. But, while Denny located the problem in a disorder particular to the German nation, other European diagnoses targeted the phenomenon of nationalism itself, in all its various manifestations. Unlike the aftermath of the First World War, when the European powers in Paris committed themselves to "getting nationalism right"—combining national self-determination with democratic and constitutional structures—the aftermath of the Second World War witnessed attempts in the West to transcend nationalism while creating deeper and broader democratic structures. If people were perhaps incapable of thinking of themselves merely as human beings, at least the inhabitants of the war-torn continent might be induced to drop their national antagonisms and think of themselves as members of a democratically oriented Europe. This would, of course, require the reframing of notions of political and social belonging and the rediscovery of what Mark Mazower has termed "democracy's quiet virtues." As was the case with Renan's notion of national belonging, this project would be based, of necessity, on powerful acts of forgetting: in Italy, statues of Mussolini were replaced by memorials to partisan freedom fighters; in France, the powerful myth of resistance quickly overshadowed much of the reality of Vichy collaborationism; in Austria, the meaning of the

1938 Anschluss was reconfigured, with Austria emerging as the "first victim" of Nazi aggression.[3] It would also require, as James Sheehan has shown, a fundamental demilitarization of individual European societies.[4] In the East, Soviet dominance brought with it the claim to have transcended history and, with it, the false promises of nationalist particularism. A new communal ideal would be forged and imposed on the Soviet sphere of influence. As the Cold War division of Europe hardened, new visions of belonging were to a great extent dependent on the ways in which the catastrophe of the Second World War was explained and understood.

From the perspective of the 1980s, the last decade of the Cold War, it seemed to many scholars that the age of nationalism had come and gone. European integration in the West was largely viewed, if not as a success, then at least as a stable and lasting mediocrity. Soviet hegemony in the East was portrayed in terms of crisis, to be sure, but without much inkling about its impending demise. Nationalist tensions were seen as having been frozen during the Cold War and essentially replaced with broader structures of belonging. In an influential 1982 work, John Breuilly saw the future relevance of nationalism being limited primarily to idiosyncratic separatist movements on the peripheries of Europe.[5] David Beetham argued that national entities would continue to become less relevant because of their disjuncture with more compelling economic and social units.[6] But by the early 1990s, scholars were busy revising their earlier reports of nationalism's demise, which had indeed been greatly exaggerated.[7] Breuilly put out a new edition of his classic text which not only contained an insightful extra chapter to take into account the momentous recent events themselves, but also altered his assessment of nationalism's future. Eric Hobsbawm reissued his 1989 *Nations and Nationalism* with a rewritten and extended final chapter less than three years later.[8] Scholarly approaches not only adjusted to make room for the revival of nationalist and ethnic hostilities after 1989, but a broader reinterpretation of the role of nationalism during the preceding Cold War period was initiated.[9] One of the most significant reinterpretations was offered by Alan Milward, who argued that the chief architects of European integration had not been intent on transcending nationalism, but rather strove to "rescue" the nation-state by creating broader economies of scale that would enable individual nation-state structures to adapt to the increasingly complex imperatives of postwar production and thereby better meet the expectations (and maintain the loyalties) of their citizens. The loss of national sovereignty was, according to Milward, fairly limited and was in any case an acceptable price to pay for the retention of most forms of political power within the salvaged nation-state system.[10] Although Milward's approach was criticized by some historians for having shortchanged the diplomatic and foreign policy aspects of the integration project, his seminal work offers powerful evidence against the notion that nationalism somehow disappeared during the Cold War. Individual nation-states were to remain indispensable features of the reimagining of social and political belonging in Europe.

Postwar post-mortems and Cold War cleavages

Fairly early in the military course of the Second World War, it became clear that the Western democracies of Europe were unable to counter Nazi aggression with any degree of success on their own, and power shifted increasingly to Washington and Moscow. The resources necessary to defeat the Nazi empire and restore independent European "civilization" were, ironically, only attainable through the sacrifice of European autonomy. So, the rival American and Soviet hegemonies that dominated Europe after the war were neither surprising nor new. The first wartime conference of the major Allied powers took place in Moscow in October 1943, when the foreign ministers of the United States, Britain, and the Soviet Union met to discuss common war aims. This was followed in late November 1943 by a personal meeting of Stalin, Churchill, and Roosevelt—the first of its kind—at the Soviet embassy in Tehran, where potential scenarios for the future of Europe were discussed in tentative and cautious terms, leaving the thorny issue of Russia's control of Polish territory unsettled.[11] The decision to accept nothing less than a complete and unconditional German surrender was reaffirmed there and on numerous subsequent occasions. The next meeting of the so-called Big Three was at the Black Sea resort of Yalta in February 1945, by which point the final victory over Nazi Germany was merely a matter of timing and procedure. While the common view holds that Roosevelt, already diminished by ill health, was outmaneuvered by Stalin at Yalta, essentially giving control of postwar Central and Eastern Europe to the Soviets, the reality is more complex.[12] For Roosevelt, who still believed Soviet assistance was necessary to defeat Japan and was therefore hesitant to press Stalin, the most important issue was to secure assent for a postwar United Nations body.[13] The final meeting of the Big Three took place at Potsdam in July 1945, with Stalin facing off against Truman, who had succeeded Roosevelt upon the latter's death in April, and Clement Attlee, who replaced Churchill midway through the conference. By that point, the fronts had already hardened considerably. Stalin's Red Army had conquered Berlin on the heels of the progressive liberation of most of Eastern Europe, and there was little incentive to compromise from the perspective of the Soviet leader. Truman, on the other hand, had been informed the day before the start of the conference of the successful test of an atomic weapon in the desert near Alamagordo, potentially reducing or even removing the need for Soviet support in defeating Japan.[14] With no ability to push back the difficult decisions to a distant future date, much of the post-Potsdam settlement in Central and Eastern Europe emerged as a fait accompli.

Both the United States and the USSR had experienced a heightened sense of nationalism during the war. As John Fousek has shown, the United States reframed itself almost completely as an "imagined community," fighting not just for freedom or civilization in an abstract sense, but explicitly in pursuit of a new universalizing American mission. Even visual conceptions of space were refashioned during the war, with the globe being transformed into an "American icon," an image that was central to U.S. policy and culture during the Cold War.[15] For the Soviet Union, the Second World War was known as the "Great Patriotic War" whose sacrifices were justified by ubiquitous references to imperial Russian history and near constant public reaffirmation of the heroism of Tsarist generals who had fought for the motherland against Napoleon.[16] Leaders in both emerging superpowers hoped to build on and universalize wartime popular mobilization by creating broader spheres of influence that would transcend individual national identities. But exactly what those spheres and those identities would mean for the individual national and state structures of postwar Europe was anything but clear. The increasingly binary division between east and west, which is often portrayed in terms of colliding tectonic plates, developed atop a complex variety of realities unfolding on the ground throughout the continent.

Before the proverbial dust had begun to settle—indeed, while some of it was still being kicked up—massive movements of people were underway. The symbol of postwar Europe was in many ways the Displaced Person, a disoriented refugee trudging along what Ben Shephard has called the "long road home."[17] But where was that home to be? Millions of Poles, Ukrainians, and inhabitants of the Baltic states (Latvia, Lithuania, and Estonia, which had been seized by Stalin in 1940) were not at all eager to live under Soviet rule.[18] In 1945, there were more than eight million uprooted refugees from across Europe stranded in German territory alone: former prisoners, forced laborers, and Eastern Europeans fleeing the advance of the Soviets.[19] At the same time, millions of Germans who had settled in other parts of the continent were forcibly expelled, often brutally and almost always with Allied approval, in what R.M. Douglas has called "an immense manmade catastrophe on a scale to put the suffering that occurred as a result of the ethnic cleansing in the former Yugoslavia in the 1990s in the shade."[20] The physical infrastructure of many European cities, particularly the housing infrastructure, had been decimated during the war, while agriculture and food supply networks had also been disrupted.[21] The crisis was especially dire for surviving European Jews, who were often transferred from the brutal conditions of Nazi concentration camps to only slightly less brutal humanitarian camps for displaced persons, many of whom fit Dan Stone's description as "betrayed persons."[22] Eastern European Jews who did return to their original homes often faced brutal persecution—particularly in Poland, as seen in the Kielce pogrom of July 1946 in which more than forty Jews were murdered by townspeople following rumors of blood libel and child kidnapping.[23]

In attempting to understand the messy and fluid nature of the postwar settlement, an examination of the cases of Poland and Germany is particularly instructive. When the new Polish state was created after the First World War, the delegates in Paris had initially plotted an eastern border that became known as the Curzon Line, named for British foreign secretary

George Curzon.[24] Following the victory of Polish troops over Soviet forces in the summer of 1920, however, the Poles established their own extended border some 150 miles eastward of the Curzon Line, encompassing large numbers of Ukrainians and Belarusians. When Stalin agreed to the Nazi–Soviet Pact in August 1939, he was motivated in large part by the desire to regain that territory, which the Red Army accomplished during the conquest of Poland the next month. At the first of the three Big Three meetings in Tehran in 1943, Stalin had pressed the issue of postwar Soviet possession of that territory, but the topic was largely sidestepped by Roosevelt and Churchill.[25] At that point, the Western Allies expected the legitimate future government of Poland to be constituted from the community of exiled Polish elites in London, despite the fact that their leader, General Władysław Sikorski, had been killed in a plane crash a few months earlier.[26] But in the summer of 1944, as the Red Army progressively liberated Polish territory from the Germans, a pro-Soviet Polish government was established in Lublin. When the Polish Home Army, which was loyal to the London Poles rather than Lublin, launched the famous Warsaw Uprising in August 1944, they expected help from the approaching Red Army. But, Soviet forces stopped their advance outside Warsaw and did nothing while German forces crushed the uprising and destroyed a major portion of the Home Army.[27] This left the pro-Soviet Lublin government in a much stronger position, and Stalin recognized its diplomatic legitimacy in January 1945. The next month, at the Yalta Conference, Stalin got much of what he wanted in regard to Poland: Roosevelt and Churchill agreed to a new Polish border roughly equivalent to the Curzon Line, allowing the Soviets to keep the territory gained in September 1939, and in exchange Stalin only had to agree that the Lublin government include some London Poles and that democratic elections should be held after the war.[28] As it turned out, those elections were delayed until early 1947, by which time only two of the former London exiles had been included in the government and much of the early absorption of Poland into the Soviet bloc had already been initiated.

Postwar policy toward Germany was shaped in part by the memory of the punitive Treaty of Versailles and its destabilizing effect on Germany and Europe. In 1945, Germany's guilt was much more extensive (and much clearer) than had been the case in 1918, but the total nature of the military defeat and the complete collapse of the Nazi regime left the Allied planners with a new and different set of challenges. The first step was a temporary one: the partition and administration of German territory by the four main Allied powers, consisting of an American zone in the south, a French zone in the southwest, a British zone in the northwest, and a Soviet zone in the east. The capital Berlin, which lay entirely within the Soviet zone, was itself divided into four sectors to mirror the broader territorial partition.

During the war, a number of territorial dismemberment proposals had been floated among the Allies. In 1943, U.S. Treasury Secretary Henry Morgenthau had put forward a plan to dismantle German industry and

MAP 7.1 The occupation zones of Germany, 1946. © *George Edward Milne, 2017. Reproduced with permission.*

divide German territory into a number of small agriculturally based units.[29] A variety of other dismemberment proposals were discussed at Yalta.[30] But what developed in reality was a slow-motion morphing of the four occupation sectors into independent administration zones, with each zone formulating its own ad hoc policies toward refugees, food supply, and economic rebuilding, taking different approaches to the restoration of transportation infrastructure, the demolition of buildings made unsafe by bombing, and the reconstitution of industry. In general terms, the British and Americans favored the rapid restoration of industrial productivity, whereas the French and Soviets looked more to the extraction of material and human resources to aid with their own massive rebuilding projects.[31] The issue of reparations was particularly vexing in light of the reparations payments from the First World War that were still unfulfilled. Stalin had insisted at Yalta that Germany be forced to pay reparations of at least $20 billion, over half of which was to be given to the Soviet Union, and Roosevelt, in his diminished state, had essentially agreed. By the time of the Potsdam Conference in July 1945, however, the American position had changed drastically and Truman reversed the earlier agreement.[32] With the broader issue of total reparations left unsettled, and with the Soviets unable to gain much industrial value from the largely agrarian nature of their own zone, the United States suspended all reparations payments from the American zone to the Soviets in May 1946.[33]

The reparations impasse was paralleled by other forms of economic divergence. In the East, the Soviet occupation authorities moved quickly to nationalize production and to break up large agricultural estates. In the West, the British and Americans began cooperating more openly to stimulate economic reconstruction, although the two powers initially differed over the extent to which public ownership of industry should be instituted.[34] In early 1947, the British and Americans merged their economic interests into "Bizonia," while beginning discussions over a possible currency union. These moves were followed by the announcement in June 1947 of the Marshall Plan, which would pump billions of U.S. dollars into Europe to aid in rebuilding and, importantly, to provide a monetary incentive for Central and Eastern European states to maintain independence from rapidly spreading Soviet influence. But, when the program began in April 1948, under the official title European Recovery Program, the vast majority of funds focused on Western Europe, with a significant portion devoted to the rebuilding of the three western zones in Germany, which had recently announced plans for more streamlined cooperation both politically and economically.[35] In June 1948, a new unified Western currency began circulating, not only in the three western zones themselves, but also in Berlin, where it proved much more attractive than the fledgling Eastern currency. In response, Soviet authorities instituted the Berlin Blockade, which sealed off the city from all Western rail access and surface traffic for nearly a year. The Western authorities, in turn, organized a massive airlift operation to keep supplies flowing to west Berlin. In May 1949, the Soviets scaled back the blockade, but began plans to transform their zone into a more durable separate state. A similar mobilization took place among the Westerners, who began writing a separate constitution and, in September 1949, announced the creation of the Federal Republic of Germany. The East followed suit, proclaiming the German Democratic Republic in October. While the division was not codified as a permanent arrangement, and while numerous visions of reunification circulated throughout the Cold War era, the two Germanies would remain separate for more than four decades.

The creation of separate state structures in Germany was not only reflective of the political and economic clash between Soviet communism and Western capitalist democracy. The German case also illustrates vastly different understandings of recent (Nazi) history and divergent diagnoses of the causes of the Second World War and the Holocaust. Contrasting interpretations of nationalism were, of course, central to these assessments. On a legal level, an initial image of unanimity was created by the central participation of all four occupying powers in the International Military Tribunal held in Nuremberg between November 1945 and October 1946.[36] A mechanism for trying Nazi leaders had been discussed at each of the Big Three meetings during the war, and in August 1945, with the French joining in, the basic parameters of the tribunal were decided. Although the Soviets had wanted the trial to take place in the capital Berlin, wartime damage to the city's infrastructure made that option logistically unworkable, whereas the *Justizpalast* in Nuremberg, within the American zone, was largely undamaged and had the further advantage of an adjoining prison complex and sufficient intact housing and amenities to handle an influx of participants and press.[37] The four presiding judges were named, one from each of the four occupying powers, who also supplied an alternate judge and a lead prosecutor, whereas the defense attorneys were drawn largely from the remnants of the German legal profession.[38] Since top Nazi leaders like Hitler, Himmler, and Goebbels had committed suicide, Hermann Goering was the most prominent of the twenty-three defendants, a number that represents not even the tip of the iceberg of German culpability. But, the tribunal was of central importance in amassing a mountain of documentary evidence and witness testimony that would take historians years to work through. The verdicts were varied, with twelve death sentences being handed down, along with three acquittals and a number of convictions with differing prison sentences.

The tribunals were envisioned as the most visible aspects of a broader denazification program to be undertaken throughout occupied Germany.[39] Here is where the approaches varied greatly between East and West. The standard ideological line in the Soviet zone, and later in East Germany, held that Nazism was the product of state-monopoly capitalism.[40] This had the effect, on the one hand, of absolving ordinary workers and farmers of complicity, since they were the victims of a criminal regime driven to expansionism and conquest by the structural contradictions of late capitalism. On the other hand, the striking particularities of Jewish victimhood were subsumed beneath a broader narrative of class struggle, which was the matrix through which experiences of repression and resistance were filtered. By way of a fairly complicated, but not ineffective, exculpatory maneuver, many East Germans were exempted from stringent denazification to the extent that they embraced the single-party rule of the Socialist Unity Party and the broader structures of Soviet influence.[41] Beyond the level of ideology, practical approaches to economic denazification were built on the conviction that nationalistic militarism was the fault of identifiable elites and class enemies—both landowning nobility and industrial magnates—whose property and assets could now be seized justifiably by the state.[42] As Benita Blessing has shown, Soviet denazification placed special emphasis on educational structures, attempting to build on earlier left-oriented innovations from the Weimar era, while fostering curricular uniformity as a remedy for continuing differences based in class, gender, and religion.[43] And while nationalism—like class and religious identities—was held to be a form of bourgeois decadence, East German communists embraced a utilitarian form of "patriotism" in contrasting their anti-fascist identity to West German capitalism and its continued potential for fascist revival.[44]

In the democratic West, the excesses of Nazism were blamed on a variety of factors, ranging from totalitarian collectivism to the failure of individual morality. The Western Allies, and particularly the United States, wanted more than anything a stable, prosperous German partner to further American interests in the face of the growing Cold War. So, while a gesture was made in the direction of justice, the emphasis on rebuilding led the Americans to hand over much of the denazification process to the Germans themselves, thereby creating major continuities, particularly among bureaucratic and professional elites, between the Third Reich and the Federal Republic.[45] Denazification authorities famously accepted what were known as *Persilscheine* (Persil certificates), which consisted of testimonials or letters of character attestation written on behalf of former Nazis to explain away their Nazi involvement, thereby cleansing them of guilt.[46] *Persil* was, of course, a leading German brand of laundry detergent.

West European integration and new forms of belonging

The civilian destruction wrought by the war in each combatant nation was unprecedented. In aggregate terms, if fatalities from disease and starvation are added to those who were shot, bombed, gassed, or worked to death, the number of European noncombatants who lost their lives between 1939 and 1945 approaches 18 million.[47] The rebuilding of physical infrastructure, which was aided by the Marshall Plan, had to be accompanied on a human level by political and moral reconstruction. The process was not always edifying, particularly for those who had in some way collaborated with the Nazi overlords.[48] In France, between one and two thousand former Vichy officials and fascist collaborators were executed in the aftermath of liberation, including former prime minister Pierre Laval and the leading right-wing journalist Robert Brasillach.[49] Elsewhere, collaborationist figures like the Dutch fascist leader Anton Mussert and the Norwegian puppet dictator Vidkun Quisling were executed.[50] With much of the radical right discredited after 1945, a number of new Christian-oriented movements and parties flourished, buoyed by a sense of moral superiority over both the evils of fascism in the West and godless communism in the East. The most notable of these were the sizable Christian Democratic parties that developed in Belgium, the Netherlands, Austria, West Germany, Italy and, on a somewhat less successful level, France.[51] These parties often overcame class-based divisions as well as internal confessional cleavages between Catholics and Protestants. They also learned to work together with moderate Social Democratic parties, which also emerged reinvigorated from the war and, in certain cases, proceeded to disavow the more radical Marxist elements of their own histories.[52] Although French communists enjoyed a brief period of relevance around 1945, the only lasting communist successes in Western Europe during the Cold War were in Italy.[53] While accepting the nation-state as the venue for practical political activity, both Christian and Social Democrats exhibited a genuine commitment to (Western) European integration, contributing to new visions of supranational belonging.

Before examining the integration process that began in earnest in the early 1950s, let us first take a brief tour through the nation-states of Western Europe in the years immediately following the war. Britain had come through the war damaged by bombing but untouched by foreign occupation, and complicated issues like collaboration and resistance were present only in very muted form.[54] By 1945, the Conservatives had dominated government for more than a decade under Stanley Baldwin, Neville Chamberlain, and then Winston Churchill, with the Labour Party holding its position on the Left without ceding significant ground to communists or radicals. In the July 1945 elections, British voters ousted Churchill, who had had barely two months to exult in the victory over Germany, replacing him with the Labour leader Clement Attlee.[55] Fear of continued high domestic unemployment was the key factor, and Attlee's Labour government built its policy on the cornerstone of attaining full employment. This brought with it a dramatic reconceptualization of the relationship between the economic and service infrastructure of the nation-state and the individual members of the nation.

Previously, balanced budgets had been seen as necessary to court the favor of the international banking sector and to maintain the stability of currency markets, even if that meant hardship for individual citizens whose services and pensions might be cut. Now, in pursuit of the economic ideas of John Maynard Keynes and William Beveridge, the Attlee government saw it as a duty of the state, especially during peacetime, to forecast the future gaps that might exist between employment and demand, and then to invest public funds to erase that gap—pursuing the goal of full employment at the expense, if need be, of balanced budgets.[56] This led also to a partial nationalization of the British coal and steel industries. Perhaps more notably, however, Labour's approach to employment policy was supplemented by a dramatic expansion of the preexisting structures of the welfare state. The National Health Service was greatly expanded and was open to all, free of charge, starting in 1948.[57] Government family assistance payments were increased, and the educational system was made more egalitarian. All this came, of course, at the price of higher taxes, and disaffection with continued shortages in foodstuffs and consumer goods grew rapidly. A series of strikes forced Labour officials to oppose certain forms of union activism, mobilizing against elements that had traditionally been in Labour's own camp, and the maintenance of Britain's overseas colonies continued to siphon massive public sums into military spending. In the elections of 1951, Winston Churchill and the Conservatives returned to power, but were unable (and to an extent, unwilling) to roll back the changes of the previous five years. The steel industry was once again privatized, but the coal and rail industries remained state enterprises.

And, expanded health and welfare benefits would have proved impossible to scale back, had the Tories made any serious attempt at it. Despite the continued sense of crisis that attended the immediate postwar years, it was the achievement of the Labour government to enable new segments of the population to envision themselves as members of a more rounded national community whose structures were directly connected to their everyday well-being, within a context of peacetime production and without the intrusions and oppressive conformity characteristic of totalitarian systems.

In the low countries—Belgium, the Netherlands, and Luxembourg—the immediate postwar years brought a fairly swift return to some sense of normalcy and stability. But, the war had also fundamentally altered conceptions of political and social belonging, both internally and within the broader context of Europe. Two of those states, Belgium and Luxembourg, had formed an initial customs union in the early 1920s, tying their economic and productive fates together in an early prefiguration of the much more extensive integrated European economic structures that would emerge at mid-century. During the war, all of the low countries had experienced German occupation, which enhanced a sense of internal national cohesion not all that dissimilar from the repercussions of Napoleonic occupation elsewhere in the early nineteenth century. In Belgium, postwar political developments were complicated not only by the problem of former fascist collaborators, such as the Rexists, but by the question of how to deal with King Leopold III, who had surrendered in problematic fashion to the Germans in 1940 and was released at the end of the war.[58] Due to concerns over possible pro-German sympathies, Leopold remained abroad for the first five postwar years, with his brother Charles ruling as regent. In 1950, a national referendum on the future of the monarchy was held, with Leopold winning a very narrow majority in favor of his return as king. Public outrage was widespread, particularly on the left, and a massive general strike was called in July 1950, forcing Leopold to abdicate in favor of his son Baudouin in early August.[59] Politically, the Belgian Socialist Party governed between 1945 and 1950, when the Christian Social Party under Gaston Eyskens came to power. With the exception of a socialist interlude between 1954 and 1958, the Christian Social Party remained in power until changing its name to the Christian People's Party in 1968.[60]

In the Netherlands, conquest at the hands of Germany had led to the flight of Queen Wilhelmina to London in May 1940, and her image, in portraits and photographs, served as a symbol of national resistance against the Germans. Her return after the war, however, elicited fairly widespread negative responses and she decided, in part due to failing health, to abdicate in favor of her daughter Juliana in May 1948. The Dutch political system was characterized by the phenomenon of "pillarization" (*Verzuiling*), in which competing political camps ("pillars") remained largely divorced from each other.[61] Attachments and loyalties were cultivated first and foremost within the context of one's sociopolitical faction: either the socialist Labor

Party, the Catholic People's Party, the secular People's Party for Freedom and Democracy, or the largely Protestant Christian Historical Union. These loyalties did not supplant broader Dutch national sentiment, but rather refracted it in idiosyncratic ways.[62]

In Luxembourg, the wartime German occupation had technically only lasted two years; in August 1942, the duchy was officially annexed and Luxembourgers became German citizens (which meant, among other things, that they could be drafted into the German military). But, opposition was widespread. The official languages of Luxembourg had been German and French, but wartime occupation stimulated the growth of Luxembourgish, which had previously been an informal dialect used primarily in the home, as a language of resistance and national self-articulation. Its grammar and vocabulary coalesced through widespread refusal to speak the language of the German occupiers, and that coalescence continued after liberation.[63] A standardized linguistic system was first published in 1946, and since then Luxembourgish has become a central vessel for "reimagining the nation," to use Kristine Horner's term, taking its place alongside German and French as an official language of state.[64] The postwar return of Duchess Charlotte, who had fled the Nazi occupation in 1940, was much less problematic than was the case with her royal counterparts in Belgium and the Netherlands, and the political system achieved a stable, if boring, level of normalcy fairly quickly under the Christian Social People's Party, which was founded in 1945 and governed until the mid-1970s.

In France, the search for national consensus and new structures of belonging was already underway before war's end, beginning with liberation in 1944. The return of Charles DeGaulle that year as the head of the Free French forces was essential in linking the heroic imagery of resistance and liberation with the French nation itself, rather than the British or Americans. De Gaulle had formed a provisional government in Paris in the late summer of 1944 but when, in October 1945, the French voted overwhelmingly against reconstituting the prewar Third Republic, he quickly grew disillusioned with the new Fourth Republic and thus resigned in early 1946. The Fourth Republic was governed during its twelve-year life by a combination of leftists (including socialists and Republican radicals) and Catholics (organized mainly under the rubric of the Popular Republican Movement). The economy was nationalized more quickly and to a greater extent than in Britain; while the rail system was already state-run, in the course of 1946, the coal, steel, and electric industries were nationalized, as were major banks, insurance companies, and the Renault automobile company. The literary critic Roland Barthes noted that the nationalization of Renault was a particular point of French national pride, amounting to "the equivalent of the construction of the large gothic cathedrals; this nationalization was a great creation of this era, [...] consumed as a mythical image by a whole nation."[65] Social services were also expanded. But, despite significant progress made by the economic reforms of Jean Monnet, who would later play a key role in European integration, dissatisfaction with the fundamental instability of the system grew, as more than twenty different governments rose and fell before the Fourth Republic itself was discarded in 1958.

Postwar Italy offers a particularly interesting and complicated case. Having switched sides during the war, Italy was the site of heavy fighting between 1943 and 1945. When hostilities ended, official Italian representatives, including Mussolini's successor Marshal Pietro Badoglio, expected to be treated favorably in the postwar settlement. Instead, Italy lost the region of Trieste to Yugoslavia (the city of Trieste was initially under international administration), while a number of Italian islands in the Aegean were given to Greece, and all Italian colonial possessions were dissolved.[66] Internally, Italian society and politics were deeply divided, and the divisions often took on a geographic dimension. In the south, which had been liberated by the Western Allies first, most Italians expected and desired a continuation of constitutional monarchy under the House of Savoy. In the north, however, the liberation had been achieved largely by communist partisans who expected a central say in the postwar political restructuring. For the first year after war's end, King Victor Emmanuel III technically remained on the throne, despite being personally tainted by his earlier support for Mussolini.[67] In the June 1946 elections, Italians voted for a republic to replace the monarchy and elected a constituent assembly to create new constitutional structures. The new Italian Republic was governed by the Christian Democrats, who came to power under Alcide De Gasperi in 1946 and remained there under his successors, through twenty consecutive administrations, until the early 1980s. Christian Social control of the prime minister's seat was shadowed over the years by the consistently strong performance of the Italian Communist Party, which averaged more than 20 percent of the popular vote under its leader Palmiro Togliatti in the Republic's first five postwar elections, before gaining even more votes under Togliatti's successors between the 1960s and 1980s.[68] There were periodic outbursts of Italian nationalism under De Gasperi, particularly in 1953 in debates over the fate of Trieste, but as Christopher Seton-Watson has noted, postwar nationalist sentiment took the form of a kind of "imperial hangover" that was ultimately overshadowed by Italy's central role in European integration.[69]

Elsewhere, on the peripheries of southwestern and northern Europe, some common trends can be noted. Spain and Portugal had begun the postwar period as semi-outcasts among the states of Western Europe, but both were integrated increasingly into the Western anti-communist consensus by the 1950s. Franco's dictatorship continued unbroken under the *Falange*, and among the Allies, there had been public calls for his removal in 1945. Relations between Roosevelt and Franco were particularly embittered.[70] Within a few years, however, Franco's willingness to allow U.S. military bases to be built in Spain brought closer economic ties with the West, including the extension of American loans, and Spain's pariah status was further ameliorated by its admittance to the United Nations in 1955. Portugal continued its authoritarian trajectory under Salazar, but because Portugal had allowed the Allies to build bases in the Azores during the war, his regime was viewed more positively than Franco's.[71] Portuguese economic development was also stimulated by loans from the United States, leading to closer economic and political ties with the West. Cold War-era conceptualizations of national identity in Portugal—the "geopolitical narratives" the Portuguese told themselves about their identity—were also shaped dramatically by the broader process of decolonization, which is discussed later in this chapter.[72]

To the north, the Scandinavian nations moved closer toward integration with each other before the broader European integration project got off the ground. Denmark had emerged from German occupation with its humanitarian image enhanced by the rescue of the Danish Jews during the Holocaust, one of the few bright spots in a broader story characterized all too often by national indifference to genocide.[73] Sweden had been both neutral and unoccupied during the war, which allowed it to serve as a haven for the Danish Jews who were ferried out of reach of the Nazis. On a much less flattering note, however, Sweden's neutrality had not been merely a mask for pro-Allied humanitarianism; in true neutral fashion, the Swedes had allowed German troops to be transported through their territory at various points and maintained trade relationships with Nazi Germany for most of the war.[74] Norway's wartime puppet regime and postwar execution of former premier Vidkun Quisling have been mentioned already. Between 1945 and 1950, however, those bitter experiences were softened somewhat by Norway's rapid economic growth, which along with Sweden, was among the most striking in Europe.[75] Loosely paralleling the Scandinavism of the mid-nineteenth century, the late 1940s and early 1950s witnessed energetic efforts to forge common notions of belonging. In 1946, the three Nordic nations founded the joint aviation venture Scandinavian Airlines, which remains the largest air carrier in the region to the present day. On a more structural level, in 1952, the Nordic Council was founded, creating an inter-parliamentary union not only between Denmark, Sweden, and Norway, but also between Iceland and Finland.[76] This Nordic union was often cited as "the Other European Community," presaging what eventually became the European Union and providing an example of the spatial and political imaginary necessary to make meaning out of such broader structures of belonging.[77] As Nordic participation increased within the broader European integration project, the twentieth-century phenomenon of Scandinavism has faded in intensity but has not disappeared.[78]

* * * *

The broad contours of the overarching European integration process are fairly well known. Against the backdrop of the loss of European independence and global influence during the early Cold War, increasing numbers of European leaders were willing to sacrifice central elements of traditional national identity in building an enhanced sense of unified (Western) Europeanness. Models of such a broad identity were either historically distant, in the form of the empires of Rome or Charlemagne; ideologically freighted, as in the case of Napoleonic Europe; or structurally unreproducible, as in the case of Latin Christendom. The latter model was, however, particularly appealing to the central architects of postwar European unity—Robert Schuman and Konrad Adenauer, for example—especially when conceived in flexible terms.[79] Schuman, a devout Catholic, was born in Luxembourg, completed all of his university studies in Germany, and opened a law practice on the eve of the First World War in Alsace-Lorraine, which was then part of the German Empire. When the region went over to French control after the German defeat in 1918, Schuman became a French citizen and decided to enter politics. Having emerged as one of the most influential parliamentary deputies in the interwar period, Schuman founded the Catholic-oriented Popular Republican Movement in 1945 and served two separate stints as French prime minister in 1947 and 1948. But, it was in his capacity as French foreign minister from 1948 to 1953 that he exercised a decisive influence in forging a unified Europe on the basis of Catholic-Christian culture, a project one scholar has called an exercise in "neoscholastic humanism."[80] Konrad Adenauer, who spent his entire life and career in Germany, did not experience the multinational influences that shaped Schuman; but as a deeply believing Catholic from Western Germany, Adenauer came to share Schuman's broad vision of a culturally unified Christian *Abendland*.[81] During the Weimar era, Adenauer had served as mayor of Cologne, but was forced out by the Nazis and remained in semi-retired seclusion for the duration of the Third Reich. Having been untainted by Nazi associations, Adenauer was particularly appealing to the Western Allies and won election as West Germany's first chancellor in 1949. Alongside Schuman and the Italian Christian Democrat Alcide De Gasperi, Adenauer used his position as West German chancellor to help forge a unified (and strongly Christian-oriented) vision of European identity.[82]

The United States also played an important background role in the initiation of European integration. Having authorized the expenditures for the Marshall Plan, U.S. officials stipulated that its funds be dispensed through a multinational European agency, which came into life in 1948 as the Organization of European Economic Cooperation (OEEC).[83] This agency was staffed with bureaucrats who became important figures in the initial drive toward European unity. The United States was also central to the creation of the North Atlantic Treaty Organization (NATO), which was founded in April 1949 in the context of the Soviet blockade of Berlin. The United States and Canada joined together with ten Western and Northern European nation-states in an alliance that bound all members to mutual defense in case of military attack. The building of common military structures under international command further enhanced the ideational plausibility of a broad Western identity based on democratic and humanitarian values.

The month after the founding of NATO, in May 1949, a new supranational parliamentary body made its first appearance: the Council of Europe. Initially envisioned as a proto-legislature for the future united Europe, the Council faced skepticism from the British in particular, who repeatedly blocked attempts to give it more authority. As a result, the Council developed into a largely symbolic body without the ability to issue binding legislation, and the movement for unity was directed primarily into economic channels over the next few years. The most significant step in that direction was the so-called Schuman Declaration, issued by French foreign minister Schuman in May 1950, which laid the foundation for the first actual forerunner of the European Union: the European Coal and Steel Community (ECSC), founded the following year. As seen in the excerpt below, Schuman's vision for the future of Europe was tied to the overcoming of the longstanding Franco-German antagonism, which is perhaps not surprising coming from a man whose personal biography was shaped so centrally by the problematic relationship between those two nations.

EXCERPT 7.1

Declaration, May 9, 1950

Robert Schuman

Europe will not be made all at once, or according to a single plan. It will be built through concrete achievements which first create a de facto solidarity. The coming together of the nations of Europe requires the elimination of the age-old opposition of France and Germany. Any action taken must in the first place concern these two countries.

With this aim in view, the French Government proposes that action be taken immediately on one limited but decisive point: It proposes that Franco-German production of coal and steel as a whole be placed under a common High Authority, within the framework of an organization open to the participation of the other countries of Europe. The pooling of coal and steel production should immediately provide for the setting up of common foundations for economic development as a first step in the federation of Europe, and will change the destinies of those regions which have long been devoted to the manufacture of munitions of war, of which they have been the most constant victims. The solidarity in production thus established will make it plain that any war between France and Germany becomes not merely unthinkable, but materially impossible.

The setting up of this powerful productive unit, open to all countries willing to take part and bound ultimately to provide all the member countries with the basic elements of industrial production on the same terms, will lay a true foundation for their economic unification. This production will be offered to the world as a whole without distinction or exception, with the aim of contributing to raising living standards and to promoting peaceful achievements.

In this way, there will be realized simply and speedily that fusion of interest which is indispensable to the establishment of a common economic system; it may be the leaven from which may grow a wider and deeper community between countries long opposed to one another by sanguinary divisions. By pooling basic production and by instituting a new High Authority, whose decisions will bind France, Germany, and other member countries, this proposal will lead to the realization of the first concrete foundation of a European Federation indispensable to the preservation of peace.[84]

Schuman's image of employing in the service of peace the productive elements typically used to wage war was compelling on a number of levels. It gave (West) Germany the possibility of heavy industrial development without the potentially problematic meddling of Allied occupation authorities. It gave France a way of influencing the inevitable reindustrialization of Germany along peaceful lines, ending the cycle of anti-French aggression that had followed nineteenth-century Prussian industrialization and the Hitlerian economic resurgence of the 1930s. And, it gave advocates of political integration a model of how common economic policy could become the "first step in the federation of Europe" on a political level.[85]

When the ECSC moved from concept to reality in 1951, it had six founding members: France, West Germany, Italy, Belgium, the Netherlands, and Luxembourg.[86] The first president of the ECSC High Authority, Jean Monnet,[87] delivered an influential speech on June 22, 1953, in which he praised the participants' eagerness to "override national differences and the rigidity of national sovereignties," forging a new mode of economic and political belonging in which decisions were being "carried out in our six countries as if they were but one country....This first Common Market, these first supranational institutions, are the beginnings of a united Europe." Monnet's vision for the type of political union that would grow out of the ECSC was ambitious, calling for a new "Political Authority based on a parliament elected by direct universal suffrage." And, his justifications for this ambitious vision were grounded in a practical view of human nature, combining the harsh lessons of history with civic idealism in the pursuit of a new identity for the people of Europe that was no longer based on fear:

Rules and institutions do not change men's natures but they do bring about a change in their behavior toward one another. That is the lesson which civilization has taught us. The rules and institutions which we are establishing will contribute essentially towards guiding the action of the peoples of Europe in the paths of peace.... After all, in this undertaking, which has begun with coal and steel, there is an ultimate objective, namely a human objective. It is the people of Europe who are concerned. Our aim must be to reestablish conditions, which eliminate fear and suspicion from human relations.[88]

Monnet's speech had also mentioned the idea of the Common Market, which officially came into being as the European Economic Community (EEC) as a result of the March 1957 Treaty of Rome.[89] The parliament mentioned by Monnet had already begun a few months before his speech, in very rudimentary form, as the Common Assembly of the ECSC. After the Treaty of Rome, it initially was renamed the European Parliamentary Assembly, before assuming the more lasting designation European Parliament in the early 1960s. By the late 1970s, the parliament had not only gained fairly substantial powers, but began to be elected by direct popular election in the individual member states. Those states, in turn, grew from the original six at the time of the founding of the ECSC to nine in 1973, when Britain, Ireland, and Denmark joined the EEC. Within two years, however, Britain held a referendum to determine whether to withdraw from the Common Market it had so recently joined. The new head of the conservative party, Margaret Thatcher, had campaigned successfully for Britain to remain in the EEC, although she eventually adopted a strongly Euroskeptical stance.[90] The 1980s witnessed three more accessions—Greece, Spain, and Portugal— so that by the end of the Cold War, the European Community numbered twelve member states. Its rechristening as the European Union and its rapid expansion since the 1990s will be discussed in the next chapter.

The European integration process, which created new ideals of geographic and political community that transcended the traditional nation-state, was paralleled outside of Europe by decolonization, which also brought about a refashioning of conceptions of belonging.[91] Most European powers had managed to hold on to their overseas colonies throughout the interwar period—with the exception, of course, of the Germans, who were stripped of their colonies by the Treaty of Versailles. Liberation movements in the colonies had been stimulated by the interwar rhetoric of national self-determination, but it was primarily in the context of the diminution of European power and legitimacy after the Second World War that the decolonization process hit high speed. The two major superpowers, the United States and the Soviet Union, encouraged postwar colonial independence movements in a variety of ways. Beginning with Lebanon and Syria during the later stages of the war, and followed after 1945 by the emergence of independent Jordan, Iraq, and

FIGURE 7.1 *Signing of the Treaty of Rome, 1957. Photo by Eric VANDEVILLE/ Gamma-Rapho via Getty Images.*

Egypt, the political map of the Middle East was fundamentally redrawn by the stark reduction in British and French power.[92] As significant as it was for the history of the Middle East, the establishment of the independent State of Israel in 1948, which was accompanied by military conflict with Egyptian, Iraqi, and Syrian forces, was a significant moment in the history of European nationalism. From the first conceptualizations of modern Zionism in circles surrounding Theodor Herzl and Nathan Birnbaum in the 1890s, the drive for a recognized Jewish homeland had represented one of the most notable offshoots of European nationalism.[93] Outside of the Middle East, British rule in the Indian subcontinent ended with the establishment of the independent states of India and Pakistan in 1947.[94] Between 1945 and 1949, the Dutch, with initial British assistance, fought a bitter and unsuccessful colonial war against nationalist insurgents in Indonesia, resulting in the establishment of the independent Republic of Indonesia under Sukarno.[95] The French, who were especially dogged in attempting to hold onto their empire, fought a series of unsuccessful colonial wars, beginning with the Indochina conflict between 1946 and 1954.[96] When the French eventually pulled out, the United States established itself as the primary enforcer of anti-communist polity in the region.[97] The entirety of France's attention, as it turned out, was required by the lengthy colonial war fought in Algeria between 1954 and 1961. After four years of fighting against the Algerian National Liberation Front, frustrated French military officers launched a bid to seize control of colonial governance in Algiers, leading to a broad political crisis in France that resulted in the demise of the Fourth Republic as a system. Charles De Gaulle returned from retirement and helped forge the more authoritarian presidential system of the Fifth Republic, which came into being in October 1958.[98] In early 1962, after more guerilla fighting and scandalous charges of military excess and torture, De Gaulle was forced to open negotiations with the National Liberation Front, resulting in Algerian independence by that summer. As Todd Shepard has shown, the loss of Algeria, which had been a fully integrated part of France for more than a century, refashioned French notions of belonging and ruptured the universalist republicanism that had been at the heart of much French nationalist discourse.[99]

The external challenges presented by decolonization were accompanied internally by a series of social and cultural movements that eventually called into question much of the political and economic consensus underpinning the postwar order in the West. It is important to note at the outset, however, that the consensus was initially broad and quite compelling. The 1950s had been characterized by remarkable economic growth and the achievement of unprecedented increases in the standard of living, particularly in West Germany, which experienced the so-called economic miracle under Konrad Adenauer and his economics minister (and eventual successor) Ludwig Erhard. Throughout the 1950s and into the 1960s, the Gross National Product of West Germany grew at an average annual rate fully twice that of the United States, whose economy was itself booming. West German export growth was also impressive, with exports as a percentage of GNP increasing from 9 percent in 1950 to nearly 20 percent in 1960.[100] The standard image of the *Wirtschaftswunder* and its creature comforts is not entirely exaggerated: millions of West German households got dishwashers and washing machines, families gathered around the television to watch dubbed episodes of American sitcoms, young adults streamed to cinemas to see James Dean movies, and teenagers listened to Elvis Presley records and danced to Bill Haley at school sock hops.[101] The Economic Miracle brought with it important consequences for West German notions of political and social belonging. In its gendered aspects, it reinforced traditional family and sex roles, with women's reproductive and moral usefulness to the nation being rewarded by a bevy of new household gadgets combined with increasingly sophisticated appeals to females as discerning consumers.[102] Economic prosperity was also linked to democratic values, unlike the depression era, when democracy was widely seen as incapable of providing economic stability and meeting basic human needs. This democratic acclimation process was accompanied by a thorough Americanization of West German culture—as indicated by the references to television, film, and music above—proving to be an increasingly valuable asset for the United States at the height of the Cold War.[103]

The principal vehicle for this unprecedented economic growth was the Social Market Economy, a hybrid capitalist system that combined private free enterprise and state involvement to guarantee social and welfare provisions, built on the concept A.J. Nicholls and others have called "freedom with responsibility."[104] As seen in the 1960 speech of economics minister Ludwig Erhard excerpted below, the Social Market Economy was more about community and belonging than about employment statistics and trade balances. The system would succeed only if, in addition to providing prosperity and sustenance, it also addressed fundamentally human needs on the level of moral and spiritual identity, forging a "new approach to life" by imparting meaning and social cohesion to individuals in an otherwise atomized world.

For Erhard, it was on the level of "one's relationship with society as a whole" and the "mental and spiritual associations" forged between members

EXCERPT 7.2

Economic Policy as a Component of Social Policy (1960)

Ludwig Erhard

Any statement of economic policy, if it is to further the dynamic expansion of our national and social life, must be constantly under review in order to link past, present and future together in one smooth and unbroken harmony. This means that the guiding principles of economic policy not only leave their mark on society but are also shaped and altered by it. The echo that economic policy finds in the minds of a nation will resound all the more if that policy succeeds not merely in fulfilling its more immediate aims but also in giving a convincing answer to contemporary spiritual problems. [...] What then is lacking? Why is it that, for all the achievements and the almost grandiose triumphs of the Social Market Economy, people are still not entirely content and society is not entirely satisfied? How is one to explain the fact that, despite security of employment and growing production in a steadily expanding economy, people are still not satisfied?

On closer reflection we may come to the conclusion that, where a democratic society such as ours has undergone tremendous industrial expansion and has been shaken to its foundations, a special effort is needed to evolve a social policy which will encourage a new approach to life in keeping with the times. [...] Seen in terms of economic policy, the problem is one of working towards a humanization of our environment in all spheres of life but particularly in the economic sphere. [...] That system can only be made secure if we bring home to the German people that their social and economic life, in all its manifestations and ramifications, is the outward expression of inner will and spiritual fulfillment.[105]

of a community that the process of postwar rebuilding would truly be made meaningful.

But, throughout the 1960s and 1970s, across much of Western Europe, new challenges arose on the basis of new notions of belonging. Particularly in Italy, France, and West Germany, student demonstrations were fueled only partially by the overcrowding of lecture halls and continued forms of restrictive elitism in university access; identification with non-Europeans and oppressed peoples was a much more decisive factor. European leaders seemed complicit in the immoral U.S. military involvement in Vietnam, and anti-war protests became a regular facet of life in university towns.[106] The postwar prosperity of their parents' generation appeared to many students as shallow and self-satisfied materialism. Unwilling to replace capitalist conformity with the regimented certainties of Marxist orthodoxy, however, students often eclectically mixed the vague collectivism of Che Guevara with individualist hedonism, sexual license, and drug experimentation. Perhaps, the most striking instance of student protest combining with other forms of discontent occurred in Paris in the spring of 1968. Beginning in March, students staged sit-ins at the new university campus in the west Parisian suburb of Nanterre, which was followed by other similar developments, culminating on May 11, 1968 in a demonstration at the Sorbonne in Paris in which hundreds were injured and hundreds more arrested. Over the ensuing days, workers joined with the growing student unrest, declaring a strike in which multiple millions of French men and women participated.[107] Student and worker unrest combined in Italy to create the largest wave of strikes in nearly fifty years during the "Hot Autumn" (*autumno caldo*) of 1969.[108] Demonstrators also took to the streets across Western Europe to advocate for greater women's rights, protest falling grain prices, and air grievances about environmental degradation, fuel scarcity, and inflationary policies. Throughout the 1970s, some radical leftists, often with roots in the student movement, turned increasingly to domestic terrorism in the belief that fundamental change could not be achieved without purgative destruction. The Red Army Faction in West Germany and the Red Brigades in Italy engaged in a series of bombings and bank robberies, in addition to undertaking a number of high profile kidnappings.[109] In Northern Ireland, decades of tensions boiled over into the "Troubles" that began in 1968 and continued for some three decades.[110] The widespread taking of life was justified in the name of restoring a unified sense of national belonging.

Social and political belonging under Soviet hegemony

The end of the Second World War had brought, from the perspective of the Soviet Union, both the hard-fought right to extend its influence throughout

Eastern and Central Europe and the pressing need to crack down internally on the organizational unruliness and perceived ideological laxity that had developed during the war. In response to the announcement of the U.S. Marshall Plan in 1947, Stalin had moved more aggressively to consolidate communist control over the governments of neighboring states, fostering or installing the so-called People's Democracies. These were, however, democracies in name only—barely even that—and it took extensive coercion and force to establish and maintain them. The consolidation process in Poland, discussed earlier in this chapter, proceeded fairly quickly and was essentially accomplished by the time of the first scheduled postwar elections in January 1947. While typically more protracted elsewhere, the process was essentially completed throughout the region by the time a separate East German state was proclaimed in the fall of 1949.

Romania had seemed initially to present the most difficult case for postwar communist consolidation. In 1940, King Carol II had abdicated and the authoritarian strongman Ion Antonescu had governed until the Soviets invaded and toppled his regime in 1944. King Carol's son Michael returned from exile, had Antonescu arrested (he was later executed), and oversaw the establishment of a provisional government under the anti-fascist military officer Nicolae Rădescu. At that point, there was very little indigenous communist organization in Romania. In February 1945, however, Stalin pressured King Michael to replace Rădescu with Petru Gorza, the pro-Soviet leader of the Ploughman's Front, which operated essentially as the rural arm of Romania's fledgling communist movement. Although Michael remained technically on the throne until late 1947, under Gorza, pro-Soviet forces moved quickly to consolidate power.[111] They rigged the November 1946 elections to give the communists and their allies nearly three-quarters of the seats in parliament. By early 1948, Stalinist stooges had achieved the absorption of the social democrats into the new communist Romanian Workers Party, which dominated the March 1948 elections with its rural partner the Ploughman's Front. At that point, Gheorghe Gheorghiu-Dej quickly emerged as the major figure among Romanian communists, establishing an effective police state and further consolidating pro-Soviet hegemony through force and brutal repression over the ensuing years.[112] Ultimately, the forcible attempt to return to earlier forms of (Leninist) universalism interacted with the problematic legacy of interwar nationalist politics to produce what Cheng Chen has identified as a distinctly Romanian brand of "illiberal nationalism," with ramifications that lasted well beyond the Cold War era.[113]

In Hungary, the rightist authoritarian regime of Miklós Horthy had been followed during the war first by Nazi occupation in the spring of 1944 and then by the Soviet invasion that fall, which initiated fierce fighting that lasted several months before Red Army forces finally prevailed. A provisional government was established under the military officer Béla Miklós, and in the first postwar elections in November 1945, the peasant Smallholders'

Party finished first by a wide margin. The party's leader, Zoltán Tildy, served for several months as prime minister before being elected President of the Hungarian Republic early the next year. In the November 1945 election, the Social Democrats had finished in second place, with the Communists coming in third, more than forty points behind the Smallholders' Party.[114] The communist leader Mátyás Rákosi, who had participated in Bela Kun's short-lived communist takeover in 1919, traveled to Moscow shortly after the election and began taking his marching orders directly from Stalin. Hungary was governed throughout 1946 by Ferenc Nagy as prime minister and Tildy as president, but with several key cabinet positions going to the communists. Under increasing pressure from Moscow and the domestic communists under Rákosi, Nagy was forced into exile in February 1947, and later that year the parliament was suspended. When Tildy was forced out as president in the summer of 1948, pro-Soviet consolidation was in full swing. Rigged elections were held in May 1949, in which a list of government-supported candidates received no less than 95.6 percent of the vote, providing Rákosi with the pretext of a popular mandate to further strengthen his hold on power.[115] In fighting against the imposition of Soviet-backed political orthodoxy, the Catholic Church in Hungary served in interesting ways as a conduit for articulations of national resistance.[116]

Czechoslovakia, which of all the new states in the interwar period had been the one in which democratic structures were most firmly maintained, had been dismantled as a result of Nazi aggression even before the Second World War began, and anti-Nazi resistance continued during the war. Following the German defeat, former Nazi collaborators were dealt with in especially merciless fashion in a purgative process of "national cleansing."[117] Several prewar democratic leaders—including President Eduard Beneš, who had gone into exile in London during the war, and Jan Masaryk, the son of founding father Tomáš Masaryk—initially hoped to reestablish a pluralistic social democratic republic with open ties to the Soviet Union and the West. Free elections were held in May 1946, and the communists, who had been strong in the interwar period, finished first by a wide margin with over 38 percent of the vote.[118] The Czech communist leader Klement Gottwald became prime minister, with Beneš continuing on as president. But over the next year, internal tensions grew, as corruption among some communist party functionaries made Gottwald's administration increasingly unpopular, leading ultimately to the resignations of the non-communist members of the government in early 1948. As discussions over new elections began, Gottwald and his interior minister Vaclav Nosek made a strike for power, using communist paramilitary forces to spark street clashes and ultimately pressuring Beneš, who was old and increasingly ill, to authorize the formation of a new and almost exclusively communist government in February 1948.[119] The face of the tragic nature of the communist takeover was provided by Jan Masaryk, who fell to his death on March 10, 1948, in what was ruled as a suicide but was likely political murder.[120] Beneš was himself forced from office a few weeks later and died in September.[121] As had been the case in the late 1930s, the democratic structures of Czechoslovakia were once again dismantled by foreign-inspired repression. The most likely window through which an inclusive vision of democratic belonging might have been maintained in east-central Europe had been forcibly closed.

To the south, among the Balkan nation-states, Soviet attempts at hegemony experienced mixed fortunes. The smoothest process of communist consolidation took place in Bulgaria, where citizens had long felt strong cultural ties to Russia. During the war, the Bulgarian monarchy had continued, but was in an increasingly complicated position, with Boris III siding with Nazi Germany enough to win important territorial concessions in 1941, while refusing to enter a full-fledged military alliance against the Soviet Union that summer. After Boris's death in late August 1943, the succession went to his six-year-old son Simeon II under a joint regency that lasted barely a week before the Soviets invaded in early September.[122] Elections in November 1945, which were only partly free, resulted in the abolition of the monarchy and the landslide victory of the Fatherland Front, a coalition of communists and radical agrarians. The moderate agrarian leader Nikola Petkov, who had earlier held a series of cabinet positions, became an increasingly outspoken oppositional figure, attempting to maintain parliamentary democracy as the Fatherland Front moved to restrict democratic freedoms. In the summer of 1947, Petkov was arrested and charged with espionage and maintaining treasonous links with Western democracies. Not wanting to risk involvement at a delicate point in the growing Cold War, British and American officials offered only weak half-protests, and Petkov was hanged in September 1947.[123] By that point, communist rule was deeply entrenched.

The situation in Yugoslavia was much more complex. During the war, it had been the indigenous communist partisans, not the Western-backed royalist Chetniks, who succeeded in ousting the Germans in 1944. That made it much easier for the communist leader Josip Broz Tito to consolidate and legitimize control after the war. His regime was extremely aggressive in purging nationalist and royalist rivals—including most notably the royalist military leader Draza Mihailovic, who was executed in the summer of 1946— and in building communist domestic structures through heavy industrial investment and the collectivization of agriculture.[124] If Tito's communist credentials were beyond question, his loyalty to Stalin certainly was not. The ambitious Tito hatched numerous self-serving plans for territorial expansion in the Balkans, and he ultimately broke with Stalin personally in an extremely bitter manner in 1948.[125] The other Soviet bloc countries, following Moscow's line, treated Tito as a pariah, and Stalin appealed to many within the Yugoslav communist establishment to abandon Tito.[126] But Tito not only managed to hang onto power but to forge his own way as the originator of the non-aligned movement, with Yugoslavia developing in relative prosperity and stability as a communist state balanced between

East and West until Tito's death in 1980. Tito was also largely successful in minimizing ethnic differences within the various Yugoslav republics in favor of a compelling form of "Socialist Yugoslav" identity.[127]

The story in Greece further diverged from broader East European patterns. In a secret (albeit now famous) meeting on the future of the Balkans between Churchill and Stalin in October 1944, Churchill had agreed to majority Soviet control elsewhere in the region in exchange for 90 percent British influence in Greece, idealized by many British as the birthplace of Western civilization and democracy.[128] Stalin had agreed, and proceeded to allow British troops to quash a communist led uprising launched in December 1944. The British goal of reestablishing the monarchy of King George II was out of the question, due to the king's problematic relationship to the prewar dictatorship of Ioannis Metaxas, but Churchill did manage to arrange a regency under the archbishop of Athens and a provisional government under Nikolaos Plastiras that lasted until late 1945.[129] Over the ensuing months, however, Greek communists launched a further series of uprisings, which initiated a protracted civil war that lasted nearly three years. In the end, the British-backed government forces prevailed against the communist insurgents, and Greece maintained a mutually beneficial relationship with the West, partaking of U.S. Marshall Plan money starting in 1949 and eventually joining NATO in 1952.[130]

Soviet responses to Western initiatives like the Marshall Plan and NATO were complex, but two broad corollaries deserve mention. In 1949, the Soviets initiated the Council for Mutual Economic Assistance (Comecon), an overarching economic organization whose founding members, in addition to the USSR, were Poland, Romania, Hungary, Czechoslovakia, and Bulgaria. Those states were joined fairly quickly by Albania and, in 1950, by East Germany. Sometimes portrayed as a straightforward counterpart to Western integration efforts, Comecon can more accurately be called a wobbly initial step on the "thorny path from political to economic integration."[131] This integration came to involve not only politics and economics, but also military considerations. Although NATO had been founded initially in 1949, it was not until 1955, when West Germany joined the transatlantic alliance, that the Soviets initiated direct countermeasures. The result was the formation of the Warsaw Pact in May 1955, which united all of the Comecon members in a broad military alliance. Against the backdrop of these larger moves toward consolidation, Soviet power in Eastern Europe experienced several direct challenges from the time of Stalin's death in 1953 to the late 1960s, challenges that were fueled by divergent visions of social and political belonging.

The first of these major challenges emerged in East Germany. As the four German occupation zones coalesced into hardened camps between 1945 and 1949, internal developments within the Soviet zone were complicated. Initially, German Communist Party (KPD), which had been banned by Hitler in 1933 but revived in 1945, resonated less among many industrial workers than the Social Democratic Party (SPD), which had also been banned by Hitler. So, Soviet authorities pressured the regional SPD leader, Otto Grotewohl, to agree to a merger with the KPD, creating the Socialist Unity Party (SED) in April 1946.[132] It was the SED under Walter Ulbricht and Erich Honecker that would govern East Germany over the ensuing decades, replacing one-party rule under the Nazis with one-party communist rule. As Mary Fulbrook has brilliantly demonstrated, the early years of the GDR were central to the forging of new "communities of experience" based on specific "structural filters" that refracted and reframed individual memory and communal belonging in the aftermath of Nazi rule.[133] In both rural areas and among industrial workers, resentment toward the state grew due to heavy industrial and agricultural quotas and housing shortages.[134] Shortly after the death of Stalin, the announcement of a new increase in norms for construction workers ignited a strike on June 16, 1953, that developed over the next day into a massive uprising in East Berlin. Students and workers threw rocks and bottles at tanks—the photos of which spread quickly around the world—and in the ensuing crackdown, dozens, perhaps hundreds, were killed.[135] Less than a decade later, in the summer of 1961, the Ulbricht regime would order the construction of the Berlin Wall which, during its twenty-eight years in existence, not only established the physical separation of East and West Berlin but also provided the Cold War with its most potent symbol.[136]

In February 1956, at the Twentieth Communist Party Congress in Moscow, new Soviet premier Nikita Khrushchev delivered his famous speech criticizing the excesses and personality cult surrounding Stalin, and launching the program of de-Stalinization.[137] The repercussions of that speech were felt throughout the Soviet sphere, as communist intellectuals began pushing for more dramatic changes—particularly in the creation of more open political dialogue and more national independence within the Eastern Bloc. In Poland, the push for change progressed without significant conflict. Demonstrations throughout the summer of 1956 brought about the return of Władysław Gomułka, who the previous decade had been leader of the communist Polish Workers Party but had been ousted in 1948 for seeking too much independence. Moscow chose not to block his return and he was able to work for modest liberalizing reforms in agriculture and in relations with the Catholic Church. According to his biographer, among his most significant achievements was the ability to combine a distinctly Polish form of communist self-articulation and a stable relationship with the Soviet Union.[138]

The reverberations of Khrushchev's de-Stalinization speech were much more turbulent in Hungary. Starting in 1953, the Hungarian premier Imre Nagy had pushed for moderate liberalizing reforms and more national control over policy, but was ousted in a power struggle in April 1955. Following Krushchev's speech, many of his supporters resumed the drive for greater independence. A group of communist academics and intellectuals hearkened back to history and the heroic nationalism of 1848, forming a literary group known as the Petőfi Circle, named for the revolutionary nationalist poet Sándor Petőfi, who had been killed in the later stages of revolutionary fighting in the summer of 1849.[139] As demonstrations built throughout the early fall, protesters became emboldened, and during the last week of October 1956, hundreds of thousands took to the streets of Budapest, toppling statues of Stalin, while unrest spread throughout much of the countryside. Imre Nagy returned to take the position of premier and after several days of street fighting, Soviet troops announced their withdrawal from Budapest. Between October 29 and November 4, Nagy initiated a series of sweeping changes, proclaiming the creation of a multiparty system, freedom of speech, and Hungary's withdrawal from the Warsaw Pact. As it turned out, however, the Soviet military withdrawal represented only a temporary repositioning, and beginning on November 4, Soviet troops and tanks launched a major offensive to retake Budapest, shelling the city and killing thousands. Nagy was arrested, taken to Romania, and held in custody for nearly two years, before being returned to Hungary, tried in secret, and executed in the summer of 1958. For many Hungarians, Nagy's death positioned him as a "martyr of the nation" on a scale even more monumental than Petőfi.[140]

Czechoslovakia also experienced various forms of unrest following the death of Stalin. In June 1953, a heavy-handed government attempt to raise production quotas—and potentially to confiscate workers' personal savings—led to a massive demonstration in Plzeň, during which the images

FIGURE 7.2 Hungarian demonstrators replacing a statue of Stalin with the Hungarian flag. *Pesti srác2/Wikimedia Commons.*

and memories of Beneš and Masaryk were explicitly invoked. While the uprising itself was suppressed, it did ultimately contribute to the institution of a more open form of socialist consumerism.[141] The most notable challenge to Soviet control in Czechoslovakia, however, emerged in the famous "Prague Spring" of 1968, which unfolded concurrent to the wave of student demonstrations sweeping Western Europe. But, unlike French, German, and Italian students, who were embracing broader forms of global community and expressing solidarity with non-Europeans, the uprising in Prague was fueled in large part by the desire for national self-articulation and the freedom with which to express it. It was in a spirit of optimism, led by young educated technocrats and communist functionaries, that the reform-oriented Alexander Dubček took over as premier in January 1968. Dubček was a committed communist and wanted to maintain, in improved form, the structures of state socialism. But, he wanted more than anything to create a model of nationally distinctive economic and political dynamism in the place of ossified and moribund bureaucracy.

In early April 1968, Dubček's government issued a new communist party program calling famously for a "Czechoslovak way to socialism," replicating the exact wording of similar calls from before the communist takeover in 1948.[142] A program of political pluralism that would perhaps mirror the cooperation between socialists and communists under Beneš and Masaryk was to be coupled with administrative decentralization and an ambitious attempt to reinvigorate and draw into political participation segments of the workforce and society that had been marginalized into lethargy.[143] Toward this end, censorship was abolished in late June 1968, which allowed an unanticipated number of radical ideas and reform programs to be published without oversight—many of which went much farther than Dubček himself was comfortable with. As the spring of optimism extended into the summer, Soviet premier Leonid Brezhnev, who had come to power four years earlier, grew increasingly concerned, particularly over the danger of the contagion of liberalization spreading to other Eastern Bloc countries. So, in August 1968, a massive invasion force of half a million troops—drawn from all the other Warsaw Pact countries—invaded Czechoslovakia and ended the brief period of openness.[144] Out of a desire to avoid the bloodshed of the 1956 Hungarian uprising, little resistance was offered and Brezhnev, in turn, felt compelled to allow Dubček to continue governing while being monitored stringently and forced to roll back the liberalizing changes of the previous months. Much of the world, including many citizens in other Eastern Bloc nations, expressed disapproval of the crackdown. Dubček, for his part, was ousted the next year and, after eventually being kicked out of the Communist Party, he retired from public life to Bratislava until reemerging to play a central role in the events of 1989.

The suppression of the Prague Spring did not stop the development of internal criticism and more open notions of social cohesion in Czechoslovakia. Among the offshoots of the events of 1968 was the formation of a Prague rock band that took the name Plastic People of the Universe, a reference to the song "Plastic People" by Frank Zappa's band, the Mothers of Invention. In the fall of 1976, the band, who performed in English as a form of dissent, were arrested by communist authorities and charged with subversion. In response, a group of intellectuals led by the poet Václav Havel and the philosopher Jan Patočka published a manifesto in January 1977, known as "Charter 77," which condemned abuses of civil rights and infringements on freedom of expression. It was signed by more than two hundred intellectuals and cultural figures in Czechoslovakia and quickly received massive international attention.[145] The Czechoslovak government responded by declaring the Charter illegal and persecuting its signatories in various ways, ranging from career dismissal to imprisonment. Vaclav Havel was arrested and ultimately sentenced to five years in prison.[146] As was the case with Alexander Dubček, Havel would return to the public eye during the so-called Velvet Revolution of 1989 and, even more so, in its aftermath.

Before examining those events in greater detail in the next chapter, let us return briefly to Poland to look briefly at developments in the 1970s and 1980s. Władysław Gomułka, who had returned to power in 1956, had brought a measure of openness to governance. In particular, peasants in the countryside were shielded from the worst effects of collectivization in the late 1950s, and the Catholic Church continued to enjoy an important measure of independence and popular prestige. As the years progressed, however, Gomułka's policies became more repressive as the Polish economy stagnated. In December 1970, following the announcement of a new spate of price increases, workers in the shipyards of Gdansk (formerly known as Danzig in German) had staged demonstrations and, eventually, strikes that spread to neighboring cities and industrial centers. In response, longtime defense minister Wojciech Jaruzelski ordered a crackdown in which dozens of protesters were killed.[147] Although the strikes were suppressed, Gomułka was forced to resign and was replaced as premier by Edward Gierek, who proceeded to roll back the program of price increases. One of the central figures in the December 1970 strikes was Lech Wałęsa, an electrician in the Gdansk shipyards, who emerged increasingly over the next decade as a skillful political organizer.[148]

In August 1980, in response to renewed rising prices and the summary dismissal of a trade union activist, a new wave of strikes and demonstrations broke out. The Gierek regime responded with an offer of concessions, but Wałęsa, who was the central figure in the growing movement that took the name Solidarity, pressed for a much more ambitious set of demands. Not wanting to replicate the bloodshed of 1970, the government agreed on August 31, 1980. In response, Soviet authorities expressed deep displeasure with the political implications of the Gdansk agreements; Gierek was forced from power in early September and replaced Stanisław Kania, who was himself replaced months later by the much more aggressive hardliner Wojciech Jaruzelski who, as defense minister, had orchestrated the bloody crackdown back in December 1970. These moves did nothing, however, to diminish the rapidly rising popularity of the Solidarity movement, which established branches throughout Poland, developed an agricultural counterpart known as Rural Solidarity, and encouraged the founding of a university students' union.[149] In December 1981, Jaruzelski decided on a quick strike to dismantle Solidarity and reduce its influence. Through the agency of the newly created Military Council of National Salvation, the Solidarity offices were occupied and its leaders arrested. Wałęsa was jailed for nearly a year, and martial law was imposed until the summer of 1983.[150]

* * * *

Wałęsa, along with Vacláv Havel and Alexander Dubček in Czechoslovakia, would return to the forefront starting in 1989. By that point, a variety of oppositional organizations and networks had begun to mobilize throughout the Eastern Bloc, advocating not only for greater political freedoms but also for economic liberalization and environmental reform. Within the context of significant changes in Soviet policy ushered in by Mikhail Gorbachev, who became Soviet premier in 1985, these various currents and trajectories would grow into a transformative wave. Conceptions of social and political belonging would once again be fundamentally altered.

8

The Politics of Belonging in Europe after the Cold War

In northwest Brussels, situated between the city's famous Atomium landmark and the King Baudouin football stadium, lies one of Europe's most striking tourist attractions. The Mini-Europe theme park consists of more than 300 scale models of famous structures from across Europe, ranging from Paris's Eiffel Tower to the Leaning Tower of Pisa to Berlin's Brandenburg Gate, all linked together by a network of outdoor walking paths, gardens, and interactive attractions. The park's promotional materials encourage tourist families and school groups to visit the Spirit of Europe installation at the end of the walking tour, where they will learn about the virtues of European integration through the "Proud to Be European" exhibit—a showcase featuring the "EU's greatest success stories"—before making a necessary stop at the park's budget-friendly restaurant facility, reminding visitors that "all this traveling makes you hungry!"[1] The official guidebook, which contains introductory welcome statements from the Presidents of the European Parliament, the European Council, and the Commission of the European Union, lays out the essential "values" at the heart of the unified structures of Europe. The first value, a "new type of European democracy," is portrayed as the glue that binds Europeans together in a harmonious community of belonging, which must be defended and preserved at all costs: "Democracy is a value worth fighting for every day." Another value, the "Spirit of Adventure," is demonstrated through reference to the expansion of Europe that began in the late fifteenth century, accompanied by a not so subtle swipe at the recent emergence of China (the attached illustration shows Columbus's *Santa Maria* towering over the tiny masts of a Chinese junk, indicating that size does apparently matter after all).[2] Other foundational principles include the "Spirit of Enterprise" and the counter-balancing values of "Christian Heritage" and "Secularism and Multiculturalism." The exact nature of the interplay between those latter ideals is, tellingly, left untouched.

The Mini-Europe park itself was created in 1989, when the Cold War was winding down and the European Community (soon to be EU) had only twelve member states.[3] In the intervening years, as the membership grew, new attractions were added to keep pace. The founding members of Europe still have the largest number of exhibits, of course, but the older model structures are now falling into disrepair, some of them dramatically. The British photographer Lewis Bush documented this decay in a recent collection of photos, focusing on the bizarre juxtapositions created by the park's mixture of cultural triumphalism and tacky touristic taste. The desired effect of the model Acropolis's noble contours is essentially destroyed by the massive multicolored waterslide located directly behind it; the presence of trash cans next to models of Europe's most revered landmarks, which are often smaller than the refuse bins themselves, is jarring; and, at least on the day Bush took his photographs, several exhibits were literally under water due to recent rains. The metaphorical image of a dilapidated and drowning Europe is almost impossible to ignore. As Bush himself noted of the discrepancies between the park's soaring rhetoric and the reality of decay: "Instead of being idealised…the result is just a weird mess of contrasts and contradictions which seem to speak to the state of the real EU."[4] While the decomposition of the Mini-Europe attractions likely stems from simple negligence and can be fixed by paint, plaster, and perhaps a better drainage system, the progressive disintegration of the consensus underlying the European Union is much deeper and more difficult to remedy, as illustrated most dramatically by the so-called Brexit, the June 2016 British vote to leave the European Union entirely.

FIGURE 8.1 The Acropolis *by Lewis Bush* © *Lewis Bush. Reproduced with permission.*

A new Europe takes shape (again)

Europe has made and remade itself repeatedly over the past two centuries, generating varying assortments of historical winners and losers who have been analyzed and categorized, often in conflicting ways, by contemporaries and scholars. Against that complicated backdrop, the events of 1989 and 1990 in Europe seemed to many to be especially significant, eliciting a striking degree of optimism in the West and engendering a veritable cottage industry of best-selling interpretations. Neo-conservative commentators like Francis Fukuyama predicted that, with the fall of the Berlin Wall and the collapse of the Soviet Union, Western-style Liberal democracy had triumphed over rival forms of social and political organization, bringing about the "end of history."[5] Fukuyama's former mentor, Samuel Huntington, further elaborated upon many of Fukuyama's ideas in his book *Clash of Civilizations*, which argued that conflict in the new post-Cold War world would no longer take the form of wars between nation-states but of epic struggles between broad civilizational systems.[6] Even more sober-minded scholars offered initially optimistic assessments.[7] In attempting to capture the spirit of 1989 in an influential essay, Michael Howard was moved to quote Wordsworth: "Bliss it was that dawn to be alive, but to be young was very heaven!"[8]

The transformation of Central and Eastern Europe in the years surrounding 1990 had deeper roots and more complex repercussions, as will be seen later in this chapter, but its most notable symbol was the breaching of the Berlin Wall in November 1989. Environmental activism and calls for political reform had grown in East Germany over the preceding decade, but the prospect of achieving change through existing channels seemed increasingly fruitless. In the context of widespread knowledge of continued party vote tampering in elections in early 1989, large numbers of East German citizens looked for other modes of expression. When Hungarian officials announced in the summer of 1989 the opening of their border with Austria, huge numbers of East German "vacationers" traveled to Hungary, which was permitted within the Eastern Bloc, in anticipation of being able to pass into Austria and thereby into the west. But as the Hungarian border continued to implement passport controls, tens of thousands of East Germans were left stranded until September 11, 1989, when the Hungarian government under Miklós Németh decided to allow them to pass essentially unchecked into Austria. Over the next three weeks more than 30,000 East Germans took advantage of this opportunity, while thousands more besieged the West German embassy in Prague, climbing over its walls to camp on its grounds while demanding passage to the west.[9] East German premier Erich Honecker initially took a hard line, and in response East German cities witnessed massive demonstrations that became increasingly unruly. When West German foreign minister Hans-Dietrich Genscher appeared at the embassy in Prague and announced on September 30 that the thousands of East Germans camped at the embassy would be accepted by the west, jubilation ensued not only among those in Prague, but also among the newly emboldened demonstrators in the cities of the GDR, whose numbers now swelled into the hundreds of thousands.[10]

These events coincided with elaborate plans to celebrate the fortieth anniversary of the GDR in early October 1989, which merely made the symbolism more powerful. The square in front of the Nikolaikirche in Leipzig became a particular center of protest, with huge crowds gathering throughout the month of October. On October 17, Honecker was forced to step down as premier and was replaced by the bland and unpopular Egon Krenz, who attempted to employ the vocabulary of openness while maintaining a bevy of older hardliners in his government.[11] By early November, the protests reached unprecedented heights, with more than half a million gathering in the streets in East Berlin on November 4 and in Leipzig two days later. On November 9, the government came to an informal decision, which had not yet been codified in writing, to allow a limited amount of emigration applications as a provisional way of relieving the tremendous pressure exerted by the ever-growing daily demonstrations. At a press conference that evening, however, an ill-informed government spokesman announced not only the provisional plan for limited emigration but, when asked by reporters about the timing, responded (without authorization) that open travel could commence immediately.[12] As that news was broadcast around the world, hundreds of thousands of East Berliners began gathering almost immediately and the crowds swelled to record numbers that evening. So rather than the orderly set of travel applications that the regime anticipated processing the next morning, it was faced with throngs of nighttime revelers who began breaching the wall; ordered by the government to stand down, the border guards allowed the joyful multitudes to pass unmolested into West Berlin, where they were greeted by crowds almost equally as jubilant.[13] Just as the Berlin Wall itself had served as an iconic symbol of Cold War division for nearly three decades, the media images and photos that evening of transgressive merrymaking quickly achieved iconic status. The nature of German belonging seemed once again open for refashioning.

Over the ensuing weeks and months, the most pressing question became how to proceed politically and structurally now that the firm boundary of the wall (and the broader border between the two Germanies) had become porous. Proposed solutions proceeded on several levels. Popularly, among ordinary Germans on both sides, optimistic visions of togetherness and national belonging proliferated amid calls for political reunification. The forty-year division seemed to many to have been an artificial Cold War device that could now be quickly overcome by combining existing linguistic and cultural commonalities with new forms of idealistic national enthusiasm, supplemented perhaps by the millions of marks in "welcome money" offered by the West German government to encourage Easterners to enjoy the fruits of capitalist consumerism. Crowds continued to gather in the streets to chant slogans of unity (*Wir sind ein Volk!*), and in the month of November 1989 alone, more than 130,000 migrated from east to west.[14] East German officials, on the other hand, had hoped to maintain as many preexisting state structures as possible in the uncertain future that faced them.[15] The Socialist Unity Party (SED) continued its existence briefly under Egon Krenz, but on December 1, 1989, the East German parliament amended the 1949 constitution to remove explicit communist terminology, and Krenz was forced out of his position, a few days later. The SED was replaced by the Party of Democratic Socialism (PDS) and preparations were made for elections in March 1990, the first truly free elections in East Germany since before the Nazi seizure of power.[16] In that election, the communist PDS, tainted as it was by its roots in the SED, garnered only 16 percent of the vote, finishing behind the reconstituted Social Democratic Party, which received 22 percent, and far behind the newly formed Alliance for Germany—an amalgamation of the Christian Democratic Union, the German Social Union, and the small splinter party Democratic Awakening—which advocated the fast-tracking of unification and collectively received 48 percent of the vote.[17]

In West Germany it was Helmut Kohl, the chancellor since 1982, who articulated perhaps the clearest vision for future reunification. Already on November 28, 1989, he presented to the Bundestag a ten-point program, the prologue of which is excerpted below. Kohl appealed directly to East German citizens and their sense of common national belonging, and praised their moral courage in having forced such dramatic social and political change.

EXCERPT 8.1

A Ten-Point Program for Overcoming the Division of Germany and Europe

Helmut Kohl

We are proud that the Germans in the GDR have, with their peaceful intervention for freedom, human rights, and self-determination, demonstrated their courage and love of freedom to the world, setting an example which has evoked praise all over the world.

We are deeply impressed by the passionate and unbroken desire for freedom shown by the people of Leipzig and many other cities. They know what they want. They want to determine their own future, in the true sense of the word.

We will, of course, respect every free decision taken by the people in the GDR. Particularly at this time, we in the Federal Republic of Germany stand side by side with our fellow countrymen. [...] Opportunities are presenting themselves for overcoming the division of Europe and hence of our fatherland. The Germans, who are now coming together in the spirit of freedom, will never pose a threat. Rather will they, I am convinced, be an asset to a Europe, which is growing more and more together.

The credit for the present transformation goes primarily to the people, who are so impressively demonstrating their will for freedom. [...] Today, as everyone can see, we have reached a new epoch in European and German history. This is an age which points beyond the status quo and the old political structures in Europe. This change is primarily the work of the people, who demand freedom, respect for their human rights, and their right to be masters of their own future.[18]

Kohl's references to a common sense of German belonging—to "fellow countrymen" and "our fatherland...coming together in the spirit of freedom"—were expressions of his particular vision of nationalism, opposed to Nazi excesses but, according to Christian Wicke, melding together earlier romantic, Liberal, and Catholic-oriented elements.[19] His appeal did not fall on deaf ears. Kohl experienced a surge of popularity in the east that was unmatched by any of the GDR's major political figures. And in the first all-German elections in October 1990, the electorate voted overwhelmingly for political reunification under the chancellorship of Helmut Kohl.

While the fall of the Berlin Wall serves as an identifiable landmark in the changing landscape of east-central Europe, revolutionary transformation was underway earlier in Hungary and Poland. In May 1988, longtime Hungarian premier János Kádár stepped down in the face of economic difficulties and was replaced by Károly Grósz.[20] The following month marked the thirtieth anniversary of the execution of Imre Nagy, and a demonstration honoring him and the other victims of the 1956 uprising was put down with a moderate measure of repressive force. But it should also be noted that a historical commission investigating the events of 1956 was allowed to publish its findings in January 1989, despite diverging from the official government line.[21] Throughout the first year of Grósz's premiership, a variety of political clubs and organizations were formed that began pushing with unprecedented vigor for increased personal freedoms and the broadening of the political system. Grósz responded by making concessions, and it was in this context that the decision was made to open the Hungarian border with Austria, which set in motion the aforementioned flurry of movement out of East Germany. In mid-June 1989, on the thirty-first anniversary of his execution, Imre Nagy was officially rehabilitated and his remains reburied in a ceremony that drew a massive crowd.[22] Throughout the summer the government engaged in extended dialogue with a "Round Table" grouping of pluralist parties, resulting in the formulation of a democratic constitution in October.[23] The next month Hungarians watched, and often cheered, the developments in East Germany that culminated in the fall of the wall, and in March 1990 Hungarian elections took place as a test of the new pluralism enshrined in the constitution. In that election several dozen parties participated and a center-right governing coalition was established; the former communists garnered less than ten percent of the vote.[24]

In Poland, the repression of the Solidarity movement and the jailing of Lech Wałęsa was followed, in 1983, by Wałęsa's selection for the Nobel Peace Prize. That international recognition was magnified in June 1987, when Pope John Paul II, the former archbishop of Krakow, returned home to give a series of sermons and outdoor masses. He chose Gdansk, where the Solidarity movement had been initiated, as the location for a particularly clear statement in support of freedom of political expression, and he visited the grave of a pro-Solidarity priest who had been killed by government security agents in 1984.[25] By early 1989, economic turmoil combined with growing political discontent moved the government to open negotiations with representatives of Solidarity, which had been officially banned and driven underground seven years earlier. The negotiations resulted in a set of agreements that legalized Solidarity and significantly opened up the political system, with new elections scheduled for June 1989. In that election the ruling communists were crushed in humiliating fashion, with Solidarity candidates and other non-communists winning virtually every seat in both the *Sejm* and the newly created Polish Senate. Wojciech Jaruzelski, who had cracked down on Solidarity and proclaimed martial law at the beginning of the decade, was only able to salvage a remnant of the regime's tattered prestige by maneuvering himself into the position of president, while the Solidarity-backed Tadeusz Mazowiecki became prime minister— the first non-communist head of government in Eastern Europe since the late 1940s.[26] Jaruzelski stepped down the next year and was replaced by Lech Wałęsa himself, whose subsequent five year tenure as president was accompanied by a level of international celebrity that the former electrician raised in humble circumstances could scarcely have imagined as a younger man. Wałęsa served as both a model of self-fashioned upward mobility and as a virtuous symbol of Polish national identity.

In Czechoslovakia, the revolutionary transformation of 1989 is often referred to as the Velvet Revolution, a name that is occasionally applied to the broader revolutions of the era.[27] As had been the case with Hungarian commemorations of the execution of Imre Nagy, in the summer of 1988 thousands of Czechoslovak citizens took to the streets to commemorate (and protest the legacy of) the Soviet-inspired invasion in 1968. That had proceeded in largely peaceful fashion. In January 1989, however, as protesters memorialized Jan Pulach, a student who had committed suicide (by self-immolation) in protest of the suppression of the Prague Spring, the government of Miloš Jakeš decided to order a number of arrests, including that of Vacláv Havel, who was subsequently imprisoned briefly. Tensions rose throughout the spring and summer, and broad public discussions took place in the context of the mass migration of East Germans to the West German embassy in Prague that September. Even after the breaching of the Berlin Wall on November 9, 1989, the Jakeš regime was intent on maintaining a hard line. But, mass protests began on November 20 and continued each night until Jakeš was forced to step down on November 24. That night two of the central veterans of the Prague Spring—Alexander Dubček and Vacláv Havel—embraced famously on a balcony overlooking Wenceslas Square, as thousands cheered. The most powerful organizational entity to emerge during the upheaval was Civic Forum, a loose grouping of oppositional forces that began meeting at Prague's Green Lantern Theater and quickly rallied behind the leadership of Vacláv Havel.[28] Following a flurry of activity over the ensuing weeks, Havel was elected President of Czechoslovakia in late December, a position he continued to hold, with the exception of a brief interlude in 1992, for the next fourteen years. Importantly, as James Krapfl has noted, the demonstrations of November 1989 had fostered unprecedented forms of social belonging throughout the country, sparking a "reconfiguration of sacrality" in which "Czechs and Slovaks experienced ontological transformation—transcendence."[29]

If Czechoslovakia experienced a velvet revolution, then a much darker and more gruesome moniker is required to describe the revolution in Romania. Claudia Moscovici has referred to the entire post-Stalinist period in Romania as an exercise in "velvet totalitarianism."[30] But whatever the label used, Romania's was the one revolution that diverged from the broader pattern of nonviolence. This was due in part to the character of the Romanian premier, Nicolae Ceaușescu, who had come to power in 1965 and was, to put it mildly, a corrupt and brutal egotist. By the 1980s, Romania was mired in crippling debt, which produced widespread rationing, fuel shortages, and planned electricity outages, while Ceaușescu and elite party functionaries lived in extreme luxury, even by western standards.[31] A state policy of forced population growth that banned abortions and certain forms of contraception led inevitably to widespread malnutrition and even starvation among poor Romanian children, especially in the inadequately funded state orphanages. Gail Kligman has documented the impact of this reproductive policy on women's lives and especially on interpersonal relationships, which were saturated with dysfunctional fears and complexes down to the most private level of sexuality and intimacy.[32] Romantic and relational notions of belonging that were ruptured by intrusive state structures were mirrored by a broader set of government intrusions that could, in the eyes of an increasing number of Romanians, only be rectified by an equally radical revolutionary rupture in the political sphere.

In the aftermath of the breaching of the Berlin Wall, Ceaușescu remained convinced that his security apparatus would protect him from any serious challenge. But when the revolutionary wave began, it originated from an unlikely and unpredictable source. A bishop within the Protestant Reformed

Church of Romania, László Tőkés, who was of Hungarian–Romanian descent and would later go on to a prominent career in the European Parliament, had emerged as a staunch critic of the regime. Under normal circumstances, this type of opposition would have been fairly easy to marginalize. But in the context of rising tensions in 1989, the government's attempt to evict Tőkés from his parish led to a popular protest in his defense on December 15, 1989. It quickly developed into a vehicle for a much broader and deeper sense of dissatisfaction with the regime, so much so that Tőkés himself appealed for less radical rhetoric.[33] Over the following days, however, demonstrations across Romania grew to massive proportions and street fighting between security forces and protesters resulted in more than 1,000 deaths, with multiple thousands wounded. The most visible casualties, of course, were Ceauşescu and his wife Elena. Ceauşescu had attempted to make a public address on December 21, but was shouted down by opponents and visibly lost his nerve. The next day he lost the support of the military and was literally chased by a mob through the administration building of the communist Central Committee, escaping from the roof via helicopter before holing up with Elena in a provincial military barracks for protection. The military leadership decided to allow Ceauşescu to be tried on charges of corruption and genocide on December 25, 1989. The trial was convened; the couple were convicted and were then hastily stood up against a wall and shot—all in the course of Christmas Day. The executions were filmed and the aftermath (including images of both bloodied bodies) broadcast on Romanian television with jubilant commentary. Had they been publicly guillotined, their heads would no doubt have been held up before the rapturous crowd. As had been the case in 1793 Paris, however, the purgative violence did not bring immediate national healing.[34]

The revolutions in Central and Eastern Europe were followed in fairly rapid succession by a series of steps ending in the dissolution of the Soviet Union, a massive transformative process that brought the Cold War officially to an end and also remade conceptions of nationhood on a scale almost as enormous as the changes ushered in by the demise of multinational empires at the end of the First World War. When Mikhail Gorbachev came to power in the USSR in 1985, few could have predicted the extent of the transformations to come. Gorbachev's initial reform policies were, however, significant enough for even linguistically challenged westerners to make almost universal use of the Russian terms themselves: *perestroika* (restructuring), which referred to the internal reform of Soviet political and economic structures, and *glasnost* (openness), which indicated a greater measure of transparency internally and externally. Far from wanting to weaken or dissolve the Soviet Union, Gorbachev's reform initiatives were intended to reinvigorate an economic and political establishment that had become moribund.[35] His loosening of restrictions on freedom of speech and press censorship was designed to make the USSR more viable in the dawning era of information technology and knowledge transfer. His willingness to engage in dialogue with U.S. President

Ronald Reagan over the reduction of nuclear weapons arsenals was envisioned as a healthy and necessary adjustment in the face of nuclear (and fiscal) reality. And his decision to allow Eastern Bloc nations greater leeway in determining their own affairs without Soviet intervention was made in pursuit of a more lasting and genuine measure of Soviet influence through flexibility, rather than through artificial and ineffective forms of coercion.[36] But regardless of his intentions, Gorbachev's reform programs were seen by hardliners in the Soviet Union as a sign of weakness and by unpopular dictators in the Soviet satellite states as a form of abandonment and perhaps even betrayal.

At the same time, oppositional activists throughout the Eastern Bloc viewed Gorbachev's policy of nonintervention as a green light for radical change, with results that were discussed earlier in this chapter. Importantly, it was interpreted in similar terms by numerous nationalities within the USSR that had been under Soviet control for decades.[37] It will be recalled that the Baltic states of Lithuania, Latvia, and Estonia had achieved independence from the Russian Empire after the First World War but were then annexed, occupied, and forcibly reincorporated into the Soviet Union during the Second World War. By the late 1980s, longstanding desires for independence began to take sharper form in what came to be known as the Baltic "singing revolutions." That phrase was coined by the Estonian journalist Heinz Valk in a June 1988 article praising the peaceful manner in which the Baltic nations were beginning to voice their demands for independence—not through "riots, barricades, burning automobiles and similar features of mass revolt by large nations," but rather by song.[38] This practice has also been described as "singing oneself into a nation."[39] In any event, the nonviolent nationalism of the Baltic states was expressed in increasingly daring calls for autonomy between 1988 and 1991, involving commemorations of those killed during the initial Stalinist occupation, the celebration of national history, and the formation of a variety of independence organizations. On August 23, 1989, the fiftieth anniversary of the signing of the Nazi–Soviet Pact that paved the way for the Soviet annexation of the Baltic states in 1940, a massive human chain dubbed the "Baltic Way" was formed, comprised of more than two million demonstrators and stretching across all three Baltic states in an innovative and visually striking mode of communal symbolic action.[40] As Mara Lazda's examination of Latvia has shown, this transnational frame of reference was more significant than the overwhelming scholarly focus on ethno-nationalism in the Baltic context would indicate.[41] National independence groups known as Popular Fronts were founded in Estonia and Latvia, while a similar role was played in Lithuania by the *Sajūdis* movement.[42] By August 1991, the three Baltic states had gained their full independence and engaged in a process of "taming" nationalism while stimulating economic growth.[43] In 2004, all three simultaneously gained membership in the European Union.[44]

National independence movements in the Soviet republics of Belarus and Ukraine proceeded along a similar timeline. In 1988, the Belarusian Popular Front was founded, engaging in more aggressive activism (and, apparently, somewhat less singing) than its Baltic Popular Front counterparts, fueled in part by outrage over the discovery of a mass grave near Minsk in which several thousand Belarusians shot by Stalin had been buried.[45] The movement also emphasized the revival of the Belarusian language as a vehicle for national revival.[46] In July 1990, the Belarusian parliament issued a Declaration of State Sovereignty and Belarus gained official independence in August 1991. In contrast to the Baltic states, however, democratic development in post-Soviet Belarus has been deeply problematic, particularly under the authoritarian Alexander Lukashenko, who has been president since 1994.[47] Even more puzzling to scholars was the initial drift under Lukashenko away from policies fostering national independence toward greater integration with Russia, which was accompanied by official discouragement of Belarusian national symbols and making Russian an official language of Belarus.[48]

In Ukraine, the fallout from the 1986 disaster at Chernobyl was political as well as nuclear, sharpening existing resentments as the policy of *perestroika* went into effect. As in Belarus, anger over Stalinist mass graves in Ukraine fueled emotional calls for independence. Starting in 1987, longstanding rumors about a mass grave near Bykivnia were supplemented by the testimonies of several who had been involved in the shootings there, but the KGB descended, stifling inquiry, and an entirely unconvincing report was issued dating the shootings to the period of German occupation between 1941 and 1943. In response, the Ukrainian "Memorial Society" was formed in the summer of 1988 to further expose and publicize the crimes of the Stalinist regime while pushing, along with a number of other independence organizations, for national autonomy over the ensuing year.[49] In July 1990, a Declaration of State Sovereignty was issued in virtual simultaneity with the similar Belarusian declaration, and in August 1991 independence was proclaimed.[50] The challenges facing post-Soviet Ukraine, particularly in connection with renewed Russian nationalist aggression under Vladimir Putin, will be discussed later in this chapter.

In Moscow, throughout 1990 and 1991 Gorbachev faced increased challenges, not least from Russian nationalists associated with the "Democratic Russia" movements.[51] His plan to draw up a new Treaty of Union in 1991, which would have transformed the USSR into a federation with increased autonomy for the national republics, sparked a coup in August launched by hardliners intent on maintaining the Soviet system. While Gorbachev was holed up in his vacation home in Crimea, it was Boris Yeltsin, president of the Russian Republic, who acted decisively to stop the coup.[52] As a result, Yeltsin's public image was greatly enhanced at the expense of Gorbachev, who was ultimately unable to recover his authority.[53] As the nations within the Soviet empire jumped ship, the Soviet Union collapsed rapidly between the summer and December 1991, when the Soviet Union was officially dissolved and replaced by the Commonwealth of Independent States (CIS).[54] Gorbachev announced his resignation in a televised address on Christmas Day 1991, by which time authority had already clearly passed to Boris Yeltsin.

MAP 8.1 The Commonwealth of Independent States, 1994. © *George Edward Milne, 2017. Reproduced with permission.*

As complex and chaotic as was the collapse of the Soviet Union and the rise of the new independent nation-states, the bloodiest repercussions of the end of the Cold War were seen in the Balkans, where the state structures of Yugoslavia disintegrated into a morass of competing identities and violence whose most visible manifestation—ethnic cleansing—represents a new chapter in the history of genocide in Europe. The following section examines both the tragedy of Balkan tribalism in the 1990s and the development of nationalist separatist movements elsewhere on the periphery of Europe.

Post-Cold War identity conflicts on the European periphery

As noted in the previous chapter, the Yugoslav leader, Josip Broz Tito, had split with Stalin in the late 1940s and proceeded to steer communist Yugoslavia along the path of non-alignment over the ensuing decades. Politically, Yugoslavia was organized as a federation of Socialist Republics with divergent ethnic, linguistic, and religious identities. The two northernmost republics, Slovenia and Croatia, were linguistically distinct but predominantly Catholic, and were shaped more fundamentally than the other republics by the legacy of Austrian control.[55] To the south and east was Bosnia-Herzegovina, which had been administered by the Austrians since the 1870s and then formally annexed in 1908; its religious composition was split roughly equally between Muslims and Christians, the latter of whom were themselves split between an Orthodox majority and a Catholic minority.[56] To the east was Serbia, the dominant Slavic power in the region since the nineteenth century, whose religious makeup was almost entirely Orthodox Christian. Two regions within Serbia—Vojvodina in the north and Kosovo, made up largely of ethnic Albanians, in the south—were accorded the status of autonomous provinces.[57] The final two Yugoslav republics, Montenegro and Macedonia, were comprised mainly of Orthodox Christians, but with notable Muslim minorities, and both were shaped decisively by the legacy of Ottoman control.[58] During Tito's time in power, religious and ethnic differences among and within the various republics were downplayed in favor of an overarching "Socialist Yugoslav" identity.[59] But while surface tensions were largely held in check for most of the Cold War era, Vjekoslav Perica and others have shown that older notions of belonging based on religion and ethnicity continued to structure the everyday lives of Yugoslav citizens to a significant degree.[60]

Tito's death in 1980 ushered in a period of crisis both economically and politically. A new constitution in 1974 had created a collective presidency that was not instituted while Tito still lived, but came into force in 1980. Over the next twelve years, until the breakup of Yugoslavia, the head of state was known as the President of the Presidency (meaning the chief position within the collective presidency) and was to be rotated each May. This plurality in governance, which came on the heels of the thirty-six year rule of Tito, led to increased instability in the face of growing economic and ethnic challenges. In the spring of 1981, ethnic Albanian protesters in Kosovo began demonstrating at the University of Pristina for greater autonomy within the Republic of Serbia.[61] Similar tensions continued throughout the decade, not only involving ethnic Albanians in Serb-controlled Kosovo, but also among increasing numbers of Croats and Slovenes to the north.

The primary advocates of Yugoslav unity were the Serbs, both those inside the Republic of Serbia and Serbs living in other Yugoslav Republics. When Slobodan Milošević became president of Serbia in 1989, he moved quickly to strip the autonomous provinces (particularly Kosovo) of much of their autonomy, while reinforcing his own autocratic rule behind the façade of multiparty reform.[62] By that point Milosevic had already initiated his personal transformation from committed communist to one of the leading exponents of Serb nationalism, using rumors of Albanian rapes of Serb women in Kosovo to infuse Serb nationalism with a strongly masculinized component.[63] But as Jasna Dragovič-Soso has shown, this revival of nationalism should not be seen as merely the artificial creation of post-Tito figures like Milosevic; its roots go back to the tradition of dissident intellectuals during the height of the Cold War.[64] In 1990, a series of elections was held in the individual Yugoslav republics, with nationalist candidates making huge gains, and in December 1990 Slovenia held a referendum on independence that passed almost unanimously.[65] In May 1991, a similar referendum was held, with similar results, in Croatia, and in June the independence of both

Croatia and Slovenia was proclaimed. Macedonia proceeded to declare its independence in September 1991, followed by Bosnia-Herzegovina in March 1992.[66] Montenegro, for its part, joined officially with Serbia to form the new Federal Republic of Yugoslavia during the spring and summer of 1992. By that time, however, the brutal conflict collectively known as the Yugoslav Wars was already well underway.

Military conflict had begun in the context of the initial independence proclamations of Slovenia and Croatia in June 1991. In the so-called Ten-Day War, the Yugoslav People's Army (JNA) attacked Slovenian territorial defense forces, making initial gains in the first days of the war before being repulsed and forced to withdraw by Slovenian troops. The independence of Slovenia was affirmed in the Brioni Declaration of July 1991, which also recognized the independence of Croatia.[67] The optimism created by the Brioni agreement was short-lived, however. Beginning later that summer low-level conflict between Croatia and the Yugoslav People's Army developed into a major conflict that lasted more than four years. V.P. Gagnon has argued that the Croatian War of Independence should not be seen primarily as an ethnic nationalist conflict, but rather as an attempt on the part of both Croatia and Serbia to thwart dynamic internal forces that threatened radical political and economic change. For Gagnon, the inflaming of nationalist sentiment was primarily a tool for the defense of entrenched interests.[68] In the end Croatian forces prevailed, but at a massive cost.

Even more costly was the Bosnian War that began in the spring of 1992. The Republic of Bosnia and Herzegovina had proclaimed its independence in March 1992 and was admitted to the United Nations two months later. But Serbs living in the new Bosnia, rallying behind Radovan Karadžić, pledged their primarily loyalty to Serbia under Milosevic. Croats living in Bosnia were also radicalized, leading to a military conflict (within the broader Bosnian War) between the breakaway Croat Republic of Herzeg-Bosnia and the legal government of the new Bosnian state. At the heart of the broader conflict, however, was enmity between Bosnia and the Serbs. The war brought to the forefront of international attention the brutality of ethnic cleansing—or the forced removal of rival identities in the pursuit of creating a homogenous ethnic hegemony—as well as the widespread use of rape as a weapon of war.[69] Infamous episodes of atrocity, such as the massacre at Srebrenica in July 1995, in which some 8,000 men and boys were killed by Bosnian Serb troops, left a massive wound in the collective memory of the region.[70]

While the Bosnian War was resolved in a virtual stalemate by the Dayton Accords in late 1995, the fighting was far from over. In February 1998, major conflict broke out between the so-called Federal Republic of Yugoslavia under Slobodan Milosevic and the Kosovo Liberation Army, which was fighting for independence. In light of the devastating level of violence already witnessed in the former Yugoslavia, the international community intervened even as large numbers of Albanian Kosovars were driven out by

Serb (Yugoslav) forces. NATO troops were mobilized and a series of NATO-led air strikes commenced in the spring of 1999, which led to a brokered peace in June. Yugoslav troops withdrew and Kosovo became an interim protectorate under the authority of the United Nations. In 2008, Kosovo declared its complete independence from Serbia, but that status is currently only partly recognized. As Jamie Munn has shown, nationalist ideology in Kosovo also appropriated masculinistic imagery on a broad scale, with sites of memory and traumatic spaces being gendered in politically useful ways.[71]

In February 2002, Slobodan Milosevic was placed on trial for genocide under the auspices of the International Criminal Tribunal for the Former Yugoslavia, which was established in The Hague by the United Nations to prosecute war crimes and atrocities committed during the Yugoslav Wars. The trial received extensive international coverage and provided a forum within which the past and present of Serbian nationalism and competing Balkan identities were debated. In one of his rambling defense speeches, excerpted below, Milosevic appealed to history as an exculpatory mechanism, claiming that Austro-Hungarian and German propagandists had fabricated the useful myth of a demonically expansionist "Greater Serbia" in the decades leading up to the First World War, creating false images of aggression that, he claimed, continued to warp perceptions of Serbia to the present day.

EXCERPT 8.2

Defense Opening Statement, August 31, 2004

Slobodan Milosevic

The red thread through all the rhetoric of the German bloc, that is to say Austria, or rather Austro-Hungary (sic), and Germany in the Balkans is the thesis of creating some kind of Greater Serbia. This danger, this key thesis, took a central place in this false indictment against me: a Greater Serbia. This thesis, this myth, was created by Austro-Hungarian propaganda as far back as the second half of the nineteenth century. It was an integral part of efforts made by a rotting empire to keep its occupied Southern Slav territories. [...] What is particularly striking is that as far back as in the Austro-Hungarian propaganda, the freeing of the people from the Austro-Hungarian yoke and the unification of the Southern Slavs, not only the Serbs, was called the expansion of the Serbian state, or a Greater Serbia. And this formulation means that there should be some kind of expansionist tendencies, tendencies of conquest among the Serbs. It is a fact that this would then mean that part of the Southern Slav peoples were under foreign rule. However, that is not true. [...]

It is well known that on the 23rd of July, 1914, the Serbian government was given an ultimatum by Austria-Hungary after false accusations of

Serbia's involvement in this assassination [of the Austrian archduke Franz Ferdinand], and a number of demands were made on Serbia which no sovereign country in the world could have accepted. The failure to meet this ultimatum was expected, and the only role of this ultimatum was to cause war, to be a pretext for war. [...]

It is general knowledge how the Kingdom of the Serbs, Croats, and Slovenes was established, later renamed Yugoslavia, as the common state of the Southern Slav peoples. The German bloc wanted to prevent this, and this state was to vanish from the face of the earth. However, the old myth of Greater Serbia remained as a smokescreen to conceal their own crimes and their own evil deeds. It is in this institution [the Hague Tribunal] that the lie of Greater Serbia found its natural foundation and grew into a monstrous construction of unprecedented magnitude.[72]

Taken in sum, the Yugoslav Wars and their aftermath not only illustrate the potential for catastrophic violence during state transitions, but also the power of centuries-old historical myths to create compelling notions of national identity and belonging. Virtually all sides in the conflict made appeals to deep history—not that of the turbulent nineteenth and twentieth centuries, as seen in Milosevic's defense, but rather stretching back to the early Middle Ages. As Patrick Geary has shown, these myths are indeed artificial, but they rely on a sense of primordial self-evidence that is extremely powerful.[73] Serb claims to Kosovo in particular were rooted in the perceived heroism of the 1389 Battle of Kosovo led by the Serbian prince Lazar Hrebeljanović against the Ottomans, in which Serb forces were decimated despite their display of exemplary courage. That battle, which came to be seen as a sort of "Serbian Golgotha," ultimately brought with it a seemingly eternal territorial mandate stretching over the centuries, regardless of the fact that the twentieth-century population of Kosovo was almost entirely Albanian, with Serbs making up only a tiny minority.[74]

The employment of history in the service of nationalist mobilization was not limited to the Balkans in the 1990s. Elsewhere on the peripheries of Europe, a variety of separatist movements articulated visions of belonging based in deep history as well. This can perhaps best be illustrated with reference to the Iberian peninsula and Northern Ireland. As noted in a previous chapter, in Basque territory (known as *Euskadi* in the Basque language) claims to a unique national identity were based in part on the very early coalescence of Basque linguistic structures, which are among the oldest in Europe. The value placed by Basque nationalists on history was increased by the consistent suppression of Basque identity over the centuries, creating a myth of heroic suffering while also absolving nationalists of the need to adhere to the objective historical record (since the "true" record lay submerged beneath layers of repression). By the early twentieth century, the Basque Nationalist Party grew in political influence. But under the Franco dictatorship, Basque identity and expressions of Basque culture and history were repressed more energetically, leading to an intensification of oppositional nationalist sentiment.

In 1959, the separatist movement ETA (in English, "Basque Country and Freedom") was founded to advocate, initially peacefully, for Basque independence from Spain.[75] Over the years, however, the group has engaged increasingly in armed paramilitary and terrorist activities.[76] One of the most notable early victims of ETA terrorism was a member of Franco's inner circle, the naval officer Luis Carrero Blanco, who had served previously as Spanish prime minister and was the sitting president of Spain when he was assassinated in December 1973.[77] A stepped up wave of ETA car bombings began in the late 1980s and stretched into the 1990s, interrupted by a few brief cease-fire interludes. As Carrie Hamilton has shown, in recent decades ETA has successfully recruited and utilized nationalist women, creating an emancipatory appeal to female agency by overcoming the traditional division between the "male warrior" and the "homefront heroine."[78] On July 10, 1997, the group kidnapped the popular politician Miguel Ángel Blanco and threatened to execute him unless a group of ETA prisoners was transferred to Basque country. A massive series of demonstrations took place over the ensuing two days demanding Blanco's release, but he was nonetheless shot execution-style in the head and left to die. He was quickly located and rushed to the hospital but died shortly thereafter.[79] The Blanco affair turned into a broader dialogue about the moral limits of nationalist violence, and a number of ETA members themselves publicly disavowed the killing. Several of them went on to form the peaceful Basque separatist organization known as the Ermua Forum.[80] It would take, however, until 2011 for a more "permanent" settlement to be arranged between ETA and the Spanish state, and even now the search for peace remains elusive.[81]

The cause of Basque nationalism, and its use of violence and terror, has evoked comparisons with the militant activism of the Irish Republican Army in Northern Ireland.[82] It will be recalled that the Provisional IRA was founded in 1969 at the beginning of the brutal period known as "the Troubles," which would last for nearly three decades. By the early 1990s, both sides were increasingly willing to negotiate. In December 1993, the so-called Downing Street Declaration was announced, signed by British prime minister John Major and Irish head of state Albert Reynolds, which paved the way (albeit somewhat indirectly) for the cease-fire that was signed in August 1994. At the heart of both peace arrangements was the pledge of national self-determination: if the citizens of Northern Ireland so voted, a transfer to the Republic of Ireland would be allowed. As Michael Cox has argued, the key to understanding these initial steps toward peace to not lay primarily in the articulation or satisfaction of nationalist longings; rather, a new conceptual "space" was opened by the ending of the Cold

War, allowing for new notions of political belonging, and this international spatial dimension was, according to Cox, the decisive factor in moving toward peace.[83] In April 1998 the so-called Good Friday Agreement was signed as a more decisive, perhaps final, step in the peace process, based as it is on the likelihood that Northern Ireland will choose to remain in the United Kingdom for the foreseeable future. The preamble of the agreement, known as the Declaration of Support, is excerpted below; it references both the brutality of past conflicts and the hope for peaceful and democratic forms of future coexistence and belonging.

EXCERPT 8.3

The Northern Ireland Peace Agreement
Good Friday, April 10, 1998

1. We, the participants in the multi-party negotiations, believe that the agreement we have negotiated offers a truly historic opportunity for a new beginning.
2. The tragedies of the past have left a deep and profoundly regrettable legacy of suffering. We must never forget those who have died or been injured, and their families. But we can best honour them through a fresh start, in which we firmly dedicate ourselves to the achievement of reconciliation, tolerance, and mutual trust, and to the protection and vindication of the human rights of all.
3. We are committed to partnership, equality and mutual respect as the basis of relationships within Northern Ireland, between North and South, and between these islands.
4. We reaffirm our total and absolute commitment to exclusively democratic and peaceful means of resolving differences on political issues, and our opposition to any use or threat of force by others for any political purpose, whether in regard to this agreement or otherwise.
5. We acknowledge the substantial differences between our continuing, and equally legitimate, political aspirations. However, we will endeavour to strive in every practical way towards reconciliation and rapprochement within the framework of democratic and agreed arrangements. We pledge that we will, in good faith, work to ensure the success of each and every one of the arrangements to be established under this agreement. It is accepted that all of the institutional and constitutional arrangements—an Assembly in Northern Ireland, a North/South Ministerial Council,

implementation bodies, a British-Irish Council and a British-Irish Intergovernmental Conference and any amendments to British Acts of Parliament and the Constitution of Ireland—are interlocking and interdependent and that in particular the functioning of the Assembly and the North/South Council are so closely inter-related that the success of each depends on that of the other.

6. Accordingly, in a spirit of concord, we strongly commend this agreement to the people, North and South, for their approval.[84]

Numerous scholars have contemplated the extent to which the Good Friday agreement represents a fundamental shift not only in Irish nationalism, but in other "peripheral nationalisms" throughout Europe.[85] Some have read it as a move toward "post-nationalism." But while the peace has held for several years, many scholars are far from convinced that the Northern Ireland issue is actually settled.[86]

Let us turn briefly from the politics of contestation on the periphery of the continent to examine central challenges to the post-Cold War order in the heart of the new Europe.

Identity challenges in the heart of the new Europe

As the Cold War wound down, the integration process in the west moved into a higher gear. To the six founding members of the European Coal and Steel Community who had signed the 1957 Treaty of Rome, there was added an initial round of expansion in the 1970s that brought the United Kingdom, Ireland, and Denmark into the community, which was then followed by further expansion in the 1980s as Greece, Portugal, and Spain joined. In the meantime, the European Parliament was, for the first time, directly elected in 1979, and a common European flag was instituted in 1986. In 1985, the French economist Jacques Delors became President of the European Commission, the executive body of the European Community, at a time when the economic stagnation and high unemployment often referred to as "eurosclerosis" had been visible for several years.[87] The solution Delors proposed was a streamlining of structures and the establishment of the Single European Act in 1986, which was an important move toward a unified market.[88] In June 1989, as Eastern and Central Europe were starting down the road to revolution, Delors outlined a plan for monetary union that would involve both a common currency and common banking institutions, with the goal of better competing with the economic dynamism of the United States and Japan. These ambitious, yet achievable, goals earned Delors praise as a "pragmatic visionary."[89] In January 1990, only two months after the fall of the Berlin Wall, Delors became the first statesman outside of Germany to publicly advocate German reunification.[90] In December 1991, the Treaty on European Union was drafted in Maastricht, the Netherlands, and was then signed by the members of the European Community in February 1992, coming into force the following year. The Maastricht Treaty, as it became known, transformed the existing structures of Europe into the European Union (EU) and laid the groundwork for the introduction of a single currency, the Euro.[91] During Delors's last year in office, 1995, another round of expansion brought Austria, Sweden, and Finland into the EU.

As the EU was streamlining and expanding, critical fault lines were emerging within its individual member states, as the post-Cold War era brought new challenges to ideals of collective belonging. In Czechoslovakia, the new democratic state produced by the Velvet Revolution of 1989 was divided only a few years later in what has been termed a "velvet divorce," as the country's two primary constituent parts split into independent Czech and Slovak Republics.[92] This division was but the official recognition of deeper attitudes toward Czech and Slovak nationality that stretched back decades. As Scott Brown has demonstrated, the Prague Spring of 1968 became, in part, a forum within which Slovak calls for federalization served as a "dress rehearsal" for the velvet divorce that eventually materialized in late 1992.[93]

In united Germany, the physical wall had come down, but a sturdy mental wall continued to exist.[94] Initial predictions of a smooth and rapid reintegration of the two German identities that had developed separately for forty years proved wildly optimistic. Westerners (*Wessis*) and easterners (*Ossis*) would experience major difficulties in finding common ground. It was recognized fairly quickly that the infrastructure in the former east was dilapidated on almost every level—especially in regard to housing stock and transportation and communications infrastructure—and the strikingly low levels of productivity there (when compared to the west) were matched by strikingly high unemployment numbers. The government of Helmut Kohl determined to fund the rebuilding of the east largely on the backs of West Germans—a potentially patronizing approach that led to bitterly sarcastic references to "Kohlonialism," but which was indispensable for the restoration of a functioning relationship between east and west.[95] Most controversially, a new "solidarity tax" (the *Soli*) was leveled on westerners at the rate of 7.5 percent, on top of an already high tax rate.[96] Many *Wessis* wondered only half-jokingly if they could exempt themselves from paying it if they personally felt no "solidarity" with *Ossis*. But the difficulties in forging a common sense of belonging were not merely the result of tax resentments. The social values inculcated in the east were vastly different from those in the capitalist west. And the nature of reunification, which was not a marriage of equals but a swallowing of the east by the west, made many former easterners feel like second class citizens in the new Germany.[97] These divisions played out against the backdrop of the continuing shift toward multiculturalism in Germany. In the course of the dramatic economic recovery in the 1950s and 1960s, gaps in the rapidly expanding German workforce led to the importation of guest workers, mainly of Turkish origin, who were originally intended to be an improvised solution to a temporary problem. But as more Turks stayed, and then had children who stayed, unrest became increasingly visible among the largely homogenous German population by the 1980s and 1990s.[98]

The twenty-first century seemed to bring with it potential moves toward overcoming, or at least better adjusting to, these internal divisions. Angela Merkel, who became chancellor in 2005, was not only the first female chancellor ever to sit in the seat of Bismarck, but also the first from the former east. She had been raised the daughter of a Catholic convert to Lutheranism, who studied theology and entered the clergy, receiving his first pastoral appointment the same year Angela was born. She grew up in a rural area north of Berlin and was a member of the socialist youth movement, although she chose Christian confirmation over the secular socialist youth consecration ceremony (the *Jugendweihe*). Without disavowing her rural roots, she studied in the cities of Leipzig and Berlin and completed a doctorate in physics before entering politics and eventually emerging after reunification as a major force within the conservative Christian Democratic Union. Thus, in her person she bridges divides on a number of levels: geographical, gender-based and, as the first German chancellor born after the end of the Nazi era, also generational. She has also been viewed increasingly as perhaps the most powerful political figure in Europe.[99]

Broader acceptance of multicultural forms of belonging also seemed to spread from an unlikely place: the football pitch. Since 2002, the German national team has finished in the top four in every World Cup competition, winning in 2014 and engendering a considerable amount of (peaceful) national pride. The strikingly multicultural nature of the national team's makeup has provided unprecedented opportunities for the millions who follow the sport to reflect in new ways on what the team's composition says about German identity in the twentieth century.[100] At the same time, however, xenophobic voices in Germany have become more strident, particularly on the political right. In 2010, Thilo Sarrazin, at the time a public official on the executive board of the German Bundesbank, published the runaway best-seller of the year, entitled *Deutschland schafft sich ab* (Germany Abolishes Itself), which criticized Germany's multicultural transformation as a form of cultural suicide.[101] The ensuing years witnessed a further uptick in Islamophobia, as seen in the founding of the movement known as *Pegida*, an acronym whose full English translation would be roughly Patriotic Europeans Against the Islamification of the West, as well as in the launching of a new populist political party, the AfD (*Alternative für Deutschland*, or Alternative for Germany). While the influence of the *Pegida* movement proved somewhat short-lived, the massive influx of Syrian and Iraqi refugees taken in by Germany—more than one million in the year 2015 alone—caused the AfD to experience significant gains in regional elections.

In France, the issue of multiculturalism has been hotly debated, often with varied terminology, for decades. France's historical relationship with North Africa, in addition to its legalistic and territorial (rather than ethnic or descent-based) approach to citizenship, have created distinctive points of conflict.[102] Disputes over the wearing of religious symbols in public schools, including the right of Muslim women to wear traditional headscarves, have engendered widespread debates about the viability of the secular republican legacy of 1789 in a globalizing pluralistic social context.[103] Over the decades, French immigration patterns have produced what some commentators have called "parallel societies" in France, in which largely unassimilated Muslim communities exist in various industrial and often poverty-stricken suburbs with very little connection to other segments of French society.[104] Some of the loudest voices in debates over cultural difference have come from leaders of the National Front, a far-right party whose origins lie in the early 1970s but which first came to prominence in the 1980s. Its founder and first leader, Jean-Marie Le Pen, emerged as an outspoken critic not only of French immigration but of membership in the European Union as well.[105] After achieving varying degrees of success in local, regional, and European elections in the 1980s and 1990s, Le Pen ran in the presidential election of 2002 and finished second to Jacques Chirac, forcing a run-off which Chirac won going away. Le Pen's prominence, and that of the National Front, faded somewhat until the emergence of Le Pen's daughter, Marine, in 2011.[106] Under her leadership, in the context of rising euroskepticism and Islamophobia, the party has experienced a renaissance; in the 2014 elections for the European Parliament, the National Front finished first.

The combination of xenophobia and euroskepticism can also be seen clearly in Austria, which entered the EU in 1995 and which witnessed the rise of the rightist Freedom Party under Jörg Haider in the ensuing years. Haider was the child of former Nazis and, as governor of the southern Austrian state of Carinthia, raised eyebrows by making sympathetic remarks about Waffen-SS veterans on more than one occasion.[107] In the 1999 parliamentary elections, the Freedom Party finished second and was brought into the governing coalition with the center-right Austrian People's Party, generating significant concern internationally. To deflect criticism, Haider stepped down as Freedom Party leader in February 2000, while continuing to influence the party decisively from behind the scenes.[108] The party experienced decline over the next several years (Haider himself was killed in a car crash in 2008), before making a stunning comeback in the context of the growing refugee crisis that started in 2015. The Freedom Party candidate in the 2016 presidential elections, Norbert Hofer, was narrowly defeated in a run-off election, demonstrating just how close Austria came to electing the first far-right extremist head of state in Europe in the post-Cold War era.

In other parts of Europe, it was the aftermath of the September 11, 2001, terrorist attacks in the United States that fostered an unprecedented upsurge in political Islamophobia, typically accompanied by the rhetoric of populist nationalism. The Belgian far-right party Flemish Block (*Vlaams Blok*), which had existed since the 1970s, rose to garner nearly 25 percent of the vote in the June 2004 parliamentary elections, placing it ahead of all other individual parties.[109] But only five months later, in November, Belgium's highest court found that the party's extreme rhetoric had violated the country's 1981 anti-racism law, resulting in the loss of all access to public campaign funds, a veritable death sentence. In response, the party simply dissolved itself and reformed under a different name, as Flemish Interest (*Vlaams Belang*), while pursuing a slightly more careful course in its radical anti-Islamic activism.[110] In the Netherlands, when the anti-Muslim filmmaker Theo van Gogh was murdered by Islamist extremists in 2004, xenophobic forces on the Dutch right were galvanized. Geert Wilders, who previously had been best known as an idiosyncratic maverick, was suddenly a relevant political figure. In 2005, he founded the Party for Freedom, which is staunchly opposed to the sneaking "Islamification" of Europe, particularly the Netherlands, and has been one of the most outspoken proponents of euroskepticism. In the 2009, Dutch elections for the European Parliament, the Party for Freedom finished second, before finishing third in Dutch parliamentary elections in 2010, at which point it accepted an invitation to form a coalition government with the center-right People's Party.[111] Scholars like Koen Vossen predicted that Wilders's version of "national populism," with its romanticized chivalrous imagery of protecting Western civilization from Islamist decimation, would provide a "new ideological master frame" for future radical xenophobic movements in Europe.[112]

It is also important to note that far-right figures have not only claimed to protect Europe, but have themselves engaged in terrorist activity against Europeans. On July 22, 2011, the Islamophobic Norwegian terrorist Anders Breivik, claiming to act in defense of the values of the Christian West, killed sixty-nine unsuspecting Norwegian youth campers and counselors on the island of Utoya, at a campsite owned by the governing Labour Party's youth group, after detonating a bomb in the government quarter of Oslo that killed eight others. In the defense statement he made at his 2012 trial, Breivik claimed to be a knightly figure riding to the defense of "ethnic Norwegians," in pursuit of the broader values of Christianity and Western civilization:

Norwegians and Europeans...will not sit quietly by while ethnic Norwegians are turned into a minority in their own country, in their own capital. We will fight against multiculturalism in the Labour Party and against all other political activists that are working towards the same goal. The attacks of July 22nd were preventive attacks, serving the defense of the Norwegian indigenous people, ethnic Norwegians, our culture, and I cannot declare myself guilty before the law for conducting them. I was acting in self-defense on behalf of my people, my culture, my religion, my city, and my country. Therefore I demand to be acquitted of all charges.[113]

Psychiatrists and commentators questioned Breivik's sanity, and with good cause. But when the Norwegian court ultimately found Breivik sane, and therefore criminally responsible, it offered as partial justification the assertion that "many people share Breivik's conspiracy theory" about the perceived Islamist threat to Western identity.[114] And Åsne Seierstad is probably not wrong in making the troubling observation that Breivik is, in many ways, "one of us."[115]

* * * *

The year 2014 was the occasion for a number of particularly significant anniversaries. In rounded numbers, it marked the 200th anniversary of the Congress of Vienna and the 100th anniversary of the outbreak of the First World War. Those inclined toward quartiles would note that it also represented the 225th anniversary of the convening of the Estates-General at Versailles and the 25th anniversary of the fall of the Berlin Wall. While there were indeed those who commemorated each of the aforementioned anniversaries, the events of 2014 themselves—particularly in regard to European nationalism—were sufficient in their own right to capture one's attention.

The most notable of these was the crisis that emerged in Ukraine. In February 2014, the Euromaidan Revolution in Kiev swept Ukrainian president Viktor Yanukovich from power and initiated dramatic political and constitutional changes. A central catalyst for the revolution had been Yanukovich's decision to move away from a planned economic agreement with the European Union and to sign instead a deal to secure loans from Russia. After the flight of Yanukovich, a provisional government was formed and plans were made to move forward with the EU agreement. At the same time, unrest broke out among Russians living in the Crimea, which had become part of Ukraine in 1954 when the unity of the Soviet Union had offered security for the roughly two-thirds of the Crimean population who were Russian. Following the collapse of the Soviet Union and the independence of Ukraine, however, those Russians living in Crimea claimed to feel stranded—somewhat akin to the "abandoned" Sudeten Germans in interwar Czechoslovakia—while authorities in Moscow appeared powerless to respond. In the weeks after the Euromaidan protests, Russians in Crimea (likely with aid from undercover forces sent by Russian President Vladimir Putin) seized and occupied the parliament building in the Crimean capital Simferopol, announcing plans for a plebiscite to decide whether Crimea would remain part of Ukraine or declare its official secession. When the referendum was held but ignored internationally, Russia annexed the region, declaring it the Crimean Federal Republic within the Russian Federation.[116]

The annexation of Crimea was followed, in the Donbass region in eastern Ukraine, by a series of uprisings among Russian-speakers there, who make up a slight majority of the population. These tensions boiled over into armed conflict in April 2014 between pro-Russian Donbass separatists and Ukrainian forces. In July, a Malaysian Airlines flight was shot down over the region, killing all of the nearly 300 passengers and crew, with both sides in the Ukrainian conflict denying responsibility. Throughout the summer, increasing numbers of troops and "volunteers" from Russia continued to arrive in eastern Ukraine to aid the separatists, although the Putin administration denied any Russian involvement for more than a year. A brief cease-fire in September was quickly abrogated and casualties continued to mount. Two other failed cease-fires were attempted in early 2015, and as this book goes to press the conflict continues—although it has most recently devolved into a stalemate punctuated by periodic skirmishes.

While the political and military narrative remains in question, this regional story took an interesting (albeit far from earth-shattering) turn in May 2016 by way of Stockholm, Sweden, where the finals of the Eurovision Song Contest were held. Ukraine won the hugely popular competition, being represented by Jamala, a woman of Crimean Tatar descent who performed a poignant and controversial song of her own writing. Entitled "1944," the song dealt with Stalin's forced deportation during the Second World War of some 200,000 Tatars, a Turkic people who had lived in Crimea for centuries. Among those deported was Jamala's great-grandmother, who lost one of her daughters to starvation along the way. Overall, tens of thousands of Tatars starved or died of exposure.[117] The title and lyrics, which were performed partly in English and partly in the Crimean Tatar language, were difficult to misconstrue and, along with Jamala's back story, received a tremendous amount of publicity long before the finals in May.[118] Some sour (losing) contestants alleged irregularities in the vote counting while others criticized Jamala's political message as a cheap ploy to win sympathy in the context of the current Ukraine crisis.[119] Both claims may be true, although it should be noted that the winner gets no prize money, just a moment of fame. Ultimately, the attention drawn to Crimea, Ukraine, and the Tatars—and broader issues of national identity, history, and violence—was perhaps the most important form of compensation.

On May 24, 2014, two months after the initial Russian annexation of Crimea, attention was focused on an Islamist terror attack at a Jewish museum in Brussels, which killed four. In retrospect that attack, despite its comparatively small death toll, initiated a sharpened tone that has continued in subsequent discussions throughout Western Europe over radical Islam and the perceived failure of multiculturalism.[120] The January 2016 shootings at the Paris offices of the satirical magazine *Charlie Hebdo*, which killed twenty, and the broader attack that November that killed over 130 in Parisian restaurants and at the Bataclan Theater simply moved the discussion further along the established ruts, as did the bombings at the

Brussels airport in March 2016, which killed more than thirty, and the brutal truck attack in Nice on Bastille Day 2016, which killed more than eighty. As with the Ukraine crisis, the continual flow of events makes it difficult to predict future responses to radical Islam and the impact of global terrorism on articulations of national belonging. It is likely that the number of existing "national conservative" governments in Europe—as illustrated by the administrations of Viktor Orbán in Hungary and Beata Szydło in Poland—will continue to grow and move increasingly in the direction of xenophobia. But history also flows in unpredictable directions.

The year 2014 was also the date set for the Scottish referendum over whether to remain part of Great Britain, to which Scotland had officially belonged since 1707, or to establish independence, as the bulk of Ireland had done in the 1920s. The Scottish National Party (SNP), the leading political force advocating for independence, had been founded before the Second World War but remained largely marginal for decades. In 1997 the SNP, alongside the Scottish Labour Party, played a significant role in establishing home rule, also known as "devolution," which created a semiautonomous Scottish Parliament and the position of First Minister, a somewhat limited counterpart to the British Prime Minister. By 2007, the SNP had become the largest party in the Scottish Parliament, and the party's leader, Alex Salmond, assumed the position of First Minister.[121] Over the ensuing years plans for an independence referendum were widely debated, with the date of September 2014 ultimately being chosen.[122] Following months of energetic stumping both by the "Yes Scotland" campaign, which endorsed independence, and by the "Better Together" campaign, which advocated remaining inside the United Kingdom, the vote itself went in favor of the latter by a somewhat unexpectedly large margin of more than ten percentage points.[123] One of the factors that helped sway public opinion toward remaining in Britain was the fear that Scotland would be forced to go through the arduous process of re-applying for membership in the European Union on its own, with a real possibility of exclusion as a result.[124]

Ironically, less than two years later, renewed talk of Scottish national independence emerged forcefully as a result of the momentous British decision to leave the EU in the so-called Brexit vote of June 2016. Following Britain's initial entrance into the European Economic Community in 1973, an initial referendum was held in 1975 over whether to remain, and "yes" votes had outnumbered "no" votes by a proportion of more than two to one. The ensuing four decades, however, witnessed the rise of British Euroskepticism fueled by a variety of concerns—the EU's often arcane bureaucracy and regulations, its vast army of unelected bureaucrats, its allowance of freedom of movement and the resulting influx of non-English-speakers into the UK—and these concerns often crossed party lines. The Conservative Party in particular was divided over the issue of EU membership, making prime minister David Cameron's promise in 2013 to hold a referendum on the issue especially complicated within his own ranks.

The emergence in 2013 of the staunchly anti-Europe UK Independence Party (UKIP) under the leadership of Nigel Farage introduced a new strident tone into debates over European, British, and English identity.[125] A new interest in England's history—singled out from the broader British context that includes Scotland, Wales, and Northern Ireland—coincided with increasing assertions that English national identity was threatened, perhaps fatally, by Britain's continued membership in the EU.[126] On June 16, 2016, just one week before the scheduled referendum, the parliamentary deputy Jo Cox, one of the most vocal political proponents of keeping Britain in the EU, was murdered publicly and in broad daylight by an attacker shouting "Britain first!" Many commentators in Britain and elsewhere expected Cox's murder to provide a rallying point for the Remain campaign to mobilize successfully in the days leading up to the vote.[127] But on referendum day, the Leave campaign prevailed on the strength of a 52 to 48 percent margin. Financial markets sank (although they rebounded fairly quickly), young British citizens lamented the perceived narrow-mindedness of older "Leavers," and fears of rising anti-immigrant nationalism were expressed widely in the media.[128]

Almost immediately, the fact that solid majorities in Scotland and Northern Ireland had voted for Remain raised the renewed prospect of separation from Britain to avoid being dragged out of the EU. Nicola Sturgeon, the successor to Alex Salmond as First Minister and leader of the SNP, was particularly vocal in calling for another Scottish independence referendum.[129] Gerry Adams, leader of the Northern Irish *Sinn Féin* party who negotiated the Good Friday Agreement in 1998, made an international push to express anger that the clear wishes of voters in Northern Ireland to remain in the EU were being discarded as a result of English (and Welsh) parochialism, noting also that leaving Europe would lead inexorably to the tragic creation of a strengthened border dividing Ireland, which remains part of the EU, and Northern Ireland—a divide that the Good Friday Agreement had done so much to reduce.[130]

* * * *

Importantly, less than three weeks after the Brexit vote, David Cameron, who had campaigned energetically to keep Britain in the EU, stepped down. His successor, both as prime minister and as leader of the Conservative Party, was Theresa May, the second woman in British history to hold both of those positions and the second to be confronted almost immediately with the issue of EU secession. The first, Margaret Thatcher, had become party leader just weeks before the initial 1975 British referendum on membership in the EEC, and one of her earliest major achievements was to advocate successfully for the "yes" campaign (she later developed, as prime minister, into a more pronounced Euroskeptic). Ironically, Theresa May, who had supported the Remain campaign, albeit somewhat tepidly, would now be tasked with the opposing endeavor: overseeing the logistical challenges of negotiating Britain's exit from the European Union. It is likely that EU leaders will impose harsh exit terms in order to discourage anti-Europe activists in other member states from launching their own versions of the Brexit campaign.

In any event, to return briefly to the image of a dilapidated Mini-Europe that opened this chapter, it is safe to say that the removal of exhibits like Big Ben and Dover Castle from the grounds of the theme park will be less messy and protracted than whatever divorce settlement is achieved between Britain and the European Union.

9

Postscript

On January 20, 2017, Donald J. Trump was inaugurated as the forty-fifth President of the United States. In his inaugural speech that day, he went to great lengths to reinforce the central idea animating the aggrieved voters who fueled his improbable rise to power: "From this day forward, it's going to be only America first. America first."[1] Leaving aside obvious questions about the real primacy of Trump's ego—not to mention widespread reports of Russian attempts to influence the election in Trump's favor—it appeared to observers near and far that a new era may indeed be dawning for the United States and the world.[2] Attempting to break almost immediately with decades of established foreign policy norms, Trump and his advisors took aim with particular venom at the forces they claimed had diminished American greatness at home and abroad, vowing to renegotiate or abrogate international treaties seen as unfavorable to U.S. interests, pursuing a cutthroat strategy of economic nationalism on all levels, pledging to fend off the pernicious forces of globalization through the imposition of border walls and travel bans, and declaring supranational agencies such as NATO to be "obsolete."

It may seem strange to conclude a book on nationalism in modern Europe with reference to the populist bloviations of an American president a continent away. But the advent of what several commentators have termed the "Trumpian moment" raises important questions about the future of Europe along several major trajectories. On the most basic level, Trump was celebrating the unabashed prioritization of national self-interest over the continued pursuit of humanitarian idealism. While the preponderance of public discourse within NATO and the EU has often focused on the values of the "west," the truth is that both organizations were founded with much more practical interests in mind. As Jean Monnet claimed in his famous 1953 speech on the need for common European economic and political structures, "rules and institutions do not change men's natures but they do bring about change in their behavior toward one another. That is the lesson which civilization has taught us."[3] In other words, the historical antagonism between France and Germany would not be overcome by appeals to "civilized" values alone, but through practical rules and common institutions within which individual and state actors could pursue their interests peacefully. As Judy Dempsey has argued insightfully, the future of a Europe currently caught between a resurgent Russian threat and an uncertain American ally may best be served by a clear articulation and defense of European interests on the practical levels of security and trade.[4] In this sense, the "Trumpian moment" may prove salutary in pushing Europe to mature in its role on the global stage.

Internally, of course, the resurgence of populist nationalism—encouraged both by the Brexit vote and Trump's political triumph—will likely continue to problematize the common "rules and institutions" underpinning the European project. It is here that the ability to foster compelling notions of belonging emerges as a central imperative. As the Congress of Vienna demonstrated more than two centuries ago, it may well be possible to maintain supranational state structures through centripetal force for a time. But in the face of the powerful appeal of nationalism, the failure of dynastic regimes in the nineteenth century to cultivate a corresponding ideal that could unify and inspire citizens with equal intensity created a constant source of potential instability. In twenty-first-century Europe, the presence of large (and often sequestered) groups of refugees and immigrants from the Muslim world provides an extra wrinkle of complication, while fears of economic uncertainty and the potential vulnerability to terror lend greater appeal to the prescriptions of xenophobes and protectionists. As this book goes to press, key elections loom in the Netherlands, France, and Germany, and it is tempting to speculate about the potential impact of their outcome. However, recognizing that attempts by historians to predict the future are often misguided at best—and noting that such prognostications usually seem outdated fairly quickly—perhaps it will be most fruitful to conclude with a brief look backward. The past offers us enough to chew on.

While this text has pursued a chronological narrative structure, several thematic elements have emerged. We have seen that nationalist ideas and movements have been remarkably effective in speaking to fundamental human needs for meaning and belonging, often successfully co-opting other markers of identity. It is true that religious identity often played a disruptive role during key moments in the nation-building process— whether recalcitrant priests falling afoul of French revolutionary radicals or oppositional Catholic bishops in Germany being jailed during the *Kulturkampf*. But on many occasions, religion played a constructive role in enhancing national cohesion, as seen in Catholic-oriented articulations of Polish or Irish identity, or in Protestant hegemony among the English or Dutch. Gendered ideals were folded into the nationalist cause during the French Revolution, as seen in the unruly mobilization of women on the streets of Paris and the soaring (if contradictory) images of Marianne leading the French into battle. The military conflicts that attended the nineteenth-century national unification projects in Italy and Germany provided a screen onto which visions of masculine vitality could be projected—although, as seen particularly in the aftermath of the First World War, such conflicts could also produce profound "crises" of masculinity, calling into question the virility of the nation. As individual men and women came increasingly to see nationality as a fundamental component of personal identity, scientific and biological metaphors helped construct the image of the "body" of the nation as an organism with its own circulatory system, which much be kept pure and free from contamination in order to survive in its Darwinian struggle against other nations. Much of the initial success of the postwar European integration project was in its creation of structures and modes of belonging that transcended the zero-sum conception of national self-interest and instead fostered collaborative peace rather than war.

We have also seen the extent to which nationalist leaders often succeeded in papering over the fundamental contradictions present within nationalist ideologies, even using these contradictions to fuel more energetic mobilization for the national cause. On the one hand, the power of Rousseau's general will lay in its inclusive appeal and its grounding of political sovereignty in the nation itself; on the other hand, the necessarily inviolable nature of the general will also authorized the exercise of coercive force against members of the nation who might deviate from its prescriptions. Nationalist rhetoric often featured triumphalist imagery of the strength and superiority of the nation, while masking a fundamental insecurity and paranoid fragility that fueled the need for constant vigilance against enemies within and without. Late eighteenth- and early nineteenth-century nationalist figures often wrapped self-interest and egocentrism within a cloak of universalism. Robespierre claimed to be animated solely by humanitarian virtue. Fichte linked the cause of German nationalists to the fate of the world ("if you go under, all humanity goes under with you, without hope of any future restoration"). Mazzini urged Italian activists to pursue their duties to humanity before their own national cause, but cautioned that if the Italian nationalist project failed, Italians would be nothing more than the "bastards of humanity." By the early twentieth century, of course, much of the humanitarian façade had been discarded in favor of a more straightforward brand of national chauvinism, with the imperatives of the nation authorizing catastrophic mass violence and genocide. Interestingly, however, despite the relatively harmonious supranational cooperation of the European integration project, the present drift toward populist nationalism most often casts universalism as the destructive threat against which more "authentic" visions of belonging are mobilized. The nation has become, in many ways, a haven and bulwark to which those mystified by the forces of globalization can retreat.

As Ernest Renan noted presciently in 1882, the ability to forget can be as important as the imperative to remember, and the lessons of the past are sometimes difficult to sell to future generations. Through wars and territorial revisions, through soaring inclusive ideals and brutal exclusionary rhetoric, through the co-optation and instrumentalization of rival forms of belonging, and through the creation of new symbolic universes of meaning and significance, European nationalism has progressed along a sweeping and convoluted trajectory, evolving as a complicated tangle of ideas, movements, and personalities. That complexity can be both fascinating and disconcerting. It may be that the current challenge of resurgent nationalism in Europe will remain limited and will call forth compelling alternatives and counter-narratives, revealing that nationalism's near monopoly on collective identity has in fact been fundamentally altered (if not entirely dislodged). But in the short term, the forlorn and dilapidated exhibits of the Mini-Europe theme park seem more appropriate than ever.

NOTES

Chapter 1

1   Robert Priest, *The Gospel According to Renan: Reading, Writing, and Religion in Nineteenth-Century France* (Oxford, 2015), 109–53.

2   For an attempt to situate Renan's earlier work on Jesus in the context of nineteenth-century nationalism, see Halvor Moxnes, *Jesus and the Rise of Nationalism: A New Quest for the Nineteenth-Century Historical Jesus* (London, 2012), 121–48.

3   Quoted in Richard Chadbourne, *Ernest Renan* (New York, 1968), 100.

4   The earliest posthumous biography of Renan devoted all of one brief sentence to the piece; Henri Desportes, *Ernest Renan: sa vie et son oeuvre* (Paris, 1893), 199.

5   Oliver Zimmer, for example, designed his historical survey to be a "more thematic and analytically focused approach [which] does not provide a chronological narrative.... My aim has not been to offer a comprehensive account"; Oliver Zimmer, *Nationalism in Europe, 1890–1940* (Houndmills, 2003), 2–3. While organized more chronologically, Timothy Baycroft's brief survey is similarly thematic; Baycroft, *Nationalism in Europe, 1789–1945* (Cambridge, 1998).

6   See David Carr, *Time, Narrative, and History* (Bloomington, 1991).

7   Simon Schama, *Citizens: A Chronicle of the French Revolution* (New York, 1989), 6.

8   Benedict Anderson, *Imagined Communities* (London, 1983).

9   Ernest Gellner, *Nations and Nationalism* (Ithaca, 1983), 1.

10 Wolfgang Mommsen, "Nationality, Patriotism, Nationalism," in Roger Michener, ed., *Nationality, Patriotism, and Nationalism* (St. Paul, 2000), 1–24.

11 In this regard, I agree with Eric Hobsbawm's approach: "As an initial working assumption, any sufficiently large body of people whose members regard themselves as members of a 'nation' will be treated as such"; Hobsbawm, *Nations and Nationalism since 1780: Programme, Myth, Reality* (Cambridge, 1990), 8. Similarly, Hugh Seton-Watson stated: "All that I can find to say is that a nation exists when a significant number of people in a community consider themselves to form a nation, or behave as if they formed one"; Hugh Seton-Watson, *Nations and States: An Enquiry into the Origins of Nations and the Politics of Nationalism* (London, 1977), 5.

12 See Montserrat Guibernau, *Belonging: Solidarity and Division in Modern Society* (Cambridge, 2013); for darker aspects, see Amin Maalouf, *In the Name of Identity: Violence and the Need to Belong* (New York, 2003).

13 Freud famously identified the oceanic feeling, which he said he did not personally share, as "a sensation of eternity, a feeling as of something limitless, unbounded—as it were, oceanic"; Sigmund Freud, *Civilization and Its Discontents* (New York, 1969), 11.

14 The concept of nationalism as an ersatz political religion was pioneered by Eric Voegelin initially in the 1930s; see his *Political Religions* (Lewiston, 1986; orig. 1938). See also Michael Burleigh, *Earthly Powers* (New York, 2005); Burleigh, *Sacred Causes* (New York, 2007).

15 For more a much more detailed analysis, see Umut Özkrimli, *Theories of Nationalism: A Critical Introduction* (Houndmills, 2010).

16 See the essays in Atsuko Ichijo and Gordana Uzelac, eds., *When Is the Nation? Towards an Understanding of Theories of Nationalism* (London, 2005).

17 Hobsbawm, *Nations and Nationalism Since 1780*, 10.

18 On Gellner's life and ideas, see John Hall and Ian Jarvie, "The Life and Times of Ernest Gellner," in Hall and Jarvie, eds., *The Social Philosophy of Ernest Gellner* (Amsterdam, 1996); also John Hall, ed., *The State of the Nation: Ernest Gellner and the Theory of Nationalism* (Cambridge, 1998).

19 John Breuilly, *Nationalism and the State* (Manchester, 1982).

20 Anderson, *Imagined Communities*, 6. Eric Hobsbawm, "Inventing Traditions," in Hobsbawm and Terence Ranger, eds., *The Invention of Tradition* (Cambridge, 1983), 1–14.

21 Among the best works on cultural aspects of nationalist thought is Joep Leersen, *National Thought in Europe: A Cultural History* (Amsterdam, 2006). For early studies of nationalism as ideology, see Carlton J.H. Hayes, *Nationalism: A Religion* (New York, 1960); Elie Kedourie, *Nationalism* (London, 1960); Karl Deutsch, *Nationalism and Social Communication* (Cambridge, MA, 1966).

22 Anthony Smith, *The Ethnic Revival in the Modern World* (Cambridge, 1981), esp. 87–95.

23 For the quintessential articulations, see Anthony D. Smith, *The Ethnic Origins of Nations* (London, 1991), and Smith, *Ethnosymbolism and Nationalism: A Cultural Approach* (London, 2009). For scholarly evaluations, see Montserrat Guibernau and John Hutchinson, eds., *History and National Destiny: Ethnosymbolism and Its Critics* (London, 2004); and Athena Leoussi and Steven Grosby, eds., *Nationalism and Ethnosymbolism: History, Culture, and Ethnicity in the Formation of Nations* (Edinburgh, 2007).

24 Early figures in what became known as the primordialist camp include Johan Huizinga and Marc Bloch; see e.g. Johan Huizinga, "Patriotism and Nationalism in European History," in Huizinga, *Men and Ideas: History, the Middle Ages and the Renaissance* (Princeton, 1959), 97–155; Peter Schöttler, "Marc Bloch as a Critic of Historiographic Nationalism in the Interwar Years," in Stefan Berger et al., eds., *Writing National Histories* (London, 1999), 125–36.

25 See the essays in Simon Forde, Lesley Johnson, and Alan Murray, eds., *Concepts of National Identity in the Middle Ages* (Leeds, 1995).

26 "Whether or not one chooses to call the concept of nation that I am discussing a form of nationalism seems to me unimportant. If modernists want to reserve the word for the kind of nationalist movements that appeared in their periods, that is fine"; Reynolds, "The Idea of the Nation as a Political Community," in Len Scales and Oliver Zimmer, eds., *Power and the Nation in European History* (Cambridge, 2005), 55. See also Reynolds, *Kingdoms and Communities in Western Europe, 900–1300* (Oxford, 1997).

27 John Armstrong, *Nations Before Nationalism* (Chapel Hill, 1982).

28 Armstrong, "Towards a Theory of Nationalism: Consensus and Dissensus," in Sukumar Periwal, ed., *Notions of Nationalism* (Budapest, 1995), 34–43.

29 See the round-table discussion of Gat's work in *Nations and Nationalism* 21 (2015): 383–402.

30 Azar Gat, *Nations: The Long History and Deep Roots of Political Ethnicity and Nationalism* (Cambridge, 2013), esp. 27–43.

31 Philip Gorski, *The Disciplinary Revolution: Calvinism and the Rise of the State in Early Modern Europe* (Chicago, 2003); also Gorski, "The Mosaic Moment: An Early Modernist Critique of Modernist Theories of Nationalism," *American Journal of Sociology* 105 (2000): esp. 1433–34.

32 Adrian Hastings, *The Construction of Nationhood: Ethnicity, Religion, and Nationalism* (Cambridge, 1997).

33 Liah Greenfeld, *Nationalism: Five Roads to Modernity* (Cambridge, MA, 1992), esp. 27–88. See also Aviel Roshwald, *The Endurance of Nationalism: Ancient Roots and Modern Dilemmas* (Cambridge, 2006), esp. 8–43.

34 Hans Kohn, *Living in a World of Revolution: My Encounters with History* (New York, 1970).

35 It was published as Hans Kohn, *The Idea of Nationalism* (New York, 1944). On the context that shaped Kohn's thinking, see Paul Lawrence, *Nationalism: History and Theory* (Harlow, 2005), 119–22.

36 See esp. Andreas Wimmer, *Waves of War: Nationalism, State Formation, and Ethnic Exclusion in the Modern World* (Cambridge, 2013).

37 On various typologies of European nationalism, see e.g. Ireneusz Paweł Karolewski and Andrzej Marcin Suszycki, *The Nation and Nationalism in Europe: An Introduction* (Edinburgh, 2011), chap. 4.

38 See Stephen Shulman, "Challenging the Civic–Ethnic and West–East Dichotomies in the Study of Nationalism," *Comparative Political Studies* 35 (2002): 554–85; David Brown, "Are There Good and Bad Nationalisms?" *Nations and Nationalisms* 5 (1999): 281–302.

39 Maria Todorova, "Is There a Weak Nationalism, and Is It a Useful Category?" *Nations and Nationalism* 21 (2015): 681–99.

40 Michael Billig, *Banal Nationalism* (London, 1995); also Michael Skey, *National Belonging in Everyday Life* (Houndmills, 2011).

41 Philip Barker, *Religious Nationalism in Modern Europe: If God Be for Us* (London, 2009).

42 Roger Friedland, "Religious Nationalism and the Problem of Collective Representation," *Annual Review of Sociology* 27 (2001): 125–52; Roger Friedland, "Money, Sex, and God: The Erotic Logic of Religious Nationalism," *Sociological Theory* 20 (2002): 381–425; Rogers Brubaker, "Religion and Nationalism: Four Approaches," *Nations and Nationalism* 18 (2012): 2–20.

43 See Nira Yuval-Davis, *Gender and Nation* (London, 1997); also Vera Tolz and Stephenie Booth, *Nation and Gender in Contemporary Europe* (Manchester, 2005).

44 Michèle Cohen, *Fashioning Masculinity: National Identity and Language in the Eighteenth Century* (London, 1996); George Mosse, *Nationalism and Sexuality* (New York, 1985); George Mosse, *The Image of Man: The Creation of Modern Masculinity* (Oxford, 1996), esp. 77–106.

45 Patrizia Albanese, *Mothers of the Nation: Women, Families, and Nationalism in Twentieth-Century Europe* (Toronto, 2006).

46 Tamar Mayer, "Gender Ironies of Nationalism: Setting the Stage," in Mayer, ed., *Gender Ironies of Nationalism: Sexing the Nation* (London, 2000), 1–24; Sasha Roseneil, ed., *Beyond Citizenship? Feminism and the Transformation of Belonging* (Houndmills, 2013); Oliver Janz and Daniel Schönpflug, eds., *Gender History in a Transnational Perspective* (New York, 2014).

47 On music and nationalist imagery, see Christopher Kelen, *Anthem Quality. National Songs: A Theoretical Survey* (Bristol, 2014); Philip Bohlman, *The Music of European Nationalism* (Santa Barbara, 2004); Philip Bohlman, *Music, Nationalism, and the Making of the New Europe* (London, 2011); Harry White and Michael Murphy, eds., *Musical Constructions of Nationalism* (Cork, 2001); Philip Ther, *Center Stage: Operatic Culture and Nation Building in Nineteenth-Century Central Europe* (West Lafayette, 2014). On sport and nationalism, see J.A. Mangan, ed., *Tribal Identities: Nationalism, Europe, Sport* (London, 1996); Alan Bairner, *Sport, Nationalism, and Globalization* (Albany, 2001); Liz Crolley and David Hand, *Football and European Identity: Historical Narratives Though the Press* (London, 2006); Christos Kassimeris, *Football Comes Home: Symbolic Identities in European Football* (Lanham, 2010); Alexandra Schwell, *New Ethnographies of Football in Europe: People, Passions, Politics* (Houndmills, 2016). On visual arts, see esp. Anthony D. Smith, *The Nation Made Real: Art and National Identity in Western Europe, 1600–1850* (Oxford, 2013).

48 Genesis 10: 31–32, *New Oxford Annotated Bible*. For a close reading of the passage by a scholar of nationalism, see Steven Grosby, "The Biblical 'Nation' as a Problem for Philosophy," *Hebraic Political Studies* 1 (2005): 7–23.

49 Genesis 17:4–5, *New Oxford Annotated Bible*. See also David Novak, *The Election of Israel: The Idea of the Chosen People* (Cambridge, 1995), esp. 10–13; and Anthony D. Smith, *Chosen Peoples: Sacred Sources of National Identity* (Oxford, 2003).

50 Israel Jacob Yuval, *Two Nations in Your Womb: Perceptions of Jews and Christians in Late Antiquity and the Middle Ages* (Berkeley, 2006).

51 Herodotus, *The History* (Chicago, 1987), Book 8, 144; quoted in Steven Grosby, *Nationalism: A Very Short Introduction* (Oxford, 2005), 2.

52 See esp. Plato's depiction of the discussion between Socrates and Glaucon contrasting Greek and barbarian identity; Allan Bloom, ed., *The Republic of Plato* (New York, 1991), 150.

53 For the initial Pauline universalization impulse, see Caroline Johnson Hodge, *If Sons, Then Heirs: A Study of Kinship and Ethnicity in the Letters of Paul* (Oxford, 2007), esp. 93–108. On later elaborations, see Michael Bland Simmons, *Universal Salvation in Late Antiquity* (Oxford, 2015), esp. 211–12.

54 Alexander Callander Murray, "Reinhard Wenskus on Ethnogenesis, Ethnicity, and the Origin of the Franks," in Andres Gillett, ed., *On Barbarian Identity: Critical Approaches to Ethnicity in the Early Middle Ages* (Turnhout, 2002), 39–68; Herwig Wolfram, *The Roman Empire and Its Germanic Peoples* (Berkeley, 1997); Walter Pohl, "Conceptions of Ethnicity in Early Medieval Studies," in Lester Little and Barbara Rosenwein, eds., *Debating the Middle Ages* (Oxford, 1998), 13–24; also Walter Pohl and Helmut Reimitz, eds., *Strategies of Distinction: The Construction of Ethnic Communities, 300–800* (Leiden, 1998).

55 Patrick Geary, *The Myth of Nations: The Medieval Origins of Europe* (Princeton, 2002). See also Walter Goffart, *Barbarian Tides: The Migration Age and the Later Roman Empire* (Philadelphia, 2010).

56 Ian Wood, "Ethnicity and the Ethnogenesis of the Burgundians," in Herwig Wolfram and Walter Pohl, eds., *Typen der Ethnogese unter besonderer Berücksichtigung der Bayern* (Vienna, 1990), 53–69; Wood, "Defining the Franks: Frankish Origins in Early Medieval Historiography," in Thomas F.X. Noble, ed., *From Roman Provinces to Medieval Kingdoms* (London, 2006), 110–19.

57 Quoted in Alan V. Murray, "Ethnic Identity in the Crusader States: The Frankish Race and the Settlement of Outremer," in Forde et al., eds., *Concepts of National Identity in the Middle Ages*, 62.

58 See Alan V. Murray, *The Franks in Outremer: Studies in the Latin Principalities of Palestine and Syria, 1099–1187* (Farnham, 2015).

59 John Gillingham, *The English in the Twelfth Century: Imperialism, National Identity, and Political Values* (Woodbridge, 2000), esp. 123–61.

60 Ardis Butterfield, *The Familiar Enemy: Chaucer, Language, and the Nation in the Hundred Years War* (Oxford, 2009).

61 Krishan Kumar, *The Making of English National Identity* (Cambridge, 2003), xi.

62 Anderson, *Imagined Communities*, 12, 16.

63 Joseph Strayer, *On the Medieval Origins of the Modern State* (Princeton, 1970).

64 Ibid., 10, 57.

65 See the programmatic article Wolfgang Reinhard, "Reformation, Counter-Reformation, and the Early Modern State: A Reassessment," *Catholic Historical Review* 75 (1989): 383–404; also Heinz Schilling, "Confessional Europe," in Thomas Brady et al., eds., *Handbook of European History, 1400–1600* (Leiden, 1995), 641–70; more generally, Heinz Schilling, *Religion, Political Culture, and the Emergence of Early Modern Society* (Leiden, 1992).

66 Joel Harrington and Helmut Walser Smith, "Confessionalization, Community, and State Building in Germany, 1555–1870," *Journal of Modern History* 69 (1997): 77–101; also Ronnie Po-Chia Hsia; see his *Social Discipline and the Reformation: Central Europe, 1550–1760* (New York, 1990).

67 Anthony Marx, *Faith in Nation: Exclusionary Origins of Nationalism* (Oxford, 2013).

68 On the longer-term contradictions inherent in the Enlightenment ideal, see Michael Mann, *The Dark Side of Democracy: Explaining Ethnic Cleansing* (Cambridge, 2005), which interprets various forms of exclusionary violence as fundamental products of, not deviations from, the Enlightenment.

69 An extensive overview is provided by Dorinda Outram, *The Enlightenment* (Cambridge, 2013); see also Roy Porter and Mikulas Teich, eds., *The Enlightenment in National Context* (Cambridge, 1981).

70 See e.g. Ken Wolf, "Hans Kohn's Liberal Nationalism," *Journal of the History of Ideas* 4 (1976): 651–72.

71 Michael Mann, *The Sources of Social Power. Volume II: The Rise of Classes and Nation-States* (Cambridge, 1993), esp. 167–213.

72 Wolfgang Reinhard, "Power Elites, State Servants, Ruling Classes, and the Growth of State Power," in Reinhard, ed., *Power Elites and State Building* (Oxford, 1996), 1–18.

73 See James Gaines, *Evening in the Palace of Reason: Bach Meets Frederick the Great in the Age of Enlightenment* (New York, 2005); T.C.W. Blanning, "Frederick the Great and Enlightened Absolutism," in H.M. Scott, ed., *Enlightened Absolutism* (London, 1990), 265–90; Derek Beales, *Joseph II: In the Shadow of Maria Theresia, 1741–1780* (Cambridge, 2008); Derek Beales, *Joseph II: Against the World, 1780–1790* (Cambridge, 2013).

74 Matthew Levinger, *Enlightened Nationalism: The Transformation of Prussian Political Culture* (Oxford, 2000).

75 H. Arnold Barton, "Gustav III of Sweden and the Enlightenment," *Eighteenth-Century Studies* 6 (1972): 1–34.

76 H. Arnold Barton, *Scandinavia in the Revolutionary Era, 1760–1815* (Minneapolis, 1986), x.

77 Marc Raeff, *The Well-Ordered Police State: Social and Institutional Change Through Law in the Germanies and Russia, 1600–1800* (New Haven, 1983); Simon Dixon, *The Modernization of Russia, 1676–1825* (Cambridge, 1999), esp. 68–73, 161–67.

78 Marc Raeff, *Origins of the Russian Intelligentsia: The Eighteenth-Century Nobility* (New York, 1966); for a brilliant evocation of Russian cultural life during the seventeenth century, see Orlando Figes, *Natasha's Dance: A Cultural History of Russia* (New York, 2002), 1–68.

79 Leo Damrosch, *Jean-Jacques Rousseau: Restless Genius* (Boston, 2005), 8–24.

80 Marc Plattner, *Rousseau's State of Nature: An Interpretation of the Discourse on Inequality* (DeKalb, 1979).

81 Anne Cohler, *Rousseau and Nationalism* (New York, 1970), 19–28; Marc Plattner, "Rousseau and the Origins of Nationalism," in Clifford Orwin and Nathan Tarcov, eds., *The Legacy of Rousseau* (Chicago, 1997), 183–99.

82 Rousseau, *The Social Contract*, trans. Henry Tozer (New York, 1895).

83 Peter Gay, "Introduction," to Rousseau, *Basic Political Writings* (Indianapolis, 1987), viii.

84 Steven Engel, "Rousseau and Imagined Communities," *Review of Politics* 67 (2005): 515–37.

85 Robert Nisbet, "Rousseau and Totalitarianism," *Review of Politics* 5 (1943): 93–114.

86 See F.M. Barnard, "National Culture and Political Legitimacy: Herder and Rousseau," *Journal of the History of Ideas* 44 (1983): 231–53; Judson Lyon, "The Herder Syndrome: A Comparative Study of Cultural Nationalism," *Ethnic and Racial Studies* 17 (1994): 224–37.

87 Herder was, however, fully engaged with Rousseau's other work, and his treatise on language was formulated as a critique of Rousseau's ideas in his *Discourse on Inequality*; see Nigel DeSouza, "Language, Reason, and Sociability: Herder's Critique of Rousseau," *Intellectual History Review* 22 (2012): 221–40.

88 For an early encapsulation, see Carlton J.H. Hayes, "Contributions of Herder to the Doctrine of Nationalism," *American Historical Review* 32 (1927): 719–36; also Royal Schmidt, "Cultural Nationalism in Herder," *Journal of the History of Ideas* 17 (1956): 407–17.

89 But for a recent argument emphasizing the political aspects of Herder's thought, see Alan Patten, "The Most Natural State: Herder and Nationalism," *History of Political Thought* 31 (2010): 657–89.

90 Anthony LaVopa, "Herder's *Publikum*: Language, Print, and Sociability in Eighteenth-Century Germany," *Eighteenth-Century Studies* 29 (1995): 5–24; also Benjamin Redekop, "Language, Literature, and Publikum: Herder's Quest for Organic Enlightenment," *History of European Ideas* 14 (1992): 235–53.

91 Frederick M. Barnard, *Herder on Nationality, Humanity, and History* (Montreal, 2003), 44–45.

92 See esp. Peter Burke, *The Fabrication of Louis XIV* (New Haven, 1992).

93 Tony Spawforth, *Versailles: Biography of a Palace* (New York, 2008). On the political symbolism of the Versailles gardens, see Chandra Mukerji, *Territorial Ambitions and the Gardens of Versailles* (Cambridge, 1997); see also Ian Thompson, *The Sun King's Garden: Louis XIV, Andre le Notre, and the Creation of the Gardens at Versailles* (London, 2006).

94 Reinhard Koselleck, *Critique and Crisis: Enlightenment and the Pathogenesis of Modern Society* (Cambridge, MA., 1988), esp. 127–86.

95 James Collins, *The State in Early Modern France*, 2nd ed. (Cambridge, 2009), esp. ix–xxv.

Chapter 2

1 Such inequality was a striking feature of eighteenth-century French society; see Daniel Gordon, *Citizens Without Sovereignty: Equality and Sociability in French Thought, 1680–1789* (Princeton, 1994). For specifics on the makeup

of the Estates-General, see the classic study of Mitchell Garrett, *The Estates General of 1789: Problems of Composition and Organization* (London, 1935); also Malcolm Crook, *Elections in the French Revolution: An Apprenticeship in Democracy, 1789–1799* (Cambridge, 1996), 8–29.

2   The metaphor of political theatricality would not be unfamiliar to many of the Revolution's leading protagonists; see Lynn Hunt's seminal study, *Politics, Culture, and Class in the French Revolution* (Berkeley, 1984), esp. 19–20.

3   On the consequences of the decision to fund intervention in North America via massive loans rather than taxes, see Eugene Nelson White, "The French Revolution and the Politics of Government Finance, 1770–1815," *Journal of Economic History* 55 (1995): 227–55.

4   For a fascinating account of the so-called Diamond Necklace Affair and its financial and political repercussions, see Schama, *Citizens*, 203–10.

5   Schama, *Citizens*, 55–60.

6   On key ideological developments, see esp. Jonathan Israel, *Revolutionary Ideas: An Intellectual History of the French Revolution from the Rights of Man to Robespierre* (Princeton, 2014), 30–52.

7   David Bell, *The Cult of the Nation in France: Inventing Nationalism, 1680–1800* (Cambridge, MA, 2001), 63–75; see also the seminal article by Jacques Godechot, "Nation, patrie, nationalisme et patriotisme en France au XVIIIe siècle," *Annales de l'histoire de la Révolution française* 206 (1971): 481–501.

8   On the complex linkage of the "people" with nationalist mobilization in the Assembly of Notables, see Vivian Gruder, *The Notables and the Nation: The Political Schooling of the French* (Cambridge, MA, 2008), 66–70.

9   The most thorough analysis of the nationalistic elements of the petitions remains Beatrice Fry Hyslop, *French Nationalism in 1789: According to the General Cahiers* (New York, 1968); but see also more generally Kenneth Margerison, *Pamphlets and Public Opinion: The Campaign for a Union of Orders in the Early French Revolution* (West Lafayette, 1998).

10   Emmanuel Joseph Sieyès, "What Is the Third Estate?" in John Hall, ed., *A Documentary Survey of the French Revolution* (New York, 1951), 43–45.

11   See more generally William Sewell, *A Rhetoric of Bourgeois Revolution: The Abbé Sieyès and What Is the Third Estate?* (Durham, 1994).

12   Graeme Fife, *The Terror: The Shadow of the Guillotine, 1792–1794* (New York, 2004), 151–52.

13   R.R. Palmer, *Twelve Who Ruled: The Year of Terror in the French Revolution* (Princeton, 1941), 12.

14   See Timothy Tackett, *Becoming a Revolutionary: The Deputies of the French National Assembly and the Emergence of a Revolutionary Culture, 1789–1791* (Princeton, 1996), 119–47.

15   Mirabeau's famous response to messengers sent by Louis XVI reflects this: "Go tell your masters that we are here by the will of the people, and that we shall be moved only at the point of a bayonet"; on Mirabeau and the broader context of the Tennis Court Oath, see Barry Shapiro, *Traumatic Politics: The Deputies and the King in the Early French Revolution* (University Park, 2009),

50–61. See also the account in Christopher Hibbert, *The Days of the French Revolution* (New York, 1980), 47–66.

16 Hans-Jürgen Lüsebrink and Rolf Reichardt, *The Bastille: History of a Symbol of Despotism and Freedom* (Durham, 1997), 88–89.

17 John Markoff, *The Abolition of Feudalism: Peasants, Lords, and Legislators in the French Revolution* (University Park, 1996), 428–48.

18 On the broader context of Lafayette's 1779 reception in France, see Laura Auricchio, *The Marquis: Lafayette Reconsidered* (New York, 2015), 77–91. Upon his initial departure for North America in 1777, Lafayette had written to his wife Adrienne linking his own personal destiny with the interests of friends of Liberty in America and around the world: "In striving for my own glory, I work for their happiness"; quoted in Stanley Idzerda, "When and Why Lafayette Became a Revolutionary," in Morris Slavin and Agnes Smith, eds., *Bourgeois, Sans-Culottes and Other Frenchmen* (Waterloo, Ont., 1981), 16.

19 On the direct influence of Rousseau on the Declaration, see J.K. Wright, "National Sovereignty and the General Will: The Political Program of the Declaration of Rights," in Dale Van Kley, ed., *The French Idea of Freedom: The Old Regime and the Declaration of Rights of 1789* (Stanford, 1994), 199–232.

20 For a good overview of the provisions of the Constitution of 1791, see Michael Fitzsimmons, *The Remaking of France: The National Assembly and the Constitution of 1791* (Cambridge, 1994).

21 See Hunt, *Politics, Culture, and Class*, 19–51.

22 Timothy Tackett, *When the King Took Flight* (Cambridge, MA, 2003), 88–118.

23 Patricia Chastain Howe, *Foreign Policy and the French Revolution* (London, 2008), 46–48.

24 Owen Connelly, *The Wars of the French Revolution and Napoleon, 1792–1815* (London, 2006), 25–26.

25 David Jordan, "The King's Longest Night: The Tuileries, August 9–10, 1792," in Jordan, *The King's Trial: The French Revolution vs. Louix XVI* (Berkeley, 1979), 1–10.

26 Timothy Tackett, "Rumor and Revolution: The Case of the September Massacres," *French History and Civilization* 4 (2011): 54–64.

27 The *Marseillaise* had been composed earlier in 1792 by the engineer Claude Joseph Rouget de Lisle and quickly became the unofficial military hymn of the Revolution before being proclaimed the official national anthem of France in 1795; see Michel Vovelle, "The Marseillaise: War or Peace," in Pierre Nora et al., eds., *Realms of Memory: The Construction of the French Past*, vol.3 (New York, 1998), 29–43.

28 Eric Hazan, *A People's History of the French Revolution* (London, 2014), 87–88. On the broader impact of nationalistic sentiment on French troop morale, see Marie-Cecile Thoral, *From Valmy to Waterloo: France at War, 1792–1815* (London, 2011), 107–11.

29 Quoted in Peter Boerner, *Goethe* (London, 2004), 65.

30 The Girondist faction was named for the Gironde, the French region from
    which many of its members came, while the "Mountain" was so named
    because its members occupied the highest seating rows of the main chamber
    of the National Convention. On the Girondists and their central ideals, see
    esp. Gary Kates, *The Cercle Social, the Girondins, and the French Revolution*
    (Princeton, 1985), esp. 175–94. For an overview of the Jacobins, see Michael
    Kennedy, *The Jacobin Clubs in the French Revolution, 1793–1795* (New York,
    2001).

31 In describing the ideational universe of the Jacobins, Patrice Higonnet noted
    that "the idea of the Nation [was] their premier mental matrix"; Higonnet,
    Goodness Beyond Virtue: Jacobins during the French Revolution (Cambridge,
    MA, 1998), 144–45.

32 On the latter, see Alexander Maxwell, *Patriots Against Fashion: Clothing and
    Nationalism in Europe's Age of Revolutions* (London, 2014), 121–29.

33 Antoine de Baecque, *Glory and Terror: Seven Deaths under the French
    Revolution* (London, 2001), 90–91; more generally, Jordan, *The King's Trial*,
    esp. 101–40.

34 Robespierre, "Against Granting the King a Trial," in Guy Carleton Lee, ed.,
    The World's Orators (New York, 1902), 99, 103–4, 110–11.

35 Susan Dunn, *The Deaths of Louis XVI: Regicide and the French Political
    Imagination* (Princeton, 1994), 95–115.

36 Adam Zamoyski, *Holy Madness: Romantics, Patriots, and Revolutionaries*
    (London, 1999), 1–2.

37 Alan Forrest, "*La patrie en danger*: The French Revolution and the First
    Levée en Masse," in Daniel Moran and Athur Waldron, eds., *The People in
    Arms: Military Myth and National Mobilization since the French Revolution*
    (Cambridge, 2003), 8–32.

38 Schama, *Citizens*, esp. 726–92; Sagan, *Citizens and Cannibals: The French
    Revolution, the Struggle for Modernity, and the Origins of Ideological Terror*
    (Lanham, 2001); Zamoyski, *Holy Madness*, esp. 55–88.

39 Higonnet, *Goodness Beyond Virtue*; Slavoj Zizek, "Revolutionary Terror from
    Robespierre to Mao," in Slavoj Zizek, ed., *In Defense of Lost Causes* (London,
    2008), 157–210; also Slavoj Zizek, ed., *Robespierre: Virtue and Terror*
    (London, 2007).

40 Timothy Tackett, *The Coming of the Terror in the French Revolution*
    (Cambridge, MA, 2015); Marisa Linton, *Choosing Terror: Virtue, Friendship,
    and Authenticity in the French Revolution* (Oxford, 2013).

41 On the discursive construction of political paranoia during the Terror, see esp.
    Caroline Weber, *Terror and Its Discontents: Suspect Words in Revolutionary
    France* (Minneapolis, 2003), 55–115.

42 Tackett, *Coming of the Terror*, 257–61. The brutal fighting in the Vendée
    lasted several years, see Ronald Secher, *A French Genocide: The Vendée* (South
    Bend, 2003).

43 Nigel Aston, *Religion and Revolution in France, 1780–1794* (Washington, DC,
    2000), 187–88; also Palmer, *Twelve Who Ruled*, 220–24.

44   See Julia Kristeva, *Severed Heads: Capital Visions* (New York, 2012), 94–95; also Jesse Goldhammer, *The Headless Republic: Sacrificial Violence in Modern French Thought* (Ithaca, 2005), chap. 1.

45   On the role of the *Enragés* in the insurrection that brought down the Girondists, see Morris Slavin, *The Making of an Insurrection: Parisian Sections and the Gironde* (Cambridge, MA, 1986), 127–41.

46   On Roux and the manifesto, see David Andress, *The French Revolution and the People* (London, 2004), 202–3; also Israel, *Revolutionary Ideas*, 467–68. See also, more generally, Robert Barrie Rose, *The Enragés: Socialists of the French Revolution?* (Sydney, 1965).

47   For a defense of Roux, see Morris Slavin, "Jacques Roux: A Victim of Vilification," *French Historical Studies* 3 (1964): 525–37. The execution of Hébert was particularly noteworthy, since he had been such a bloodthirsty advocate of the guillotine in the early stages of the Terror. As Simon Schama notes: "There was a strong emotion of *Schadenfreude* among the crowd, who plainly enjoyed seeing the man who had so celebrated the guillotine quail visibly at the prospect of his own destruction"; Schama, *Citizens*, 816.

48   David Lawday, *The Giant of the French Revolution: Danton, A Life* (New York, 2009), 252–60.

49   See the accounts in Ruth Scurr, *Fatal Purity: Robespierre and the French Revolution* (New York, 2006), 353–58; and Peter McPhee, *Robespierre: A Revolutionary Life* (New Haven, 2012), 204–20.

50   Stephen Clay, "The White Terror: Factions, Reactions, and the Politics of Vengeance," in Peter McPhee, ed., *A Companion to the French Revolution* (Oxford, 2013), 359–77. More generally, see Bronislaw Baczko, *Ending the Terror: The French Revolution After Robespierre* (Cambridge, 1994).

51   See Martyn Lyons, *France Under the Directory* (Cambridge, 1975), 18–23.

52   For a thorough overview of Church personnel and holdings in France, see John McManners, *Church and Society in Eighteenth-Century France* (Oxford, 1998).

53   David Garrioch, *Neighbourhood and Community in Paris, 1740–1790* (Cambridge, 1986), 149–57.

54   Quoted in Aston, *Religion and Revolution in France, 1780–1794*, 133.

55   On the attitudes of pro-revolutionary clergy, see Joseph Byrnes, *Priests of the French Revolution: Saints and Renegades in a New Political Era* (University Park, 2014), 40–46; on the Civil Constitution more generally, see Aston, *Religion and Revolution in France, 1780–1794*, 140–62.

56   Aston, *Religion and Revolution in France, 1780–1794*, 164–65.

57   See Burleigh, *Earthly Powers*, 102–3.

58   David Lloyd Dowd, *Pageant-Master of the Republic: Jacques-Louis David and the French Revolution* (Lincoln, 1948), 122–25.

59   Citations drawn from John W. Boyer, "The Festival of the Supreme Being (8 June 1794)," in Keith Michael Baker, ed., *University of Chicago Readings in Western Civilization*, vol.7 (Chicago, 1987), 384–91.

60 Quoted in Zamoyski, *Holy Madness*, 110.

61 For a fascinating dramatic account by a German convert to Catholicism, published coincidentally in the same year that Hitler came to power, see Gertrud von Le Fort, *The Song at the Scaffold* (San Francisco, 2011; German original 1933).

62 See James McMillan, *France and Women, 1789–1914: Gender, Society, and Politics* (London, 2000), 9–11.

63 "Declaration of Rights of Woman and the Female Citizen," reprinted in Baker, ed., *University of Chicago Readings in Western Civilization*, 263–67. For thorough treatment of the subject, see John Cole, *Between the Queen and the Cabby: Olympe de Gouges's "Rights of Woman"* (Montreal, 2011); and Carol Sherman, *Reading Olympe de Gouges* (New York, 2013).

64 It was primarily her close relationship with Brissot and the Girondists that proved fatal; see Sophie Mousset, *Women's Rights and the French Revolution: A Biography of Olympe de Gouges* (New Brunswick, 2007), chap. 4.

65 Darlene Levy and Harriet Applewhite estimate the number of female demonstrators that day to be approximately 7,000; see their "Women and Militant Citizenship in Revolutionary Paris," in Sara Melzer and Leslie Rabine, eds., *Rebel Daughters: Women and the French Revolution* (Oxford, 1992), esp. 83–86.

66 Dominique Godineau, *The Women of Paris and Their French Revolution* (Berkeley, 1998), 119–34.

67 See Maurice Agulhon, *Marianne Into Battle: Republican Imagery and Symbolism in France, 1789–1880* (Cambridge, 1981), chap. 1.

68 On Napoleon's Corsican upbringing and family background, see esp. David Bell, *Napoleon: A Concise Biography* (Oxford, 2015), 14–24; also Andrew Roberts, *Napoleon: A Life* (New York, 2014), 3–28. For a classic interpretation from a French Marxist perspective, see Georges Lefebvre, *Napoléon* (Paris, 1935), chap. 1.

69 Quoted in Frank McLynn, *Napoleon: A Biography* (New York, 2011), 37–38.

70 Roberts, *Napoleon: A Life*, 54–56.

71 Robert Asprey, *The Rise of Napoleon Bonaparte* (New York, 2000), 111–12.

72 See Owen Connelly, *Blundering to Glory: Napoleon's Miliary Campaigns* (Lanham, 2006), 47–60. On the team of scholars and scientists that accompanied Napoleon's forces on the Egyptian expedition and famously discovered the Rosetta Stone, see Nina Burleigh, *Mirage: Napoleon's Scientists and the Unveiling of Egypt* (New York, 2007), esp. 209–19.

73 On the importance of economic factors in consolidating Napoleon's power, including the February 1800 founding of the new Bank of France, see J. Christopher Herold, *The Age of Napoleon* (New York, 2002; orig. 1963), 130–32.

74 Clive Emsley, *Napoleon: Conquest, Reform, and Reorganisation* (London, 2015), 32–56.

75 See the extended discussion in Aston, *Religion and Revolution in France, 1780–1794*, 316–35, quote from p. 324.

76 Michael Hughes, *Forging Napoleon's Grande Armée: Motivation, Military Culture, and Masculinity in the French Army, 1800–1808* (New York, 2012).

77 Asprey, *The Rise of Napoleon Bonaparte*, 147–51.

78 These reforms included the introduction of the metric system and a geographic reorganization of Italian territory into *départments* and *arondissements*; Philip Dwyer, *Citizen Emperor: Napoleon in Power* (New Haven, 2012), 185–89.

79 See Owen Connelly, *Napoleon's Satellite Kingdoms* (New York, 1966), chap. 2.

80 Alexander Grab, *Napoleon and the Transformation of Europe* (London, 2003), 166–69.

81 Susan Vandiver Nicassio, *Imperial City: Rome under Napoleon* (Chicago, 2005).

82 As Lucy Riall has noted: "It would be hard to overestimate the importance of the French occupation for future developments in Italy"; Lucy Riall, *Risorgimento: The History of Italy from Napoleon to Nation State* (London, 2009), 5.

83 Charles Esdaile, *Fighting Napoleon: Guerrillas, Bandits, and Adventurers in Spain, 1808–1814* (New Haven, 2004).

84 Scott Eastman, *Preaching Spanish Nationalism Across the Hispanic Atlantic, 1759–1823* (Baton Rouge, 2012), esp. 45–68.

85 On the early intertwining of agrarian reform and Danish identity, see Uffe Østergård, "Peasants and Danes: The Danish National Identity and Political Culture," *Comparative Studies in Society and History* 34 (1992): 3–27.

86 Arnold Barton, *Scandinavia in the Revolutionary Era, 1760–1815*, 222–23.

87 Ole Feldbaek, *The Battle of Copenhagen, 1801: Nelson and the Danes* (London, 2002).

88 Michael Bregnsbo, "The Motives Behind the Foreign Political Decisions of Frederick VI during the Napoleonic Wars," *Scandinavian Journal of History* 39 (2014): 335–52.

89 Henrika Tandefelt, "The Image of Kingship in Sweden, 1770–1809," in Pasi Ihalainen et al., eds., *Scandinavia in the Age of Revolution: Nordic Political Cultures, 1740–1820* (Farnham, 2011), 41–54.

90 The Riksdag was transformed into a bicameral parliamentary body only in 1866; Torbjörn Bergman and Niklas Bolin, "Swedish Democracy," in Torbjörn Bergman and Kaare Strøm, eds., *The Madisonian Turn: Political Parties and Parliamentary Democracy in Nordic Europe* (Ann Arbor, 2013), 251–93.

91 Jennifer Orr, *Literary Networks and Dissenting Print Culture in Romantic-Period Ireland* (London, 2015), 88–89.

92 Ian Haywood, "The 'Most Distressful Country': The Irish Rebellion of 1798," in Haywood, *Bloody Romanticism: Spectacular Violence and the Politics of Representation, 1776–1832* (London, 2006), 103–33.

93 Richard Gott, *Britain's Empire: Resistance, Repression, and Revolt* (London, 2011), 130–37.

94 Quoted in Patrick Geoghegan, *Robert Emmet: A Life* (Montreal, 2002), 15.

95   See esp. Leith Davis, *Acts of Union: Scotland and the Literary Imagination of the British Nation, 1707–1830* (Stanford, 1998), 107–42. On connections with Irish romanticism, Christopher Whatley, "The Political and Cultural Legacy of Robert Burns in Scotland and Ulster, 1796–1859," in John Kirk, ed., *Cultures of Radicalism in Britain and Ireland* (London, 2016), 79–94.

96   Bob Harris, "Volunteers, the Militia, and the United Scotsmen," in Bob Harris, ed., *The Scottish People and the French Revolution* (London, 2008), 147–84.

97   John Barrell, "Putting Down the Rising," in Leith Davis et al., eds., *Scotland and the Borders of Romanticism* (Cambridge, 2004), 130–38.

98   Michael Rapport, *Nationality and Citizenship in Revolutionary France: The Treatment of Foreigners, 1789–1799* (Oxford, 2000), 292–93.

99   See e.g. Iain Gale, *Scotland Forever: The Scots Greys at Waterloo* (Edinburgh, 2015).

100   For a fascinating account of the impact of the Napoleonic wars on the home front in Britain, see Jenny Uglow, *In These Times: Living in Britain Through Napoleon's Wars, 1793–1815* (New York, 2015).

101   On the national significance of Nelson and the "highly selective cult of heroism" that surrounded him, see Linda Colley, *Britons: Forging the Nation, 1707–1837* (New Haven, 1992), 183–88.

102   See esp. Oscar Cox Jensen, *Napoleon and British Song, 1797–1822* (London, 2015).

103   Roy Adkins, *Nelson's Trafalgar: The Battle that Changed the World* (New York, 2005), 282–307.

104   The anniversary symbolism, combined with uncommonly clear and sunny weather that day, enhanced the sense that the victory at Austerlitz was foreordained as part of France's national destiny; Alistair Horne, *How Far from Austerlitz? Napoleon, 1805–1815* (New York, 1994), 159–90.

105   Robert Goetz, *1805 Austerlitz: Napoleon and the Destruction of the Third Coalition* (London, 2005), 294–98.

106   Katherine Aaslestad, "Napoleonic Rule in German Central Europe," in Michael Broers et al., eds., *The Napoleonic Empire and the New European Political Culture* (London, 2012), 160–72.

107   Joachim Whaley, *Germany and the Holy Roman Empire: From the Peace of Westphalia to the Dissolution of the Reich, 1648–1806* (Oxford, 2013), 623–44.

108   Clive Emsley, *Napoleon: Conquest, Reform, and Reorganization* (London, 2003), 57–72. On the gendered impact of Napoleonic reforms in Baden and Bavaria, the two most significant members of the Confederation of the Rhine, see Isabel Hull, *Sexuality, State, and Society in Germany, 1700–1815* (Ithaca, 1996), chaps. 9–10.

109   On the relationship between conceptions of the German "nation" and the Holy Roman Empire, see John Gagliardo, *Reich and Nation: The Holy Roman Empire as Idea and Reality, 1763–1806* (Bloomington, 1980); and, most recently, Peter Wilson, *Heart of Europe: A History of the Holy Roman Empire* (Cambridge, MA, 2016), esp. 255–93.

110 On the naval blockade and the corresponding Continental System established by Napoleon, see Silvia Marzagalli, "The Continental System: A View from the Sea," in Katherine Aaslestad and Johan Joor, eds., *Revisiting Napoleon's Continental System* (London, 2014), 83–97.

111 For an insightful interpretation of the psychological impact of the 1806 Prussian campaign, see Peter Paret, *The Cognitive Challenge of War: Prussia 1806* (Princeton, 2009), esp. 33–70.

112 Fichte, *Addresses to the German Nation*, trans. R.F. Jones and G.H. Turnbull (Ashland, 1922), 52–54.

113 See David James, "The Role of Language in Fichte's Construction of the Nation," in James, ed., *Fichte's Republic: Idealism, History, and Nationalism* (Cambridge, 2015), 181–218.

114 See Arash Abizadeh, "Was Fichte an Ethnic Nationalist?" *History of Political Thought* 26 (2005): 334–59.

115 Fichte, *Addresses to the German Nation*, 56.

116 See the classic and still-useful studies of J.R. Seeley, *The Life and Times of Stein* (Cambridge, 1878); Guy Stanton Ford, *Stein and the Era of Reform in Prussia, 1807–1815* (Princeton, 1922). In German, Gerhard Ritter's *Stein: Eine politische Biographie* (Stuttgart, 1931) remains indispensable.

117 The issue of opening the officer corps increasingly to non-nobles was contested among some reform-oriented figures, such as Ludwig Yorck von Wartenburg; see Peter Paret, *Yorck and the Era of Prussian Reform* (Princeton, 1966), 157–70.

118 "While this rationalizing impulse of the Prussian reform movement had its roots in eighteenth-century governing traditions, Stein and Hardenberg fused this prerevolutionary legacy with an effort to forge a politically active nation"; Levinger, *Enlightened Nationalism*, 5.

119 Walter Langsam, *The Napoleonic Wars and German Nationalism in Austria* (New York, 1930).

120 See F. Gunther Eyck, *Loyal Rebels: Andreas Hofer and the Tyrolean Uprising of 1809* (Washington, DC, 1986).

121 Laurence Cole, *Andreas Hofer: The Social and Cultural Construction of a National Myth in Tirol, 1809–1909* (Florence, 1994).

122 Kálmán Benda, "Hungary," in Otto Dann and John Dinwiddy, eds., *Nationalism in the Age of the French Revolution* (London, 1988), 132–33.

123 R.J.W. Evans, *Austria, Hungary, and the Habsburgs: Central Europe, 1683–1867* (Oxford, 2006), 134–46. On Joseph II's Germanization policies, see T.C.W. Blanning, *Joseph II* (London, 2013), 70–72.

124 See Paul Bödy, "The Hungarian Jacobin Conspiracy of 1794–95," *Journal of Central European Affairs* 22 (1962): 3–26; Peter Sugar, "The Influence of the Enlightenment and French Revolution in Eighteenth-Century Hungary," *Journal of Central European Affairs* 17 (1958): 331–55; and most recently, Paul Lendvai, "Abbot Martinovics and the Jacobin Plot: A Secret Agent as Revolutionary Martyr," in Lendvai, *The Hungarians* (Princeton, 2003), 183–90.

125 The primary force behind the rejection of Napoleon's offer was the concern of Hungarian nobles over the possible loss of traditional privileges; see Lendvai, *The Hungarians*, 545.

126 On the poor performance of Hungarian troops in the key 1809 Battle of Raab, though, see Richard Bassett, *For God and Kaiser: The Imperial Austrian Army, 1619–1918* (New Haven, 2015), 264–65.

127 For a solid overview of the three partitions, see Jerzy Lukowski, *The Partitions of Poland: 1772, 1793, 1795* (London, 1999).

128 See esp. Janusz Duzinkiewicz, *Fateful Transformations: The Four Years' Parliament and the Constitution of May 3, 1791* (New York, 1993); and the essays in Samuel Fiszman, ed., *Constitution and Reform in Eighteenth-Century Poland: The Constitution of 3 May 1791* (Bloomington, 1997). For the text of the constitution in English, see Jerzy Lukowski, *Disorderly Liberty: The Political Culture of the Polish-Lithuanian Commonwealth in the Eighteenth Century* (London, 2010), 261–71.

129 Quoted in Adam Zamoyski, *Phantom Terror: Political Paranoia and the Creation of the Modern State, 1789–1815* (New York, 2015), 38.

130 Zamek Krlewski, *New Constitution of the Government of Poland, Established by the Revolution, the Third of May 1791* (London, 1791), 3–5.

131 Alex Storozynski, *The Peasant Prince: Thaddeus Kosciuszko and the Age of Revolution* (New York, 2009), 237–38. Kosciuszko had earlier been proclaimed an honorary citizen of France; ibid., 166–67.

132 Jarusław Czubaty, "What Lies Behind the Glory? A Balance Sheet of the Napoleonic Era in Poland," in Ute Planert and Frank Blackaby, eds., *Napoleon's Empire: European Politics in Global Perspective* (London, 2015), 174–75.

133 Storozynski, *The Peasant Prince*, 239–45.

134 See Jarusław Czubaty, *The Duchy of Warsaw, 1807–1815* (London, 2016), esp. 45–62.

135 Hans Rogger, *National Consciousness in Eighteenth-Century Russia* (Cambridge, MA, 1960), 136–37.

136 Lukoswki, *Disorderly Liberty*, 225–26.

137 Janet Hartley, *Alexander I* (London, 1994), 13–14.

138 Michael Adams, *Napoleon and Russia* (London, 2006), 177–88.

139 Alexander Niven, *Napoleon and Alexander I: A Study in Franco-Russian Relations* (Washington, DC, 1978); Marie-Pierre Rey, *Alexander I: The Tsar Who Defeated Napoleon* (DeKalb, 2012), chap. 13.

140 On Napoleon's rationale behind the invasion, see most recently Alan Forrest, "Napoleon's Vision of Empire and the Decision to Invade Russia," in Janet Hartley et al., eds., *Russia and the Napoleonic Wars* (London, 2015), 43–56.

141 Ruth Leiserowitz, "Polish Volunteers in the Napoleonic Wars," in Christine Krüger and Sonja Levsen, eds., *War Volunteering in Modern Times: From the French Revolution to the Second World War* (Houndmills, 2010), 59–77.

142 Luibov Melnikova, "Orthodox Russia against 'Godless' France: The Russian Church and the 'Holy War' of 1812," in Hartley et al., eds., *Russia and the Napoleonic Wars*, 179–95.

143 The bloodiest engagement was the Battle of Borodino in early September; see Christopher Duffy, *Borodino and the War of 1812* (New York, 1973).

144 The causes of the fire, whether accidental or deliberate, remain disputed, although the general consensus holds the Russians primarily responsible; see Alexander Mikaberidze, *The Burning of Moscow: Napoleon's Trial by Fire, 1812* (London, 2014), esp. 145–65.

145 Adam Zamoyski, *Moscow 1812: Napoleon's Fatal March* (New York, 2005), 397–405.

146 Ibid., 536.

147 The Convention of Tauroggen, which codified this act, was published five days later; see Paret, *Yorck*, 192–95.

148 See the excellent overview of the Battle of the Nations in Munro Price, *Napoleon: The End of Glory* (Oxford, 2014), 135–52.

Chapter 3

1 Donald Emerson, *Metternich and the Political Police: Security and Subversion in the Habsburg Monarchy, 1815–1830* (Dordrecht, 1968), 31–56. The best recent biography is Wolfram Siemann, *Metternich, Stratege und Visionär: Eine Biographie* (Munich, 2016).

2 John Bew, *Castlereagh: A Life* (Oxford, 2012), 537–50.

3 Jean Orieux, *Talleyrand: The Art of Survival* (New York, 1974), 414–24.

4 On Nesselrode's later career see Harold Ingle, *Nesselrode and the Russian Rapprochement with Britain, 1836–1844* (Berkeley, 1976).

5 Brian Vick, *The Congress of Vienna* (Cambridge, MA, 2014), 142–45.

6 Burleigh, *Sacred Causes*, 119.

7 Krüdener quoted in Elena Gretchanaia, "Between National Myth and Transnational Ideal: The Representation of Nations in the French-Language Writings of Russian Women, 1770–1819," in Amelia Sanz et al., eds., *Women Telling Nations* (Amsterdam, 2014), 390.

8 R.S. Alexander, *Bonapartism and the Revolutionary Tradition in France: The Fédérés of 1815* (Cambridge, 2002).

9 Andrew Roberts, *Waterloo: Napoleon's Last Gamble* (New York, 2005); Jeremy Black, *The Battle of Waterloo* (New York, 2010).

10 Christopher Hibbert, *Waterloo: Napoleon's Last Campaign* (New York, 2003), 143–44.

11 Price, *End of Glory*, 258–65.

12 Michael John Thornton, *Napoleon After Waterloo: England and the St. Helena Decision* (Stanford, 1968), 124–43.

13 Alan Davies, *The Crucified Nation: A Motif in Modern Nationalism* (Sussex, 2009), chap. 1.

14 Alan Kahan, *Liberalism in Nineteenth-Century Europe: The Political Culture of Limited Suffrage* (Houndmills, 2003).

15 Theodore Hamerow, *Restoration, Revolution, Reaction: Economics and Politics in Germany, 1815–1871* (Princeton, 1958), 70–71.

16 See Jennifer Mitzen, *Power in Concert: The Nineteenth-Century Origins of Global Governance* (Chicago, 2013), 102–39.

17 Rasmus Glenthøj and Morten Nordhagen Ottosen, *Experiences of War and Nationality in Denmark and Norway, 1807–1815* (London, 2014).

18 Bjarne Jønaes, *The Sculptor Bertel Thorvaldsen* (Copenhagen, 2012).

19 See Alan Palmer, *Bernadotte: Napoleon's Marshal, Sweden's King* (London, 1990), chaps. 14–15.

20 Colley, *Britons*, 102–47.

21 Robert Poole, "The March to Peterloo: Politics and Festivity in Late Georgian England," *Past and Present* 192 (August 2006): 109–53.

22 Cheryl Schonhardt-Bailey, *From the Corn Laws to Free Trade* (Cambridge, MA, 2006), 283–90.

23 See Antonia Fraser, *Perilous Question: The Drama of the Great Reform Bill, 1832* (London, 2013).

24 Jonathan Parry, *The Politics of Patriotism: English Liberalism, National Identity, and Europe, 1830–1886* (Cambridge, 2006), esp. 86–126.

25 Philip Mansel, *Louis XVIII* (London, 1981), 220–21.

26 Munro Price, *The Perilous Crown: France between Revolutions, 1814–1848* (London, 2007), 56–62.

27 Robert Alexander, *Re-Writing the French Revolutionary Tradition: Liberal Opposition and the Fall of the Bourbon Monarchy* (Cambridge, 2003), 37–61.

28 Jonathan Sperber, *Revolutionary Europe, 1780–1850* (Harlow, 2000), 326.

29 Darrin McMahon, *Enemies of the Enlightenment: The French Counter-Enlightenment and the Making of Modernity* (Oxford, 2001), 182–84.

30 Juan Luis Simal, "Letters from Spain: The 1820 Revolution and the Liberal International," in M. Isabella and K. Zanou, eds., *Mediterranean Diasporas* (London, 2016), 25–42.

31 The French invading forces called themselves the "Hundred Thousand Sons of Saint Louis"; see Mark Jarrett, *The Congress of Vienna and Its Legacy* (London, 2013), 341–42.

32 Sporadic fighting continued for nearly a year after Carlos's exile; see Mark Lawrence, *Spain's First Carlist War, 1833–1840* (London, 2014), and John Coverdale, *The Basque Phase of Spain's First Carlist War* (Princeton, 1984).

33 Guy Thomson, *The Birth of Modern Politics in Spain: Democracy, Association, and Revolution, 1854–1875* (London, 2010), 253–92.

34 Markus Prutsch, *Making Sense of Constitutional Monarchism in Post-Napoleonic France and Germany* (London, 2013), chap. 3.

35 On Hormayr's writings between 1807 and 1814, see esp. "Joseph von Hormayr: Austria and Germany," in Balász Trencsényi and Michal Kopeĉek, eds., *Discourses of Collective Identity in Central and Southeast Europe, 1770–1945*, vol. 2 (Budapest, 2007), 27–32.

36 John Toews, *Becoming Historical: Cultural Reformation and Public Memory in Early Nineteenth-Century Berlin* (Cambridge, 2004), 117–40.

37 Joshua Hagen, "Architecture, Urban Planning, and Political Authority in Ludwig I's Munich," *Journal of Urban History* 35 (2009): 459–85.

38 Ursula Heinzelmann, The Munich Oktoberfest: Generator and Vehicle of Bavarian Identity (M.A. Thesis, University of Canterbury, 2007), esp. 30–42.

39 Hans Pohlsander, *National Monuments and Nationalism in Nineteenth-Century Germany* (New York, 2008), 129–46.

40 David Laven, *Venice and Venetia under the Habsburgs* (Oxford, 2002).

41 See Ayşe Ozil, *Orthodox Christians in the Late Ottoman Empire* (Cambridge, 2013); Frederick Anscombe, *State, Faith, and Nation in Ottoman and Post-Ottoman Lands* (Cambridge, 2014), 21–32.

42 Misha Glenny, *The Balkans: Nationalism, War, and the Great Powers, 1804–2011* (New York, 2012), esp. 6–22.

43 Anatole Mazour, *The First Russian Revolution, 1825: The Decembrist Movement* (Stanford, 1937), 64–85.

44 Patrick O'Meara, *The Decembrist Pavel Pestel: Russia's First Republican* (London, 2003).

45 Ludmilla Trigos, *The Decembrist Myth in Russian Culture* (New York, 2009).

46 David Saunders, *Russia in the Age of Reaction and Reform, 1801–1881* (London, 2014), 87–115.

47 Nicholas Riasonovsky, *Nicholas I and Official Nationality in Russia, 1825–1855* (Berkeley, 1959).

48 Nicholas Riasanovsky, *Russian Identities: A Historical Survey* (Oxford, 2005), 130–65.

49 For an insightful overview, see Tim Blanning, *The Romantic Revolution: A History* (New York, 2011).

50 Gerald Izenberg, *Impossible Individuality: Romanticism, Revolution, and the Origins of Modern Selfhood* (Princeton, 1992), esp. 18–52.

51 Stephen Bann, "Romanticism in France," in Roy Porter and Mikula S. Teich, eds., *Romanticism in National Context* (Cambridge, 1988), esp. 240–48.

52 Anne Frey, *British State Romanticism: Authorship, Agency, and Bureaucratic Nationalism* (Stanford, 2010).

53 David Aram Kaiser, *Romanticism, Aesthetics, and Nationalism* (Cambridge, 1999); Marc Redfield, *The Politics of Aesthetics: Nationalism, Gender, Romanticism* (Stanford, 2003).

54 Ina Ferris, *The Romantic National Tale and the Question of Ireland* (Cambridge, 2009), 1–17.

55 Murray Pittock, "Strumming and Being Hanged: The Irish Bard and History Regained," in Murray Pittock, ed., *Scottish and Irish Romanticism* (Oxford, 2008), 92–119.

56 On O'Connell's nationalism in light of romanticism, see Sue Chaplin, "Literary and Cultural Contexts," in Sue Chaplin, ed., *The Romanticism Handbook* (London, 2011), 45–46. See also the two-volume biography by Patrick Geoghegan, *King Dan O'Connell, 1775–1829* (Dublin, 2010); and Patrick Geoghegan, *Liberator: The Life and Death of Daniel O'Connell, 1830–1847* (Dublin, 2010).

57 J.D. Clarkson, *Labor and Nationalism in Ireland* (New York, 1925), esp. 144–45. More generally, James Epstein, *The Lion of Freedom: Feargus O'Connor and the Chartist Movement, 1832–1842* (London, 1982).

58 Kevin Anderson, "Ireland: Nationalism, Class, and the Labor Movement," in Kevin Anderson, ed., *Marx at the Margins* (Chicago, 2015), esp. 118–23.

59 See Marilyn Butler, "Burns and Politics," in Robert Crawford, ed., *Robert Burns and Cultural Authority* (Iowa City, 1997), 86–112; more generally, Robert Crawford, *The Bard, Robert Burns: A Biography* (Princeton, 2009).

60 Toby Benis, "The Scottish Martyrs and the Narrative of Reform," in Toby Benis, ed., *Romantic Diasporas* (London, 2009), 107–30.

61 Julian Meldon D'Arcy, *Subversive Scott: The Waverley Novels and Scottish Nationalism* (Reykjavik, 2005).

62 Michael Keating and David Bleiman, *Labour and Scottish Nationalism* (London, 1979), esp. 25–27.

63 Atsuko Ichijo, *Scottish Nationalism and the Idea of Europe: Concepts of Europe and the Nation* (London, 2004), 36–37.

64 The constitution remains in force to the present day, and 17 May is still celebrated as Constitution Day; see Karen Gammelgaard and Eirik Holmøyvik, eds., *Writing Democracy: The Norwegian Constitution, 1814–2014* (New York, 2014).

65 Oscar Falnes, *National Romanticism in Norway* (New York, 1933), esp. 21–26.

66 Raymond Lindgren, *Norway-Sweden: Union, Disunion, and Scandinavian Integration* (Princeton, 1959), 47.

67 H. Arnold Barton, *Sweden and Visions of Norway: Politics and Culture, 1814–1905* (Carbondale, 2003), 93–94. See also Ragnhild Galtung, ed., *The Army of Truth: Selected Poems by Henrik Wergeland* (Madison, 2003).

68 On Wergeland's public support for the July Revolution, see Knut Gjerset, *History of the Norwegian People*, vol. 2 (New York, 1915), 467–68.

69 Rossini had been named director of Paris's Théâtre-Italien in 1824, and *Il viaggio a Reims* is widely seen as a major step in Rossini's progression from classicism to romanticism; see Benjamin Walton, *Rossini in Restoration Paris* (Cambridge, 2010), 68–107.

70 Jeremy Popkin, *Press, Revolution, and Social Identities in France, 1830–1835* (University Park, 2002), 44–45.

71　Pamela Pilbeam, *The French Revolution of 1830* (Houndmills, 1991), 60–79.

72　Lloyd Kramer, *Lafayette in Two Worlds: Public Cultures and Personal Identities in an Age of Revolutions* (Chapel Hill, 1996), 230–32.

73　Janneke Weijermars, *Stepbrothers: Southern Dutch Literature and Nation-Building under Willem I, 1814–1834* (Leiden, 2015). For an account of contemporaneous efforts to integrate the border region of French Flanders into dynamic conceptions of French nationhood, see Timothy Baycroft, *Culture, Identity, and Nationalism: French Flanders in the Nineteenth and Twentieth Centuries* (Woodbridge, 2004), esp. 21–44.

74　Sonia Slatin, "Opera and Revolution: *La Muette di Portici* and the Belgian Revolution of 1830 Revisited," *Journal of Musicological Research* 3 (1979): 45–62.

75　Joel Schulem Fishman, *The London Conference of 1830 and the Belgian Revolt* (PhD Diss., Columbia University, 1972).

76　Samuel Humes, *Belgium: Long United, Long Divided* (London, 2014), 131–36.

77　Joep Leersen, "Novels and Their Readers, Memories and Their Social Frameworks," in Karin Tilmans et al., eds., *Performing the Past: Memory, History, and Identity in Modern Europe* (Amsterdam, 2010), 235–53.

78　Frank Delmartino, "Accommodating Flemings and Francophones in a Federal Arrangement: The Cultural and Religious Dimension of the Belgian Experience," in Ferran Requejo and Klaus Jürgen Nagel, eds., *The Politics of Religion and Nationalism* (New York, 2015), 167–80.

79　Carl Strikwerda, "The Low Countries: Between the City and the *Volk*," in Timothy Baycroft and Mark Hewitson, eds., *What Is a Nation? Europe, 1789–1914* (Oxford, 2006), 81–99.

80　Marnix Beyen, "Belgium: A Nation That Failed to Be Ethnic," in Linas Eriksonas and Leos Müller, eds., *Statehood Before and Beyond Ethnicity* (Brussels, 2005), 341–52.

81　See esp. Riall, *Risorgimento*, passim.

82　Harry Hearder, *Italy in the Age of the Risorgimento 1790–1870* (New York, 2013), 178–82.

83　Robert Goldstein, *Political Repression in Nineteenth Century Europe* (New York, 1983), 150–51.

84　Derek Beales and Eugenio Biagini, *The Risorgimento and the Unification of Italy* (New York, 2013), 40–46.

85　Denis Mack Smith, *Mazzini* (New Haven, 1994), 4–17.

86　Lucy Riall, *Garibaldi: Invention of a Hero* (New Haven, 2008), 33–34.

87　Garibaldi, *An Autobiography* (London, 1861).

88　Ibid., 43–47.

89　Mosse, *Nationalization*, esp. 21–46.

90　Quoted in Leighton James, *Witnessing the Revolutionary and Napoleonic Wars in German Central Europe* (London, 2013), 160.

91 Christiane Eisenberg, "Charismatic National Leader: Turnvater Jahn," in Richard Holt et al., eds., *European Heroes: Myth, Identity, Sport* (London, 2013), 14–27.

92 Sperber, *Revolutionary Europe*, 340.

93 Stan Landry, *Ecumenism, Memory, and German Nationalism, 1817–1917* (Syracuse, 2014), chap. 1.

94 On Görres's early romantic phase, see Jan Vanden Heuvel, *A German Life in the Age of Revolution: Joseph Görres, 1776–1848* (Washington, DC, 2001), 104–8.

95 Quoted in Hans Kohn, *The Age of Nationalism* (New York, 1962), 9.

96 Quoted in Zamoyski, *Holy Madness*, 165. Arndt's 1813 poem "Des Deutschen Vaterland" became perhaps the most influential of all German nationalist hymns; see Barbara Eichner, *History in Mighty Sounds: Musical Constructions of German National Identity* (Woodbridge, 2012), 10–11.

97 Leersen, *National Thought in Europe*, 130.

98 James Brophy, *Popular Culture and the Public Sphere in the Rhineland, 1800–1850* (Cambridge, 2007), 41–46.

99 Mosse, *Nationalization*, 85.

100 Serhiy Bilenky, *Romantic Nationalism in Eastern Europe* (Stanford, 2012), 17–42.

101 Roman Koropeckyj, *Adam Mickiewicz: The Life of a Romantic* (Ithaca, 2008), 29–30.

102 Halina Goldberg, *Music in Chopin's Warsaw* (Oxford, 2008), 50–52, 173–78.

103 Peter Cochran et al., eds., *Poland's Angry Romantic: Two Poems and a Play By Juliusz Słowacki* (Cambridge, 2009), 1–30.

104 On the centrality of Wallenrod imagery during the uprising, see Monika Coghen, "Polish Romanticism," in Paul Hamilton, ed., *The Oxford Handbook of European Romanticism* (Oxford, 2016), 561–62.

105 Marian Kukiel, *Czartoryski and European Unity, 1770–1861* (Princeton, 1955), 159–65.

106 Brian Porter-Szűcs, *Poland in the Modern World: Beyond Martyrdom* (Oxford, 2014). On the massive influence of Mickiewicz on Polish self-perceptions down to the present day, Porter-Szűcs notes that Mickiewicz "is to Poles what William Shakespeare is to Anglophones"; ibid., 11.

107 Jonathan Bellman, *Chopin's Polish Ballade: Op. 38 as Narrative of National Martyrdom* (Oxford, 2010), 55–85.

108 Mickiewicz, "To a Polish Mother," trans. Jewell Parish, in *Konrad Wallenrod and Other Writings of Adam Mickiewicz* (Berkeley, 1925), 128–29.

109 See Lucian Leustean, "Orthodox Christianity and Nationalism," in Lucian Leustean, ed., *Orthodox Christianity and Nationalism in Nineteenth-Century Southeastern Europe* (New York, 2014), 1–13.

110 Religious motivations were, however, often intertwined with nationalist ideals; see Ioannis Grigioriadis, *Instilling Religion in Greek and Turkish Nationalism: A "Sacred Synthesis"* (London, 2013), esp. 13–37.

111 Peter Mackridge, *Language and National Identity in Greece, 1766–1976* (Oxford, 2013), 57–58.

112 Paschalis Kitromilides, *Enlightenment and Revolution: The Making of Modern Greece* (Cambridge, MA, 2013), 200–29; more generally, Christopher Woodhouse, *Rhigas Velestinlis: Proto-Martyr of the Greek Revolution* (Limni, 1997).

113 Stathis Gourgouris, *Dream Nation: Enlightenment, Colonization, and the Institution of Modern Greece* (Stanford, 1996), 90–112.

114 Stephen George Chaconas, *Adamantios Korais: A Study in Greek Nationalism* (New York, 1942).

115 Korais, "Report on the Present State of Civilization in Greece," in Elie Kedourie, ed., *Nationalism in Asia and Africa* (London, 1970), 183–84.

116 Richard Stites, *The Four Horsemen: Riding to Liberty in Post-Napoleonic Europe* (Oxford, 2014), 185–86.

117 K.E. Fleming, *The Muslim Bonaparte: Diplomacy and Orientalism in Ali Pasha's Greece* (Princeton, 1999).

118 Charles Frazee, *The Orthodox Church and Independent Greece, 1821–1852* (Cambridge, 1969), 18–22.

119 Quoted in Thomas Gallant, *Modern Greece* (London, 2001), 21–22.

120 William St. Clair *That Greece Might Still Be Free: The Philhellenes in the War of Independence* (Oxford, 1972), 150–55.

121 Roderick Beaton, *Byron's War: Romantic Rebellion, Greek Revolution* (Cambridge, 2014), esp. 228–46.

122 William Parry, *The Last Days of Lord Byron* (London, 1825), esp. 128–35. See also Benita Eisler, *Byron: Child of Passion, Fool of Fame* (New York, 2000), 734–48.

123 Lucien Frary, *Russia and the Making of Modern Greek Identity, 1821–1844* (Oxford, 2015), 18–53.

124 Douglas Dakin, *The Greek Struggle for Independence, 1821–1833* (Berkeley, 1973), 226–34.

125 For a positive evaluation of Kapodistrias, see Christopher Woodhouse, *Capodistria: The Founder of Greek Independence* (Oxford, 1973).

126 P. Dimitrakis, *Greece and the English: British Diplomacy and the Kings of Greece* (London, 2009), 3–16.

127 John Petropolus, *Politics and Statecraft in the Kingdom of Greece, 1833–1843* (Princeton, 1968), 218–40; see also Eleni Bastéa, "Athens," in *Capital Cities in the Aftermath of Empires* (London, 2010), 29–44.

128 Peter Jelavich, *Munich and Theatrical Modernism* (Cambridge, MA, 1985), 20.Jelavich, *Munich*, 20.

129 Price, *Perilous Crown*, 187–88.

130 See David Kerr, *Caricature and French Political Culture, 1830–1848* (Oxford, 2000), 66–67.

131 Eric Martone, "Not Just the Uprising of *Les Misérables*: The Legacy of the June Revolution of 1832 in Paris," in Eric Martone, ed., *Royalists, Radicals, and Les Misérables: France in 1832* (Cambridge, 2013), 123–74.

132 Jonathan House, *Controlling Paris: Armed Forces and Counter-Revolution, 1789–1848* (New York, 2014), 47–48.

133 Pamela Pilbeam, *The Constitutional Monarchy in France, 1814–1848* (London, 2000), 60–65.

134 John Baughman, "The French Banquet Campaign of 1847–48," *JMH* 31 (1959): 1–15.

135 On Lamartine's romantic orientalism, see C.W. Thompson, *French Romantic Travel Writing: Chateaubriand to Nerval* (Oxford 2012), 111–20.

136 Mark Traugott, *Armies of the Poor: Determinants of Working-Class Participation in the Parisian Insurrection of June 1848* (Princeton, 1985).

137 William Fontescue, *France and 1848: The End of Monarchy* (London, 2005), 134–54.

138 Fenton Bresler, *Napoleon III: A Life* (New York, 1999), 227–32.

139 Andre de Vries, *Flanders: A Cultural History* (Oxford, 2007), 13.

140 Jonathan Sperber, *Karl Marx: A Nineteenth-Century Life* (New York, 2013), 161–64.

141 Brison Gooch, *Belgium and the February Revolution* (The Hague, 1963), 52–60.

142 Jonathan Sperber, *The European Revolutions, 1848–1851* (Cambridge, 2005), 120–21; see also Mike Rapport, *1848: Year of Revolution* (New York, 2008), 116–17.

143 Bernard Cook, *Belgium: A History* (New York, 2005), 66.

144 Horst Lademacher, "The Netherlands and Belgium: Notes on the Causes of Abstinence from Revolution," in Dieter Dowe, ed., *Europe in 1848* (New York, 2000), 259–88.

145 Joachim Remak, *A Very Civil War: The Swiss Sonderbund War of 1847* (Boulder, 1993).

146 Marc Lerner, *A Laboratory of Liberty: The Transformation of Political Culture in Republican Switzerland, 1780–1848* (Leiden, 2011), chap. 7.

147 Oliver Zimmer, *Contested Nation: History, Memory, and Nationalism in Switzerland, 1761–1891* (Cambridge, 2003). For an insightful discussion of the extent to which the Swiss case problematizes attempts to create tidy categories of civic and ethnic nationalism, ibid., 8–14.

148 John Cunningham, "'Tis Hard to Argue Starvation into Quiet': Protest and Resistance, 1846–47," in Enda Delaney and Breandán Mac Suibhne, eds., *Ireland's Great Famine and Popular Politics* (New York, 2016), 10–33.

149 See Helen Mulvey, *Thomas Davis and Ireland: A Biographical Study* (Washington, DC, 2003).

150 From Thomas Osborne, *The Spirit of the Nation: Ballads and Songs by the Writers of "The Nation"* (Dublin, 1845), 274–75.

151 Cian McMahon, *The Global Dimensions of Irish Identity: Race, Nation, and the Popular Press, 1840–1880* (Chapel Hill, 2015), 37–39.

152 Christine Kinealy, *The Great Irish Famine: Impact, Ideology, and Rebellion* (Houndmills, 2002), 182–210.

153 Robert Sloan, *William Smith O'Brien and the Young Irelander Rebellion of 1848* (Dublin, 2000), 219.

154 Lawrence Fenton, *The Young Ireland Rebellion and Limerick* (Cork, 2010), 184–94.

155 Sloan, *William Smith O'Brien and the Young Irelander Rebellion of 1848*, 286–89.

156 On the legacy of the rebellion, see Christine Kinealy, *Repeal and Revolution: 1848 in Ireland* (Manchester, 2009), 276–94.

157 Falnes, National Romanticism in Norway (New York, 1933).

158 Gjerset, *History of the Norwegian People*, vol. 2, 508–9.

159 Anne-Lise Seip, "The Revolution of 1848 on the Norwegian Scene," in Dieter Dowe, ed., *Europe in 1848*, 316.

160 Inger Furseth, *A Comparative Study of Social and Religious Movements in Norway, 1780–1905* (Lewiston, 2002), 169–73.

161 Harold Naess, *A History of Norwegian Literature* (Lincoln, 1993), 95.

162 Quoted in Arne Ruth, "The Second New Nation: The Mythology of Modern Sweden," *Daedalus* 113:2 (Spring 1984): 54.

163 Göran Nilsson, "Sweden 1848: On the Road to the 'Middle Way'," in Dieter Dowe, ed., *Europe in 1848*, 325–26.

164 Göran Nilsson, *The Founder: André Oscar Wallenberg, 1816–1886* (Stockholm, 2005).

165 Nilsson, "Sweden 1848," 330–32.

166 Roger Congleton, *Improving Democracy through Constitutional Reform: Some Swedish Lessons* (Dordrecht, 2003), 24–27.

167 T.K. Derry, *A History of Scandinavia* (Minneapolis, 1979), 79.

168 Peter Thaler, *Of Mind and Matter: The Duality of National Identity in the German-Danish Borderlands* (West Lafayette, 2009), esp. 69–108.

169 Knud J.V. Jespersen, *A History of Denmark* (Houndmills, 2011), 64–66.

170 See the overview in Nick Svendsen, *The First Schleswig-Holstein War, 1848–1850* (Solihull, 2007).

171 Martin Klatt, "Mobile Regions: Competitive Regional Concepts (not only) in the Danish-German Border Region," in D.J. Anderson et al., eds., *The Border Multiple: The Practicing of Borders between Public Policy and Everyday Life* (New York, 2012), 55–74.

172 H. Schulze, *The Course of German Nationalism* (Cambridge, 1991), 66–67.

173 J. Deak, *Forging a Multinational State* (Stanford, 2015), 107–8.

174 Quoted in R.S. Alexander, *Europe's Uncertain Path, 1814–1914* (Oxford, 2012), 68.

175 Andrea Komlosy, "Imperial Cohesion, Nation-Building, and Regional Integration in the Habsburg Monarchy, 1804–1918," in Stefan Berger and Alexei Miller, eds., *Nationalizing Empires* (Budapest, 2015), 385–86.

176 Larry Wolff, *The Idea of Galicia: History and Fantasy in Habsburg Political Culture* (Stanford, 2010), 178–83.

177 Hans Henning Hahn, "The Polish Nation in the Revolution of 1846–49," in Dieter Dowe, ed., *Europe in 1848*, 171–74.

178 Bruce Seymour, *Lola Montez: A Life* (New Haven, 1997), 102–5.

179 Pieter Judson, *Exclusive Revolutionaries: Liberal Politics, Social Experience, and National Identity in the Austrian Empire, 1848–1914* (Ann Arbor, 1996), 29–67.

180 Monika Baar, *Historians and Nationalism* (Oxford, 2010), 29–34.

181 Sperber, *The European Revolutions*, 203–5.

182 Pieter Judson, *The Habsburg Empire: A New History* (Cambridge, MA, 2016), 164. On Kossuth's broader revolutionary activities, see Istvan Deak, *The Lawful Revolution: Louis Kossuth and the Hungarians, 1848–1849* (New York, 1979).

183 Paul Lendvai, *The Hungarians: A Thousand Years of Victory in Defeat* (Princeton, 2003), 222–41.

184 Christoph Dipper and Ulrich Speck, *1848: Revolution in Deutschland* (Frankfurt, 1998), 115–16; Gisela Mettele, *Bürgertum in Köln 1775–1870* (Munich, 1998), 296–97.

185 David Barclay gives the figure of 303 civilians killed; Barclay, "Revolution and Counter-Revolution in Prussia, 1840–1850," in Philip Dwyer, ed., *Modern Prussian History, 1830–1947* (New York, 2013), 74.

186 Martin Kitchen, *A History of Modern Germany, 1800 to the Present* (Oxford, 2012), 69

187 Norman Davies, *God's Playground: A History of Poland*, vol. 2 (Oxford, 2005), 88–89.

188 Quoted in Lewis Namier, *1848: The Revolution of the Intellectuals* (Oxford, 1992; orig. 1944), 88.

189 Brian Vick, *Defining Germany: The 1848 Frankfurt Parliamentarians and National Identity* (Cambridge, MA, 2002).

190 Abigail Green, *Fatherlands: State-Building and Nationhood in Nineteenth-Century Germany* (Cambridge, 2001).

191 Steven Soper, *Building a Civil Society: Associations, Public Life, and the Origins of Modern Italy* (Toronto, 2013), 21–24.

192 Clara Maria Lovett, *Carlo Cattaneo and the Politics of the Risorgimento, 1820–1860* (The Hague, 1972), 38–44.

193 Michael Embree, *Radetzky's Marches: The Campaigns of 1848 and 1849 in Upper Italy* (London, 2013).

194 Frank Coppa, *The Origins of the Italian Wars of Independence* (New York, 1992), 23–40.

195 Ibid., 54–56.

196 See G.M. Trevelyan, *Garibaldi's Defense of the Roman Republic* (London, 1907).

197 Denis Mack Smith, *Garibaldi* (New Haven, 1994), 64–76.

198 David Rowley, "Guiseppe Mazzini and the Democratic Logic of Nationalism," *Nations and Nationalism* 18 (2012): 39–56.

Chapter 4

1 Hermione Hobhouse, *The Crystal Palace and the Great Exhibition: Art, Science, and Productive Industry* (London, 2002), 16–21.

2 Christine MacLeod, *Heroes of Invention: Technology, Liberalism, and British Identity, 1750–1914* (Cambridge, 2007), 212–13.

3 Jeffrey Auerbach, *The Great Exhibition of 1851: A Nation on Display* (New Haven, 1999), 3–4. See also Jo Briggs, *Novelty Fair: British Visual Culture between Chartism and the Great Exhibition* (Manchester, 2016), 111–34.

4 Jeffrey Auerbach and Peter Hoffenberg, eds., *Britain, the Empire, and the World at the Great Exhibition of 1851* (Aldershot, 2008); Louise Burbrick, ed., *The Great Exhibition of 1851: New Interdisciplinary Essays* (Manchester, 2001).

5 Geoffrey Cantor, *Religion and the Great Exhibition of 1851* (Oxford, 2013), 102–27.

6 Tom Kemp, *Industrialization in Nineteenth-Century Europe* (London, 1985); Lenard Burlanstein, ed., *The Industrial Revolution and Work in Nineteenth Century Europe* (New York, 1992); Roy Porter and Mikulas Teich, eds., *The Industrial Revolution in National Context* (Cambridge, 1996).

7 Andrew Lees and Lynn Hollen Lees, *Cities and the Making of Modern Europe* (Cambridge, 2007).

8 Norman Rich, *The Age of Nationalism and Reform* (New York, 1970), 1–13; Michael Forman, *Nationalism and the International Labor Movement* (University Park, 2007), 115–66.

9 See esp. Abigail Green, "Representing Germany? The Zollverein at the World Exhibitions, 1851–1862," *JMH* 75 (2003): 836–63; John Davis, "The Great Exhibition and the German States," in Jeffrey A Auerbach and Peter H. Hoffenberg, eds., *Britain, the Empire, and the World*, 147–72.

10 For a comparative overview, see Daniel Ziblatt, *Structuring the State: The Formation of Italy and Germany and the Puzzle of Federalism* (Princeton, 2006); also John Breuilly, "Nationalism and National Unification in Nineteenth-Century Europe," in John Breuilly, ed., *The Oxford Handbook of the History of Nationalism* (Oxford, 2013), 149–74.

11 For the best overview in Italian, see the pathbreaking Alberto Banti, *La nazione del Risorgimento* (Turin, 2006).

12 Bruce Haddock, "Political Union without Social Revolution: Vincenzo Gioberti's Primato," *Historical Journal* 41 (1998): 705–23. On Gioberti's influence on the vocabulary of Italian nationalism, see Silvana Patriarca, "National Identity or National Character? New Vocabularies and Old Paradigms," in Albert Ascoli and Krystyna von Henneberg, eds., *Making and Remaking Italy: The Cultivation of National Identity Around the Risorgimento* (Oxford, 2001), 309–10.

13 Riall, *Risorgimento*, 57.

14 John Dowling, *The Life and Reign of Pope Pius the Ninth* (New York, 1849), 661.

15 G.F.-W. Berkeley, *Italy in the Making, 1815 to 1846* (Cambridge, 1968), 257–66.

16 John Gilmary Shea, *The Life of Pope Pius IX* (New York, 1877), 110–11.

17 Frank Coppa, *Cardinal Giacomo Antonelli and Papal Politics in European Affairs* (Albany, 1990), 47–56.

18 Eric Frattini, *The Entity: Five Centuries of Secret Vatican Espionage* (New York, 2008), 149–50.

19 Ciaran O'Caroll, "Pius IX: Pastor and Prince," in James Corkery and Thomas Worcester, eds., *The Papacy Since 1500: From Italian Prince to Universal Pastor* (Cambridge, 2010), 125–42.

20 Denis Mack Smith, *Mazzini* (New Haven, 1994), 151.

21 Michael Burleigh has aptly characterized Mazzini's ideas as "a religion of cosmopolitan Romantic nationalism"; *Earthly Powers*, 185.

22 Mazzini, *The Duties of Man*, trans. E.A. Venturi (London, 1863), 60–65.

23 On Garibaldi's gradual transformation into a moderate constitutional monarchist, see Christopher Hibbert, *Garibaldi: Hero of Italian Unification* (New York, 2008), 133–37.

24 Harry Hearder, *Cavour* (London, 2013), 9–11.

25 Denis Mack Smith, *Cavour: A Biography* (New York, 1985), 31.

26 See e.g. Mario Loria, "Cavour and the Development of the Fertilizer Industry in Piedmont," *Technology and Culture* 8 (1967): 159–77.

27 Stefano Fenoaltea, *The Reinterpretation of Italian Economic History* (Cambridge, 2011), 135–36, 170–73.

28 Denis Mack Smith, *Modern Italy: A Political History* (Ann Arbor, 1997), 21–22.

29 Russell King, *The Industrial Geography of Italy* (New York, 2015), 22–50. On revisionist debates over economic developments in the south, see Marta Petrusewicz, *Latifundium: Moral Economy and Material Life in a European Periphery* (Ann Arbor, 1996); and Lucy Riall, "Which Road to the South? Revisionists Revisit the Mezzogiorno," *Journal of Modern Italian Studies* 5 (2000): 89–100.

30 J.A. Davis, "Technology and Innovation in an Industrial Late-Comer: Italy in the Nineteenth Century," in Davis and P. Mathias, eds., *Technology and Innovation from the Eighteenth Century to the Present* (Oxford, 1991), 62–106.

31 Riall, *Risorgimento*, 143.

32 Christopher Duggan, *The Force of Destiny: A History of Italy since 1796* (New York, 2008), 189–90.

33 Jack Fairey, *The Great Powers and Orthodox Christendom: The Crisis over the Eastern Church in the Era of the Crimean War* (New York, 2015), 4–13.

34 Andrew Rath, *The Crimean War in Imperial Context, 1854–1856* (New York, 2015).

35 John Sweetman, *The Crimean War* (London, 2013), 69–71.

36 Roger Absalom, *Italy Since 1800: A Nation in the Balance?* (London, 2014), 36–37.

37 On the 1858 event as the forerunner of Turin's subsequent exhibitions, see esp. Cristina Della Coletta, *World's Fairs Italian Style: The Great Expositions in Turin and Their Narratives* (Toronto, 2006), 20–21.

38 On the meeting at Plombières, see James Macmillan, *Napoleon III* (London, 2013), 83–85.

39 Arnold Blumberg, *A Carefully Planned Accident: The Italian War of 1859* (Toronto, 1990).

40 Max Boot, *Invisible Armies: An Epic History of Guerilla Warfare* (New York, 2013), 115–16.

41 The Swiss observer Henri Dunant was so shaken by the images at Solferino that he founded the International Red Cross in response; see Caroline Moorehead, *Dunant's Dream: War, Memory, and the History of the Red Cross* (London, 1998).

42 Frederick Schneid, *The Second War of Italian Unification* (Oxford, 2012), 82–84.

43 Ivan Scott, *The Roman Question and the Powers, 1848–1865* (The Hague, 1969), 161–70.

44 See the classic study of G.M. Trevelyan, *Garibaldi and the Thousand: May 1860* (London, 1909).

45 Lucy Riall, *Garibaldi: The Invention of a Hero* (New Haven, 2008), 207–25.

46 The most thorough account in English is Denis Mack Smith, *Cavour and Garibaldi, 1860: A Study in Political Conflict* (Cambridge, 1954).

47 See Sabina Donati, *A Political History of National Citizenship and Identity in Italy, 1861–1950* (Stanford, 2013), 16–20.

48 Suzanne Stewart-Steinberg, *The Pinocchio Effect: On Making Italians, 1860–1920* (Chicago, 2007), 1–2.

49 See the insightful analysis of MacGregor Knox, *To the Threshold of Power, 1922–33: Origins and Dynamics of the Fascist and National Socialist Dictatorships* (Cambridge, 2007), 19–57.

50 Abigail Green, *Fatherlands; State Building and Nationhood in Nineteenth Century Germany* (Cambridge, 2001), 22–61; Mark Hewitson, *Nationalism in Germany, 1848–1866: Revolutionary Nation* (Houndmills, 2010), 160–82; Lawrence Flockerzie, "State-Building and Nation-Building in the 'Third Germany'," *Central European History* 24 (1991): 268–92.

51 Quoted in Jelavich, *Munich*, 20.

52 See George Windell, *The Catholics and German Unity, 1866–1871* (Minneapolis, 1954), 3–27.

53 John Deak, *Forging a Multinational State: State Making in Imperial Austria from the Enlightenment to the First World War* (Stanford, 2015), 99–108.

54 Roy Austensen, "Austria and the 'Struggle for Supremacy' in Germany, 1848–1864," *Journal of Modern History* 52 (1980): 195–225.

55 On the continuation of earlier patterns, see Markus Cerman, "Proto-Industrial Development in Austria," in Sheilagh Ogilvie and Markus Cerman, eds., *European Proto-Industrialization* (Cambridge, 1996), 171–87.

56 David Good, *The Economic Rise of the Habsburg Empire, 1750–1914* (Berkeley, 1984), 80–81.

57 Rolf Dumke, "Tariffs and Market Structure: The German Zollverein as a Model for Economic Integration," in W.R. Lee, ed., *German Industry and German Industrialization* (London, 1991), 77–115.

58 Herbert Matis, "Austria: Industrialization in a Multinational Setting," in Mikulas Teich and Roy Porter, eds., *Industrial Revolution in National Context*, 228.

59 On the construction of the Votivkirche as a celebration of the "national triumph" over ethnically motivated revolutionaries, see Rachel Hoffmann, "The Age of Assassination: Monarchy and Nation in Nineteenth-Century Europe," in Jan Rüger and Nikolaus Wachsmann, eds., *Rewriting German History: New Perspectives on German History* (New York, 2015), 121–41.

60 See Daniel Unowsky, *The Pomp and Politics of Patriotism: Imperial Celebrations in Habsburg Austria, 1848–1916* (West Lafayette, 2005), esp. 12–25.

61 Judson, *Exclusive Revolutionaries*, 77–84.

62 Dennis Showalter, *Railroads and Rifles: Soldiers, Technology, and the Unification of Germany* (Hamden, 1976).

63 For a concise biographical overview in German, see Eberhard Kolb, *Bismarck: Eine Biographie* (Munich, 2014).

64 Edgar Feuchtwanger, *Bismarck: A Political History* (New York, 2002), 84–85.

65 Katherine Lerman, *Bismarck* (London, 2004), 83–90.

66 John Breuilly, "From Revolution to Unification," in John Breuilly and Mary Fulbrook, eds., *Germany Since 1800* (London, 1997); also John Breuilly, *The Formation of the First German Nation-State* (London, 1996).

67 L.D. Steefel, *The Schleswig-Holstein Question* (Cambridge, MA, 1932).

68 On the November Constitution in the context of nationalist ideas, see esp. Jason Jensen and John Hall, "The Decomposition of the Danish Imperial Monarchy," *Nations and Nationalism* 20 (2014): 742–59.

69 J.V. Clardy, "Austrian Foreign Policy during the Schleswig-Holstein Crisis of 1864," *Diplomacy & Statecraft* 2 (1991): 254–69.

70 Geoffrey Wawro, *The Austro-Prussian War* (Cambridge, 1997), 50–51.

71 Wawro, *Austro-Prussian War*, 273–75.

72 Evans, *Austria, Hungary, and the Habsburgs*, 266–92.

73 Peter Katzenstein, *Disjointed Partners: Germany and Austria since 1815* (Berkeley, 1976), 97–110.

74 Allan Mitchell, "Bonapartism as Model for Bismarckian Politics," *JMH* 49 (1977): 181–99.

75 James Sheehan, *German Liberalism in the Nineteenth Century* (Chicago, 1976), 123–40; Gordon Mork, "Bismarck and the 'Capitulation' of German Liberalism," *JMH* 43 (1971): 59–75.

76 Windell, *The Catholics and German Unity, 1866–1871*, 84–115.

77 Georges Bonin, *Bismarck and the Hohenzollern Candidature for the Spanish Throne* (London, 1957); also H.S. Halperin, "The Origins of the Franco-Prussian War Revisited: Bismarck and the Hohenzollern Candidature for the Spanish Throne," *JMH* 45 (1973): 83–91.

78 The best overview in English remains Geoffrey Wawro, *The Franco-Prussian War: The German Conquest of France in 1870–1871* (Cambridge, 2003).

79 See Robert Tombs, *The Paris Commune, 1871* (London, 1999).

80 Raffael Scheck, *Germany, 1871–1945: A Concise History* (London, 2008), 27–28.

81 For one of the earliest articulations of this concept, see Friedrich Darmstaedter, *Bismarck and the Creation of the Second Reich* (London, 1948), xiv.

82 On the broader context and significance of the Kulturkampf, see Margaret Lavinia Anderson, "The Kulturkampf and the Course of German History," *CEH* 19 (1986): 82–115.

83 For a brief overview, see Otto Pflanze, *Bismarck and the Development of Germany* (Princeton, 1990), 179–206. On the persecution of the Jesuits in particular, see Roisin Healy, *The Jesuit Specter in Imperial Germany* (Leiden, 2003), chap. 2.

84 Rebecca Bennette, *Fighting for the Soul of Germany: The Catholic Struggle for Inclusion after Unification* (Cambridge, MA, 2012).

85 Jonathan Sperber, *Popular Catholicism in Nineteenth-Century Germany* (Princeton, 1984).

86 David Blackbourn, *Marpingen: Apparitions of the Virgin Mary in Nineteenth-Century Germany* (New York, 1993).

87 Michael Gross, *The War against Catholicism: Liberalism and the Anti-Catholic Imagination in Nineteenth-Century Germany* (Ann Arbor, 2005).

88 Ronald Ross, *The Failure of Bismarck's Kulturkampf: Catholicism and State Power in Imperial Germany, 1871–1887* (Washington, DC, 1998).

89 Ellen Lovell Evans, *The German Center Party, 1870–1933: A Study in Political Catholicism* (Carbondale, 1981).

90 Helmut Walser Smith, *German Nationalism and Religious Conflict: Culture, Ideology, Politics, 1870–1914* (Princeton, 1995); Lisa Zwicker, *Dueling Students: Conflict, Masculinity, and Politics in German Universities, 1890–1914* (Ann Arbor, 2011).

91 Quoted in Bonnie Smith, *Changing Lives: Women in European History since 1700* (Boston, 1989), 257.

92 Mark Seymour, "Keystone of the Patriarchal Family? Indissoluable Marriage, Masculinity, and Divorce in Liberal Italy," *Journal of Modern Italian Studies* 10 (2005): 297–313.

93 See Clare Midgley, *Women Activists in Imperial Britain, 1790–1865* (London, 2007), esp. 123–46.

94 Marcella Pellegrino Sutcliffe, *Victorian Radicals and Italian Democrats* (Woodbridge, 2014).

95   On the broader move to integrate southern Italy, see Nelson Moe, *The View from Vesuvius: Italian Culture and the Southern Question* (Berkeley, 2002).

96   Maura O'Connor, "Civilizing Southern Italy: British and Italian Women and the Cultural Politics of European Nation Building," *Women's Writing* 10 (2003): 253–68. See also Axel Körner, *The Politics of Culture in Liberal Italy: From Unification to Fascism* (London, 2009), 210–11.

97   George Mosse, "Nationalism and Respectability: Normal and Abnormal Sexuality in Nineteenth-Century Europe," *JCH* 17 (1982): 221–46; more generally, George L. Mosse,, *Nationalism and Sexuality: Respectability and Abnormal Sexuality in Modern Europe* (New York, 1985).

98   Steven Halliday, *The Great Stink of London: Sir Joseph Bazalgette and the Cleansing of the Victorian Metropolis* (Stroud, 1999).

99   David Barnes, *The Great Stink of Paris and the Nineteenth-Century Struggle against Filth and Germs* (Baltimore, 2006).

100 See Richard Evans, *Death in Hamburg: Society and Politics in the Cholera Years* (New York, 2005).

101 On western Europe see Richard Olsen, *Science and Scientism in Nineteenth Century Europe* (Urbana, 2008). For other parts of the continent, see Faidra Papanelopoulou et al., eds., *Popularizing Science and Technology in the European Periphery, 1800–2000* (Farnham, 2009).

102 Owen Chadwick, *The Secularization of the European Mind in the Nineteenth Century* (Cambridge, 1975), esp. 161–88.

103 Stuart Hayashi, *Hunting Down Social Darwinism: Will This Canard Go Extinct?* (Lanham, 2015), 27.

104 Mark Francis, *Herbert Spencer and the Invention of Modern Life* (Ithaca, 2007), 3–4.

105 Patrick Barnard, *Herder on Nationality, Humanity, and History* (Montreal, 2003), 45.

106 Wallace, "The Origin of Human Races and the Antiquity of Man Deduced from the Theory of Natural Selection," *Journal of the Anthropological Society of London* 2 (1864): 164–65.

107 See Michael Biddiss, *Father of Racist Ideology: The Social and Political Thought of Count Gobineau* (London, 1970).

108 Steven Kale, "Gobineau, Racism, and Legitimism: A Royalist Heretic in Nineteenth-Century France," *Modern Intellectual History* 7 (2010): 33–61.

109 The work was translated into English by Henry Hotze and published as *The Moral and Intellectual Diversity of Races: With Particular Reference to Their Respective Influence in the Civil and Political History of Mankind* (Philadelphia, 1856).

110 On the application of Gobineau's ideas to the identity of Africans and the issue of slavery in the United States, particularly by his translator Henry Hotze, see Lonnie Burnett, *Henry Hotze, Confederate Propagandist* (Tuscaloosa, 2009), esp. 3–5.

111 Michael Biddiss, "Gobineau and the Origins of European Racism," *Race & Class* 7 (1966): 255–70.

112 Leon Poliakov, *The Aryan Myth: A History of Racist and Nationalist Ideas in Europe* (New York, 1970), 233–35.

113 See esp. Gavin Langmuir, *History, Religion, and Antisemitism* (Berkeley, 1990); William Nicholls, *Christian Antisemitism: A History of Hate* (Lanham, 1993).

114 On the centrality of Gobineau to this transformation, see Alan Davies, *Infected Christianity: A Study of Modern Racism* (Montreal, 1988), 23–27, 59–63.

115 Leon Poliakov, *The History of Anti-Semitism. Volume Four: Suicidal Europe, 1870–1933* (Philadelphia, 2003), chaps. 1–2.

116 John Klier, *Russians, Jews, and the Pogroms of 1881–1882* (Cambridge, 2011).

117 See Andersen's account in his memoir, Hans C. Andersen, *A Poet's Bazaar: Pictures of Travel in Germany, Italy, Greece and the Orient* (New York, 1871), 92–93. On Andersen's other poetry in that era, see Jackie Wullschlager, *Hans Christian Andersen: The Life of a Storyteller* (New York, 2000), 179–96.

118 Marie Louise Svane, "Introduction to Danish Romanticism," in Stephen Prickett, ed., *European Romanticism* (London, 2010), 31–32.

119 Mette Bligaard, "The Image of Denmark: Museums as Sanctuaries of Identity," in J.M. Fladmark, ed., *Heritage and Museums: Shaping National Identity* (London, 2014), 290–91.

120 Bruce Baum, *The Rise and Fall of the Caucasian Race: A Political History of Racial Identity* (New York, 2009), 130–31.

121 J. Laurence Hare, *Excavating Nations: Archaeology, Museums, and the German-Danish Borderlands* (Toronto, 2015), 45–46. For a broader view, see the insightful work of Chris Manias, *Race, Science, and the Nation: Reconstructing the Ancient Past in Britain, France, and Germany* (New York, 2013).

122 Richard McMahon, "Anthropological Race Psychology, 1820–1945: A Common European System of Ethnic Identity Narratives," *Nations and Nationalism* 15 (2009): 575–96. More generally, see Richard McMahon, *The Races of Europe: Construction of National Identities in the Social Sciences, 1839–1939* (London, 2016).

123 Jonas Harvard, "Connecting the Nordic Region: The Electric Telegraph and the European News Market," in Jonas Harvard and Peter Stadius, eds., *Communicating the North: Media Structures and Images in the Making of the Nordic Region* (Farnham, 2013).

124 David Kirby, *The Baltic World, 1772–1993: Europe's Northern Periphery in an Age of Change* (New York, 2013), 123–24.

125 John Peter Collett, "The Christiana University's Fifty Years Celebration in 1861: National Pride and Scandinavian Solidarity," in Pieter Dhondt, ed., *National, Nordic, or European? Nineteenth-Century University Jubilees and Nordic Cooperation* (Leiden, 2011), 73–98.

126 For a broad overview, see Robert Kann, *The Multinational Empire: Nationalism and National Reform in the Habsburg Monarchy, 1848–1918* (New York, 1950).

127 Lawrence Orton, *The Prague Slav Congress of 1848* (Boulder, 1978).

128 Glenny, *Balkans*, 11.

129 Branimir Anzluovic, *Heavenly Serbia: From Myth to Genocide* (New York, 1999), 13–17.

130 Ibid., 51–60.

131 Petar II Petrović Njegoš, "The Mountain Wreath," in Balázs Trencsényi and Michal Kopeček, eds., *Discourses of Collective Identity in Central and Southeast Europe, 1770–1945. Volume II: National Romanticism* (Budapest, 2007), 435, "The Mountain Wreath," in, *Discourses,*.

132 For an insightful perspective emphasizing the merging of religious and ethnic ideals, see Jack Fairey, "Russia's Quest for the Holy Grail: Relics, Liturgics, and Great Power Politics in the Ottoman Empire," in Lucien Frary and Mara Kozelsky, eds., *Russian-Ottoman Borderlands: The Eastern Question Reconsidered* (Madison, 2014), 131–64.

133 Roumen Daskalov, *The Making of a Nation in the Balkans: Historiography of the Bulgarian Revival* (Budapest, 2004), 197–225.

134 Barbara Jelavich, *Russia's Balkan Entanglements, 1806–1914* (Cambridge, 1991), esp. 170–78.

135 Andre Gerolymatos, *The Balkan Wars: Conquest, Revolution, and Retribution from the Ottoman Era to the Twentieth Century and Beyond* (New York, 2002), 203–5.

136 William Norton Endicott, *The Congress of Berlin and After: A Diplomatic History of the Near Eastern Settlement, 1878–1880* (London, 1963), esp. 205–61.

137 László Bencze, *The Occupation of Bosnia and Herzegovina in 1878* (Boulder, 2006).

138 See the essays in Chima Korieh and R.C. Njoku, eds., *Missions, States, and European Expansion in Africa* (New York, 2007).

139 For an insightful account of the linkages between expansionist impulses in imperialist and nationalist projects, see Hannah Arendt's classic essay "Imperialism, Nationalism, Chauvinism," *Review of Politics* 7 (1945): 441–63.

140 Stephen Brown, "First Among Equals: Jan Pieterszoon Coen and the Dutch East India Company," in Stephen Brown, ed., *Merchant Kings: When Companies Ruled the World, 1600–1800* (New York, 2009), 7–56.

141 See esp. Philip Stern, *The Company-State: Corporate Sovereignty and the Early Modern Foundations of the British Empire in India* (Oxford, 2011).

142 Christopher Hibbert, *The Great Mutiny: India, 1857* (New York, 1980); Jill Bender, *The 1857 Indian Uprising and the British Empire* (Cambridge, 2016).

143 Lawrence James, *The Raj: The Making and Unmaking of British India* (New York, 1997), 292–94.

144 On the impact of the Mutiny on literary self-representation, see Gautram Chakravarty, *The Indian Mutiny and the British Imagination* (Cambridge, 2005).

145 Crane and Mohanram, *Imperialism as Diaspora: Race, Sexuality, and History in Anglo-India* (Liverpool, 2013), 22–54.

146 Steven Patterson, *The Cult of Imperial Honor in British India* (New York, 2009), 1.

147 Zachary Karabell, *Parting the Desert: The Creation of the Suez Canal* (New York, 2003), 245–59.

148 See esp. Alice Conklin, *In the Museum of Man: Race, Anthropology, and Empire in France, 1850–1950* (Ithaca, 2013).

149 See Margaret Majumdar, *Postcoloniality: The French Dimension* (New York, 2007), 22–23.

150 From Paul Robiquet, ed., *Discours et Opnions de Jules Ferry* (Paris, 1897), 199–201.

151 Matthew Fitzpatrick, *Liberal Imperialism in Germany: Expansionism and Nationalism, 1848–1884* (New York, 2008).

152 Thomas Pakenham, *The Scramble for Africa: White Man's Conquest of the Dark Continent, 1876–1912* (New York, 1991), 470–86.

153 Adam Hochschild, *King Leopold's Ghost: A Story of Greed, Terror, and Heroism in Colonial Africa* (New York, 1998), 91–92.

154 Martin Ewans, *European Atrocity, African Catastrophe: Leopold II, the Congo Free State, and Its Aftermath* (London, 2002), 113–15.

155 Arendt, *The Origins of Totalitarianism* (New York, 1951), 224.

156 Gerwarth and Malinowski, "Hannah Arendt's Ghosts: Reflections on the Disputable Path from Windhoeck to Auschwitz," *Central European History* 42 (2009): 279–300. See also Sarah Danielsson, "Pan-Nationalism Reframed: Nationalism, 'Diaspora', the Role of the Nation-State, and the Global Age," in Daphne Halikiopoulou and Sofia Vasilopoulou, eds., *Nationalism and Globalisation: Conflicting or Complementary?* (London, 2011), 41–60.

157 Baranowski, *Nazi Empire: German Colonialism from Bismarck to Hitler* (Cambridge, 2011); Eley, "Empire by Land or Sea? Germany's Colonial Imaginary," in Bradley Naranch and Geoff Eley, eds., *German Colonialism in a Global Age* (Durham, 2014), 19–44.

Chapter 5

1 Erich Eyck, *Bismarck and the German Empire* (New York, 1968), 274.

2 John C.G. Röhl, *The Kaiser and His Court: Wilhelm II and the Government of Germany* (Cambridge, 1994), 13. See also John Röhl, *Young Wilhelm: The Kaiser's Early Years, 1859–1888* (Cambridge, 1998).

3 On the late nineteenth century as the key moment for these domestic linkages, see George Mosse, "Racism and Nationalism," *Nations and Nationalism* 1 (1995): 163–73.

4 Hobsbawm, *Nations and Nationalism since 1780*, 81–82.

5   Eugen Weber, *Peasants into Frenchmen: The Modernization of Rural France, 1870–1914* (Stanford, 1976). But see also James Lehning, *Peasants and French: Cultural Contact in Rural France during the Nineteenth Century* (Cambridge, 1995).

6   Celia Applegate, *A Nation of Provincials: The German Idea of Heimat* (Berkeley, 1990); Alon Confino, *The Nation as a Local Metaphor: Württemberg, Imperial Germany, and National Memory, 1871–1918* (Chapel Hill, 1997).

7   Caroline Ford, *Creating the Nation in Provincial France: Religion and Political Identity in Brittany* (Princeton, 1993).

8   See Moshe Zimmermann, *Wilhelm Marr: The Patriarch of Anti-Semitism* (Oxford, 1986), 70–71.

9   Harry Liebersohn, *Religion and Industrial Society: The Protestant Social Congress in Wilhelmine Germany* (Philadelphia, 1986), 8–10.

10 Peter Pulzer, *The Rise of Political Anti-Semitism in Germany and Austria*, rev. ed. (Cambridge, MA, 1988; orig. 1964), chap. 10.

11 Götz Aly, *Why the Germans? Why the Jews? Envy, Race Hatred, and the Prehistory of the Holocaust* (New York, 2014), 81.

12 Richard Levy, *The Downfall of the Antisemitic Political Parties in Imperial Germany* (New Haven, 1975).

13 Geoff Eley, *Reshaping the German Right: Radical Nationalism and Political Change after Bismarck* (New Haven, 1980).

14 Roger Chickering, *We Men Who Feel Most German: A Cultural History of the Pan-German League, 1886–1914* (Boston, 1984).

15 Smith, *German Nationalism and Religious Conflict*, 206–32.

16 Kristin Kopp, *Germany's Wild East: Constructing Poland as a Colonial Space* (Ann Arbor, 2012), 59–64.

17 Geoff Eley, "Reshaping the Right: Radical Nationalism and the German Navy League, 1898–1908," *Historical Journal* 21 (1978): 327–54.

18 Patrick Kelly, *Tirpitz and the Imperial German Navy* (Bloomington, 2011), 129–65.

19 Marilyn Shevin Coetzee, *The German Army League: Popular Nationalism in Wilhelmine Germany* (Oxford, 1990).

20 Andrew Whiteside, *The Socialism of Fools: Georg Ritter von Schönerer and Austrian Pan-Germanism* (Berkeley, 1975).

21 Deak, *Forging a Multinational State*, 223–25.

22 Gary Cohen, *The Politics of Ethnic Survival: Germans in Prague, 1861–1914* (Princeton, 1981).

23 See esp. Daniel Unowsky, "Local Violence, Regional Politics, and State Crisis: The 1898 Anti-Jewish Riots in Habsburg Galicia," and Michael Frankl, "From Boycott to Riot: The Moravian Anti-Jewish Violence of 1899 and Its Background," both in Robert Nemes and Daniel Unowsky, eds., *Sites of European Antisemitism in the Age of Mass Politics, 1880–1918* (Waltham, 2014).

24 John Boyer, *Political Radicalism in Late Imperial Vienna: Origins of the Christian Social Movement, 1848–1897* (Chicago, 1981), 316–41.

25 John Boyer, *Culture and Political Crisis in Vienna: Christian Socialism in Power, 1897–1918* (Chicago, 1995), 19–22.

26 Brigitte Hamann, *Hitlers Wien: Lehrjahre eines Diktators* (Munich, 1998), chap. 10.

27 T. Mills Kelly, *Without Remorse: Czech National Socialism in Late-Habsburg Austria* (New York, 2006).

28 Andrew Whiteside, *Austrian National Socialism Before 1918* (The Hague, 1962), 112–13.

29 Don Rawson, *Russian Rightists and the Revolution of 1905* (Cambridge, 1995), esp. 56–61.

30 Hans Rogger, "Was There a Russian Fascism? The Union of Russian People," *JMH* 36 (1964): 398–415.

31 Walter Laqueur, *Black Hundred: The Rise of the Extreme Right in Russia* (New York, 1993); George Gilbert, *The Radical Right in Late Imperial Russia: Dreams of a True Fatherland?* (New York, 2016), esp. 8–10.

32 See Edmund Levin, *A Child of Christian Blood: Murder and Conspiracy in Tsarist Russia* (New York, 2014), esp. 35–39, 51–55.

33 Peter Rutkoff, *Revanche and Revision: The Ligue des Patriotes and the Origins of the Radical Right in France, 1882–1900* (Athens, 1981).

34 Kevin Passmore, *The Right in France from the Third Republic to Vichy* (Oxford, 2013), 68–70.

35 Frederic Seager, *The Boulanger Affair: Political Crossroad of France, 1886–1889* (Ithaca, 1969), 27–30.

36 Patrick Hutton, "Popular Boulangism and the Advent of Mass Politics in France, 1886–1890," *JCH* 11 (1976): 85–106.

37 Patrick Hutton, *The Cult of the Revolutionary Tradition: The Blanquists in French Politics, 1864–1893* (Berkeley, 1981), esp. 143–61.

38 Philip Nord, *The Politics of Resentment: Shopkeeper Protest in Nineteenth-Century Paris* (Princeton, 1986), 302–50.

39 William Irvine, *The Boulanger Affair Reconsidered* (Oxford, 1989), 122–23.

40 Frederick Busi, *The Pope of Antisemitism: The Career and Legacy of Edouard-Adolphe Drumont* (Washington, DC, 1986).

41 David Lewis, *Prisoners of Honor: The Dreyfus Affair* (New York, 1994), 213–14.

42 Ruth Harris, *Dreyfus: Politics, Emotion, and the Scandal of the Century* (New York, 2010), 105–34.

43 For an extensive exploration of these divisions, see Frederick Brown, *For the Soul of France: Culture Wars in the Age of Dreyfus* (New York, 2011).

44 On Dreyfus's life, see Michael Burns, *Dreyfus: A Family Affair* (New York, 1993).

45 Eugen Weber, *Action Française: Royalism and Reaction in Twentieth-Century France* (Stanford, 1962), 18–20.

46 See esp. Michael Sutton, *Nationalism, Positivism, Catholicism: The Politics of Charles Maurras and French Catholics, 1890–1914* (Cambridge, 1982).

47 Ernst Nolte, *The Three Faces of Fascism: Action Française, Italian Fascism, National Socialism* (New York, 1966).

48 Zeev Sternhell, *Neither Right nor Left: Fascist Ideology in France* (Princeton, 1986); Zeev Sternhell, *The Birth of Fascist Ideology: From Cultural Rebellion to Political Revolution* (Princeton, 1994).

49 Eugen Weber, "Nationalism, Socialism, and National Socialism in France," *FHS* 2 (1962): 273–307.

50 As Stanley Payne has noted, Barrès "tried to combine the search for energy and a vital style of life with national rootedness and a sort of Darwinian racism. His nationalism stressed cross-class interests"; Stanley Payne, *A History of Fascism, 1914–1945* (Madison, 1995), 46.

51 George Mosse, "The French Right and the Working Classes: Les Jaunes," *JCH* 7 (1972): 185–208.

52 Shlomo Aveneri, *Herzl: Theodor Herzl and the Foundation of the Jewish State* (London, 2013), 114–40.

53 From Theodor Herzl, *A Jewish State*, trans. Sylvie D'Avigdor (New York, 1904), xvi–xvii, 4–5.

54 The term "Zionism" had been initially coined by the Austrian Jewish journalist Nathan Birnbaum around 1890; see Jess Olson, *Nathan Birnbaum and Jewish Modernity: Architect of Zionism, Yiddishism, and Orthodoxy* (Stanford, 2013), 44–45.

55 John C.G. Röhl, "Herzl and Kaiser Wilhelm II: A German Protectorate in Palestine?" in Ritchie Robertson and E. Timms, eds., *Theodor Herzl and the Origins of Zionism* (Edinburgh, 1997), 27–35.

56 R.L. Trask, *The History of Basque* (London, 1997), 35–36.

57 Daniele Conversi notes that Arana's goal was "not so much to preserve the language as to preserve a sense of 'unique' Basque racial purity"; Daniele Conversi, *The Basques, the Catalans, and Spain: Alternative Routes to Nationalist Mobilization* (Reno, 1997), 60.

58 Angel Smith, *The Origins of Catalan Nationalism, 1770–1880* (Houndmills, 2014), 8–38.

59 Jaume Subirana, "National Poets and Universal Catalans," in J. Manuel Barbeito et al., eds., *National Identities and European Literatures* (New York, 2008), 248–49.

60 See esp. Giovanni Cattini, "Myths and Symbols in the Political Culture of Catalan Nationalism, 1880–1914," *Nations and Nationalism* 21 (2015): 445–60.

61 Josep Llobera, "The Idea of *Volksgeist* in the Formation of Catalan Nationalist Ideology," *Ethnic and Racial Studies* 6 (1983): 332–50; also Josep Llobera, *Foundations of National Identity: From Catalonia to Europe* (New York, 2004), 78–79.

62 See Sune Laegaard, "Liberal Nationalism and the Nationalization of Liberal Values," *Nations and Nationalism* 13 (2007): 37–55.

63 France. K Offen, "Depopulation, Nationalism, and Feminism in fin-de-siècle France," *AHR* 89 (1984): 648–76; Repp, *Reformers, Critics, and the Paths of German Modernity* (Cambridge, MA, 2000).

64 Christopher Clark, *Sleepwalkers: How Europe Went to War in 1914* (London, 2012).

65 See also Sean McMeekin, *The Russian Origins of the First World War* (Cambridge, MA, 2013).

66 David MacKenzie, *Apis, the Congenial Conspirator: The Life of Colonel Dragutin T. Dimitrijević* (Boulder, 1989), 41–49.

67 See more generally Mary Sparks, *The Development of Austro-Hungarian Sarajevo, 1878–1918* (London, 2014).

68 David MacKenzie, "Serbia as Piedmont and the Yugoslav Idea, 1804–1914," *East European Quarterly* 28 (1994): 155–82.

69 Henry Gilfond, *The Black Hand at Sarajevo* (Indianapolis, 1975).

70 Barbara Tuchman, *The Guns of August: The Outbreak of World War I* (New York, 1962), 12–13.

71 Mark Hewitson, *Germany and the Causes of the First World War* (Oxford, 2004), 65.

72 Friedrich Bernhardi, *Germany and the Next War*, trans. Allen Powles (New York, 1914), 16–19.

73 Quoted in Walter Adamson, *Avant-Garde Florence: From Modernism to Fascism* (Cambridge, MA, 1993), 88.

74 Günter Berghaus, *Futurism and Politics: Between Anarchist Rebellion and Fascist Reaction* (New York, 1996).

75 Alexander DeGrand, *The Italian Nationalist Association and the Rise of Fascism* (Lincoln, 1978), esp. 122–23.

76 Payne, *A History of Fascism, 1914–1945*, 63.

77 Cinzia Sartini Blum, *The Other Modernism: F.T. Marinetti's Futurist Fiction of Power* (Berkeley, 1996).

78 Adrian Lyttleton, ed., *Italian Fascisms from Pareto to Gentile* (New York, 1975), 212.

79 Mark Antliff, *Avant-Garde Fascism: The Mobilization of Myth, Art, and Culture in France, 1909–1939* (Durham, 2007), chaps. 2–3.

80 Yvonne Servais, *Charles Péguy: The Pursuit of Salvation* (Cork, 1953).

81 See Robert Wohl, *The Generation of 1914* (Cambridge, MA, 1979), 5–41.

82 Under the pseudonym of Agathon Henri Massis and Alfred de Tarde, "Young People of Today," in John Boyer, ed., *University of Chicago Readings in Western Civilization*, vol. 9, 16, 22–25, 34–35.

83 David Sobek, *The Causes of War* (London, 2009), 131.

84 Edward Erickson, *Defeat in Detail: The Ottoman Army in the Balkans, 1912–1913* (Westport, 2003), 211–42; On the Ottoman perspective in the context of nationalism, see Eyal Ginio, "Mobilizing the Ottoman Nation during the Balkan Wars, 1912–1913," *War in History* 12 (2005): 156–77.

85   S. Skendi, *The Albanian National Awakening, 1878–1912* (Princeton, 1967), 438–63.

86   Richard Hull, *The Balkan Wars, 1912–1913: Prelude to the First World War* (New York, 2002).

87   Hannah Arendt, *The Origins of Totalitarianism* (New York, 1951), 267.

88   Lavender Cassels, *The Archduke and the Assassin* (London, 1984).

89   On the various policy implications of the assassination, see Samuel Williamson, "Influence, Power, and the Policy Process: The Case of Franz Ferdinand, 1906–1914," *Historical Journal* 17 (1974): 417–34.

90   Sean McMeekin, *July 1914: Countdown to War* (New York, 2013), 23–46.

91   Ulrich Trumpener, "War Premeditated? German Intelligence Operations in July 1914," *CEH* 9 (1976): 58–85; Imanuel Geiss, "The Outbreak of the First World War and German War Aims," *JCH* 1 (1966): 75–91.

92   George F. Kennan, *The Fateful Alliance: France, Russia, and the Coming of the First World War* (Manchester, 1984).

93   For a harsh critique of British involvement, see Niall Ferguson, *The Pity of War: Explaining World War I* (New York, 1998).

94   For a critical view of this image of euphoria, see Jeffrey Verhey, *The Spirit of 1914: Militarism, Myth, and Mobilization in Germany* (Cambridge, 2000); also Ferguson, *The Pity of War*, 174–211.

95   On the much more sober responses to mobilization in the German countryside, see Benjamin Ziemann, *War Experiences in Rural Germany, 1914–1923* (Oxford, 2007), esp. 15–28.

96   On the confluence of Jaurès's funeral and mobilization euphoria, see Peter Jackson, *Beyond the Balance of Power: France and the Politics of National Security in the Era of the First World War* (Cambridge, 2013), 87–88.

97   The common view of widespread national enthusiasm for war in the British context has also been challenged; see Catriona Pennell, *A Kingdom United: Popular Responses to the Outbreak of the First World War in Britain and Ireland* (Oxford, 2012), 22–56; see also more generally Adam Hochschild, *To End All Wars: How the First World War Divided Britain* (New York, 2011).

98   Norman Dubeski, "Victory Myths and the Battle of Tannenberg," *Journal of Political and Military Sociology* 29 (2001): 282–92.

99   Anna Von der Goltz, *Hindenburg: Power, Myth, and the Rise of the Nazis* (Oxford, 2009), 14–42.

100   For a partial debunking of the Taxis of the Marne myth, see esp. Holger Herwig, *The Marne, 1914* (New York, 2011), 261–64.

101   Annette Becker, *War and Faith: The Religious Imagination in France, 1914–1930* (Oxford, 1998).

102   John Ellis, *Eye-Deep in Hell: Trench Warfare in World War I* (Baltimore, 1976).

103   Ernst Jünger, *Storm of Steel*, trans. Michael Hofmann (New York, 2004).

104   For a classic account of the brutalities of trench warfare, see Eric Leed, *No Man's Land: Combat and Identity in World War I* (Cambridge, 1981).

105 Martin Gilbert, *The Somme: Heroism and Horror in the First World War* (New York, 2007).

106 Paul Fussell, *The Great War and Modern Memory* (Oxford, 1977).

107 Philipp Witkop, ed., *German Students' War Letters*, trans. A.F. Wedd (London, 1929), 1–2, 17–18, 368.

108 See esp. Taner Akçam, *The Young Turks' Crime Against Humanity: The Armenian Genocide and Ethnic Cleansing in the Ottoman Empire* (Princeton, 2012).

109 See Erik Zürcher, *The Young Turk Legacy and Nation Building: From the Ottoman Empire to Atatürk's Turkey* (London, 2010), 73–84.

110 Şükrü Hanioğlu, "Turkish Nationalism and the Young Turks, 1897–1908," in Fatma Müge Göçek, ed., *Social Constructions of Nationalism in the Middle East* (Albany, 2002), 85–98; David Fromkin, *A Peace to End All Peace: The Fall of the Ottoman Empire and the Creation of the Modern Middle East* (New York, 1989), 40–49.

111 Donald Bloxham, *The Great Game of Genocide: Imperialism, Nationalism, and the Destruction of the Ottoman Armenians* (Oxford, 2005).

112 Peter Balakian, *The Burning Tigris: The Armenian Genocide and America's Response* (New York, 2003), 378.

113 See R.J.B. Bosworth, *Italy and the Approach of the First World War* (London, 1983); Simon Mark Jones, *Domestic Factors in Italian Intervention in the First World War* (New York, 1986).

114 John Gooch, *The Italian Army and the First World War* (Cambridge, 2014), 53–96.

115 Alvin Jackson, *Home Rule: An Irish History, 1800–2000* (Oxford, 2003), 24–37.

116 Paul Bew, *Enigma: A New Life of Charles Stewart Parnell* (Dublin, 2011).

117 Alan O'Day, *Irish Home Rule, 1867–1921* (Manchester, 1998), 92–121.

118 Ibid., 240–65.

119 Leon Ó'Broin, *Revolutionary Underground: The Story of the Irish Republican Brotherhood, 1858–1924* (Lanham, 1976).

120 Tom Corfe, *The Phoenix Park Murders: Conflict, Compromise, and Tragedy in Ireland, 1879–1882* (London, 1968).

121 Brian Feeney, *Sinn Féin: A Hundred Turbulent Years* (Madison, 2003), 18–43.

122 See esp. Joseph Finnan, *John Redmond and Irish Unity, 1912–1918* (Syracuse, 2004).

123 For details see Fearghal McGarry, *The Rising: Ireland, Easter 1916* (Oxford, 2010).

124 Seán Farrell Moran, *Patrick Pearse and the Mind of the Easter Rising, 1916* (Washington, DC, 1994), 2.

125 In early 1917, German foreign minister Arthur Zimmermann offered Mexico territorial rewards in Texas, New Mexico, and Arizona if Mexico agreed to attack the United States from the south; see Justus Doenecke, *Nothing Less*

Than War: A New History of America's Entry into World War I (Lexington, 2014).

126   David Welch, *Germany and Propaganda in World War I: Pacifism, Mobilization, and Total War* (London, 2014), 238–52.

127   Nick Lloyd, *Hundred Days: The Campaign that Ended World War I* (New York, 2014).

128   Lothar Machtan, "Germany's Ersatz Kaiser? The Political Opportunities of Max von Baden," in Heidi Mehrkens and Frank Lorenz Müller, eds., *Sons and Heirs: Succession and Political Culture in Nineteenth-Century Europe* (Houndmills, 2015), 263–79.

129   Wolfgang Schivelbusch, *The Culture of Defeat: On National Trauma, Mourning, and Recovery* (New York, 2001), 203–7.

130   Eric Weitz, "From the Vienna to the Paris System: International Politics and the Entangled Histories of Human Rights, Forced Deportations, and Civilizing Missions," *AHR* 113 (2008): 1313–43.

131   Margaret MacMillan, *Paris 1919: Six Months That Changed the World* (New York, 2001), esp. 53–108.

132   Fritz Fischer, *Germany's Aims in the First World War* (New York, 1968).

133   Subsequent conferences established the figure of $35 billion, but that figure itself was altered several times. Germany did not finish paying its reparations obligations from the First World War until the fall of 2010; for an account of the early payments (and non-payments) see Leonard Gomes, *German Reparations, 1919–1932: A Historical Survey* (Houndmills, 2010).

134   See e.g. R.W. Connell, *Masculinities* (Berkeley, 2005).

135   Jason Crouthamel, *An Intimate History of the Front: Masculinity, Sexuality, and German Soldiers in the First World War* (Houndmills, 2014), 147–69.

136   Jessica Meyer, *Men of War: The First World War and Masculinity in Britain* (Houndmills, 2009), 97–127.

137   Carole Poore, *Disability in Twentieth Century German Culture* (Ann Arbor, 2007), esp. 7–18; Heather Perry, *Recycling the Disabled: Army, Medicine, and Modernity in World War I Germany* (Manchester, 2014); Deborah Cohen, *The War Come Home: Disabled Veterans in Britain and Germany, 1914–1939* (Berkeley, 2001).

138   Paul Lerner, *Hysterical Men: War, Psychiatry, and the Politics of Trauma in Germany, 1890–1930* (Ithaca, 2003); Fiona Reid, *Broken Men: Shell Shock, Treatment, and Recovery in Britain, 1914–1930* (London, 2010), esp. 13–14.

139   Albrecht Ritschl, "The Pity of Peace: Germany's Economy at War," in Stephen Broadberry and Mark Harrison, eds., *The Economies of World War I* (Cambridge, 2005), 41–76.

Chapter 6

1   See Susan Pedersen, *The Guardians: The League of Nations and the Crisis of Empire* (Oxford, 2015).

2   Patricia Clavin, "Europe and the League of Nations," in Robert Gerwarth, ed., *Twisted Paths: Europe, 1914–1945* (Oxford, 2008), 325; see also Clavin *Securing the World Economy: The Reinvention of the League of Nations, 1920–1946* (Oxford, 2013).

3   Lindgren, *Norway-Sweden*, 112–14.

4   Fridtjof Nansen, *Norge og foreningen med Sverige* (Oslo, 1905).

5   In his overview of the roots of interwar humanitarianism, Bruno Cabanes devotes an entire chapter to Nansen; Cabanes, *The Great War and the Origins of Humanitarianism, 1918–1924* (Cambridge, 2014), 133–88.

6   Rebecka Lettevall, "Cosmopolitanism in Practice: Perspectives on the Nansen Passports," in Ulrike Ziemer and Sean Roberts, eds., *East European Diasporas, Migration, and Cosmopolitanism* (New York, 2013), 13–24.

7   Mona Siegel, *The Moral Disarmament of France: Education, Pacifism, and Patriotism, 1914–1930* (Cambridge, 2004).

8   Norman Ingram, *The Politics of Dissent: Pacifism in France, 1919–1939* (Oxford, 1991).

9   Gearóid Barry, *The Disarmament of Hatred: Marc Sangnier, French Catholicism, and the Legacy of the First World War, 1914–1945* (New York, 2012).

10 Daniel Laqua, *The Age of Internationalism and Belgium, 1880–1930* (Manchester, 2013), 1.

11 Martin Ceadel, *Pacifism in Britain, 1914–1945* (Oxford, 1980), 1.

12 Ceadel, *Semi-Detached Idealists: The British Peace Movement and International Relations, 1854–1945* (Oxford, 2000), esp. 187–238.

13 Baldwin, *On England, and Other Addresses* (London, 1926), 2–9.

14 See Passmore, *The Right in France from the Third Republic to Vichy*, 206–33.

15 On the fascinating yet tragic case of Deschanel, see Gregory Thomas, *Treating the Trauma of the Great War: Soldiers, Civilians, and Psychiatry in France, 1914–1940* (Baton Rouge, 2009), 1–6.

16 Benjamin Martin, *France and the Apres Guerre, 1918–1924* (Baton Rouge, 1999), 51–52.

17 Walter McDougall, *France's Rhineland Policy, 1914–1924* (Princeton, 1978), esp. 250–92.

18 Paul Jankowsky, *Stavisky: A Confidence Man in the Republic of Virtue* (Ithaca, 2002), esp. 221–22.

19 Jonathan Vance, *Death So Noble: Memory, Meaning, and the First World War* (Vancouver, 2000).

20 Jay Winter, *Sites of Memory, Sites of Mourning: The Great War in European Cultural History* (Cambridge, 1995), 204–22.

21 George Mosse, *Fallen Soldiers: Reshaping the Memory of the World Wars* (Oxford, 1990), 32–33.

22 Philip Longworth, *The Unending Vigil: A History of the Commonwealth War Graves Commission, 1917–1967* (London, 1967).

23   Gaynor Kavanaugh, "Museum as Memorial: The Origins of the Imperial War Museum," *JCH* 23 (1988): 77–97.

24   Terry Charman, "A Museum of Man's Greatest Lunatic Folly: The Imperial War Museum and Its Commemoration of the Great War," in Michael Howard, ed., *A Part of History: Aspects of the British Experience of the First World War* (London, 2008), esp. 99–103.

25   Paul Cornish, "Sacred Relics: Objects in the Imperial War Museum, 1917–1939," in Nicholas Saunders, ed., *Matters of Conflict: Material Culture, Memory, and the First World War* (New York, 2004), 35–50.

26   Mark Connelly, *The Great War, Memory, and Ritual: Commemoration in the City and East London, 1916–1939* (Woodbridge, 2002).

27   David Lloyd, *Battlefield Tourism: Pilgrimage and the Commemoration of the Great War in Britain, Australia, and Canada, 1919–1939* (Oxford, 1998).

28   Gabriel Koureas, *Memory, Masculinity, and National Identity in British Visual Culture* (Farnham, 2007), 79–80.

29   See esp. Michèle Barrett, "Death and the Afterlife: Britain's Colonies and Dominions," in Santanu Das, ed., *Race, Empire, and First World War Writing* (Cambridge, 2011), 301–20.

30   Daniel Sherman, "Art, Commerce, and the Production of Memory in France after World War I," in John R. Gillis, ed., *Commemorations: The Politics of National Identity* (Princeton, NJ, 1996), 186–214.

31   Christopher Fischer, "National Sacrifices, Local Losses: Politics and Commemoration in Interwar Alsace," in Patricia Lorcin and Daniel Brewer, eds., *France and Its Spaces of War: Experience, Memory, Image* (New York, 2009), 133–48; Alice Conklin, *A Mission to Civilize: The Republican Idea of Empire in France and West Africa, 1895–1930* (Stanford, 1997), esp. 142–71.

32   Karen Shelby, *Flemish Nationalism and the Great War* (New York, 2014).

33   Nuala Johnson, *Ireland, the Great War, and the Geography of Remembrance* (Cambridge, 2003).

34   Michael Laffan, *The Resurrection of Ireland: The Sinn Féin Party, 1916–1923* (Cambridge, 1999), 160–68.

35   Robert Lynch, *Revolutionary Ireland, 1912–1925* (London, 2015), 61–62; the Declaration is reprinted in ibid., Document 7.

36   Gerard Noonan, *The IRA in Britain: "In the Heart of Enemy Lines"* (Liverpool, 2014).

37   Jason Knirck, *Imagining Ireland's Independence* (Lanham, 2006), esp. 75–109.

38   Thomas Hennessey, *A History of Northern Ireland* (New York, 1999), 6–20.

39   On the broader social and political elements of the war, see Gavin Foster, *The Irish Civil War and Society* (Houndmills, 2015).

40   Maryann Gialanella Valiulis, *Portrait of a Revolutionary: General Richard Mulcahy and the Founding of the Irish Free State* (Lexington, 1992), 172–98.

41   Richard Dunphy, *The Making of Fianna Fáil Power in Ireland, 1923–1948* (Oxford, 1995).

42 See Shlomo Ben-Ami, *Fascism from Above: The Dictatorship of Primo de Rivera in Spain, 1923–1930* (Oxford, 1983), which differentiates between Spanish authoritarianism and full-blown fascism.

43 Arendt, *The Origins of Totalitarianism*, 269–89; Roshwald, *Ethnic Nationalism*, 198–217. Aviel Roshwald, *Ethnic Nationalism and the Fall of Empires* (London, 2001), 198-217.

44 On the broader context, see John W. Boyer, "Silent War and Bitter Peace: The Austrian Revolution of 1918," *Austrian History Yearbook* 34 (2003): 1–56.

45 Quoted in Peter Thaler, *The Ambivalence of Identity: The Austrian Experience of Nation-Building in a Modern Society* (West Lafayette, 2001), 68–69.

46 Quoted in Thomas Čapek, "The Past and the Future of Bohemia," *Czechoslovak Review* 3:1 (January 1919): 4.

47 Mark Mazower, "Minorities and the League of Nations in Interwar Europe," *Daedalus* 126 (1997): 47–63.

48 "Czechoslovak Republic Consolidated," *Czechoslovak Review* 3:1 (January 1919): 1.

49 *Czechoslovak Review* 3:12 (December 1919): 385–86.

50 Bennett Kovrig, *The Hungarian People's Republic* (Baltimore, 1970), 15–16.

51 György Borsányi, *The Life of a Communist Revolutionary: Bela Kun* (Boulder, 1993).

52 Paul Hanebrink, *In Defense of Christian Hungary: Religion, Nationalism, and Antisemitism, 1890–1944* (Ithaca, 2006), 86–89; also Robert Gerwarth, "Fighting the Red Beast: Counter-Revolutionary Violence in the Defeated States of Central Europe," in Gerwarth and John Horne, eds., *War in Peace: Paramilitary Violence in Europe After the Great War* (Oxford, 2012), esp. 63–69.

53 Thomas Sakmyster, *Hungary's Admiral on Horseback: Miklós Horthy, 1918–1944* (New York, 1994).

54 Victoria Brown, "The Movement for Reform in Rumania after World War I: The Parliamentary Bloc Government of 1919–1920," *Slavic Review* 38 (1979): 456–72.

55 V. Drapac, *Constructing Yugoslavia: A Transnational History* (Houndmills, 2010), 96–99.

56 Ivo Banac, *The National Question in Yugoslavia* (Ithaca, 1984), 393–405.

57 Drapac, *Constructing Yugoslavia: A Transnational History*, 135–41. On the assassination, see Allen Roberts, *The Turning Point: The Assassination of Louis Barthou and King Alexander I of Yugoslavia* (New York, 1970).

58 John Bell, *Peasants in Power: Alexander Stamboliski and the Bulgarian Agrarian National Union* (Princeton, 1977).

59 George Mavrogordatos, *Stillborn Republic: Social Coalitions and Party Strategies in Greece, 1922–1936* (Berkeley, 1983), 33–34.

60 Mieczyslaw Biskupski, "The Invention of Modern Poland: Pilsudski and the Politics of Symbolism," in Stanislav Kirschbaum, ed., *Central European History and the European Union* (New York, 2007), 102–22.

61 Raymond Pearson, *National Minorities in Eastern Europe, 1848–1945* (Houndmills, 1983), 148–72.

62 Brian Porter, *When Nationalism Began to Hate: Imagining Modern Politics in Nineteenth-Century Poland* (Oxford, 2000), 10.

63 Alfonsas Eidintas, *Antanas Smetona and His Lithuania: From the National Liberation Movement to an Authoritarian Regime, 1893–1940* (Leiden, 2015), 58–65.

64 Vejas Liulevicius, *War Land on the Eastern Front: Culture, National Identity, and German Occupation in World War I* (Cambridge, 2000), 201–05.

65 V. Stanley Vardys and Judith Sedaitis, *Lithuania: The Rebel Nation* (Boulder, 1997), 28–45.

66 Eidintas, *Antanas Smetona and His Lithuania*, 178–201. On the authoritarian turn more generally, see Algimantas Kasparavičius, "The Historical Experience of the Twentieth Century: Authoritarianism and Totalitarianism in Lithuania," in Jerzy Borejsza and Klaus Ziemer, eds., *Totalitarian and Authoritarian Regimes in Europe* (New York, 2006), 297–312.

67 John Wheeler Bennett, *The Treaty of Brest-Litovsk and Germany's Eastern Policy* (Oxford, 1939).

68 Smith, "One Day There Will Be an Estonian State," in David Smith et al., eds., *The Baltic States: Estonia, Latvia, and Lithuania* (London, 2002), 14.

69 Koehl, "A Prelude to Hitler's Greater Germany," *AHR* 59 (1953): 43–65.

70 See Deniss Hanovs and Valdis Tēraudkalns, *Ultimate Freedom—No Choice: The Culture of Authoritarianism in Latvia, 1934–1940* (Leiden, 2013).

71 Mark Mazower, *Dark Continent: Europe's Twentieth Century* (New York, 1998), esp. 138–81.

72 Ibid., xii.

73 Timothy Snyder, *Bloodlands: Europe Between Hitler and Stalin* (New York, 2010).

74 Domenico Settembrini, "Mussolini and the Legacy of Revolutionary Socialism," *JCH* 11 (1976): 239–68.

75 On his war service and its subsequent exaggeration, see Peter Neville, *Mussolini* (London, 2004), 36.

76 Julie Dashwood, "Futurism and Fascism," *Italian Studies* 27 (1972): 91–103.

77 Barbara Spackman, *Fascist Virilities: Rhetoric, Ideology, and Social Fantasy in Italy* (Minneapolis, 1996), 22–24.

78 Michael Ebner, *Ordinary Violence in Mussolini's Italy* (Cambridge, 2011), 23–47.

79 Alexander De Grand, *The Hunchback's Tailor: Giovanni Giolitti and Liberal Italy from the Challenge of Mass Politics to the Rise of Fascism, 1882–1922* (Westport, 2001), 242–48.

80 On the march on Rome in the context of Mussolini's fixation on Rome, see Borden Painter, *Mussolini's Rome: Rebuilding the Eternal City* (New York, 2005), 3–4.

81 From Michael Oakeshott, ed., *The Social and Political Doctrines of Contemporary Europe* (Cambridge, 1947), 164–67.

82 Mauro Canali, "The Matteotti Murder and the Origins of Mussolini's Totalitarian Fascist Regime in Italy," *Journal of Modern Italian Studies* 14 (2009); 143–67.

83 No firm evidence has emerged to show that Mussolini directly ordered the hit, and it is possible that it was initiated by more radical elements within the fascist leadership; see John Pollard, *The Fascist Experience in Italy* (London, 1998), 51–52.

84 Paul Corner, *The Fascist Party and Popular Opinion in Mussolini's Italy* (Oxford, 2013), 1–2.

85 Adrian Lyttelton, *The Seizure of Power: Fascism in Italy, 1919–1929*, 3rd ed. (New York, 2004), 165–68.

86 David Kertzer, *The Pope and Mussolini* (New York, 2014), 98–115.

87 Adolf Hitler, *Mein Kampf*, trans. Ralph Mannheim (Boston, 1943; orig. 1925), 283.

88 "Doctrine of Fascism," in Oakeshott, ed., *The Social and Political Doctrines of Contemporary Europe*, 65–66.

89 On the influence of Rousseau, see Henry Silton Harris, *The Social Philosophy of Giovanni Gentile* (Urbana, 1960); also A. James Gregor, *Mussolini's Intellectuals: Fascist Social and Political Thought* (Princeton, 2005), 147–48.

90 Hitler, *Mein Kampf*, 170–71.

91 Michele Sarfatti, *The Jews in Mussolini's Italy* (Madison, 2006).

92 Hitler, *Mein Kampf*, 13.

93 Frederic Spotts, *Hitler and the Power of Aesthetics* (New York, 2002), 123–37.

94 Brigitte Hamann, *Hitler's Vienna: A Dictator's Apprenticeship* (Oxford, 1999), 52–66; Ian Kershaw, *Hitler, 1889–1936: Hubris* (New York, 1998), 60–67.

95 Peter Fritzsche, *Germans into Nazis* (Cambridge, MA, 1998), 1–10.

96 Thomas Weber, *Hitler's First War: Adolf Hitler, the Men of the List Regiment, and the First World War* (Oxford, 2010), 140–41.

97 Adam Seipp, *The Ordeal of Peace: Demobilization and the Urban Experience in Britain and Germany, 1917–1921* (Farnham, 2009), 177–80.

98 Dietrich Orlow, *The Nazi Party, 1919–1945* (New York, 2013), 33–43.

99 So named because it began with the capture of Bavarian government leaders during a meeting in a local beer hall; Harold Gorden, *Hitler and the Beer Hall Putsch* (Princeton, 1972).

100 Richard Rolfs, *Sorcerer's Apprentice: The Life of Franz von Papen* (Washington, DC, 1995).

101 Hans Mommsen, "The Reichstag Fire and Its Political Consequences," in H.W. Koch, ed., *Aspects of the Third Reich* (London, 1984), 62–80.

102 Harold Marcuse, *Legacies of Dachau: The Uses and Abuses of a Concentration Camp, 1933–2001* (Cambridge, 2001), 21–26.

103 While that was the largest vote total gained by any party in German history to that point, the important fact is that, even in March 1933, more than 56 percent of Germans were voting for parties other than the Nazis.

104 The Enabling Act gave Hitler authority to legislate by decree, making parliament superfluous, and to negotiate with foreign powers and, if need be, go to war on his own authority, without consulting parliament; see the prescient early survey, Karl Loewenstein, "Dictatorship and the German Constitution, 1933–1937," *University of Chicago Law Review* 4 (1937): 537–74.

105 Max Gallo, *The Night of Long Knives* (New York, 1972).

106 Eleanor Hancock, "The Purge of the SA Reconsidered: An Old Putschist Trick?" *CEH* 44 (2011): 669–83.

107 Mary Devereaux, "Beauty and Evil: The Case of Leni Riefenstahl's *Triumph of the Will*," in Jerrold Levinson, ed., *Aesthetics and Ethics: Essays at the Intersection* (Cambridge, 1998), 227–56.

108 Richard Meran Barsam, *Filmguide to Triumph of the Will* (Bloomington, 1975), 44.

109 Martin Loiperdinger and David Culbert, "Leni Riefenstahl, the SA, and the Nazi Party Rally Films, Nuremberg, 1933–1934," *Historical Journal of Film, Radio, and Television* 8 (1988): 3–38.

110 On the conflicted legacy of the Ehrentempel and the sarcophagi, see Gavriel Rosenfeld, *Munich and Memory: Architecture, Monuments, and the Legacy of the Third Reich* (Berkeley, 2000), 87–92.

111 Rogers Brubaker, *Nationalism Reframed* (Cambridge, 1996), 26–29.

112 Ronald Suny, *The Soviet Experience* (Oxford, 1998), 141.

113 Yuri Slezkine, "The USSR as a Communal Apartment, or How a Socialist State Promoted Ethnic Particularism," *Slavic Review* 53 (1994): 414–52.

114 Terry Martin, *The Affirmative Action Empire: Nations and Nationalism in the Soviet Union, 1923–1939* (Ithaca, 2001).

115 Zimmer, *Nationalism in Europe, 1890–1940*, 119.

116 Suny, *The Soviet Experience*, 218–31.

117 C.E. Edmondson, *The Heimwehr and Austrian Politics, 1918–1936* (Athens, 1982).

118 Tim Kirk, "Fascism and Austrofascism," in Günter Bischof et al., eds., *The Dollfuss-Schuschnigg Era in Austria* (New Brunswick, 2003), 10–31.

119 Laura Gellot, *The Catholic Church and the Authoritarian Regime in Austria, 1933–1938* (New York, 1987).

120 John Lauridsen, *Nazism and the Radical Right in Austria, 1918–1934* (Copenhagen, 2007), 417–30.

121 Payne, *A History of Fascism*, 250–51.

122 Evan Burr Bukey, *Hitler's Austria: Popular Sentiment in the Nazi Era, 1938–1945* (Chapel Hill, 2000), 25–41.

123 Maria Ormos, *Hungary in the Age of the Two World Wars, 1914–1945* (New York, 2007), 265–85.

124 Nicholas Nagy-Talavera, *The Green Shirts and the Others: A History of Fascism in Hungary and Rumania* (Stanford, 1970).

125 Irina Livezeanu, *Cultural Politics in Greater Romania: Regionalism, Nation Building and Ethnic Politics* (Ithaca, 1995).

126 Paul Quinlan, *The Playboy King: Carol II of Romania* (Westport, 1995).

127 Radu Ioanid, *The Sword of the Archangel: Fascist Ideology in Romania* (Boulder, 1990).

128 On the initiation rituals, see Payne, *A History of Fascism*, 285; see also Eugen Weber, "The Men of the Archangel," *JCH* 1 (1966): 101–26.

129 Radu Ioanid, *The Holocaust in Romania* (Chicago, 2000); Dennis Deletant, *Hitler's Forgotten Ally: Ion Antonescu and His Regime, 1940–1944* (New York, 2006).

130 Diamantino Machado, *The Structure of Portuguese Society: The Failure of Fascism* (Westport, 1991).

131 Alejandro Quiroga, *Making Spaniards: Primo de Rivera and the Nationalization of the Masses, 1923–1930* (Houndmills, 2007).

132 Martin Blinkhorn, *Fascism and the Right in Europe, 1919–1945* (London, 2000), 54–57.

133 Payne, *A History of Fascism*, 262–63.

134 Antony Beevor, *The Battle for Spain: The Spanish Civil War, 1936–1939* (New York, 1982), 96–97.

135 Christopher Othen, *Franco's International Brigades: Adventurers, Fascists, and Christian Crusaders in the Spanish Civil War* (New York, 2013).

136 R. Dan Richardson, *Comintern Army: The International Brigades and the Spanish Civil War* (Lexington, 1982).

137 Robert Soucy, *French Fascism: The First Wave, 1924–1933* (New Haven, 1986); Samuel Kalman, *The Extreme Right in Interwar France: The Faisceau and the Croix de Feu* (Farnham, 2008).

138 Scholars have debated the extent to which the Croix de Feu should be seen as an outright fascist entity; William Irvine, "Fascism in France and the Strange Case of the Croix de Feu," *JMH* 63 (1991): 271–95; Robert Soucy, "French Fascism and the Croix de Feu: A Dissenting Interpretation," *JCH* 26 (1991): 159–88.

139 Robert Soucy, *French Fascism: The Second Wave, 1933–1939* (New Haven, 1997), 38–40.

140 Georges Valois, who had founded Le Faisceau, was later arrested by the Nazis and killed in the Bergen-Belsen camp, whereas François de la Rocque, after briefly supporting the collaborationist Vichy regime, was active in resistance circles and arrested by the Gestapo; see Jules Levey, "Georges Valois and the Faisceau: The Making and Breaking of a Fascist," *FHS* 8 (1973): 279–304.

141 William Brustein, "The Political Geography of Belgian Fascism: The Case of Rexism," *ASR* 53 (1988): 69–80.

142 Martin Conway, *Collaboration in Belgium: Léon Degrelle and the Rexist Movement, 1940–1944* (New Haven, 1993).

143 Jennifer Foray, "An Old Empire in a New Order: The Global Designs of the Dutch Nazi Party, 1931–1942," *EHQ* 43 (2013): 27–52.

144 On earlier stages of the Dutch-German Nazi relationship, Dietrich Orlow, "A Difficult Relationship of Unequal Relatives: The Dutch NSB and Nazi Germany, 1933–1940," *EHQ* 29 (1999): 349–80.

145 Stephen Dorril, *Blackshirt: Sir Oswald Mosley and British Fascism* (London, 2007).

146 Frank McDonough, *Hitler, Chamberlain, and Appeasement* (Cambridge, 2002).

147 For an insightful analysis that places the pact in the context of the longstanding German and Russian refusal to accept the legitimacy of the Polish nation-state created after the First World War, see Snyder, *Bloodlands*, 119–54.

148 John Mosier, *The Blitzkrieg Myth* (New York, 2003).

149 The primary military conflict in late 1939 and early 1940 was the so-called Winter War between the Soviet Union and Finland; see Gordon Sander, *The Hundred Day Winter War: Finland's Gallant Stand Against the Soviet Army* (Lawrence, 2013).

150 See the interesting account in Bertram Gordon, "Warfare and Tourism: Paris in World War II," *Annals of Tourism Research* 25 (1998): 616–38.

151 Richard Overy, *The Battle of Britain: The Myth and the Reality* (New York, 2000).

152 David Stahel, *Operation Barbarossa and Germany's Defeat in the East* (Cambridge, 2011), 139–52.

153 David Stahel, *Kiev 1941: Hitler's Battle for Supremacy in the East* (Cambridge, 2012).

154 For an extensive discussion of the decision-making timetable and varying scholarly assessments of it, see Christopher Browning, *The Origins of the Final Solution* (Lincoln, 2007), 309–51.

155 Thomas Kühne, *Belonging and Genocide: Hitler's Community, 1918–1945* (New Haven, 2010).

156 Christian Gerlach, "The Wannsee Conference, the Fate of German Jews, and Hitler's Decision in Principle to Eradicate All European Jews," *JMH* 70 (1998): 759–812.

157 Christopher Browning, *Ordinary Men* (New York, 1992), xv–xvi.

158 Karl Schleunes, *The Twisted Road to Auschwitz* (Chapel Hill, 1970).

159 Ibid., 62–91; also Saul Friedländer, *Nazi Germany and the Jews: The Years of Persecution, 1933–1939* (London, 1997), 20–24.

160 Dan Silverman, "Nazification of the German Bureaucracy Reconsidered: A Case Study," *JMH* 60 (1988): 496–539.

161 A reconvoluted formula identifying full Jews, half-Jews, and various levels of *Mischlinge* was constructed; see Marion Kaplan, *Between Dignity and Despair: Jewish Life in Nazi Germany* (Oxford, 1998), 74–93.

162 Herbert A. Strauss, "Jewish Emigration from Germany: Nazi Policies and Jewish Responses," *Leo Baeck Institute Yearbook* 25 (1980): 313–61.

163 Gordon Horwitz, *Ghettostadt: Łodz and the Making of a Nazi City* (Cambridge, MA, 2010); Yisrael Gutman, *The Jews of Warsaw* (Bloomington, 1989); also Dan Michman, ed., *The Emergence of Jewish Ghettos during the Holocaust* (Cambridge, 2011).

164 Richard Rhodes, *Masters of Death: The SS-Einsatzgruppen and the Invention of the Holocaust* (New York, 2002), esp. 5–11.

165 Christopher Browning, "Nazi Resettlement Policy and the Search for a Solution to the Jewish Question, 1939–1941," *GSR* 9 (1986): 497–519.

166 Eric Jennings, "Writing Madagascar Back into the Madagascar Plan," *HGS* 21 (2007): 187–217.

167 Browning, *Ordinary Men*, passim; Martin Dean, *Collaboration in the Holocaust: Crimes of the Local Police in Belorussia and Ukraine, 1941–1944* (New York, 2000).

168 Timothy Snyder, *Black Earth: The Holocaust as History and Warning* (New York, 2015), 42–43.

169 Yitzhak Arad, *Belzec, Sobibor, Treblinka: The Operation Reinhard Death Camps* (Bloomington, 1999).

170 Laurence Rees, *Auschwitz: A New History* (New York, 2006).

171 See Primo Levi, *Survival in Auschwitz* (New York, 1996).

172 Kühne, *Belonging and Genocide*, 4–8.

173 Götz Aly, *Hitler's Beneficiaries: Plunder, Racial War, and the Nazi Welfare State* (New York, 2006).

174 Michael Burleigh and Wolfgang Wippermann, *The Racial State: Germany, 1933–1945* (Cambridge, 1993).

175 Michael Burleigh, *Death and Deliverance: Euthanasia in Germany, 1900–1945* (Cambridge, 1995).

176 Michelle Mouton, *From Nurturing the Nation to Purifying the Volk: Weimar and Nazi Family Policy, 1918–1945* (Cambridge, 2007), 153–96, 215–27.

177 John Paul Himka, "Ukrainian Collaboration in the Extermination of the Jews during the Second World War," in Jonathan Frankel, ed., *The Fate of the European Jews, 1939–1945* (Oxford, 1997), 170–89.

178 Jan T. Gross, *Neighbors: The Destruction of the Jewish Community in Jedwabne, Poland* (Princeton, 2001).

179 Porter, *When Nationalism Learned to Hate*, 189–232.

180 Anthony Beevor, *Stalingrad: The Fateful Siege, 1942–1943* (New York, 1999).

181 MacGregor Knox, *Hitler's Italian Allies* (Cambridge, 2000), 1–3.

182 Greg Annussek, *Hitler's Raid to Save Mussolini* (New York, 2006).

183 Anthony Beevor, *The Fall of Berlin 1945* (New York, 2002), 354–69.

184 Robert Hilderbrand, *Dumbarton Oaks: The Origins of the United Nations and the Search for Postwar Security* (Chapel Hill, 1990).

Chapter 7

1 "Harold Denny, 56, Journalist, Dead," *NYT* (July 4, 1945), 13.

2 Denny, "The World Must Not Forget," *NYT* (May 6, 1945).

3 Mazower, *Dark Continent*, xi.

4 James Sheehan, *Where Have All the Soldiers Gone? The Transformation of Modern Europe* (Boston, 2008).

5 Breully, *Nationalism and the State*, 352–53.

6 David Beetham, "The Future of the Nation-State," in Gregor McLennan et al., eds., *The Idea of the Modern State* (Milton Keynes, 1984), 208–22.

7 Some scholars continued to predict the "end of the nation-state" well into the 1990s, particularly in regard to economic structures; see Kenichi Ohmae, *The End of the Nation-State: The Rise of Regional Economies* (New York, 1995).

8 Hobsbawm, *Nations and Nationalism Since 1780*, 2nd ed., 163–92.

9 Malcolm Anderson, *States and Nationalism in Europe Since 1945* (London, 2000); André Gerrits, *Nationalism in Europe since 1945* (New York, 2015).

10 Alan Milward, *The European Rescue of the Nation State* (Berkeley, 1992); see also William Wallace, "Rescue or Retreat? The Nation-State in Western Europe, 1945–1993," *Political Studies* 42 (1994): 52–76.

11 L. Douglas Keeney, *The Eleventh Hour: How Great Britain, the Soviet Union, and the U.S. Brokered the Unlikely Deal that Won the War* (New York, 2015).

12 S.M. Plokhy, *Yalta: The Price of Peace* (New York, 2010); Fraser Harbutt, *Yalta 1945: Europe and America at the Crossroads* (Cambridge, 2010).

13 William Hitchcock, *The Struggle for Europe: The Turbulent History of a Divided Continent* (New York, 2004), 19–25.

14 On the scholarly debate over "atomic diplomacy" and its impact on the hardening of the US position at Potsdam, see Gar Alperovitz, *Atomic Diplomacy, Hiroshima, and Potsdam: The Use of the Atomic Bomb and the American Confrontation with Soviet Power* (London, 1965); and Gregg Herken, *The Winning Weapon: The Atomic Bomb in the Cold War, 1945–1960* (Princeton, 1981), esp. 4–8.

15 John Fousek, *To Lead the Free World: American Nationalism and the Cultural Roots of the Cold War* (Chapel Hill, 2000), 91–102.

16 James Wertsch, "National Narratives and the Conservative Nature of Collective Memory," *Neohelicon* 34 (2007): 23–33; also Dmitri Loza, *Fighting for the Soviet Motherland: Recollections from the Eastern Front* (Lincoln, 1998).

17 Ben Shephard, *The Long Road Home: The Aftermath of the Second World War* (New York, 2010).

18 Gerard Daniel Cohen, *In War's Wake: Europe's Displaced Persons in the Postwar Order* (Oxford, 2012).

19 Anna Holian, *Between National Socialism and Soviet Communism: Displaced Persons in Postwar Germany* (Ann Arbor, 2011), 3.

20 R.M. Douglas, *Orderly and Humane: The Expulsion of the Germans after the Second World War* (New Haven, 2012), 2.

21 Ian Buruma, *Year Zero: A History of 1945* (New York, 2013), 131–68; Lizzie Collingham, *The Taste of War: World War II and the Battle for Food* (New York, 2012), 467–501.

22 Dan Stone, *The Liberation of the Camps: The End of the Holocaust and Its Aftermath* (New Haven, 2015), 139–77.

23 Jan Gross, *Fear: Antisemitism in Poland After Auschwitz* (New York, 2006), 81–117.

24 Piotr Eberhardt, "The Curzon Line as the Eastern Boundary of Poland: Origins and Political Background," *Geographia Polonica* 85 (2012): 5–21.

25 Churchill was, however, open to Soviet control of eastern Poland, provided the reconstituted Polish state gained compensatory territory in the west at the expense of Germany; see Paul Mayle, *Eureka Summit: Agreement in Principle and the Big Three at Tehran, 1943* (Newark, 1987), 78–79.

26 Leon Waszak, *Agreement in Principle: The Wartime Partnership of General Władysław Sikorski and Winston Churchill* (New York, 1996).

27 Norman Davies, *Rising '44: The Battle for Warsaw* (New York, 2004).

28 Michael Dobbs, *Six Months in 1945: FDR, Stalin, and Churchill from World War to Cold War* (New York, 2012), 57–76.

29 Warren Kimball, *Swords or Ploughshares? The Morgenthau Plan for Defeated Germany, 1943–1946* (Philadelphia, 1976).

30 Michael Beschloss, *The Conquerors: Roosevelt, Truman, and the Destruction of Germany, 1941–1945* (New York, 2002), 181–83.

31 Andrew Szanajda, *The Allies and the German Problem, 1941–1949* (New York, 2015), 41–62.

32 J.E. Farquharson, "Anglo-American Policy on Reparations from Yalta to Potsdam," *EHR* 112 (1997): 904–26.

33 John Gimbel, "The American Reparations Stop in Germany: An Essay on the Political Uses of History," *Historian* 37 (1975): 276–96.

34 James Van Hook, "From Socialization to Co-Determination: The US, Britain, Germany, and Public Ownership in the Ruhr, 1945–1951," *HJ* 45 (2002): 153–78.

35 Werner Abelshauser, "American Aid and West German Economic Recovery," in Charles Maier and Günter Bischof, eds., *The Marshall Plan and Germany* (Oxford, 1991), 367–409.

36 There were twelve of these tribunals in total; see Kevin Jon Heller, *The Nuremberg Military Tribunals and the Origins of International Criminal Law* (Oxford, 2011).

37 Joseph Persico, *Nuremberg: Infamy on Trial* (New York, 1995), 39–40.

38 Robert Conot, *Justice at Nuremberg* (New York, 2009), 62–68.

39 Frederick Taylor, *Exorcising Hitler: The Occupation and Denazification of Germany* (London, 2011).

40 Andreas Dorpalen, *German History in Marxist Perspective: The East German Approach* (Detroit, 1985), 393–98.

41 Timothy Vogt, *Denazification in Soviet-Occupied Germany: Brandenburg, 1945–1948* (Cambridge, MA, 2000).

42 Norman Naimark, *The Russians in Germany: A History of the Soviet Zone of Occupation, 1945–1949* (Cambridge, MA, 1995), 7–10.

43 Benita Blessing, *The Antifascist Classroom: Denazification in Soviet-Occupied Germany, 1945–1949* (New York, 2006); Charles Lansing, *From Nazism to Communism: German Schoolteachers under Two Dictatorships* (Cambridge, MA, 2010).

44 Dirk Spilker, *The East German Leadership and the Division of Germany: Patriotism and Propaganda, 1945–1953* (Oxford, 2006), 58–60.

45 See the recent edited translation of Theodor Adorno's insightful *Guilt and Defense: On the Legacies of National Socialism in Postwar Germany* (Cambridge, MA, 2010).

46 Michael Hughes, *Shouldering the Burdens of Defeat: West Germany and the Reconstruction of Social Justice* (Chapel Hill, 1999), 36–37.

47 Robert Paxton, *Europe in the Twentieth Century* (Fort Worth, 1997), 517.

48 Istvan Deak, *Europe on Trial: The Story of Collaboration, Resistance, and Retribution During World War II* (Boulder, 2015), 211–24.

49 J. Kenneth Brody, *The Trial of Pierre Laval France* (New Brunswick, 2010); Alice Kaplan, *The Collaborator: The Trial and Execution of Robert Brasillach* (Chicago, 2000).

50 On Mussert, see Ido de Haan, "Failures and Mistakes: Images of Collaboration in Postwar Dutch Society," in Roni Stauber, ed., *Collaboration with the Nazis* (New York, 2011), 71–90; on Quisling, H.F. Dahl, *Quisling: A Study in Treachery* (Cambridge, 1999).

51 See Stathis Kalyvas, *The Rise of Christian Democracy in Europe* (Ithaca, 1996); also Thomas Kselman and Joseph Buttigeig, eds., *European Christian Democracy* (Notre Dame, 2003).

52 Sheri Berman, *The Primacy of Politics: Social Democracy and the Making of Europe's Twentieth Century* (Cambridge, 2006), 177–99.

53 Cyrille Guiat, *The French and Italian Communist Parties* (London, 2003).

54 Peter Hennessey, *Never Again: Britain, 1945–1951* (London, 2006).

55 Nicklaus Thomas-Symonds, *Attlee: A Life in Politics* (London, 2010), 129–36.

56 See the new edition of William Beveridge's foundational William Beveridge, *Full Employment in a Free Society: A Report* (New York, 2015; orig. 1943).

57 Charles Webster, *The National Health Service: A Political History* (Oxford, 2002).

58 One of the primary Belgian collaborator figures, the Rexist founder Leon Degrelle, had escaped to Spain during the war. He was granted Spanish citizenship by Franco in 1954 and lived in Spain until his death in 1994; see David Messenger, *Hunting Nazis in Franco's Spain* (Baton Rouge, 2014), 67–68.

59 E. Ramón Arango, *Leopold III and the Belgian Royal Question* (Baltimore, 1963).

60 Kris Deschouwer, *The Politics of Belgium: Governing a Divided Society* (New York, 2012).

61 H.H.G. Post, *Pillarization: An Analysis of Dutch and Belgian Society* (Aldershot, 1989); Arend Lijphart, *The Politics of Accommodation: Pluralism and Democracy in the Netherlands* (Berkeley, 1975).

62 Johan den Hertog, "The Pillars of Nation: Inside the Dutch State," in Linas Eriksonas and Leos Müller, eds., *Statehood Before and Beyond Ethnicity* (Brussels, 2005), 353–62.

63 Melanie Wagner and Winifred Davies, "The Role of World War II in the Development of Luxembourgish as a National Language," *Language Problems and Language Planning* 33 (2009): 112–31. For developments in the 1970s and 1980s, see Nuria Garcia, "The Paradox of Contemporary Linguistic Nationalism: The Case of Luxembourg," *Nations and Nationalism* 20 (2014): 113–32.

64 Kristine Horner, "Reimagining the Nation: Discourses of Language Purism in Luxembourg," in Nils Langer and Winifred Davies, eds., *Linguistic Purism in the Germanic Languages* (Berlin, 2005), 166–87; see also Pit Péporté et al., *Inventing Luxembourg* (Leiden, 2010), esp. 267–94.

65 Quoted in Bertrand Jacquillat, *Nationalization and Privatization in Contemporary France* (Stanford, 1988), 4–5.

66 The United Nations gave Italy brief administrative control of Somaliland in 1950, and an arrangement with Yugoslavia in 1954 gave Italy the city of Trieste and part of the surrounding province; see Maura Hametz, *Making Trieste Italian, 1918–1954* (London, 2005), 43–46.

67 In the spring of 1944, under pressure from the Allies, Victor Emmanuel had appointed his son Umberto to rule on his behalf, while retaining the title of king for himself; see Denis Mack Smith, *Italy and Its Monarchy* (New Haven, 1989), 323–30.

68 Joan Barth Urban, *Moscow and the Italian Communist Party: From Togliatti to Berlinguer* (London, 1986).

69 Christopher Seton-Watson, "Italy's Imperial Hangover," *JCH* 15 (1980): 169–79.

70 Joan Maria Thomás, *Roosevelt, Franco, and the End of the Second World War* (New York, 2011), 187–99.

71 Fernando Rosas, "Portuguese Neutrality in the Second World War," in Neville Wylie, ed., *European Neutrals and Non-Belligerents During the Second World War* (Cambridge, 2002), 268–82.

72 James Sidaway and Marcus Power, "The 'Tears of Portugal': Empire, Identity, Race, and Destiny in Portuguese Geopolitical Narratives," *Environment and Planning* 23 (2005): 527–54.

73 Emmy Werner, *A Conspiracy of Decency: The Rescue of the Danish Jews during World War II* (Boulder, 2002).

74 John Gilmour, *Sweden, the Swastika, and Stalin: The Swedish Experience in the Second World War* (Edinburgh, 2011), 115–22.

75 Francis Sejersted, *The Age of Social Democracy: Norway and Sweden in the Twentieth Century* (Princeton, 2011), 205–41.

76 Stanley Anderson, *The Nordic Council: A Study of Scandinavian Regionalism* (Seattle, 1967).

77 Barry Turner and Gunilla Nordquist, *The Other European Community: Integration and Cooperation in Nordic Europe* (New York, 1982); Erik Solem, *The Nordic Council and Scandinavian Integration* (New York, 1977).

78 Caroline Howard Grøn et al., "Still the 'Other' European Community? The Nordic Countries and the European Union," in Caroline Howard Grøn et al., eds., *The Nordic Countries and the European Union* (New York, 2015), 1–12.

79 Gary Wilton, "Christianity at the Founding: The Legacy of Robert Schuman," in Gary Wilton and Jonathan Chaplin, eds., *God and the EU: Retrieving the Christian Inspirations of the European Project* (New York, 2016), 13–32.

80 Alan Paul Fimister, *Robert Schuman: Neoscholastic Humanism and the Reunification of Europe* (Brussels, 2008).

81 Ronald Granieri, *Ambivalent Alliance: Konrad Adenauer, the CDU/CSU, and the West, 1949–1966* (New York, 2006).

82 Thomas Maulucci, *Adenauer's Foreign Office: West German Diplomacy in the Shadow of the Third Reich* (Dekalb, 2012).

83 Herbert Simon, "The Birth of an Organization: The Economic Cooperation Administration," *Public Administration Review* 13 (1953): 227–36.

84 "The Schuman Declaration, 9 May 1950," http://europa.eu/about-eu/basic-information/symbols/europe-day/schuman-declaration/index_en.htm.

85 See Milward, *European Rescue*, 64–82.

86 John Gillingham, *Coal, Steel, and the Rebirth of Europe, 1945–1955* (Cambridge, 1991), 299–347.

87 Frederic Fransen, *The Supranational Politics of Jean Monnet: Ideas and Origins of the European Community* (Westport, 2001); Francois Duchene, *Jean Monnet: First Statesman of Interdependence* (New York, 1994).

88 Jean Monnet, "Red Letter Day for European Unity," in John W. Boyer and Jan E. Goldstein, eds., *Readings in Western Civilization*, vol. 9, doc. 41.

89 See the essays in David Phinnemore and Alex Warleigh-Lack, eds., *Reflections on European Integration: Fifty Years of the Treaty of Rome* (Houndmills, 2008).

90 Cary Fontana and Craig Parsons, "'One Woman's Prejudice': Did Margaret Thatcher Cause Britain's Anti-Europeanism?" *Journal of Common Market Studies* 53 (2015): 89–105.

91 John Springhall, *Decolonization Since 1945: The Collapse of European Overseas Empires* (New York, 2001).

92 Fred Halliday, *The Middle East in International Relations* (Cambridge, 2005), 75–129.

93   Aviel Roshwald, "Jewish Identity and the Paradox of Nationalism," in
      Michael Berkowitz, ed., *Nationalism, Zionism, and the Mobilization of the
      Jews in 1900 and Beyond* (Leiden, 2004), 11–24.

94   Yasmin Khan, *The Great Partition: The Making of India and Pakistan* (New
      Haven, 2007).

95   On British participation, see Richard McMillan, *The British Occupation of
      Indonesia, 1945–1946* (New York, 2006).

96   Pierre Brocheux and Daniel Hémery, *Indochina: An Ambiguous Colonization,
      1858–1954* (Berkeley, 2011), 336–74.

97   Arthur Dommen, *The Indochinese Experience of the French and the
      Americans* (Bloomington, 2001).

98   Nicholas Atkin, *The Fifth French Republic* (Houndmills, 2005), 38–59.

99   Todd Shepard, *The Invention of Decolonization: The Algerian War and the
      Remaking of France* (Ithaca, 2008).

100   Economic statistics taken from Kitchen, *Modern Germany*, 316–17.

101   Arnold Sywottek, "From Starvation to Excess? Trends in Consumer
      Society from the 1940s to the 1970s," in Hanna Schissler, ed., *The Miracle
      Years: A Cultural History of West Germany, 1949–1968* (Princeton, 2001),
      341–58.

102   Robert Moeller, *Protecting Motherhood: Women and the Family in the
      Politics of Postwar West Germany* (Berkeley, 1993).

103   See esp. Ute Poiger, *Jazz, Rock, and Rebels: Cold War Politics and American
      Culture in a Divided Germany* (Berkeley, 2000).

104   A.J. Nicholls, *Freedom with Responsibility: The Social Market Economy in
      Germany, 1918–1963* (Oxford, 2000); see also James Van Hook, *Rebuilding
      Germany: The Creation of the Social Market Economy, 1945–1957*
      (Cambridge, 2004).

105   Ludwig Erhard, "Economic Policy as a Component of Social Policy," in John
      W Boyer and Jan E. Goldstein, eds., *Readings*, vol. 9, doc. 38. See also Alfred
      Mierzejewski, *Ludwig Erhard: A Biography* (Chapel Hill, 2004), 27–42.

106   Wilfried Mausbach, "America's Vietnam in Germany, Germany in America's
      Vietnam: On the Relocation of Spaces and the Appropriation of History," in
      Belinda Davis et al., eds., *Changing the World, Changing Oneself: Political
      Protest and Collective Identities in West Germany and the U.S. in the 1960s
      and 1970s* (New York, 2012), 41–64; also Martin Klimke, *The Other
      Alliance: Student Protest in West Germany and the United States in the
      Global Sixties* (Princeton, 2010).

107   Michael Seidman, *The Imaginary Revolution: Parisian Students and Workers
      in 1968* (New York, 2004), 161–214.

108   Roberto Franzosi, *The Puzzle of Strikes: Class and State Strategies in Postwar
      Italy* (Oxford, 1995), 257–99.

109   See Karrin Hanshew, *Terror and Democracy in West Germany* (Cambridge,
      2012); Alessandro Orsini, *Anatomy of the Red Brigades: The Religious
      Mindset of Modern Terrorists* (Ithaca, 2011).

110 Gary McGladdery, *The Provisional IRA in England* (Dublin, 2006); Timothy Shanahan, *The Provisional Irish Republican Army and the Morality of Terrorism* (Edinburgh, 2009).

111 Cristian Vasile, "Propaganda and Culture in Romania at the Beginning of the Communist Regime," in Vladimir Tismaneanu, ed., *Stalinism Revisited* (Budapest, 2009), 367–86.

112 Dennis Deletant, *Communist Terror in Romania: Gheorghiu-Dej and the Police State, 1948–1965* (New York, 1999).

113 Cheng Chen, "The Roots of Illiberal Nationalism in Romania," *East European Politics and Societies* 17 (2003): 166–201.

114 Eric Roman, *Hungary and the Victor Powers, 1945–1950* (London, 1996), 99–106.

115 Mark Gilbert, *Cold War Europe: The Politics of a Contested Continent* (Lanham, 2015), 34–35; on Rákosy's influence as communist leader, see Lendvai, *The Hungarians*, 430–48.

116 Peter Kenez, "The Hungarian Communist Party and the Catholic Church, 1945–1948," *JMH* 75 (2003): 864–89.

117 Benjamin Frommer, *National Cleansing: Retribution against Nazi Collaborators in Postwar Czechoslovakia* (Cambridge, 2005).

118 The Czech Communist Party got just over 31 percent and the allied Slovak communists got 7 percent; see Mary Heimann, *Czechoslovakia: The State That Failed* (New Haven, 2009), 166–67.

119 Josef Korbel, *The Communist Subversion of Czechoslovakia, 1938–1948* (Princeton, 1959), 194–98.

120 Claire Sterling, *The Masaryk Case* (New York, 1969).

121 Zbyněk Zeman and Antonín Klimek, *The Life of Eduard Beneš, 1884–1948* (Oxford, 1997), 281–82.

122 The young Simeon was spared, but all three of the regents, including his uncle Prince Kyril, were executed; see R.J. Crampton, *A Concise History of Bulgaria* (Cambridge, 2003), 173–74.

123 Marietta Stankova, *Bulgaria in British Foreign Policy, 1943–1949* (London, 2014), 154–55.

124 Melissa Bokovoy, "Collectivization in Yugoslavia: Rethinking Regional and National Interests," in Constantin Iordachi and Arnd Bauerkämper, eds., *The Collectivization of Agriculture in Communist Eastern Europe* (Budapest, 2014), 329–68.

125 Jeronim Petrovic, "The Tito-Stalin Split: A Reassessment in Light of New Evidence," *Journal of Cold War Studies* 9 (2007): 32–63.

126 Ivo Banac, *With Stalin Against Tito: Conformist Splits in Yugoslav Communism* (Ithaca, 1988).

127 Hilde Katrine Haug, *Creating a Socialist Yugoslavia: Tito, Communist Leadership, and the National Question* (London, 2012).

128 Albert Resis, "The Churchill-Stalin Secret 'Percentages' Agreement on the Balkans, Moscow, October 1944," *AHR* 83 (1978): 368–87.

129 Dimitrakis, *Greece and the English*, 70–75.

130 Evanthis Hatzivassiliou, *Greece and the Cold War* (New York, 2006), 17–23.

131 Adam Zwass, *The Council for Mutual Economic Assistance* (Armonk, 1988), 3.

132 Monika Kaiser, "Change and Continuity in the Development of the Socialist Unity Party of Germany," *JCH* 30 (1995): 687–88.

133 Mary Fulbrook, "East Germans in a Post-Nazi State: Communities of Experience, Connection, and Identification," in Mary Fulbrook and Andrew Port, eds., *Becoming East German: Socialist Structures and Sensibilities after Hitler* (New York, 2013), 33–55.

134 See Andrew Port's insightful study of the agricultural and industrial region around Saalfeld; Andrew Port, *Conflict and Stability in the German Democratic Republic* (Cambridge, 2007), 21–45.

135 On the contested death toll and, especially, on the social impact of memory of the uprising, see Richard Millington, *State, Society, and Memories of the Uprising of 17 June 1953 in the GDR* (Houndmills, 2014).

136 Frederick Taylor, *The Berlin Wall: A World Divided, 1961–1989* (New York, 2007).

137 William Taubman, *Khrushchev: The Man and His Era* (New York, 2003), 270–99.

138 Anita Pramzowska, *Władysław Gomułka: A Biography* (London, 2015), chap. 9.

139 See Eniko Basa, *Sándor Petőfi* (Boston, 1980); László Deme, "National Interests and Cosmopolitan Goals in the Hungarian Revolution of 1848–49," *Austrian History Yearbook* 12 (1976): 36–44.

140 Karl Benziger, *Imre Nagy, Martyr of the Nation* (Lanham, 2008), 59–80.

141 Kevin McDermott, "Popular Resistance in Communist Czechoslovakia: The Plzeň Uprising, June 1953," *Contemporary European History* 19 (2010): 287–307.

142 Peter Hruby, *Fools and Heroes: The Changing Role of Communist Intellectuals in Czechoslovakia* (London, 1980), 154–55.

143 Kieran Williams, *The Prague Spring and Its Aftermath: Czechoslovak Politics, 1968–1970* (Cambridge, 1997), 3–28.

144 Mark Kramer, "The Prague Spring and the Soviet Invasion in Historical Perspective," in Günter Bischof et al., eds., *The Prague Spring and the Warsaw Pact Invasion of Czechoslovakia in 1968* (Lanham, 2010), 35–60.

145 Jonathan Bolton, *Worlds of Dissent: Charter 77, the Plastic People of the Universe, and Czech Culture under Communism* (Cambridge, MA, 2012).

146 Michael Zantovsky, *Václav Havel: A Life* (New York, 2014), 185–93.

147 Roman Laba, *The Roots of Solidarity: A Political Sociology of Poland's Working Class Democratization* (Princeton, 1991), 15–56.

148 See Rebecca Stefoff, *Lech Walesa: The Road to Democracy* (New York, 2011).

149 Andrzej Paczkowski and Malcolm Byrne, "The Polish Crisis: Internal and
      International Dimensions," in Andrzej Paczkowski and Malcolm Byrne, eds.,
      From Solidarity to Martial Law: The Polish Crisis of 1980–1981 (Budapest,
      2007), 19–22.

150 George Sanford, *Military Rule in Poland: The Rebuilding of Communist
      Power, 1981–1983* (London, 1986).

Chapter 8

1   Quotes taken from the promotional brochure *Mini-Europe: The Best of the
        Best* (Brussels, 2016).

2   *Mini-Europe: Catalog Guide* (Brussels, 2016), 2–3.

3   Tuuli Lähdesmäki, "The Politics of Cultural Marking in Mini-Europe:
        Anchoring European Cultural Identity in a Theme Park," *Journal of
        Contemporary European Studies* 20 (2012): 29–40.

4   Tom Seymour, "Inside the European Union Theme Park," *British Journal of
        Photography* (April 1, 2016).

5   Francis Fukuyama, *The End of History and the Last Man* (New York, 1992).

6   Samuel Huntington, *The Clash of Civilizations and the Remaking of World
        Order* (New York, 1996).

7   See e.g. Angela Stent, *Russia and Germany Reborn: Unification, the Soviet
        Collapse, and the New Europe* (Princeton, 1998).

8   Michael Howard, "The Springtime of Nations," *Foreign Affairs* 69 (1990):
        17–32.

9   Serge Schmemann, "East Germans Swell Embassy in Prague," *New York
        Times* (September 29, 1989).

10   Konrad Jarausch, *The Rush to Germany Unity* (New York, 1994), 21–22.

11   Richard Leiby, *The Unification of Germany, 1989–1990* (Westport, 1999),
        15–16.

12   Mary Elise Sarotte, *The Collapse: The Accidental Opening of the Berlin Wall*
        (New York, 2014), 105–26.

13   See esp. the colorful account in Robert Darnton, *Berlin Journal, 1989–1990*
        (New York, 1991), 112–19.

14   Gilbert, *Cold War Europe*, 257.

15   See esp. Dietrich Orlow, *Socialist Reformers and the Collapse of the German
        Democratic Republic* (Houndmills, 2015).

16   Peter Barker, "From the SED to the PDS: Continuity or Renewal?" in
        Barker, ed., *The Party of Democratic Socialism in Germany: Modern Post-
        Communism or Nostalgic Populism* (Amsterdam, 1998), 1–17.

17   Lothar Kettenacker, *Germany 1989: In the Aftermath of the Cold War*
        (Harlow, 2009), 164.

18   Helmut Kohl, "A Ten-Point Program for Overcoming the Division of
        Germany and Europe," in Harold James and Marla Stone, eds., *When the
        Wall Came Down: Reactions to German Unification* (London, 1992), 33–35.

19 Christian Wicke, *Helmut Kohl's Quest for Normality: His Representation of the German Nation and Himself* (New York, 2015).

20 Joszef Bayer, "The Process of the Change of the Political System in Hungary: Deepening Crisis, Emerging Opposition," *East European Quarterly* 39 (2005): 129–47.

21 Gilbert, *Cold War Europe*, 251.

22 Rudolf Tőkés, *Hungary's Negotiated Revolution: Economic Reform, Social Change, and Political Succession* (Cambridge, 1996), 320–29.

23 László Bruszt and David Stark, "Remaking the Political Field in Hungary: From the Politics of Confrontation to the Politics of Competition," *Journal of International Affairs* 45 (1991): 201–45.

24 Barnabas Racz, "Political Pluralisation in Hungary: The 1990 Elections," *Soviet Studies* 43 (1991): 107–36.

25 John Anderson, "The Catholic Contribution to Democratization's 'Third Wave': Altruism, Hegemony, or Self-Interest?" *Cambridge Review of International Affairs* 20 (2007): 383–99.

26 Grzgorz Ekiert and Jan Kubik, *Rebellious Civil Society: Popular Protest and Democratic Consolidation in Poland, 1989–1993* (Ann Arbor, 2001), 49–54.

27 Bernard Wheaton and Zdenek Kavan, *The Velvet Revolution: Czechoslovakia, 1988–1991* (Boulder, 1992). See also Miroslav Vaněk and Pavel Mücke, *Velvet Revolutions: An Oral History of Czech Society* (Oxford, 2016), which is based on more than 300 interviews and uses the term to refer to the individual experiences of ordinary participants and observers.

28 See Timothy Garten Ash, *The Magic Lantern: The Revolution of '89 Witnessed in Warsaw, Budapest, Berlin, and Prague* (New York, 1993), esp. 84–90.

29 James Krapfl, *Revolution with a Human Face: Politics, Culture, and Community in Czechoslovakia, 1989–1992* (Ithaca, 2013), 102.

30 Claudia Moscovici, *Velvet Totalitarianism: Post-Stalinist Romania* (Lanham, 2009).

31 For a sensationalized yet interesting account, see Ion Mihai Pacepa, *Red Horizons: The True Story of Nicolae and Elena Ceauşescu's Crimes, Lifestyle, and Corruption* (Washington, DC, 1987).

32 Gail Kligman, *The Politics of Duplicity: Controlling Reproduction in Ceauşescu's Romania* (Berkeley, 1998).

33 Peter Siani-Davies, *The Romanian Revolution of December 1989* (Ithaca, 2005), 56–60.

34 On Romanian politics after Ceauşescu's death, see Tom Gallagher, "A Feeble Embrace: Romania's Engagement with Democracy, 1989–1994," *Journal of Communist Studies and Transition Politics* 12 (1996): 145–72.

35 Padma Desai, *Perestroika in Perspective: The Design and Dilemmas of Soviet Reform* (Princeton, 1989).

36 Archie Brown, *Seven Years that Changed the World: Perestroika in Perspective* (Oxford, 2009), 103–34.

37 The important nationalist movements in Soviet Central Asia and elsewhere are beyond the geographic scope of this study; but see Oliver Roy, *The New Central Asia: Geopolitics and the Birth of Nations* (London, 2007).

38 Guntis Šmidchens, *The Power of Song: Nonviolent National Culture in the Baltic Singing Revolution* (Seattle, 2014), 3.

39 Karsten Brüggemann and Andres Kasekamp, "Singing Oneself into a Nation? Estonian Song Festivals as Rituals of Political Mobilisation," *Nations and Nationalism* 20 (2014): 259–76.

40 On the legacy of that iconic demonstration, see Daina Eglitis and Laura Ardava, "The Politics of Memory: Remembering the Baltic Way 20 Years After 1989," *Europe-Asia Studies* 64 (2012): 1033–59.

41 Mara Lazda, "Reconsidering Nationalism: The Baltic Case of Latvia in 1989," *International Journal of Politics, Culture, and Society* 22 (2009): 517–36.

42 Stefan Hedlund, *The Baltic States and the End of the Soviet Empire* (London, 1993).

43 Dovile Budryte, *Taming Nationalism? Political Community Building in the Post-Soviet Baltic States* (New York, 2005).

44 Richard Mole, *The Baltic States from Soviet Union to European Union: Identity, Discourse, and Power in the Post-Communist Transition of Estonia, Latvia, and Lithuania* (New York, 2012), 143–64.

45 Alexandra Goujon, "'Genozid', a Rallying Cry in Belarus: A Rhetoric Analysis of Some Belarusian Nationalist Texts," *Journal of Genocide Research* 1 (1999): 353–66; also David Marples, "Kuropaty: The Investigation of a Stalinist Historical Controversy," *Slavic Review* 53 (1994): 513–23.

46 Alexandra Goujon, "Language, Nationalism, and Populism in Belarus," *Nationalities Papers* 27 (1999): 661–77.

47 David Marples, "Outpost of Tyranny? The Failure of Democratization in Belarus," *Democratization* 16 (2009): 756–76.

48 David Marples, *Belarus: A Denationalised Nation* (London, 1999); Timothy Snyder, *The Reconstruction of Nations: Poland, Ukraine, Lithuania, Belarus, 1569–1999* (Oxford, 2003), 278–80. For a nuanced argument against viewing Belarus as a "failed" nation, see Natalia Leschenko, "Two Nation-Building Strategies in Post-Soviet Belarus," *Nations and Nationalism* 10 (2004): 333–52.

49 See the fascinating account of the Bykivnia investigation and the Memorial Society in Karel Berkhoff, "Bykivnia: How Grave Robbers, Activists, and Foreigners Ended Official Silence About Stalin's Mass Graves Near Kiev," in Elizabeth Anstett and Jean-Marc Dreyfus, eds., *Human Remains and Identification: Mass Violence, Genocide, and the "Forensic Turn"* (Manchester, 2015), 59–82.

50 Serhii Plokhy, *The Gates of Europe: A History of Ukraine* (New York, 2015), 307–22.

51 Archie Brown, *The Gorbachev Factor* (Oxford, 1997), 188–89.

52 Timothy Colton, *Yeltsin: A Life* (New York, 2011), 196–210.

53 See the public reactions in Victoria Bonnell et al., eds., *Russia at the Barricades: Eyewitness Accounts of the August 1991 Coup* (Armonk, NY, 1994).

54 Ronald Grigor Suny, *The Revenge of the Past: Nationalism, Revolution, and the Collapse of the Soviet Union* (Stanford, 1993); also David Marples, *The Collapse of the Soviet Union, 1985–1991* (London, 2004).

55 Oto Luthar, *The Land Between: A History of Slovenia* (New York, 2013), 325–61; Marcus Tanner, *Croatia: A Nation Forged in War* (New Haven, 2001), 66–108.

56 Catherine Carmichael, *A Concise History of Bosnia* (Cambridge, 2015), 38–59.

57 Mark Mazower, *The Balkans: A Short History* (New York, 2002), 124–25.

58 Elizabeth Roberts, *Realm of the Black Mountain: History of Montenegro* (Ithaca, 2007); Andrew Rossos, *Macedonia and the Macedonians: A History* (Stanford, 2008).

59 Hilde Katrine Haug, *Creating a Socialist Yugoslavia: Tito, Communist Leadership, and the National Question* (London, 2012).

60 Vjekoslav Perica, *Balkan Idols: Religion and Nationalism in Yugoslav States* (Oxford, 2004).

61 Julie Mertus, *Kosovo: How Myths and Truths Started a War* (Berkeley, 1999), 17–55.

62 Gregory Hall, "The Politics of Autocracy: Serbia under Slobodan Milosevic," *East European Quarterly* 33 (1999): 233–49.

63 Wendy Bracewell, "Rape in Kosovo: Masculinity and Serbian Nationalism," *Nations and Nationalism* 6 (2000); 563–90.

64 Jasna Dragovič-Soso, *"Saviours of the Nation": Serbia's Intellectual Opposition and the Revival of Nationalism* (Montreal, 2002).

65 Officially the "yes" vote was nearly 95 percent, although there have been questions raised about the format and framing of the survey on which the referendum was based; see Donald Rubin, Hal Stern, and Vasja Vehovar, "Handling 'Don't Know' Survey Responses: The Case of the Slovenian Plebiscite," *Journal of the American Statistical Association* 90 (1995): 822–38.

66 John Lampe, *Yugoslavia as History: Twice There Was a Country* (Cambridge, 2000), 332–64.

67 Catherine Baker, *The Yugoslav Wars of the 1990s* (Houndmills, 2015), chap. 4.

68 V.P. Gagnon, *The Myth of Ethnic War: Serbia and Croatia in the 1990s* (Ithaca, 2004).

69 Ruth Seifert, "War and Rape: A Preliminary Analysis," in Alexandra Siglmayer, ed., *Mass Rape: The War against Women in Bosnia-Herzegovina* (Lincoln, 1994), 54–72.

70 Stevan Weine, *When History Is a Nightmare: Lives and Memories of Ethnic Cleansing in Bosnia-Herzegovina* (New Brunswick, 1999).

71 Jamie Munn, "The Hegemonic Male and Kosovar Nationalism, 2000–2005," *Men and Masculinities* 10 (2008): 440–56.

72 "Tuesday, 31 August 2004, Defense Opening Statement," from http:// www.icty.org/x/cases/ slobodan milosevic/trans/en/040831ED.htm, 32188–93.

73 Patrick Geary, *The Myth of Nations: The Medieval Origins of Europe* (Princeton, 2003).

74 Thomas Emmert, *Serbian Golgotha: Kosovo, 1389* (Boulder, 1990); see also Florian Bieber, "Nationalist Mobilization and Stories of Serb Suffering: The Kosovo Myth from the 600th Anniversary to the Present," *Rethinking History* 6 (2002): 95–110.

75 John Sullivan, *ETA and Basque Nationalism: The Fight for Euskadi, 1890–1986* (London, 1988).

76 Cameron Watson, *Basque Nationalism and Political Violence: The Ideological and Intellectual Origins of ETA* (Reno, 2007).

77 Julen Agirre, *Operation Ogro: The Execution of Admiral Luis Carerro Blanco* (New York, 1975).

78 Carrie Hamilton, *Women and ETA: The Gender Politics of Radical Basque Nationalism* (Manchester, 2007), 84–124.

79 Cecilia Garza, "Spain's Mobilization Against Terrorism: The Death of Miguel Angel Blanco," *International Journal on World Peace* 15 (1998): 91–99.

80 See Justin Crumbaugh, "Are We All (Still) Miguel Ángel Blanco? Victimhood, the Media Afterlife, and the Challenge of Historical Memory," *Hispanic Review* 75 (2007): 365–84.

81 See Theresa Whitfield, *Endgame for ETA: Elusive Peace in the Basque Country* (Oxford, 2014).

82 See esp. John Bew, Martyn Frampton, and Inigo Gurruchaga, *Talking to Terrorists: Making Peace in Northern Ireland and the Basque Country* (New York, 2009).

83 Michael Cox, "Bringing in the 'International': The IRA Ceasefire and the End of the Cold War," *International Affairs* 73 (1997): 671–93.

84 "The Northern Ireland Peace Agreement (Good Friday Agreement)," http://peacemaker.un.org/uk-ireland-good-friday98.

85 Joseph Ruane and Jennifer Todd, "A Changed Irish Nationalism? The Significance of the Good Friday Agreement of 1998," in Joseph Ruane, Jennifer Todd, and Anne Mandeville, eds., *Europe's Old States and the New World Order: The Politics of Transition in Britain, France, and Spain* (Dublin, 2004), 121–45.

86 See e.g. Paul Bew, "Myths of Consociationalism: From Good Friday to Political Impasse," in Michael Cox et al., eds., *A Farewell to Arms? Beyond the Good Friday Agreement* (Manchester, 2006), 57–69. See also Thomas Taafe, "Images of Peace: The News Media, Politics, and the Good Friday Agreement," in Jörg Neuheiser and Stefan Wolff, *Peace at Last? The Impact of the Good Friday Agreement on Northern Ireland* (New York, 2004), 111–32.

87 Mancur Olson, "The Varieties of Eurosclerosis: The Rise and Decline of Nations since 1982," in Nicholas Crafts and Gianni Toniolo, eds., *Economic Growth in Europe Sine 1945* (Cambridge, 2002), 72–94.

88 Nicola Fielder, *Western European Integration in the 1980s: The Origins of the Single Market* (New York, 1997).

89   Helen Drake, *Jacques Delors: Perspectives on a European Leader* (London, 2000), 78.

90   George Ross, *Jacques Delors and European Integration* (Oxford, 1995), 49–50.

91   The Euro was to be introduced in 1999 to run concurrently with local currencies for a three-year period, before becoming the sole currency of the Eurozone members in 2002; see more generally David Marsh, *The Euro: The Battle for the New Global Currency* (New Haven, 2011).

92   Otto Ulc, "Czechoslovakia's Velvet Divorce," *East European Quarterly* 30 (1996): 331–52; Paal Sigurd Hilde, "Slovak Nationalism and the Breakup of Czechoslovakia," *Europe-Asia Studies* 51 (1999): 647–65.

93   Scott Brown, "Prelude to a Divorce? The Prague Spring as Dress Rehearsal for Czechoslovakia's 'Velvet Divorce'," *Europe-Asia Studies* 60 (2008): 1783–1804.

94   John Rodden, *The Walls That Remain: Eastern and Western Germans Since Reunification* (New York, 2008).

95   Kitchen, *History of Modern Germany*, 400.

96   See Michael Münter and Roland Sturm, "Economic Consequences of German Unification," *German Politics* 11 (2002): 179–94.

97   On the impact of the continuing east–west divide on notions of German nationalism in the decade after reunification, see Irene Götz, "The Rediscovery of the 'National' in the 1990s: Contexts, New Cultural Forms and Practices in Reunified Germany," *Nations and Nationalism* 22 (2016): 408–30.

98   Rita Chin, *The Guest Worker Question in Postwar Germany* (Cambridge: Cambridge University Press, 2007).

99   Matthew Qvortrup, *Angela Merkel: Europe's Most Influential Leader* (New York: Overlook, 2016).

100   Several of the national team's fixtures over the past several years have been of mixed ethnicity: Sami Khedira is Tunisian–German, Jerome Boateng is Ghanaian–German, Mesut Özil is Turkish–German; see Jacqueline Gehring, "Race, Ethnicity, and German Identity: A Media Analysis of the 2010 World Cup Men's National Soccer Team," *Ethnic and Racial Studies* 39 (2016). For a somewhat more pessimistic analysis, see Maria Stehle and Beverly Weber, "German Soccer, the 2010 World Cup, and Multicultural Belonging," *German Studies Review* 36 (2013): 103–24.

101   Martina Wasner, "Public Debates and Public Opinion on Multiculturalism in Germany," in Raymond Taras, ed., *Challenging Multiculturalism: European Models of Diversity* (Edinburgh, 2013), 163–89.

102   Rogers Brubaker, *Citizenship and Nationhood in France and Germany* (Cambridge, MA, 1998).

103   Elisa Beller, "The Headscarf Affair: The Conseil d-État on the Role of Religion and Culture in French Society," *Texas International Law Journal* 39 (2004): 581–623; see also the comparative insights of Leora Auslander, "Bavarian Crucifixes and French Headscarves: Religious Practices and the Postmodern European State," *Cultural Dynamics* 12 (2000): 183–209.

104   Syros Sofos and Roza Tsagarousianou, "Muslims in Europe: Balancing between Belonging and Exclusion," in their *Islam in Europe: Public Spaces and Civic Networks* (New York, 2013), 10–27

105   Jonathan Marcus, *The National Front and French Politics: The Resistible Rise of Jean-Marie Le Pen* (New York, 1995); Edward DeClair, *Politics on the Fringe: The People, Policies, and Organization of the French National Front* (Durham, 1999).

106   Nonna Mayer, "From Jean-Marie to Marine Le Pen: Electoral Change on the Far Right," *Parliamentary Affairs* 66 (2013): 160–78.

107   Jacob Heilbrunn, "A Disdain for the Past: Jörg Haider's Austria," *World Policy Journal* 17 (2000): 71–78.

108   Lothar Höbelt, *Defiant Populist: Jörg Haider and the Politics of Austria* (West Lafayette, 2003), 187–93.

109   Stefaan Walgrave and Knut De Swert, "The Making of the (Issues of) the Vlaams Blok," *Political Communication* 21 (2004): 479–500.

110   Jan Erk, "From Vlaams Blok to Vlaams Belang: The Belgian Far Right Renames Itself," *West European Politics* 28 (2005): 493–502.

111   Matthijs Rooduijn, "Vox Populismus: A Populist Radical Right Attitude Among the Public?" *Nations and Nationalism* 20 (2014): 80–92.

112   Koen Wassen, "Classifying Wilders: The Ideological Development of Geert Wilders and His Party for Freedom," *Politics* 31 (2011): 179–89.

113   Breivik later claimed to identify more with Odin than with Christianity; Cato Hemmingby and Tore Bjorgo, "The Trial and Sentencing," in idem, *The Dynamics of a Terrorist Targeting Process: Anders B. Breivik and the 22 July Attacks in Norway* (New York, 2015), 79–80.

114   Quoted in Kenneth Weiss, "At a Loss for Words: Nosological Impotence in the Search for Justice," *Journal of the American Academy of Psychiatry and the Law* 44 (2016): 38.

115   Åsne Seierstad, *One of Us: The Story of Anders Breivik and the Massacre in Norway* (New York, 2015).

116   Jeffrey Mankoff, "Russia's Latest Land Grab: How Putin Won Crimea and Lost Ukraine," *Foreign Affairs* (May/June 2014). See also the deeply insightful analysis in Plokhy, *The Gates of Europe*, 347–54.

117   Greta Lynn Uehling, *Beyond Memory: The Crimean Tatars' Deportation and Return* (New York, 2004), 56.

118   See Alisa Sopova, "Ukraine Sings Its Frustration with Russia," *New York Times* (February 23, 2016).

119   While the references are carefully couched, Jamala stated that she wrote the song thinking not only about the second World War history, but about the present Russian intervention; see Fred Bronson, "Eurovision 2016: Ukraine Wins with Jamala's '1944'," *Billboard* (May 14, 2016).

120   Daniel Byman and Jeremy Shapiro, "Homeward Bound? Don't Hype the Threat of Returning Jihadists," *Foreign Affairs* 93:6 (November–December 2014): 37–46.

121 See esp. James Mitchell, Lynne Bennie, and Rob Johns, *The Scottish National Party: Transition to Power* (Oxford, 2012), 109–10.

122 Iain McLean, Jim Gallagher, and Guy Lodge, *Scotland's Choices: The Referendum and What Happens Afterwards* (Edinburgh, 2013), 8–9.

123 Eberhard Bort, "The Annals of the Parish: Referendum Year 2014," *Scottish Affairs* 24 (2015): 1–21.

124 Kenneth Armstrong, "An Independent Scotland in the European Union," *Cambridge Journal of International and Comparative Law* 3 (2014): 181–95.

125 On the UKIP rise, see esp. Robert Ford and Matthew Goodwin, *Revolt on the Right: Explaining Support for the Radical Right in Britain* (New York, 2014).

126 For an illustration of the growing attention to English history, see Robert Tombs, *The English and Their History* (London, 2015). For an insightful analysis, see also Keith Thomas, "Was There Always an England?" *New York Review of Books* (May 12, 2016), 73–75; Fintan O'Toole, "Brexit Is Being Driven by English Nationalism," *Guardian* (June 18, 2016).

127 See Geoffrey Wheatcroft, "Europhobia: A Very British Problem," *Guardian* (June 21, 2016); Roger Cohen, "Jo Cox and Britain's Place in Europe," *New York Times* (June 20, 2016); Gideon Rachman, "Why True Democrats Should Vote to Remain in the EU," *Financial Times* (June 20, 2016).

128 See e.g. Andrew Solomon, "A Perilous Nationalism at Brexit," *New Yorker* (June 28, 2016).

129 See Mure Dickie and Vincent Boland, "Scotland's Referendum Backing for Remain Threatens Union," *Financial Times* (June 24, 2016).

130 Gerry Adams, "Brexit and Irish Unity," *New York Times* (July 12, 2016); see also John Manley, "Irish Nationalism Reawakened by Brexit Vote," *Irish Times* (June 27, 2016).

Chapter 9

1 David Graham, "'America First': Donald Trump's Populist Inaugural Address," *The Atlantic* (January 20, 2017).

2 This sense was palpable on the eve of the inauguration: see Steven Erlanger, "As Trump Era Arrives, A Sense of Uncertainty Grips the World," *New York Times* (January 16, 2017).

3 Monnet, "Red Letter Day for European United," in Boyer and Goldstein, eds., *Readings in Western Civilization*, vol. 9, doc. 41. The context of Monnet's speech is discussed in Chapter 7 above.

4 Judy Dempsey, "What Trump Should Mean for Europe," *Carnegie Europe* (January 23, 2017). See also Erin Jenne, *Nested Security: Lessons in Conflict Management from the League of Nations and the European Union* (Ithaca, 2016), esp. chap. 5.

SELECT BIBLIOGRAPHY

Absalom, R. *Italy since 1800: A Nation in the Balance?* London, 2014.

Agulhon, M. *Marianne into Battle.* Cambridge, 1981.

Albanese, P. *Mothers of the Nation.* Toronto, 2006.

Anderson, B. *Imagined Communities.* London, 1983.

Applegate, C. *A Nation of Provincials.* Berkeley, 1990.

Arendt, H. *The Origins of Totalitarianism.* New York, 1951.

Armstrong, J. *Nations Before Nationalism.* Chapel Hill, 1982.

Ash, T.G. *The Magic Lantern.* New York, 1993.

Aston, N. *Religion and Revolution in France, 1780–1794.* Washington, DC, 2000.

Baar, M. *Historians and Nationalism.* Oxford, 2010.

Bairner, A. *Sport, Nationalism, and Globalization.* Albany, 2001.

Banac, I. *The National Question in Yugoslavia.* Ithaca, 1984.

Baranowski, S. *Nazi Empire: German Colonialism from Bismarck to Hitler.* Cambridge, 2011.

Barker, P. *Religious Nationalism in Modern Europe: If God Be for Us.* London, 2009.

Barnard, F. *Herder on Nationality, Humanity, and History.* Montreal, 2003.

Baycroft, T. *Nationalism in Europe, 1789–1945.* Cambridge, 1998.

Bell, D. *The Cult of the Nation in France.* Cambridge, MA, 2001.

Berger, S. et al., eds. *Writing National Histories.* London, 1999.

Bilenky, S. *Romantic Nationalism in Eastern Europe.* Stanford, 2012.

Billig, M. *Banal Nationalism.* London, 1995.

Blessing, B. *The Antifasicst Classroom.* New York, 2006.

Blinkhorn, M. *Fascism and the Right in Europe, 1919–1945.* London, 2000.

Bloxham, D. *The Great Game of Genocide.* Oxford, 2005.

Bohlman, P. *The Music of European Nationalism.* Santa Barbara, 2004.

Bohlman, P. *Music, Nationalism, and the Making of the New Europe.* London, 2011.

Boyer, J. *Political Radicalism in Late Imperial Vienna.* Chicago, 1981.

Boyer, J. *Culture and Political Crisis in Vienna.* Chicago, 1995.

Breuilly, J. *The Formation of the First German Nation-State.* London, 1996.

Breuilly, J. *Nationalism and the State.* Manchester, 2002.

Browning, C. *Ordinary Men.* New York, 1992.

Brubaker, R. *Nationalism Reframed.* Cambridge, 1996.

Budryte, D. *Taming Nationalism?* New York, 2005.

Bukey, E. *Hitler's Austria.* Chapel Hill, 2000.

Burleigh, M. *Earthly Powers.* New York, 2005.

Burleigh, M. *Sacred Causes.* New York, 2007.

Chadwick, O. *The Secularization of the European Mind.* Cambridge, 1975.

Chickering, R. *We Men Who Feel Most German*. Boston, 1984.

Clark, C. *Sleepwalkers: How Europe Went to War in 1914*. London, 2012.

Cohen, G. *The Politics of Ethnic Survival*. Princeton, 1981.

Cohler, A. *Rousseau and Nationalism*. New York, 1970.

Colley, L. *Britons: Forging the Nation, 1707–1837*. New Haven, 1992.

Collins, J. *The State in Early Modern France*. Cambridge, 2009.

Confino, A. *The Nation as a Local Metaphor*. Chapel Hill, 1997.

Crouthamel, J. *An Intimate History of the Front*. Houndmills, 2014.

Daskalov, R. *The Making of a Nation in the Balkans*. Budapest, 2004.

Davies, A. *The Crucified Nation: A Motif in Modern Nationalism*. Sussex, 2009.

Deak, J. *Forging a Multinational State*. Stanford, 2015.

Deutsch, K. *Nationalism and Social Communication*. Cambridge, MA, 1966.

Eastman, S. *Preaching Nationalism Across the Hispanic Atlantic*. Baton Rouge, 2012.

Eley, G. *Reshaping the German Right*. New Haven, 1980.

Falnes, O. *National Romanticism in Norway*. New York, 1933.

Ferguson, N. *The Pity of War*. New York, 1998.

Fitzpatrick, M. *Liberal Imperialism in Germany*. New York, 2008.

Ford, C. *Creating the Nation in Provincial France*. Princeton, 1993.

Fritzsche, P. *Germans into Nazis*. Cambridge, MA, 1998.

Frommer, B. *National Cleansing*. Cambridge, 2005.

Fussell, P. *The Great War and Modern Memory*. Oxford, 1977.

Gagnon, V.P. *The Myth of Ethnic War*. Ithaca, 2004.

Gallant, T. *Modern Greece*. London, 2001.

Gat, A. *Nations*. Cambridge, 2013.

Geary, P. *The Myth of Nations*. Princeton, 2002.

Gellner, E. *Nations and Nationalism*. Ithaca, 1983.

Gilbert, M. *Cold War Europe: The Politics of a Contested Continent*. Lanham, 2015.

Glenny, M. *The Balkans*. New York, 2012.

Goltz, A. von der *Hindenburg*. Oxford, 2009.

Granieri, R. *Ambivalent Alliance*. New York, 2006.

Green, A. *Fatherlands*. Cambridge, 2001.

Greenfield, L. *Nationalism: Five Roads to Modernity*. Cambridge, MA, 1992.

Grigioriadis, I. *Instilling Religion in Greek and Turkish Nationalism*. London, 2013.

Gross, J. *Neighbors*. Princeton, 2001.

Gross, J. *Fear: Antisemitism in Poland after Auschwitz*. New York, 2006.

Gruder, V. *The Notables and the Nation*. Cambridge, MA, 2008.

Guibernau, M. *Belonging: Solidarity and Division in Modern Society*. Cambridge, 2013.

Hamann, B. *Hitlers Wien*. Munich, 1998.

Hancock, E. *Ernst Röhm: Hitler's SA Chief of Staff*. New York, 2008.

Hanebrink, P. *In Defense of Christian Hungary*. Ithaca, 2006.

Hanshew, K. *Terror and Democracy in West Germany*. Cambridge, 2012.

Hare, J.L. *Excavating Nations*. Toronto, 2015.

Hastings, A. *The Construction of Nationhood*. Cambridge, 1997.

Hayes, Carlton. *Nationalism: A Religion*. New York, 1960.

Hewitson, M. *Nationalism in Germany, 1848–1866*. Houndmills, 2010.

Hewitson, M. *Germany and the Causes of the First World War*. Oxford, 2014.

Higonnet, P. *Goodness Beyond Virtue*. Cambridge, MA, 1998.

Hitchcock, W. *The Struggle for Europe*. New York, 2004.

Höbelt, L. *Defiant Populist*. West Lafayette, 2003.

Hobsbawm, E. *Nations and Nationalism since 1780*. Cambridge, 1990.

Hochschild, A. *King Leopold's Ghost*. New York, 1998.

Holian, A. *Between National Socialism and Soviet Communism*. Ann Arbor, 2011.

Hyslop, B. *French Nationalism in 1789*. New York, 1968.

Ijicho, A. *Scottish Nationalism and the Idea of Europe*. London, 2004.

Ijicho, A. and G. Uzelac, eds. *When Is the Nation?* London, 2005.

Ionanid, R. *The Sword of the Archangel: Fascist Ideology in Romania*. Boulder, 1990.

Ionanid, R. *The Holocaust in Romania*. Chicago, 2000.

Jarausch, K. *The Rush to German Unity*. New York, 1994.

Johnson, L. and A. Murray, eds. *Concepts of National Identity in the Middle Ages*. Leeds, 1995.

Judson, P. *Exclusive Revolutionaries*. Ann Arbor, 1996.

Judson, P. *The Habsburg Empire*. Cambridge, MA, 2016.

Karolewski, P. and A.M. Suszycki, *The Nation and Nationalism in Europe*. Edinburg, 2011.

Kedourie, E. *Nationalism*. London, 1960.

Kohn, H. *The Idea of Nationalism*. New York, 1944.

Kohn, H. *The Age of Nationalism*. New York, 1962.

Kopp, K. *Germany's Wild East: Constructing Poland as a Colonial Space*. Ann Arbor, 2012.

Kühne, T. *Belonging and Genocide*. New Haven, 2010.

Kumar, K. *The Making of English National Identity*. Cambridge, 2003.

Lawrence, P. *Nationalism: History and Theory*. Harlow, 2005.

Leersen, J. *National Thought in Europe*. Amsterdam, 2006.

Lerner, P. *Hysterical Men*. Ithaca, 2003.

Levinger, M. *Enlightened Nationalism*. Oxford, 2000.

Levy, R. *Downfall of the Antisemitic Political Parties in Imperial Germany*. New Haven, 1973.

Liulevicius, V. *War Land on the Eastern Front*. Cambridge, 2000.

Llobera, J. *Foundations of National Identity*. New York, 2004.

Mackridge, P. *Language and National Identity in Greece*. Oxford, 2013.

Macmillan, M. *Paris 1919: Six Months That Changed the World*. New York, 2001.

Manias, C. *Race, Science, and the Nation*. New York, 2013.

Marcuse, H. *Legacies of Dachau*. Cambridge, 2001.

Marples, D. *Belarus: A Denationalised Nation*. London, 1999.

Martin, T. *The Affirmative Action Empire*. Ithaca, 2001.

Marx, A. *Faith in Nation: Exclusionary Origins of Nationalism*. Oxford, 2013.

Maxwell, A. *Patriots against Fashion*. London, 2014.

Mazower, M. *Dark Continent*. New York, 1998.

Milward, A. *The European Rescue of the Nation State*. Berkeley, 1992.

Moeller, R. *Protecting Motherhood*. Berkeley, 1993.

Moran, S.F. *Patrick Pearse and the Mind of the Easter Rising, 1916*. Washington, DC, 1994.

Mosse, G. *The Nationalization of the Masses*. Ithaca, 1975.

Mosse, G. *Nationalism and Sexuality*. New York, 1985.

Özkrimli, U. *Theories of Nationalism*. Houndmills, 2010.

Palmer, R.R. *Twelve Who Ruled*. Princeton, 1941.

Parry, J. *The Politics of Patriotism*. Cambridge, 2006.

Passmore, K. *The Right in France from the Third Republic to Vichy*. Oxford, 2013.

Patterson, S. *The Cult of Imperial Honor in British India*. New York, 2009.

Paxton, R. *Europe in the Twentieth Century*. Fort Worth, 1997.

Payne, S. *A History of Fascism, 1914–1945*. Madison, 1995.

Pederson, S. *The Guardians*. Oxford, 2015.

Perica, V. *Balkan Idols*. Oxford, 2004.

Poiger, U. *Jazz, Rock, and Rebels*. Berkeley, 2000.

Port, A. *Conflict and Stability in the German Democratic Republic*. Cambridge, 2007.

Porter, Brian. *When Nationalism Began to Hate*. Oxford, 2000.

Pulzer, P. *The Rise of Political Anti-Semitism in Germany and Austria*. Cambridge, 1988.

Quiroga, A. *Making Spaniards*. Houndmills, 2007.

Raeff, M. *The Well-Ordered Police State*. New Haven, 1983.

Rapport, M. *Nationality and Citizenship in Revolutionary France*. Oxford, 2000.

Riall, L. *Garibaldi: Invention of a Hero*. New Haven, 2008.

Riall, L. *Risorgimento*. London, 2009.

Riasanovsky, N. *Nicholas I and Official Nationality in Russia*. Berkeley, 1959.

Rich, N. *The Age of Nationalism and Reform*. New York, 1970.

Rogger, H. *National Consciousness in Eighteenth-Century Russia*. Cambridge, MA, 1960.

Rosenfeld, G. *Munich and Memory*. Berkeley, 2000.

Roshwald, A. *The Endurance of Nationalism*. Cambridge, 2006.

Schama, S. *Citizens: A Chronicle of the French Revolution*. New York, 1989.

Schissler, H. ed. *The Miracle Years*. Princeton, 2001.

Schivelbusch, W. *The Culture of Defeat*. New York, 2001.

Schulze, H. *The Course of German Nationalism*. Cambridge, 1991.

Seipp, A. *The Ordeal of Peace*. Farnham, 2009.

Seton-Watson, H. *Nations and States*. London, 1977.

Sheehan, J. *German Liberalism in the Nineteenth Century*. Chicago, 1981.

Sheehan, J. *Where Have All the Soldiers Gone?* Boston, 2008.

Shelby, K. *Flemish Nationalism and the Great War*. New York, 2014.

Shepard, T. *The Invention of Decolonization*. Ithaca, 2008.

Shephard, B. *The Long Road Home*. New York, 2010.

Skendi, S. *The Albanian National Awakening, 1878–1912*. Princeton, 1967.

Skey, M. *National Belonging in Everyday Life*. Houndmills, 2011.

Smith, A. *The Ethnic Revival in the Modern World*. Cambridge, 1981.

Smith, A. *The Ethnic Origins of Nations*. London, 1991.

Smith, A. *Chosen Peoples: Sacred Sources of National Identity*. Oxford, 2003.

Smith, A. *Ethnosymbolism and Nationalism*. London, 2009.

Smith, A. *The Nation Made Real*. Oxford, 2013.

Smith, A. *The Origins of Catalan Nationalism*. Houndmills, 2014.

Smith, H.W. *German Nationalism and Religious Conflict*. Princeton, 1995.

Snyder, T. *The Reconstruction of Nations*. Oxford, 2003.

Snyder, T. *Bloodlands: Europe Between Hitler and Stalin*. New York, 2010.

Snyder, T. *Black Earth: The Holocaust as History and Warning*. New York, 2015.
Sperber, J. *Revolutionary Europe, 1780–1850*. Harlow, 2000.
Sperber, J. *The European Revolutions, 1848–1851*. Cambridge, 2005.
Sternhell, Z. *Neither Right nor Left: Fascist Ideology in France*. Princeton, 1986.
Sternhell, Z. *The Birth of Fascist Ideology*. Princeton, 1994.
Stone, Dan. *The Liberation of the Camps*. New Haven, 2015.
Strayer, J. *On the Medieval Origins of the Modern State*. Princeton, 1970.
Suny, R. *The Revenge of the Past*. Stanford, 1993.
Tackett, T. *The Coming of the Terror in the French Revolution*. Cambridge, MA, 2015.
Taylor, F. *Exorcising Hitler*. London, 2011.
Unowsky, D. *The Pomp and Politics of Patriotism*. West Lafayette, 2005.
Vick, B. *Defining Germany*. Cambridge, MA, 2002.
Watson, C. *Basque Nationalism and Political Violence*. Reno, 2007.
Weber, E. *Peasants into Frenchmen*. Stanford, 1976.
Weber, T. *Hitler's First War*. Oxford, 1920.
Whaley, J. *Germany and the Holy Roman Empire*. Oxford, 2013.
Wicke, C. *Helmut Kohl's Quest for Normality*. New York, 2015.
Wimmer, A. *Waves of War*. Cambridge, 2013.
Winter, J. *Sites of Memory, Sites of Mourning*. Cambridge, 1995.
Wohl, R. *The Generation of 1914*. Cambridge, MA, 1979.
Wolff, L. *The Idea of Galicia*. Stanford, 2010.
Yuval-Davis, N. *Gender and Nation*. London, 1997.
Zamoyski, A. *Holy Madness*. London, 1999.
Zamoyski, A. *Phantom Terror*. New York, 2015.
Zimmer, O. *Contested Nation*. Cambridge, 2003.
Zimmer, O. *Nationalism in Europe, 1890–1945*. Houndmills, 2003.

INDEX

Louis Napoleon. *See* Napoleon III
Louis Philippe (France) 63–4, 77–8, 85
Ludendorff, Erich 144, 154
Ludwig I (Bavaria) 58–9, 76, 85, 100
Lueger, Karl 127, 133
Lukashenko, Alexander 241
Lusitania, sinking of 150
Luther, Martin 68
Luxembourgish 211
Lvov, Georgi 150

Maastricht Treaty 250
MacDiarmada, Seán 149
MacDonald, Ramsay 159
Madagascar Plan 193
Mahmoud II (Ottoman sultan) 74
Manzoni, Alessandro 93
Marat, Jean Paul 28
March on Rome 173–4, 179
Maria Theresia (Austria) 13
Marie Antoinette (France) 22, 35
Marinetti, Filippo 138, 173
Marr, Wilhelm 125
Marseillaise 28, 143
Marshall Plan 206, 208, 214, 222, 225
Martinovics, Ignac 46
Marx, Karl 79
Masaryk, Jan 223, 228
Masaryk, Tomas 166–7, 223
Massis, Henri 139–40
Matteotti, Giacomo 175
Maurras, Charles 131
Mavromichalis, Petrobey 74–6
Maximilian II (Bavaria) 85, 100
May, Theresa 257
Mazowiecki, Tadeusz 237
Mazzini, Giuseppe 67–8, 80, 88, 92–4, 107, 261
Menotti, Ciro 67
Merkel, Angela 251
Metaxas, Ioannis 225
Metternich, Klemens von 51–2, 85, 100
Michael I (Romania) 185, 222
Mickiewicz, Adam 70–2
Mierosławski, Ludwik 86
Mihailovic, Draza 224
Miklós, Béla 222
Mill, John Stuart 107

Millerand, Alexandre 160
Milošević, Slobodan 243–6
Mini-Europe 231–2, 258, 262
Mirabeau, Honoré Gabriel de 24
Mochnacki, Maurycy 70–1
Modernist interpretation (of nationalism) 5–6
Monnet, Jean 211–12, 216–17, 259
Montez, Lola 85
Morgenthau, Henry 204
Mosley, Oswald 189
Mozzoni, Anna Maria 107
Muir, Thomas 41, 62
Murat, Joachim 39
Mussert, Anton 208
Mussolini, Benito 164, 172–7, 196, 200, 212

Nagy, Ferenc 223
Nagy, Imre 226–7, 236–7
Nansen, Fridtjof 158
Napoleon I (France) 32, 36–9, 41–3, 46–50, 52–3, 191, 203
Napoleon III (France) 77–8, 97–8, 105
National Antisemitic League (France) 129, 131
National Assembly (France) 24
National Democracy (Poland) 169
National Fascist Party (Italy) 173
National Front (France) 252
National Guard (France) 26–7, 35
National Health Service (Britain) 209
National Liberal Party (Romania) 168
National Peasant Party (Romania) 168
National Social Party (Bohemia) 127
National Socialist German Workers' Party (Germany) 179–82
National Socialist movement (Netherlands) 189
National Socialist Party (France) 132
National Syndicalism (Portugal) 186
NATO. *See* North Atlantic Treaty Organization
Naval League (Germany) 126
Nazi-Soviet Pact 189, 204
Nelson, Horatio 41
Németh, Miklós 233
Nesselrode, Karl 52
Nicholas I (Russia) 60, 70, 75, 128